EXPLAINING HUMAN BEHAVIOR

EXPLAINING HUMAN BEHAVIOR

Consciousness, Human Action and Social Structure

PAUL F. SECORD
Editor

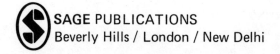

SAGE PUBLICATIONS
Beverly Hills / London / New Delhi

For information address:

SAGE Publications, Inc.
275 South Beverly Drive
Beverly Hills, California 90212

SAGE Publications India Pvt. Ltd.
C-236 Defence Colony
New Delhi 110 024, India

SAGE Publications Ltd
28 Banner Street
London EC1Y 8QE, England

Printed in the United States of America

Library of Congress Cataloging in Publication Data

Main entry under title:

Explaining human behavior.

Bibliography: p.
Includes index.
1. Psychology—Philosophy—Addresses, essays,
lectures. 2. Consciousness—Addresses, essays,
lectures. 3. Social psychology—Philosophy—
Addresses, essays, lectures. 4. Social structure—
Psychological aspects—Addresses, essays, lectures.
I. Secord, Paul F.
BF38.E87   302'.12   82-868
ISBN 0-8039-1822-4   AACR2

FIRST PRINTING

Table of Contents

About the Contributors

KURT W. BACK is James B. Duke Professor of Sociology at Duke University. He has been working on several applications of social psychology such as aging, fertility control, and encounter groups, and is also concerned with the theoretical and methodological bases of the field.

ROY BHASKAR is Lecturer in Philosophy at the University of Edinburgh and currently Visiting Research Fellow at the University of Sussex. His main interests are in the philosophy of science and the human sciences. He is the author of *A Realist Theory of Science* (1975), *The Possibility of Naturalism* (1979), *Dialectic Materialism and Human Emancipation* (1982), and *Philosophical Ideologies* (1982).

KENNETH J. GERGEN is Professor of Psychology at Swarthmore College. He has been primarily concerned with the generation of new forms of study in social psychology. His most recent books are *Toward Transformation in Social Psychology* (1982), *Self Concept* (edited with M. Lynch and A. Norem-Hebeisen) and *Social Psychology* (with M.M. Gergen).

MARY M. GERGEN is a research associate in Psychology at Swarthmore College. Her research has been particularly concerned with foreign relations, social narratives, and explanations in aging. With K. J. Gergen, she has authored a text, *Social Psychology,* and is currently working on a volume, *Historical Social Psychology.*

ANTHONY GIDDENS is a Fellow of King's College, Cambridge, England. Among other books, he is the author of *Studies in Social and Political Theory* (1977), *Central Problems in Social Theory* (1979), and a *Contemporary Critique of Historical Materialism* (1981). He is an Associate Editor of the *Journal for the Theory of Social Behavior.*

7

D. W. HAMLYN is Professor of Philosophy at Birkbeck College, University of London, and the editor of *Mind*. He is the author of *The Psychology of Perception* (1957), *Sensation and Perception* (1961), *The Theory of Knowledge* (1971), *Experience and the Growth of Understanding* (1978), *Perception, Learning and the Self* (1982), as well as books on Aristotle and Schopenhauer. Philosophy of psychology has been a primary interest of his for many years, along with epistemology and metaphysics and certain aspects of the history of philosophy.

ROM HARRÉ is a Fellow of Linacre College and a member of the Philosophy Faculty at the University of Oxford. His books include *Principles of Scientific Thinking* (1970); (with P. Secord) *The Explanation of Social Behavior* (1972); (with E. Madden) *Causal Powers: A Theory of Natural Necessity* (1975); (with Peter Marsh and Elizabeth Rosser) *Rules of Disorder* (1978); (with Jane Morgan) *Nicknames: Their Origins and Social Consequences* (1979); and *Social Being: A Theory for Social Psychology* (1979).

IVAN KARP is Associate Professor of Anthropology at Indiana University. He is a social anthropologist interested in modes of thought, the interpretation of experience, and has conducted field research in Kenya. He is author of *Fields of Change Among the Iteso of Kenya* (1978) and co-editor of *Explorations in African Systems of Thought* (1980).

MARTHA B. KENDALL is Associate Professor of Anthropology at Indiana University. She is primarily interested in linguistic and semantic anthropological questions as they reflect on social process. Her field work has been in North America and West Africa.

JUSTIN LEIBER is Professor of Philosophy at the University of Houston. His work is with the underlying issues that connect linguistics, cognitive psychology, and primatology. His books include *Noam Chomsky: A Philosophic Overview* (1975), *Structuralism* (1978), and *Beyond Rejection* (1980).

PETER T. MANICAS, Professor of Philosophy at Queens College, City University of New York, has been primarily interested in the foundations of the human sciences and in political and social theory. His articles have appeared in a variety of interdisciplinary and philosophical journals, and his most recent book is The *Death of the State* (1974). He is an Associate Editor of the *Journal for the Theory of Social Behavior.*

JOHN P. SABINI is Associate Professor in the Department of Psychology at the University of Pennsylvania. His major research interests are in the area of moral judgments. With Maury Silver, he is co-author of *Moralities of Everyday Life* (1982).

PAUL F. SECORD is currently Professor of Psychology and Education at the University of Houston. A social psychologist, he has maintained a strong interest in interdisciplinary theory and research throughout his career. In 1970, with Rom Harré, he founded the *Journal for the Theory of Social Behavior* and has remained its General Editor since that time. He is the author of seven books, including (with Rom Harré) *The Explanation of Social Behavior,* and (with Marcia Guttentag) the forthcoming *Too Many Women: The Sex Ratio Question.* His interests extend beyond psychology to sociology and to the philosophy of mind and of science. He has been a Visiting Professor at Princeton University, Yale University, and Oxford University, and is Past President of the Society for Philosophy and Psychology and of the Division of Personality and Social Psychology of the American Psychological Association. He has also served as Chief Executive Officer of the Society for Experimental Social Psychology.

MAURY SILVER is an Assistant Professor of Psychology at The Johns Hopkins University. His major research interests are in the field of moral judgments. He is co-author (with John Sabini) of *Moralities of Everyday Life* (1982).

CHARLES W. SMITH is an Associate Professor of Sociology at Queens College, C.U.N.Y. His primary interest has been various forms of reasoning and consciousness and their social grounds. He is the author of *A Critique of Sociological Reasoning* (1979) and *The Mind of the Market: A Study of Stock Market Philosophies, their Uses, and their Implications* (1981). He is an Associate Editor of the *Journal for the Theory of Social Behavior.*

CHARLES TAYLOR is Professor of Political Science at McGill University. The conceptual foundations of psychology and the social sciences has been one of his primary concerns. His books include *The Explanation of Behavior* (1964) and *Hegel* (1975).

STEPHEN TOULMIN has been a Professor in the Committee for Social Thought at the University of Chicago since 1973. Among his many books are *The Ancestry of Science*, Vols. 1-3 (1962-1965); *Human Understanding* (1972); *Wittgenstein's Vienna* (1973); *Knowing and Acting* (1976); and *An Introduction to Reasoning* (1979).

Preface

This volume is part of a continuing effort by a group of philosophers and behavioral scientists to explore theoretical issues at the interface of philosophy and the behavioral sciences. The volume was planned by the editor in collaboration with several of the scholars regularly participating in this work. For each volume, participants worked for a year or more preparing their contributions, and then, after exchanging papers, convened for a three-day discussion of the ideas therein. The conference for the present volume was held at the University of Houston in December 1979. We are especially grateful for the support of Chancellor Barry Munitz and the Conference Center of the University.

The continuing interdisciplinary collaboration began in the 1960s under the energetic and wise leadership of the late Theodore Mischel. The initial meeting of philosophers and psychologists focused on issues relating to the philosophy of mind and the explanation of human behavior. A conference held in 1967 was followed by the publication in 1969 of the volume, *Human Action*. Subsequent volumes, all edited by Theodore Mischel, but each having a somewhat different topic and set of contributors, were *Cognitive Development and Epistemology* (1971), *Understanding Other Persons* (1974), and *The Self: Psychological and Philosophical Issues* (1977). The last volume was published shortly after Mischel's death in December 1976.

The topic of the present volume departs somewhat from earlier ones, in examining the interface between philosophy, psychology, and the social sciences with a view to conceptualizing adequate explanations of human consciousness and behavior. In addition to the contributors to this volume, Thomas Beidelman of New York University participated in the conference discussions.

Those of us who had the privilege of working with and knowing Ted Mischel greatly lament his untimely death, both in the loss to the world of ideas and in our loss of a warm and enjoyable colleague. This book is dedicated to his memory.

P. F. Secord

CHAPTER 1

Interfacing the Personal
and the Social

PAUL F. SECORD

This book addresses what is perhaps the most difficult but also the most important question of the social and behavioral sciences: how we generate explanations of social behavior through articulating a mix of:

1. objective conditions in the physical and social world;
2. actors' conciousness and understanding of themselves in the social world; and
3. background, social context, or social structures which are not part of the actor's consciousness or understandings.

The theme represented by these questions has many roots in the past. It relates the old arguments in social theory between *Naturwissenschaften* and *Geisteswissenschaften,* idealism and materialism, positivism and anti-positivism, naturalism and anti-naturalism, and methodological individualism and holism. During the past few decades, approaches taken by psychologists, sociologists, anthropologists, and others have often emphasized one or more of the thematic perspectives at the expense of others. As a result, their views of human nature and their explanations of social behavior are usually one-sided and make only limited contributions to our understanding. For example, behaviorism in its most extreme form has simply evaded the issue by ruling out the subjective side of the question. Other well-known approaches such as interpretive sociology, humanistic psychology, and symbolic interactionism have emphasized the subjective pole of the question while sacrificing the remaining perspectives. No single book could possibly provide a complete answer to the many ramifications of this theme, but hopefully partial progress can be accomplished by a varied series of efforts. The original contributions offered here take up some facet of this theme in the attempt to achieve a better articulation of the various approaches.

Among the many questions raised by this core theme are the following:

(1) Are phenomenology, action-theory, notions of rule-governed behavior, ethnomethodology, ethogeny, and dramaturgy (granting differences between these) limited to a "clarification of what is thought about the social world by those living in it" (Giddens, 1976, pp. 17ff, 32)? Do these approaches confuse or assimilate description and "interpretation" with "explanation," assuming that we can get clear on these ideas?

(2) If it be granted that social reality is constituted by the beliefs and acts of participants, and that "understanding" is "the very ontological condition of human life," how does one bring in the "objective conditions"? If we deny that there are any, aren't we into idealism with its problems? Are objective conditions determining conditions in some sense? In what sense? Are they mediated by consciousness? All of them? Do we appeal to Durkheimian "social facts"? To "structures" (whatever *they* are)? What is the role of "cause" in social science? How does it articulate with the various perspectives of our core theme?

(3) Can actors be wrong about their own social reality? Can the ground of action be opaque to the actors? Can it be determined by conditions not mediated by consciousness? How do we negotiate differences in accounts provided by actors? Or differences between accounts and theoretical explanations? What of false consciousness?

(4) What do we mean by the explanation of social behavior? What counts as an explanation? What are we trying to explain? Individual actions? Classes of actions? Forms of life? Institutions? Societies? Are these different *levels* of explanation (e.g., psychological, sociological, biological)? If so, how are they related to each other?

(5) Is social psychology part of psychology, or really part of sociology? That is, if general psychology can be understood as an attempt to detail the "generative mechanisms" of behavior (perception, learning, and the like), perhaps all we need for it is a causal account (à la Australian materialism; Armstrong, 1968). But social psychology seems in stark contrast, in that it is *historical* in being concerned with social acts at specific times and places. And *social* acts have meanings to the actors and involve their understanding.

(6) Is there a useful methodological division of labor between micro- and macro-sociology? What is the flaw, if any, in seeing Goffman- (1974) and Garfinkel- (1967) type inquiries as explanations of interpersonal

behavior? Is it the case that such inquiries are limited or mystifying unless institutions, power differentials, and so forth are part of the study? If so, how do we connect the explication of human action at the interpersonal level with the properties of social institutions and structures?

All of the contributors in this book address themselves directly to one or more of the questions. The following shows how each of the chapters bears upon the central theme, and indicates the tentative lines taken in order to advance our knowledge.

In Chapter 2, Charles Taylor raises one facet of our core theme: the inadequate treatment of consciousness in modern cognitive psychology and the question of its proper role in the explanation of behavior. He first notes that the modern functionalist form of cognitive psychology treats consciousness as marginal—it has only a peripheral role in explaining behavior. Underlying this marginal view is the notion that functions can ultimately be described in physicalist terms, including conscious action. This is not a crude, but a sophisticated reductionism. In this version, computer programs provide an analogue for the functions of behavior: a computer can be said to compute in the same way that humans compute, although the computational process of the human in the analogical sense is at least partially below awareness or outside of consciousness. The reductionism is more sophisticated because it recognizes that radically different forms of hardware could be programmed to represent the same process.

Taylor asks why this functionalist view has such a strong hold on many behavioral scientists. He suggests that the answer is rooted in absolutism—the idea that the world must be grasped entirely apart from observation of it; subject-related properties must be purged; the realm of body must be separate from that of mind. But the Cartesian-empiricist tradition did not achieve this; it retained an interactionism between mind and body—perception and desires entered into explanation. Functionalism rejects any form of interactionism because interactionism would require that nonphysical events trigger physical ones; hence Taylor notes that the choice between seeing consciousness as marginal or adopting an interactionist view of body and mind seems forced only if these two views are the only ones possible. He offers an alternative, called the significance feature, which is not always seen as a view of consciousness, but which actually emphasizes consciousness as a feature of human action. To understand this alternative, one must first see what is inadequate about assuming an essential identity between the functional processes of machines and those of humans.

A machine *does something* when it does what we have designed it to do. This, Taylor argues, is the flaw in the functionalist view, because in fact the attribution of such action terms to machines is relative to our interests and projects. But there is no answer to the question of what the machine is *really* doing. Clearly, this question is relevant to human action but not to machines. Actions are essentially constituted by their purposes, machines are not. This purposive quality of human action is its "significance feature."

This objection may not be decisive for the computative process—both human and machine—but Taylor considers it decisive in the case of human emotions. For some features of human behavior, such as calculating, the functionalist could still argue that awareness is peripheral and unnecessary; our behavior can be understood without it. But this becomes impossible for human emotions. The case of "shame," for example, seems conclusive. Shame requires a self-feeling, a sense of agency. Humans can feel ashamed of having made a mistake; computers cannot. Shame cannot be regarded as an inessential mental phenomenon; it is too heavily implicated in describing and understanding important human actions; it is inescapably involved in our functioning as human beings. To try to reduce it to physiology, moreover, is futile, because such a reduction would require a fundamentally different logic from that involved in human action.

Taylor concludes, then, that consciousness is at the core of our understanding of human action; it is an achievement of agents with the aid of language, and it is mistaken to view it as a representation of an independent reality. No boundary can be drawn between the mental and the physical, for this would exclude explanations in terms of their most significant feature. This breaks fundamentally with the view dominant today in much philosophy and cognitive psychology.

In Chapter 3, Stephen Toulmin continues the issue of how to understand consciousness and its place in the behavioral and social sciences. Like Taylor, he too rejects a dualistic view of mind and body, a view in which the scientist identifies consciousness with the inner and private, and thus dismisses it as inappropriate for inclusion in any scientific system. But though Toulmin's and Taylor's views are not incompatible, Toulmin's approach and use of argument is different from Taylor's.

Toulmin begins by asking why, for 350 years, the central problems of epistemology and the philosophy of mind have so often been formulated around the mind-body distinction, in terms of a contrast between the inward, private character of experience (consciousness) and the public, interpersonal language of thought. Quite possibly, he suggests, concrete practical terms like "deciding" and "intending," which have functional uses in ordinary life, have historically been subtly transformed into private, interior terms of "experience." Philosophers, in attempting to construct a general account of knowledge, have unquestionably played an important part in this unfortunate transformation.

Toulmin approaches the problem by starting with an analysis of the senses in which "consciousness" is used. These are: (1) sensibility, in the sense of lapsing into unconsciousness when asleep but regaining it when awake; (2) attentiveness, in the sense of consciously paying attention to what one is doing or to what is going on; and (3) articulateness, in the sense of having explicit motives, intentions, and plans in carrying out a line of action.

Each of these is in turn a condition for the next sense of consciousness; without sensibility one could not monitor progress in carrying out one's intentions or plans. In other words, the senses are not separable from one another except in an abstract sense; they have essential connections. As we will see, moreover, they are linked to a fourth sense as yet to be identified.

The second sense, attentiveness, allows sociological aspects of consciousness to enter in, in such senses as "consciousness of class" or "consciousness-raising." Psychoanalytic senses (unconscious, preconscious, conscious) do not yet fully enter in, although some types of pathological disabilities would fall here, such as paranoid/overattention to trivial events or neurotic inattention to significant ones. In the third sense, one will be unable to give a coherent account of one's actions or will give an account that is discrepant from what an ordinary observer can plainly see. Social consciousness, as it is expressed in Marxism or other critical views of society, also falls under this third sense.

Toulmin next asks: In what order did these senses come into use? He suggests starting with the third sense. And seeking the origins of these senses leads ultimately to the identification of a fourth sense of consciousness: that of several agents formulating jointly coordinated states of mind, plans, or actions. The roots of this fourth sense are found in the Latin origins of the word *consciousness,* and its historical origins are found in Roman law. The upshot is that basic sensibility can hardly be thought of as primary; even the famous "stream of consciousness" phrase is an improper one, for it ignores the roots of the word "consciousness" in social life.

The final and most difficult question posed by Toulmin asks how consciousness ever acquired the private meanings that have characterized the past few centuries and offers some highly tentative answers. Ultimately, then, the parallel between Taylor's and Toulmin's versions of consciousness is complete; both find their roots in what is essentially public: the intentionality of human action. While Toulmin emphasizes the concerted, multiperson nature of consciousness and Taylor does not, this interpersonal, social characteristic of intentional action is nevertheless implicit in any adequate account of consciousness.

In Chapter 4, John Sabini and Maury Silver tackle the difficult question of distinctions between subjectivity and objectivity. All too often, behavioral scientists oversimplify these distinctions; the analysis here effectively brings out the complexities involved in articulating what is meant by saying that something is subjective or objective. Subjectivity is central to the core theme of this book as, for example, in asking how the interpretive sociology of Weber is to be articulated with, say, the "social facts" of Durkheim, or how the phenomenological perspective is to be articulated with "objectively" described behavior.

Sabini and Silver develop eight senses of subjectivity/objectivity. What becomes clear in the course of their analysis is that subjectivity and objectivity are not necessarily in opposition or even inconsistent with one another—in fact, some senses of subjectivity require a corresponding sense of objectivity even to be understandable. Most of the senses of subjectivity appear to be rooted in personal differences—for instance differences in perspectives or in values; and, because of this, can sometimes be seen objectively by different individuals, as in the case where each is capable of taking the other's point of view, or where the ends of individuals may be different, and yet are understood in terms of common standards or commonly understood ways to reach ends, even idiosyncratic ends. Not all differences among individuals are rooted in an irredeemable subjectivity; it is possible to have different points of view which are not subjective—in the sense of distorted. The account of a play by a critic and by a member of the audience may be quite different, yet both may be objective.

Toward the end of their chapter, Sabini and Silver explore the implications of their analysis for understanding human action. They conclude that, while it may be difficult to find criteria for judging human action, there is no irreducible subjectivity about human action. Moreover, objectivity doesn't always depend on shared criteria; the fact that people disagree with each other shows that they treat the focus of their disagreement as objective. Often disagreement arises about the nature of the object; in this case, observers may differ, but their differences need not imply that the issue is subjective: the observers, in disagreeing, treat the issue as real.

The authors go on to distinguish ambiguity from subjectivity, and then raise the issue of whether or not moral actions must necessarily be judged subjectively. Here, the most relevant sense of subjectivity is that of ends—observers may see the ends of an action differently, as where an attack upon a person might be seen as having an aggressive intent or as the intent to defend oneself. But there are ways in which such ends can be further analyzed, ultimately leading to an agreement among the observers that is objective in content. The authors conclude that morality is not necessarily subjective; observers from the same culture can sometimes arrive objectively at agreements that certain actions are right or wrong and good or bad.

In Chapter 5, Rom Harré starts from the premise "that the structure of ordinary language reflects and in part creates the psychology of the people who use that language" (p. 93). By now this premise has been accepted in many quarters (see the anthology, *The Psychology of Ordinary Explanations of Social Behavior*), although many behavioral scientists resist or ignore it. But its acceptance is crucial to understanding the thrust of Harré's treatment of psychological dimensions. The point is that the activities of persons are inextricably intertwined with the everyday language used to describe, refer, grasp, perceive, or even enact them. So if psychology is to be relevant to everyday life, its theories and concepts must provide a place for this domain.

The move, long favored by many behavioral scientists, to substitute for everyday understanding a more technical language in which human action is to be described may be sound in principle, but in practice it has taken only simple-minded, wholly objectionable forms (e.g., stimulus-response psychology). The ever-present danger of such a move is that human action is apt to be described in grossly distorted, inappropriate, or even imaginary forms having little resemblance to real-life action. No artificially constructed language has appeared which can even begin to approach the richness and subtlety of natural languages.

Yet, psychologists need not remain solely within this ordinary language domain. Psychology must be articulated with it, but need not be limited to it. Harré undertakes to analyze certain aspects of this language domain, aspects that might be referred to as folk psychology. He performs a dimensional analysis of selected mentalistic concepts and attempts to identify their roots in a systematic, three-dimensional space. Folk psychology is incomplete and does not provide an adequate analytical scheme for many psychological processes. One purpose of the analysis is to insure that terms that are not a part of folk psychology are appropriately articulated with folk psychology, especially those arising through new discoveries about human action.

Harré develops a space consisting of three dimensions that are orthogonal to each other: private-public, individual-collective, and personal order versus social order. He is particularly concerned to reject the Cartesian inner-outer dimension which has been so pervasive in both philosophy and psychology. Further, Harré takes as given that: (1) human life is inescapably social; and (2) that the display in different societies of certain psychological attributes (e.g., emotions) varies markedly. These givens entail that at least some human attributes will have both an individual and collective realization, and these considerations provide a basis for the three dimensions offered.

Harré goes on to illustrate how various human attributes may be mapped on his three-dimensional space. Intelligence, for example, is continuous from pole to pole of the personal order versus social order dimension, but is mapped toward the individual and the private poles of the other two dimensions. Interesting considerations arise in the attempt to map memory in the three-dimensional space, while memory has traditionally been mapped in the private-individual-social order sector. Harré demonstrates that the growth of technical aids and institutional practices involving memory are apt to shift the conceptual status of memory somewhat toward the collective and the public poles. Clearly, the three-dimensional scheme has important implications for other attributes like intention and the emotions.

Finally, Harré applies the schema to the concept of consciousness. He finds a marked parallel between his analysis and that of Toulmin (this volume). Using three root ideas—awareness, attention, and reflexiveness—he finds that the first is a prerequisite for the second, and the second a prerequisite for the third. Each of these three senses is seen as a type of relation between the person and the object of his or her consciousness. Consciousness falls in the private-individual-personal order sector in the three-dimensional space. But the social dimension enters in at the second level: attention is partly determined by an individual's system of categories which, of course, have their origin in society. And at the third level, the social component arises in a more complex way, in that reflexivity requires a working concept of the self.

Justin Leiber, in Chapter 6, makes use of the distinction, common in biology, between analogy and homology to understand and resolve these three issues:

(1) The debate about nonhuman primate linguistic abilities.
(2) "What is the normal form for psychological descriptions; can they be the tables of a universal Turing machine?"

(3) The supposed subjectivity (or double indeterminacy) of claims in the psychological/social sciences. If societies have wholly arbitrary cultures, and can be known only through the meanings that humans attach to them, must they only be known subjectively?

The distinction between analogy and homology is clear. Two organs in two different species are homologous if they have a common form of biological development; if they have the same phylogeny. Thus, the whiskers of cats and the antennae of insects are only analogous in their capacity to determine proximity to objects; they are not homologous because they lack a phylogenic relationship. And the maturing of biology can be characterized as the gradual replacement of analogy by homology.

Taking first the issue of the normal form of psychological description, Leiber reminds us that "Turing suggested in effect that any computer that could be said to have the same Turing machine table as a human would therefore bear the same cognitive predicates, the psychological description. Only if the machine and we share something like the same table for addition, can we both be said to know that $5 + 7 = 12$, etc." If this form of functionalism were true, it should be possible to give a complete description of a human mind by indicating the routines or programs it currently has on hand. Leiber then shows that this argument is relatively weak; it is more like an analogy than a homology. He does this by developing another analogy between human locomotion and a universal machine that locomotes, and by demonstrating that sharing the same locomotion tables does not entail that their locomotion is similar. It is not that Turing is wrong, but rather that the computer analogy is just that, and provides only a weak basis for describing and understanding human cognitive states.

Leiber goes on to suggest that the use of sign language by Washoe, the chimpanzee, is a borderline case of language. In a functional and analogical sense, it is reasonable to say that Washoe is something of a person, a person with something comparable to the moral status of a human. And if this is a criterion for having language, then Washoe does have language. But Washoe does not have language in the homological sense; it is not natural to her. We cannot describe her language in the developmental and phylogenetic terms that we can apply to human linguistic capacity.

The discussion leads to skepticism as to whether there is a universal, normal form of psychological description for any member of the species of human thinkers. Instead, we may share normal forms of descriptions for some faculties but not others. And the basis for identifying normal component or subdescriptions should be homological—species-wide, organ-systematic, comparative, developmental, and phylogenetic. By this criterion, to describe a language is to give it generative grammar; that is, to specify the device for generating sentences of the language. Arguing from homology, this amounts to the claim that there is a "language organ," a claim that legitimizes linguistics as an independent science.

Finally, Leiber turns to the supposed gulf between the subjectivity of the social and psychological sciences and the objectivity of the natural sciences. If we conceive of a language organ as emanating from maturation and development in a given setting, then language is not an exterior, wholly social-cultural entity, but one that is integral with the biology of humans, and with their developmental capacities. The conception can be extended to the cultures of society: it seems unlikely that we can think of them as wholly autonomous; rather, they can only be understood within the context of naturally developing humans as biological entities. Thus the biological mode of explanation provides a bridge or homological framework within which sociological generalizations can be placed. And so Leiber concludes that, so long as biology is regarded as a natural science, the methods of natural science are appropriate to the investigation of language, cognitive processes, and society.

In Chapter 7, Kenneth and Mary Gergen examine forms of explanation in ordinary experience as well as their close counterparts in psychology. Their central theme is that explanations that compete with one another often map the real world in incommensurate ways. The evidence or observations pertaining to one explanatory form do not overlap or overlap only partially with the evidence or observations relevant to another explanatory form. This makes it difficult or impossible to favor on the basis of empirical evidence one explanatory form over another.

Gergen and Gergen suggest that the major forms of explanation found in ordinary usage as well as in psychology can be classified under two headings: empowered or enabled. The *empowered* explanation is one that "bestows on the explanatory source a determinative control." Typically, the determinative control is found in the situational conditions that prevail at the time the behavior occurs. What springs to mind here is the ubiquitous use of the phrase among Skinnerian behaviorists: "the behavior has come under the control of . . . ." *Enabled* explanations focus on the person as the generative source of the behavior. Phenomenological or cognitive explanations are apt here. The Gergens run through a variety of cases which epitomize these two contrasting explanatory forms.

In their original form, empowered and enabled explanations are incommensurate because the terms in which the observations or evidence are described have no common basis. But Gergen and Gergen go on to note that, in principle, a person-based explanation can be located for every situation-based explanation, and vice versa. This is accomplished by translating the terms of one explanatory form into the other. Since this is always possible, there is no way of eliminating either the person-based theorist or the situation-based theorist in favor of the other.

They close their inquiry by illustrating how explanation is confounded in social learning theory. Bandura (1977) makes use of the power of the behaviorist tradition, but at the same time tries to amplify it by bringing in social constructs. He starts out by emphasizing the effects of external events on the activity of the individual in terms of reinforcement contingencies, but allows them to recede into the background as the cognitive apparatus comes to the fore as a basis of explanation. Gergen and Gergen see this as juxtaposing conflicting explanatory forms in an unwarranted fashion.

Chapter 8, by Peter Manicas, takes up another facet of our core theme, this time the nature of psychology and its relation to the social sciences. The leading idea, startling until it is understood, is the rejection of the common belief that the human sciences are aimed at *explaining behavior* (a term which here includes not only movements or responses, but also actions). Manicas's view is that psychology *is* neuropsychology and is continuous with the biological sciences. Its special task is the explanation of psychological processes, such as learning, perception, cognition, and the like in terms of their generative mechanisms. Note that this is a broad conception of neuropsychology, since it includes perception and learning, and is not neuropsychology as it is sometimes narrowly conceived. But the aim of psychology, properly conceived, is not to explain behavior, not the particular acts of individuals, nor classes of actions characterized in general terms. It would instead aim at an understanding of *how* humans are able to do the things they do.

This view is based upon recent developments which represent a radical departure from conventional philosophy of science. First, the orthodox assumption that the nature of the world permits the use of the formula, "whenever these conditions, then this event" is rejected. This thesis, derived from Hume, that scientific laws are statements of constant conjunctions between events, is no longer believed to apply to the natural world. Along with this thesis came the idea that events are to be explained by subsuming them under scientific laws; this, too, is to be discarded and replaced by a more defensible notion of explanation. Worth noting is that while the radical behaviorism of Skinner is the most explicit modeling in psychology of these outmoded ideas, they have seriously affected all of psychology.

What needs emphasis is that, for some events (at least), the world is radically *open*. Because of this, science must "aim at knowledge of something other than laws construed as constant conjunctions of events." According to Manicas (and Bhaskar, this volume), "science aims at producing knowledge of 'real structures which endure and operate independently of our knowledge, our experiences and the conditions which allow us access to them.'" In the case of psychology, this means that we might eventually come to understand human powers and capacities far better than we now do, but still not be able to explain or predict the everyday actions of people. The latter cannot be an aim of *science* because, with few exceptions, such as the movement of heavenly bodies, the world is an open system. Behavior *never* operates under conditions of closure in the everyday world. Only in the experimental laboratory is it possible to achieve closure (and partially at that). And the purpose of such experimentation is to identify generative mechanisms or processes that account for or explain the behavior that occurs in the laboratory. But this is done only in the service of understanding how certain behaviors are generated by structures or processes that can be conceived in theoretical terms.

The philosophy of mind, inspired by Ryle's (1949) *The Concept of Mind* and the later writings of Wittgenstein, takes us one step further. Focusing on human action, arguments against the very possibility of causal explanations of behavior emerged. Ordinary everyday explanations of behavior were often more appropriate than those based on scientific psychology, it was argued. This assumption, if accepted, would appear to make scientific psychology impossible. But Manicas pinpoints the error made here by *both* sides: the idea that it is the task of a scientific psychology to explain behavior as it occurs in everyday life. If this assumption is dropped, then it is quite possible to accept the idea that many of our ordinary explanations are perfectly sound without being in conflict with psychology. A psychology does not have to reject all this accumulated knowledge and start from scratch; on the other hand, it might at times refine and improve our knowledge. But this would occur largely through a greater insight into our powers and limitations; psychology as a science is properly confined to the laboratory. The intention here is not to rule out those areas of psychology such as personality, industrial, and clinical, but rather to bring out that their task is radically different from that of the laboratory psychologists; most importantly, they must bring in many extrascientific forms of knowledge and skills. Any attempt to understand and explain the behavior of individuals in the everyday world necessarily brings in biographical, social, historical, and situational factors. These cannot be incorporated within a science which requires the achievement of closure in the laboratory; thus, those disciplines of psychology which deal with everyday behaviors are forms of inquiry that relate more closely to the other social sciences, like sociology and anthropology, than they do to experimental psychology.

Turning back to psychology as a laboratory science, Manicas reemphasizes its linkage with biology. Humans are natural organisms with an evolutionary history. Efforts to understand how linguistic, intellectual, and social powers are developed and "represented" in the maturing nervous system thus seem to dovetail with psychology as a biological science; many facets of cognitive psychology, too, fit in here. This does not require that psychology be reductionistic; phenomenology will remain an integral part of it. A neuropsychology will not escape its dependence upon the use of ordinary terms for describing the behavior that is generated; these constitute a different and irreducible level from that of neurology or physiology.

Since human action is inherently social, a biological psychology cannot and should not strive to explain or understand social behavior, but it can contribute by uncovering the basis of social powers (e.g., language). Yet it cannot explain the contents of mind, which have their origins in the social world. So social psychology is a "transitionary discipline in that it links our knowledge of human powers as physiologically explained and human powers as they are realized socially," a definition that comes close to that of George Herbert Mead (1934). Social psychology is clearly a social, not a biological science because it is built around the concept of the person as we know and understand it in our everyday lives. And it is therefore historical and situational.

Finally, the role of sociology and the other social sciences, like psychology, is specialized, and likewise should not be understood as having as its central purpose the explanation of everyday behavior within the context of various societies. No more than psychology, sociology is not to be conceived of as *replacing* our ordinary explanations of everyday behavior, but has as its distinct theoretical interest an understanding of "social structures"—the relatively enduring *products* and *media* of all human action. That is, social structures, e.g., language, pre-exist for individuals; they thus *enable* persons to become persons and to act; and at the same time they are "coercive," limiting the ways we *can* act. Yet social structures are *constituted* by actions which either reproduce or transform the very structures which are its medium" (p. 167 this volume).

In closing, Manicas stresses the point that so long as the human sciences are conceived as concerned with explaining behavior, they are doomed to fail, because persons are biologically and culturally a mix that cannot be dealt with scientifically. But we can come to better understand ourselves if we accept this fact and acknowledge our interest in ourselves both as *persons* (with all the social/biographical implications of that word), and conduct social inquiry with that in mind, and also as *organisms,* with special capacities or powers acquired through a long evolutionary history, and conduct a psychological inquiry into the origins of those capacities or powers.

The previous chapters have more or less emphasized the psychological aspects of the problems raised by the core theme of this book. In the remaining chapters the emphasis is more on the sociological aspects of these problems. Of course, no absolute distinction is intended, nor is it possible.

Chapter 9, by Anthony Giddens, provides his perspective on how first steps might be taken to resolve these problems. As such, it also provides a helpful orientation to the remaining chapters.

Giddens first calls attention to the prevailing insularity of sociology and philosophy, even though they often address themselves to common problems. This is partly due, he believes, to the emphasis in the extensive philosophical literature pertaining to human action on individuals and their intentions and reasons at the expense of attention to the unintended consequences of such action. In contrast, much of sociology has brushed aside the idea of individuals as knowledgeable actors, preferring to stress impersonal conditions, processes, or structures as central determinants of behavior. And it is one of the strong themes of this book that these two polar perspectives need to be articulated with each other. Giddens suggests a way in which this might be done.

The chapter focuses on three issues:

(1) "What should a theory of action involve in the social sciences—how should we best conceptualize 'human action' in sociology?
(2) "How should we best conceptualize the notion of 'structure' in sociology?
(3) "What conceptual connections should be supposed to exist between these two—between the ideas of action and structure—in sociological explanations" (this volume, p. 176)?

Giddens observes that symbolic interactionism in sociology (e.g., that of Goffman) constitutes a minority position: it emphasizes intentional human action but slights institutional and structural analysis. Sociology more commonly has "stressed the primacy of object over subject, of social structure or social system over the purposeful, capable social actor." This is true both of structuralism in France and functionalism in the English-speaking world.

In large outline, Giddens proposes to resolve the antithesis between purposeful action and the systematic or functional control of human behavior through what he terms a *stratification model* of action. This model starts with the unacknowledged conditions of action as a context. Within it, purposive action occurs: its three components are motivation, the "rationalization of action," and the reflexive monitoring of action. But all such actions extend beyond the purposive action itself; they have unintended consequences. Finally, and most important, these unintended consequences act back to qualify the action that takes place, and to reproduce or transform the unacknowledged conditions of action.

Action, moreover, involves a duality; that of *discursive consciousness* and *practical consciousness*. The actor is usually capable of reflecting upon and describing his actions—giving an account—but actions also have a tacit component: individuals enact many performances for which they cannot give an adequate account. Finally, the knowledgeability of humans is always bounded by the unacknowledged conditions of action on one side, and by its unintended consequences on the other.

In addition, the concept of *structure* plays a vital role. While not accepting the views of structuralists as given, Giddens believes that certain ideas inherent in their views are vital to social theory. Functionalists, he notes, stress function at the expense of structure, which has remained more implicit or taken for granted among them. Most often it has taken the form of constraints, à la Durkheim. Structure is to be distinguished from system, which is taken to cover the social relations among individuals as well as collectivism, in terms of regularly recurring patterns. In Giddens's sense, structure involves "recursively organized rules and resources. Structure only exists as 'structural properties.'" Structuration involves "conditions governing the continuity or transformation of structures, and therefore the reproduction of systems."

Just as human action has a duality in terms of discursive consciousness versus practical consciousness, structure, too, is dually comprised. Social life is recursive; the structural properties of social systems are both medium and outcome of the practices that constitute those systems. The analogy is to language: syntactical rules are the medium whereby one generates grammatical sentences, but in generating sentences one reproduces the language, including the rules implicated in it.

Giddens concludes by reiterating his major points. Institutions do not just work behind the backs of actors; both their discursive knowledge and practical consciousness are involved in reproducing the institutions over time. One final point: structures involve both rules and resources; the latter are the key to social power, which has not been sufficiently emphasized in either philosophical or sociological discussions.

In Chapter 10, David Hamlyn takes to task a central theme in Berger and Luckmann's (1967) classic work, *The Social Construction of Reality*. This is the idea that social reality is socially constructed: that it is normative and conventional. Hamlyn finds fault with this view on epistemological grounds: there is no sense in which *reality* (whether physical or social) can be "constructed." For any sense which refers to reality cannot be merely subjective; the very meaning of reality requires a concept of truth: knowledge of reality must in principle be accessible to other persons. While there is a sense in which reality becomes known through social interaction with other persons, it is not constructed. If it is to be *knowledge* of reality, then that knowledge must have grounds for being correct or not. Having a conception of reality requires that we be both conscious and social. But it is not *merely* social; if it were, then it would not be reality.

Berger and Luckmann acknowledge a debt to Mead (1934) and Schutz (1966), so Hamlyn turns to these scholars to search for the possible origins of the idea of the social construction of reality. Neither Mead nor Schutz, he notes, had a primary concern for setting out an epistemology which would provide an account of claims to knowledge of the world; their interest was in how individuals understood or grasped the social world. Both emphasized relations with other persons as a primary source of such understanding. But they were very different in certain respects; Mead emphasized social behavior with little reference to consciousness of it, while Schutz, as a phenomenologist, did emphasize it. Nevertheless, both writers offer an account of sorts of the relation between social considerations and knowledge of reality, an account that Hamlyn finds to be seriously wrong. It is perhaps this erroneous account which Berger and Luckmann take as their starting point.

As Hamlyn notes, Schutz and Mead take very different stances in respect to consciousness. Schutz begins with individuals conscious of their lives and actions; for Mead, consciousness emerges only out of interactions with others, thus entering late in the account. For Hamlyn, consciousness lies somewhere in between these extremes: the most basic form of consciousness is awareness of an object (in a formal sense). This elementary sense becomes elaborated through interaction with others in ways that lead to the acquisition of knowledge, and further, through its relation to our social actions. But this requisite social factor does not imply that reality is constructed; rather, we come to know reality.

An important source of confusion in Berger and Luckmann's thought, according to Hamlyn, is their confounding of knowledge with belief; they think of the different modes of consciousness arising from social differences as forms of *knowledge*. For them, knowledge might be legitimized belief. But this would imply that what is known is what society says is so. The fact, however, that the notions of right and wrong are social does not entail that "what is right is simply what society says is so." In the end, there is no such thing as social reality; there is only reality itself.

In Chapter 11, Charles Smith emphasizes the social roots of mind and the mental pluralism which these roots produce. Mind is conceived of as a specific life form, reaching its present state through a process of biological and cultural evolution. The four modalities of mind described here have some relation to—and some differences from—the various social science perspectives that we have been at pains to articulate to each other. Smith's major aim is to provide a scheme for determining the relative significance of the modalities of mind in different situations. Under what circumstances does intentional human action take front and center; under what social conditions do only inarticulate feelings get expressed? With cultural evolution, mind has become so complex that it seems highly advisable to identify those components that are analytically distinct as well as the social situations or environmentally distinct stances in which these components become important.

In Smith's scheme, the four modalities of mind differ along dimensions such as their foci of concern, their meanings and ends, their perspectives, their view of reality, and their degree of reflectivity. The four modalities are:

(1) The organism-libido context, where mind functions primarily to protect the organism as an organism.
(2) The social relations context, where jurisdiction and power come to the fore.
(3) The physical world context, which the mind orders and clarifies, usually in a pragmatic way.
(4) The symbolic, meaning-ordered world context, in which the mind operates to reduce contradictions and to impose clarity and order.

Smith emphasizes that these modalities are not entirely distinct from one another; they can be identified only analytically. And often two or more modalities are operating simultaneously. Yet the distinctions are useful and become apparent under the special circumstances that call forth particular modalities. For example, when the organism is the focus of concern (e.g., when in a state of extreme hunger), mind is exercised only in the biological and ecological viability of the organism; the other components of mind are greatly subdued. Or where adaptation to the physical world is forced by a crisis situation, categorizing, clarifying, and ordering its features looms large.

The social relations modality is itself multifaceted. Relating to other people may produce pleasure and pain, simultaneously invoking the organic modality; but also, since social relations involve complex understanding of other persons, this modality involves a high degree of self-reflectivity.

As might be anticipated, the modality involving symbolic meaning is the most complex; possibly because of its inherent self-reflective character. Smith wonders whether this modality is an evolutionary accident: "Other species have done quite well in adapting to their physical environment, regulating their own organisms, and establishing working orders without mind as we normally understand it (p. 217)." He notes that man himself often seems to do better in many endeavors by not thinking. So why the evolutionary emergence of mind? Smith suggests, paralleling Durkheim's claim, that the primary survival value of mind is the generation of a new form of social solidarity. Symbolic meanings have made it possible for humans to share a common world view which in turn provides a basis for an emergent type of social bonding and solidarity.

Smith finds a paradox in the functions of the modalities: all are engaged in simplifying and ordering the world; yet mind itself, by making the world meaningful, in this sense complicates our world. For example, meanings obliterate the spatial-temporal boundaries which exist for other creatures and things, and meanings involve things and events which are distant from us in time and place. The problem for the sociologist, though, is to know when one modality dominates and then another, as well as to understand how the modalities might work in concert or in opposition to one another. Of especial importance is to discover empirically and theoretically how different social structures favor specific modalities, which in return act on the structures. This not only depends upon external conditions, but social scientists with different predilections themselves have modality biases. Understanding the part played by these different modalities of mind, then, can assist us in the task of articulating in a more adequate fashion the varying social science perspectives, so as to achieve a more complete, encompassing comprehension of the social world.

In Chapter 12, Kurt Back, perhaps at the risk of caricaturing different social science views, identifies three models: the biological, the structural, and the interactional. He classes with the biological model all treatments in which individual behavior is the data base, and he sees the underlying theory/method as based upon formal mathematics. The structuralist model takes language as a human reality and makes central underlying abstract concepts that are universal. The interactionist model is that of the symbolic interactionist, in which the intentional actions of humans as agents constitute the primary data. Back sees the interactionists as focusing on the phenomenology of actors in relation to each other, as largely excluding other perspectives, and thus as assigning merely a descriptive status to social science.

Given these three models, the problem for Back becomes that of finding a way to resolve the incommensurabilities of three models that focus, respectively, on formal mathematics, linguistic abstractions, and ordinary language descriptions of social behavior. He finds a first step toward resolution in the possibility of new formal methods that would bridge mathematics, logic, and everyday language. In the latter part of his chapter he describes briefly two new mathematical approaches that have recently emerged: fuzzy set theory and catastrophe theory.

Chapter 13, by Ivan Karp and Martha Kendall, brings out rather dramatically a limitation of contemporary sociology that Giddens has emphasized. They do this indirectly by outlining the difficulties which field anthropologists encounter in just grasping the forms of everyday life characteristic of a native society. While this is not the sole aim of field workers, it appears to be a crucial first step in reaching an understanding of societies other than ours. This effort revolves around the anthropologist gaining an understanding of what Giddens would call the "discursive consciousness" of the natives—their accounts of their lives. As we have seen, the mainstream of contemporary sociology has neglected to provide an adequate place for this form of life in most of its theoretical formulations.

Karp and Kendall go on to note that anthropologists not only need to gain secure knowledge of natives' accounts, but to form adequate theories, to go beneath or beyond to underlying structures and processes which the natives are unable to articulate. In this effort we might expect to find some guidance for social science in general as to how to articulate discursive consciousness, practical consciousness, and social structures—the central issue dealt with in this book.

Karp and Kendall note the great heterogeneity of views among an-

thropologists concerning field work, ranging from the belief that no training is necessary, to commitment to positivistic, recipe-like methods, and
point out that the idea of standard field-work methods is essentially a
myth (reminiscent of Feyerabend's (1978) theme in *Against Method*).
One popular approach among anthropologists consists of making analogies between field work and various common forms of role-taking. Field
anthropologists have been likened to children undergoing socialization,
second-language learners, quasi-kinsmen, natural historians, strangers,
and so on. Karp and Kendall discuss critically the senses in which each of
these analogous roles may be helpful or misleading.

From their discussion of roles they point up the paradox of field work,
in that it requires a peculiar combination of engrossment and distance. In
a sense, field work may succeed best where it is least self-conscious,
because of the immersion in native life. Yet it clearly cannot be the same
thing as immersion, for one then would not be at all reflective, or even
observing. One common type of experience that frequently disrupts
engrossment is the shock aroused by experiencing the unexpected. This
produces the discovery of background knowledge, as Garfinkel (1967)
has so strongly emphasized.

Karp and Kendall also offer justifications for the importance of describing human actions. Here, Bhaskar's (this volume) point that intentional
human action is not reducible to another kind of explanation, but must be
independently considered, dovetails with their justifications.

Their discussion is consistent with that of Giddens and many of the
other contributors to this volume, to the effect that field work requires
attention to describing the character of everyday life, as well as the uncovering of background, taken-for-granted stances which natives do not
include in their accounts, and finally, to sketching the theoretical or abstract structures that can be articulated with these forms of knowledge.
We see here a recognition of the different senses of consciousness as
stressed by Toulmin and by Giddens (this volume). Toulmin's "public" or
"group" consciousness parallels Giddens's discursive consciousness. For
Karp and Kendall, participant observers gradually gain a sense of discursive consciousness, followed by Giddens's practical consciousness (tacit
knowledge). But through adopting a reflexive stance as a scientific ideal,
they must arrive at a truer consciousness which encompasses the conditions of their own existence as well as those of their subjects.

Chapter 14, by Roy Bhaskar, is not easy to describe except in very
general terms. Bhaskar has undertaken to resolve, all by himself, virtually
all of the aspects of the problem that is the theme of this book. Underpin-

ning his contribution are two published volumes by him, as well as most of a third, projected volume. Since his chapter is a masterful effort at synthesis, I will here only anticipate his major themes.

Bhaskar outlines his purposes succinctly: "In this chapter I want to consider the forms of explanation appropriate to the ontological setting of the human sciences; to outline a heuristic for the understanding of social life; to criticize a prevalent assumption in the meta-theory of the human sciences; and to advance a counter-position (p. 275)." He notes that the philosophy of science has been confined to an ontology of empirical realism which has been the source of many of its troubles. Once this is transcended, many of its problems are resolved. In natural science, the objects of investigation are structures, not events; these are not empirical and they, not observations per se, form the real ground for causal laws. Moreover, in the human sciences, empirical invariances are not epistemically significant; what is required is knowledge of structures and generative mechanisms.

Bhaskar offers what he terms a "transformational model of social activity" (TMSA). On this model, the logical structure of human activity is conceived as consisting in the transformation by intentional agency of pre-given material, both natural and social. This recursive feature of the TMSA makes for a strong ontological distinction between natural and social science inquiry: social mechanisms and structures generating social phenomena are themselves social products, and so are given to and reproduced in human agency like any other social object. Nothing remotely resembling this characterizes the natural sciences.

Agreeing with Giddens, Bhaskar identifies a duality of structure: "In the TMSA, then, society is conceived of both as the ever-present *condition* and the continually reproduced *outcome* of human agency ... agents reproduce in their substantive motivated productions the unmotivated conditions governing (and employed in) those productions, and society is both the unconscious medium and nonteleological product of this activity. In the TMSA, society and agents are seen as *existentially interdependent* but *essentially distinct*, for whereas society exists only in virtue of human agency and human agency (or being) always presupposes (and expresses) some or other definite social form, they cannot be reduced to or reconstructed from one another" (pp. 284-285).

This conception allows us to specify a double set of errors in traditional social science views: the ontological errors of reification and voluntarism, and the epistemological ones of social determinism and methodological individualism. Society is not created by human agency in any full sense (voluntarism), but neither does it exist independently of it (reification). And individual action does not completely determine social forms (methodological individualism), nor do social forms completely determine human action (determinism). "In the TMSA, unintended consequences, unacknowledged conditions, and tacit skills limit the actor's understanding of the social world, while unacknowledged (unconscious) motivation limits one's understanding of oneself" (p. 286).

This historical dimension is important and cannot be ignored. Relations between the elements of the social totality change along with the elements themselves, so regional theories must always be historically specific, intermediate sciences: social psychology is one such science; it can only hope to be applicable within a given timespan.

In another section, Bhaskar clarifies several common misunderstandings about the accounts of agents. Noting that the central error of hermeneutic approaches to social science is to consider the accounts of agents as the base or foundation of social knowledge, he argues that such accounts are intrinsically corrigible. On the other hand, they are not merely contingently conjoined with human action. Their significance lies instead in the fact that such accounts are internally related to and constitutive of social life itself. Finally, Bhaskar argues persuasively that social science is inextricably bound to values, and that it is *necessarily* nonneutral.

References

Armstrong, D. M. *A materialist theory of the mind.* London: Routledge & Kegan Paul, 1968.

Bandura, A. *Social learning theory.* Englewood Cliffs, NJ: Prentice-Hall, 1977.

Berger, P., & Luckmann, T. *The social construction of reality.* London: Allen Lane, 1967.

Feyerabend, P. *Against method: Outline of an anarchistic theory of knowledge.* London: Verso, 1978.

Garfinkel, H. *Studies in ethnomethodology.* Englewood Cliffs, NJ: Prentice-Hall, 1967.

Giddens, A. *New rules of sociological method.* New York: Basic Books, 1976.

Goffman, E. *Frame Analysis: An essay on the organization of experience.* New York: Harper & Row, 1974.

Mead, G. *Mind, self and society.* Chicago: University of Chicago Press, 1934.

Ryle, G. *The concept of mind.* New York: Barnes & Noble, 1949.

Schutz, A. *Alfred Schutz: Collected papers* (Vols. I-III). The Hague: Martinus Nijhoff, 1966.

CHAPTER 2

Consciousness

CHARLES TAYLOR

What is consciousness? The question is almost never directly discussed, but there are two very different understandings implicit in the philosophical literature.

The first tends in fact to marginalize consciousness. This understanding is the heir of the Cartesian-empiricist tradition, but which has now taken a physicalist turn. It is taken as given that a proper account of behavior will eventually be given in physical terms, i.e., in terms of neurophysiology, or in the language of physics and chemistry. It follows from this that the *functions* which we describe in terms of consciousness in ordinary life—thinking, feeling, conscious action—can ultimately be picked out in physical terms, and that it is under these descriptions that they will receive their most satisfactory explanation. When I calculate, for instance, we can assume that some physical processes are going on in my brain and nervous system rather like those in an electronic computer. These processes, like those in the computer, can be understood as the physical realization of a computing program.

According to "functionalism"—the now dominant view among thinkers of this orientation—this account involves descriptions on two levels: that of the computing program, and that of the physical realization. These may not be nomologically linked. That is, we may be able to discover laws which explain my calculative and other performances on the level of the program that my organism somehow realizes, but without being able to discover comparable laws on the level of physical description. This is because, as Fodor and others have argued, the same program can be realized physically in a host of different ways. This is something that experience with computing machines has driven home to us. The whole group of physical realizations of a given program may easily fail to form a class subject to the same physical laws. For instance, a program may be instantiated on an electronic device and on another which operates with gears. If we are tempted to protest that in our case the "physical realization" of our thinking is pretty similar from case to case, that we are all in other words human organisms, the answer is that we have every reason to believe that our thinking performances can also be matched eventually by electronic devices (see the discussion in Fodor, 1975, pp. 9-26).

This answer turns out to beg an important question, as I shall argue later—the issue of whether we can really be said to calculate in the same sense as the nonliving devices that somehow match our performances. But it is central to the whole attempt to account for our thinking in such computational terms that this assumption be taken as valid, and once it is made, it is clear that the distinction has to be made between the two levels.

This distinction differentiates functionalism from an older, cruder form of physicalist reductionism. But the two are basically at one concerning the issue that I want to discuss in this chapter, the understanding of consciousness. For the two levels are not to be identified with the traditionally understood terms, "mental" and "physical," respectively. This should be immediately evident from the fact that the operation of machines is also to be described on two levels, even though these have no mental life and are not conscious in any but some highly metaphorical way.

The program level is not to be identified with our awareness of our action, feeling, thinking, and so forth. On the contrary, functionalists go out of their way to stress that our awareness of what we are doing may be very faulty and partial. We are not at all aware of complicated calculations going on in us when we reach for the ball which has been thrown to us, or when we respond with just the right nuance in the course of a delicate conversation. Yet this is what functionalist theory supposes must be going on, mainly because, on the assumption that we are to be understood as complex computing devices analogous to the machines we are now familiar with, there is no other plausible account to be offered of our high level of performance (catching the ball, or saying the right thing). Thus, functionalists constantly repeat their warnings and admonitions not to put too much confidence in phenomenology. It can be a very bad guide to underlying reality.

In this, they are just following in the footsteps of a venerable tradition. The scientific revolution of the 17th century gets under way through heroic feats of ignoring phenomenology, as one can see from the debates between Galileo and his opponents. *Of course* it looks as though the sun were going around the earth; *of course* it feels as though an object tends to stop whenever we stop pushing it. But we have all learned from this and other cases how misleading our everyday awareness of such processes may be. Why should it be any different with my awareness of what goes on in me when I think? Indeed, we already know that it is no different with my awareness of what goes on in me during certain disorders: the pain in my arm really comes from a malfunction in the heart; the pain I feel in the area of the heart, in my hypochondriac panic, really comes from somewhere else. So why should my action, feeling, or thinking be privileged in this regard?

This argument, plausible as it sounds, is plainly rooted in the Cartesian-empiricist tradition. For it assumes that for the purposes of this discussion, consciousness can be treated as a representation of a distinct reality. My awareness of what I am doing, feeling, and so forth is assessed as a representation of what is going on in my organism, and not, indeed, of what is going on in merely physical terms, but of a computation that is being realized in me. For the purposes of this assessment, awareness has no relevance to whether a computation is going on in me or not, any more than it has in the case of an electronic computer. In the last analysis, this is to be decided on the basis of the input-output schedules.

It is clear that as a representation of this, consciousness is not very reliable, no more so than for the relative movements of sun and earth. But it is also clear that this way of looking at the issue of consciousness, at assessing its role in our actions, feelings, and so on marginalizes consciousness. It plays no role in explaining what we do, feel, and/or think. This is not to say that the underlying processes which are supposed to underpin our awareness have no part; that is not at all what functionalists want to claim. On the contrary, they defend the view that what goes on in us can be understood as computation, that therefore some of our inner states can be understood as representations of outer reality. They explicitly eschew the kind of physicalism which wants to give mental performance predicates of this kind no role in explanation, as Skinner does, in the name of some misconceived fastidiousness in avoiding "mentalism."

But what is given a role here is the underlying mechanism characterizable in terms of mental performance predicates. Experienced *awareness,* on the other hand, is marginalized by the same considerations. For it is declared to be a bad guide to that which the performance predicates ("calculating," "representing," "deducing," and the like) properly apply to in our explanatory theory (as against our looser, ordinary language use). And these predicates are meant to apply in the same sense to machines who have no experienced awareness. This assumption, as we saw, played a key role in the functionalist refutation of crude physical reductionism. Consequently, this awareness is construed by functionalism as a representation of something which plays a role in explanation, but as not itself playing a role. It is rather a byproduct (in certain systems, e.g., organic ones) of the function which is well characterized in terms of performance predicates applied on the basis of input-output schedules; or on the basis of a mapping of our physical states onto the formulae of some computing language in such a way as to match the semantic relations among the formulae appropriate for such predicates as "deduces" or "calculates" (see discussion in Fodor, 1975, pp. 73-74).

That is what I mean by saying that this theory marginalizes consciousness or awareness, and that in this it is at one with the cruder forms of physicalist reductionism that it is at pains to refute. Its roots in the Cartesian-empiricist tradition should be evident, for this tradition made central the conception of consciousness as a representation of a distinct reality. This is, of course, not just a matter of blindly carrying on a philosophical tradition. It is, rather, that the motivations behind the 17th-century construal of mind are in some cases still operative today.

One of the strongest reasons for the representative view of the mind was that it made possible the epistemological enterprise which was so important to the 17th century. The attempt to found our knowledge in a systematic way, to check its credentials thoroughly, seemed to require that we unearth some ultimate foundations which would not in turn need further grounding. The notion of the "idea" or the "impression," an intramental representation of extramental reality, seemed to fill this requirement perfectly. All our knowledge of the "external world" must come to us through such ideas, or else this knowledge can have no rational foundation at all. (Maybe it has no such foundation anyway, even though based on "ideas," as many were tempted to argue, or feared might be the case, but the only hope of a rational foundation lay in this kind of grounding.)

This was one of the motives of the thoroughgoing dualism, the radical distinction between mind and "external" reality, which has had such a fateful influence since. But alongside this rationalist motive, there were others as well. Another very powerful one arose out of the climate of

17th-century science. We can call it the requirement of absolutism, borrowing a term from Bernard Williams (1978) in his book, *Decartes.*

The 17th-century revolution in scientific thought which we associate with the names of Bacon, Galileo, Descartes, and Newton had to fight its way free from a conception of the cosmos as meaningful order, an order which was to be understood in what we would today recognize as semiological terms. This order was to be rejected as a mere projection of our minds onto reality, a set of "idols of the mind," as Bacon put it.

Against this, they held that understanding the world requires that we grasp it not as it appears in human awareness, but as it is even outside this awareness. This means that the world ought to be understood without recourse to what we might call subject-related properties. By that I mean properties which apply to things only insofar as they are objects of experience of a certain kind of subject. The paradigm examples of such in the 17th-century discussion were the so-called secondary properties, such as color or perceived temperature. Clearly, in a universe without sighted creatures we could no longer speak of things having color. The light waves bouncing off them would go on having certain wavelengths, but the language of color would have no application.

A description of things purged of subject-related properties can be called an absolute description. And the requirements of scientific explanation that it do without such properties can be called a requirement of absolutism. This requirement was central to the 17th-century scientific revolution, and it contributed in its own way to the mind-body dualism that comes to us from that time.

The requirement, at least in an obvious construal, seemed to demand that we account for all bodily reality in terms purged of mental predicates, and that means in purely bodily terms. The realm of body must be separate from that of mind, which must in turn be purely immaterial. The requirement of absolutism therefore seemed to lead quite ineluctably to dualism, and in this it dovetailed nicely with the rationalist motive. It seemed evident that mind was separate from bodily reality, and that its most important relation with this external stuff was representational. (There was also a volitional relation, but this was even more mysterious.)

To the extent that rationalism, that is, the drive to examine the foundations of our beliefs, and the requirement of absolutism, are widely adhered to in contemporary philosophy, we can see why a standpoint on consciousness born in the 17th century is still so influential. It is not so much a matter of blind hewing to tradition as of like causes producing like effects.

This is not to say that the early dualism is equivalent to the modern position, one variant of which I tried to identify as functionalism. On the contrary, it is evident that the standard 17th-century view did not marginalize consciousness in the sense I mean above. Rather, perceptions and desires were thought to play a crucial role in explanation, precisely qua experienced states. But what this view amounts to is a kind of interactionism between mind and body; the physical world produces an effect in the mind, a representation characteristically, and this in turn can give rise to some motivational state, some "unease," which in turn can trigger action.

What characterizes the contemporary understanding of consciousness, common to both functionalism and cruder forms of reductionism, is its rejection of any interaction theory of this kind. But this only seems plausible if one ignores the complexity of the body as a physical system. Once one reflects what must be involved in a neurophysiological account of behavior, an interactionist perspective begins to seem much more implausible to most people. It seems to involve our acknowledging gaps and intermissions in our account of the body as a physical system. It does not, of course, seem implausible to everyone. Interactionism is still alive, as we can see from the recent work of Sir Karl Popper and Sir John Eccles, but most philosophers find it distasteful.

A characteristic reaction can be seen in this argument of Dan Dennett's (1978, p. 252), presented in capsule form as an argument for nonspecialists, but nevertheless purporting to give the general line of a refutation of interactionist dualism. This is ruled out, because if it were so, then "since the occurrence of *non-physical* events . . . would be required to trigger unproblematically physical events in the brain, the conservation laws of physics would be violated."

But what is common to both the earlier view and the presently fashionable functionalism is the assumption that these two are the only alternatives. Either awareness is marginalized, i.e., it plays no explanatory role, or else it plays a role in an interactionist manner. What underlies this assumption is a very profound dualism. By "profound," I mean here not a view which is deeply insightful, but rather one which is held at a relatively deep and unconscious level, so that its protagonists are scarcely aware that they have taken one out of a gamut of possible views on a key question, but rather confuse their opinion with one of the limiting principles of rational thinking in the domain concerned.

The alternative—marginalization/interactionism—seems exhaustive once one accepts the basically dualist idea that two domains can be distinguished, or at least that a domain of the unambiguously physical can be demarcated. If this is so, then either the events within it are explanatorily self-sufficient, that is, can be explained in physical terms, and if this is so, then we have no alternatives but to marginalize consciousness; or else we take the alternative view, that some physical events have nonphysical explanations, which is the essence of an interactionist position.

This deep dualist assumption is at the base of the first understanding of consciousness I have been examining here, in the representative form of functionalism. The other construal, to which I now want to turn, involves a rejection of this dualism.

This alternative view is not immediately recognizable as a conception of consciousness. Those who have espoused it have generally steered clear of the word, due to its heavy associations with the dualist tradition. Heidegger is a case that springs to mind. But I want to see this alternative as a view of consciousness because it gives quite another understanding of our experienced awareness, which is the common reality which all philosophical views have to recognize, and gives it quite a different place in our action, feeling, and so forth.

Another reason that this alternative view may not be seen as a view about consciousness is that it doesn't isolate it, but rather sees it in the context of a more basic feature of living things. This is what I want to call the "significance feature," for reasons which I hope will soon be evident.

The best way to introduce the significance feature is by challenging the assumption of functionalism mentioned above, that we can speak of human beings and machines as "calculating," "deducing," and so on for the various mental performance terms, in the same sense. But this is far from self-evident. Can we really attribute action to a machine, in the normal sense?

Why do we want to say that a machine computes, or for that matter that a machine moves gravel, or stacks bottles? Partly because the machine operates in such a way as to get these tasks done in the proper circumstances. But also, and more strongly, as in the case of computers, because the way the machine gets these tasks done has a certain structural resemblance to the way we do them. Characteristically, the machine's operation involves breaking down the task into subtasks, the fulfillment of which can be seen as logical stages to the completion of the computation. This breaking down into subtasks is also essential to what we call computation when *we* compute: you wouldn't say someone was computing if he gave the answer straight off without any analytical reflection.

More generally, to borrow Fodor's formulation, we can see a physical system as a computational device if we can map different physical states of that system onto formulae of some language of computation in such a way that the relation between the physical states matches the logical relations among the formulae. "The idea is that, in the case of organisms as in the case of real computers, if we get the right way of assigning formulae to the states it will be feasible to interpret the sequence of events that *causes* the output as a computational *derivation* of the output (Fodor, 1975, p. 73)."

Third, we say that a machine "does" something when we have designed it to accomplish the task. All three factors apply in the case of computers, and at least two in the case of bottle-stackers. But there could be objects which we would describe as phi-ing just because they were very useful at accomplishing the task of getting something phi-ed, even though they were discovered in nature and not manufactured.

It is clear from this that the attribution of an action term to such artifacts or useful objects is relative to our interests and projects. A machine phi-s because we have manufactured it to phi, or we use it to phi, or we are interested in it in respect of the phi-ing it gets done. If we ask why we want to say that it is phi-ing and not psi-ing, where "things being psi-ed" is a description of some other outcome of the machine's operation (our computer also hums, heats up the room, keeps George awake, increases our electricity bill), the answer is that psi-ing is not what we use it for, or what we built it for.

Of course, we would normally say quite unproblematically that the machine hums, heats the room, and so forth, but where we want to make a distinction between that which it is really engaged in, as against just incidentally bringing about (it's a computer, dammit, not a room-heater), we do so by reference to our interests, projects, or designs. A changed economic picture or the demands of a new technology could make it the case that psi-ing was suddenly a very important function, and then we might think of the same machine as a psi-er and as psi-ing (provided it was also an efficient device for this end). Indeed, we could imagine two groups, each with quite different demands, sharing time on the same device for quite different purposes. The computer also makes clicks in strange patterns, very much valued by some eccentric group of meditation adepts. For them, the machine is a "mantric clicker," while for us it is computing payrolls or chi squares.

But what is it *really* doing? There is no answer to this question for a machine. We tend to think in this case that it is really computing, because we see it as made for this purpose, and only by accident serving the purpose of helping meditation. But this is a contingent, external fact, one external, that is, to the machine's makeup and function. It could have been designed by some mad yogi with a degree in electronic engineering, and just happens to serve as a computer. Or it could have just come into existence by some cosmic accident: a bolt of many-tongued lightning fused all this metal into just the structure needed to fulfill both of these functions.

Attributions of action terms to such devices are relative to our interests and purpose. As Fodor puts it: "It is *feasible* to think of such a system as a computer just insofar as it is possible to devise some mapping which pairs physical states of the device with formulae in a computing language in such a fashion as to preserve the desired semantic relations among the formulae" (1975, emphasis added). And, he adds later: "Patently, there are indefinitely many ways of pairing states of the machine with formulae in a language which will preserve (the right) sort of relation."

But the same is not true of ourselves. There is an answer to the question, "What is he doing?" or "What am I doing?" (when it is not taken in the bland form such that any true description of an outcome eventuating in the course of my action can provide an answer) which is not simply relative to the interests and purposes of the observer, for action is directed activity. An action is such that a certain outcome is privileged—that which the agent is seeking to encompass in the action. The distinction between action and non-action (events in inanimate objects, or reflex-type events in ourselves, or lapses, breakdowns, and the like) is made on this basis.

In contradistinction to machines, we can be said to act in the strong sense, such that our behavior is purposively directed toward ends. Thus there is an answer to the question, "What are you doing?" which is not relative to the interests and purposes of an observer. Of course, there are issues between different action descriptions which may be settled by the interests of the observer, for any action may bear a number of descriptions. Notoriously, there are further and more immediate purposes, broader and narrower contexts of relevance. Thus we can say, severely, "I know you just wanted to do the best by him, but did you physically prevent him from leaving the house?" or "I know you only meant to scare him, but did you shoot the dog?" and so on.

Nevertheless, there are other descriptions of things which get done when I act which I can repudiate as action descriptions, at least in any full-blooded sense, e.g., that I move molecules of air when I talk, or even give clicks with my teeth which are highly prized by the eccentric meditation circle. We can imagine that they hire me to come and give lectures in philosophy, and that I am puzzled why they keep inviting me back, because they do not seem interested in what I say, and indeed sink into a deep trance when I talk. There is some sense in which "putting them to sleep" is an action description applying to me, but we recognize that this applies in quite a different way than, for instance, the description "lecturing on philosophy." Hence we have a barrage of reservation terms like "unwittingly," "inadvertently," "by accident," "by mistake," and so on.

Now *this* distinction, between what I am full-bloodedly doing and what is coming about inadvertently, is not relative to observers' or designers' interests and purposes. Unlike the case of the artifact, it remains true of me that what I am doing in the full-blooded sense is lecturing on philosophy, and not mantric clicking; even though I may be much more useful as a device to accomplish the second end than the first, may do it more efficiently, and so on; or even though everyone else becomes interested in mantric clicking, and no one even knows what philosophy is anymore besides me.

Nor can we account for this difference by casting me in the role of crucial observer and saying that the crucial description is the one relative to my interests. For this neglects the crucial difference, that with the artifact the observer's interests are distinguishable from the machine. Thus it makes sense to speak of a machine as surviving with its functioning intact even when no one is interested anymore in its original purpose, and it serves quite another one, or none at all. But an action is essentially constituted by its purpose. The attempt to make a comparable distinction to the one we make with artifacts, between external movement and some separable inner act of will breaks down, as is now notorious, for the inner act shrinks to vanishing point. Our ordinary conception of an act of will is parasitic on our ordinary understanding of action.

Mental performance terms like "calculating" have a different sense when attributed to artifacts than when attributed to humans. In the latter case, we mean to describe actions in the strong sense, in a way which is not merely observer- or user- or designer-relative. Let me say quickly, as a sort of parenthesis, that this represents as yet no decisive objection against functionalism; it just puts the issue in clearer perspective. It is a point about the logic of our action-attributions. It does not show by itself that what goes on when people calculate is something very different from what goes on in computers. For all we know at this stage, a computer-type, observer-relative "calculation" may underlie every act of calculating; and, it may provide the best explanation for our performance.

The point is only that our language of action attributes something quite different to us agents, namely, action in the strong sense, something for which there is no basis whatever in machines, nor in the functioning of the organism understood analogously to that of a machine; and indeed, for which one cannot easily conceive of any basis being found in a machine.

I have made the point in terms of action, but the same point goes for other "functional" states of machines in contrast to ourselves. We might try to find states of machines which parallel our desires and emotions. A machine might be said to "want to go" when it is all primed and started, and only being held back by a brake. But it is clear that an analogous distinction applies here to the case of action. What the machine "desires" is determined by the observer's interest or fiat, or that of the user or designer, while this is not so for the human agent. Actually, the temptation does not exist here, as it does in the case of action, to apply such terms to machines, except as a kind of anthropomorphic joke.

The crucial place of the significance feature is even more evident here, as the clear upshot of the previous discussion is that human and animal agents are beings for whom the question arises of what significance things have for them. I am using the term "significance" here as a term of art to cover what is peculiar to the force of action, emotion, and similar terms when applied to animate beings, namely, that there is a non-observer-relative answer to the question, "What are they doing?" (what purpose are they trying to effect?), or "What are they feeling?" or "What do they want?" We can try to formulate this force by saying that things have a significance for such agents: their actions, the things they desire, are averse to, the things they fear, hope for, find provoking, and that in a nonrelative sense.

For there is, of course, another, weaker sense in which we can speak of things having significance for inanimate beings. Something can be dangerous for my car, or good for my typewriter, and so on. But these significances are only predictable in the light of extrinsic, observer-relative or user-relative purposes. By contrast, the significances we attribute to agents in our language of action and desire are their own. To treat a being as an agent is to treat him or her as a center of significance such that there are nonrelative answers to such questions as, "What is (s)he doing?" and "What does (s)he want?"

Beings we treat in this way can be said to have the significance feature attributed to them, and that is how I want to use this term of art, as a way of summing up what is involved in our nonrelative attributions of actions, feelings, and desires.

As I mentioned above, the fact that our ordinary language deals with agents as possessing the significance feature does not by itself show functionalism to be mistaken. This feature differentiates us from machines, and ourselves qua agents from our organisms understood as machines, or at least this difference is marked by our language. But a functionalist can still reply (can he not?) that this alleged feature in fact plays no role in an adequate, truly explanatory theory of why and how we perform as we do, that it is a feature we are led to attribute to ourselves in our own self-experience, that it is part of our experienced awareness of ourselves, and that it does not need to be taken any more seriously than those other features of things which arose in immediate awareness, such as the movements of the sun around the earth, which the 17th-century revolution knew to set aside.

In fact, as I hope to show, this short way with the significance feature will not do. Indeed, once one appreciates its importance, the issue between functionalism and its opponents must be seen in a new light. But the main purpose here ought to be to show how appreciating the significance feature is the basis for an alternative conception of consciousness. I would like to build toward both these conclusions by drawing out some further consequences of the discussion so far.

I have argued that our language marks an important distinction between agents and non-agents in the presence of the significance feature. But in fact the distinction is greater than I have yet described. When we look at action terms like "calculation," we might think that the difference was that entities without the significance feature can only bear some lesser, relative version of full-blooded action predicates. If this were all, then at least non-agents could bear all the same ranges of predicates as agents, albeit in the reduced form.

But when we look at our emotion terms, we see that the gap is greater. Take an emotion term like "shame." Shame is what we feel in a characteristic type of situation, one in which we are humiliated, or shown up, in which something shameful is revealed about us. To say that we feel shame is to say that the situation has a certain import for us. But when we try to analyze what kind of import this is, we see that it is of a kind which could only hold for a being with the significance feature.

This is true for two reasons. The first is a more general one, that there is clearly something gratuitously anthropomorphic in attributing feelings of any kind to a non-agent. But the second bites deeper. Someone can only feel shame who has a sense of himself as an agent, hence as a center of significance. I feel ashamed of what I am like—of how I appear as a subject among subjects. Only a being who is reflexively aware of himself as an agent can have the feeling of shame. This is a matter of the nature of the import that defines the emotion of shame. You do not experience shame by virtue of the sensations or raw feel of your emotions, but by virtue of the import of the situation, and this is one which makes essential reference to my qualities as a subject among others.

That is why it would be an expression of fantasy to speak of a computer as being ashamed. Without a qualm, we happily speak of its calculating, because we use it for that, designed it for that, and its performance in many ways is structured analogously to ours (in other ways, of course, not at all). Here the only (only?) difference is that the term is applied relatively to the machine. If this were the only type of difference between agent and non-agent, we might run away with the idea that the significance feature was simply an honorific mark we attach to the former. We might think that analogous predicates applied to both, that for any predicate we applied to agents we could construct an analogous one applying to non-agents by focusing on the features of performance which defined it. And this might make us think that what was left out, the significance feature, corresponded to no important, explanatory empirical feature, but was rather a tag of honor we accorded to agents, that they should bear their predicates nonrelatively.

But this impression is totally dissipated when we look at an emotion like shame. Here there is plainly nothing analogous in machine existence, nor can there be. The significance feature does not play the role of adding something to the criteria by which we can also apply the term to inanimate beings, as we might think (even here wrongly) in the case of action. Rather, this feature is an essential part of the background against which the criteria for "shame" make sense. We could not begin to pick out the kind of situations and responses characteristic of shame without reference to it.

We might take shame as an example of what we could call an intrinsically human significance. These are significances which it only makes sense to attribute to human agents. Terms relating to these contrast with terms like "calculating," and "stacking bottles," which can easily be applied to machines in the usual relative way.

The importance of these intrinsically human significances in our ordinary account of ourselves shows that the significance feature is much more deeply embedded in our self-understanding than those infected with the dualist tradition usually appreciate. I said above that functionalists could reply to this identification of the significance feature in our ordinary talk of action by claiming that it need play no role in a satisfactory explanation of our performances, of what we do and how we react to our surroundings. We could treat it as an aspect of our awareness of reality which was not matched by reality itself, like the appearance of the sun's movement in the sky.

But once we appreciate the importance of the intrinsically human significances, this line becomes much more difficult to sustain. To say that the significance feature plays no role in an adequate explanation is to say that such motives as shame, a sense of dignity, a sense of integrity, a desire for mutual love, an aspiration to community, and the like, which only make sense against the background of the significance feature, play no role in an adequate explanation. But this is very hard to credit. It may sound plausible to believe that whatever is specific to my action in calculating, which is not part of the supposed underlying program running in my neurons, plays no part in the explanation. It is tempting to think that that specific element simply consists in a "mental" representation, a monitoring which takes place in a marginalized consciousness, or a symptom of the underlying process.

But this model of things breaks down when we consider my meeting a humiliating situation, experiencing shame, and responding appropriately (perhaps by flight, by hiding myself, by aggressive accusation, or whatever). Here, what belongs to the significance level cannot be understood as a marginal monitoring, or a symptom, since whatever we may be able to construct in the way of an underlying account in nonsignificance terms will have a fundamentally different logic. There will be no room in it for such terms as "shame" and "humiliation," and consequently no way of identifying the class of humiliating situations, or of accounting for why one is more humiliating than another, or anything of the kind. In short, here the significance feature is essential to the explanatory factors, and that is why it is more difficult to imagine it being marginalized.

What emerges from this is that on closer examination, the whole idea of treating our experienced awareness as a possibly misleading representation of an independent reality, as strictly analogous to our immediate perceptions of the movements of heavenly bodies, turns out to be profoundly mistaken. It quite fails to appreciate the crucial place of the significance feature in our understanding and explanation of our own and others' actions and feelings. But I have still understated the case. It is not just that the significance feature seems to be an essential part of any plausible explanation for much of what we do and feel. It is also that we cannot choose to abandon this way of looking at ourselves.

For it is inescapably involved in our functioning as human beings. The significance feature is at the center of human life, because we come to understandings with people about the significance of things. There is no relationship, from the most external and frosty to the most intimate and defining, which is not based on some understanding about the significances of things. In the most important cases, of course, one of the things whose significance is understood between us is our relationship itself.

That is why the significance perspective is not an arbitrary one among human beings, one way of explaining how these organisms work among other possible ones. It is not even primarily a theoretical perspective on our behavior. We could not function as human beings, that is, as humans among other humans, for five minutes outside of this perspective. (I think this is what emerges from the very interesting analysis by Peter Strawson [1974] in his article, "Freedom and Resentment.")

This is what makes the disanalogy with the immediate perception of the sun's movements. The significance feature is constitutive of our understanding of *ourselves* in ordinary life, as this must be if we are to function normally as human beings. We could have no relations at all if we did not treat ourselves and others as agents (by which I do not mean at all to treat them ethically, or as ends in themselves, even though our exploitative behavior in the vast majority of cases takes our victims as agents. It can be argued, of course, that there is a profound connection between our status as agents and the validity of such moral precepts as those of Kant). This self-understanding is part of the reality it purports to understand.

This is what is wrong with trying to treat our experienced awareness as a possibly misleading representation of an independent reality, as I put it above. Possibly misleading it certainly is. Not only psychoanalytic theory but ordinary experience makes us very aware of this. But it cannot for all that be understood as the representation of an independent reality. Our repressions, distorted self-images, and fond self-delusions do not bear on an emotional life and character which exists quite independently of them. On the contrary, they help to form emotions and character. To overcome some repression, to climb out of some delusion, is not to leave the object of distorted awareness unchanged. Unrepressed emotions are transformed emotions.

All this is understandable on the significance perspective, for from this vantage, consciousness is understood in a quite different light. The significance feature is seen as the basic fact. This is something we attribute to agents in general, including those that are minimally conscious. Consciousness is seen as an achievement of some agents (i.e., especially that species which is human) over some range of what is significant to them, with some degree of distortion. In particular, our consciousness is something we attain to and develop with language.

But a significance of which we become conscious, which we become able to formulate in language, cannot remain unchanged. Things have a different significance for us by the very fact that we can articulate this significance, that we can discriminate more exactly what it amounts to, distinguish it from others, and so on, not to speak of the tensions, dilemmas, and reversals which come from our greater awareness of what we feel and want.

Seen in the context of the significance feature, consciousness cannot therefore be understood as the representation of an independent reality. Rather, our understanding of the significance things have for us helps to constitute this significance. On this view, consciousness cannot be marginalized. Since we explain our action in terms at least partly of the significance things have for us, anything which affects this significance, as greater awareness does, is relevant to our explanatory account.

But neither is it interactionist. An explanation of human action in terms of the significance feature does not allow that we can treat behavior as belonging to a physical domain, in principle explicable normally in purely physical terms, but subject to interference from beyond. On the contrary, explanation in terms of significance cuts across the division between mental and physical. It does not recognize the validity of this dualism. The kinds of significance things can have for us are often essentially bound up with our being bodily agents—as is true particularly of the example I have been using above, shame, which concerns how we *appear* in public space before others. And yet these bodily features cannot be understood purely in terms of physics.

Instead of drawing the boundary between the "mental" and the "physical," the significance perspective marks a crucial distinction between agents and non-agents. But this draws a boundary within the physical universe, and not around it. Beings which have the significance feature are to be explained, at least for part of their behavior, in terms of factors that have no role in explaining inanimate things.

What underlies this rejection of dualism is a rejection of one of its strongest motives, the requirement of absoluteness. This is not indeed rejected as a principle of explanation for inanimate beings, where it has amply shown its validity in the last three centuries. But it is disastrous to attempt to apply it across the board to animate beings. It would exclude totally explanations in terms of significance, for these clearly violate the requirement, since significance is paradigmatically a subject-related property of things. In a world without human subjects, there could be no enticing, no humiliating, no joyful or saddening situations.

The alternative construal of consciousness, that from the significance perspective, therefore breaks fundamentally with the one dominant today in much philosophy and cognitive psychology. It breaks with the deep-seated dualist assumptions of the latter, which is why the protagonists of cognitive psychology seem often to have trouble envisaging it as an alternative. But once the issue is put in focus, it seems hard not to see the force of the significance perspective, or at least so it seems to me.

This puts a severe dent in functionalism in the form in which it is at present defended, but it does not mean that the whole option of mechanist explanations of mind and action is closed. The debate can be joined again, but I believe it will have to be in different terms, ones which remove some of the shine of plausibility that the mechanist option has enjoyed in a fundamentally dualist philosophical culture. But that is a thesis that I will not try to defend here.

References

Dennett, D. C. *Brainstorms: Philosophical essays on mind and psychology.* Montgomery, VT: Bradford Books, 1978.

Fodor, J. *The language of thought.* New York: Crowell, 1975.

Strawson, P. *Freedom and resentment.* London, 1974.

Williams, B. *Descartes: The project of pure inquiry.* Sussex, Eng: Harvester Press, 1978.

CHAPTER 3

The Genealogy of "Consciousness"

STEPHEN TOULMIN

I

For some 350 years, ever since the time of Descartes, the central problems in the theory of knowledge and the philosophy of mind have repeatedly been formulated using large, general abstractions such as Mind, Will, Thought, Feeling, Experience, and Consciousness; and the same philosophical dialectics and difficulties have ensued in each case. The contrast between, on the one hand, the seemingly *inward* character typical of so many of the relevant phenomena and, on the other hand, the *public* criteria for judging the correctness or incorrectness of their descriptions, has exposed us to a recurrent tension between the supposedly private, inward character of personal thought, experience, mental life, or consciousness and the public, interpersonal language in which thought, experience, and so forth have to be described.

In this way, a string of concrete, practical terms, all of them having familiar, colloquial uses—whether as verbs ("Do you mind?"), as adverbs ("consciously"), or as adjectives ("experienced")—have been converted, in turn, into so many broad and general abstract nouns, which have then been construed as names for the most personal, private flux of sensory inputs, kinesthetic sensations, and so on. Starting from such practical idioms as "I think it's time to go" and "She thought out the solution to the chess problem," we have been exhorted to recognize in Thought an internal process paralleling the external activities of Things. Starting from "I don't mind" and "He was not minded to do it"—meaning "I don't object" and "He was not inclined to do it"—we have been expected, similarly, to accept the grand abstraction, Mind, as the totality of what is personal and hidden in our mental life. And, again, behind "He is an experienced commercial pilot, with 4,000 hours as captain," we have been asked to perceive the pilot's "experiences," i.e., his visual and auditory inputs, and the feelings in the pit of his stomach as he pulls the plane out of a dive.

During the 20th century, the leading candidate for naming the essentially "interior" aspects of our mental life and activities—just those which, if Wittgenstein is right, are also the most *un-name-able*—is the term *consciousness*. The word was adopted for this purpose at the beginning of the present century, although with reservations, by William James, and also, more enthusiastically, by Bertrand Russell. In the present chapter, we shall see just how closely its own transformation has followed the same course as that of its precursors: Mind, Thought, Experience, and the rest. In the case of "consciousness," a family of words whose historic use and sense had to do with the public articulation of shared plans and intentions has been taken over into philosophical theory, as providing a name for the most private and *un*shared aspects of mental life. Whereas lawyers and jurists formerly considered how several agents may create and share their "consciousness" (i.e., their *con-scientia,* or mutual understanding) by concerting their plans, 20th-century philosophers have concentrated rather on the consciousness of individuals (i.e., my or your, his or her consciousness) as being what sensibility confers on each one of us independently. The term "consciousness" has thus become the name for a flux of sensory inputs that is seemingly neither *con-,* since each individual supposedly has his or her own, nor *-sciens,* since the sensory flux is thought of as "buzzing and booming" rather than cognitively structured or interpreted.

Whichever key term is chosen to play the leading part in the resulting epistemological debate, we face some real difficulties at the outset. As a contribution to the "theory of knowledge," indeed, the step from the public domain of joint actions, pooled understandings, and interpersonal meanings into the private, individual domain of hidden thoughts, sensations, and feelings may well appear a retrograde step, especially since the philosophers concerned have all too often argued as though the stream of inner mental life, or "conscious experience," were not merely *one possible* source of true knowledge, but even the *sole available* source. This conclusion would surely be an odd one, if only because knowledge is like any other currency. It has value, meaning, and significance only to the extent that it is capable of being assessed or exchanged in the interpersonal marketplace of rational discussion. In a nutshell: We have no more reason to associate "knowledge" with sensations than we do "market value" with sentiments. So there is, from the beginning, something intrinsically odd about philosophers constructing a general account of *knowledge* on the basis of "purely personal" data rather than on the results of public, collaborative observations and agreed meanings. It is very much as though economists, say, set out to construct a general theory of *value* on the basis, not of exchange values, labor inputs, and other interpersonal measures, but rather on each individual's personal thrills, distastes, and "sentimental values."

Whichever key has been chosen, again, the grandiloquence of the abstractions involved has tended to conceal the modest practical issues and idioms that underlie them. Only very recently, in fact, have philosophers begun to recognize how much may be gained, if only we set out to bring those practical matters back into the center of the picture. John Austin did this quite strikingly in the case of Will, Gilbert Ryle and his successors did something of the same kind for Mind, but little has been done so far in the case of Consciousness. That is a task on which we can usefully embark here. In this chapter, accordingly, I shall begin by teasing out some representative strands from the tangled skein of ideas associated with such terms and phrases as "conscious," "half-conscious," "the unconscious," "consciously," "self-consciousness," and the like. Here and elsewhere, this preliminary analysis of usage will not (of course) be the "be-all and end-all" of our investigation: still—to borrow a phrase from Austin—such an analysis may well be the "begin-all" for anyone who is concerned with the general significance of "consciousness" and the difficulties that it creates for epistemology.

The philosophical dividends to be hoped for from such an investigation should not need underlining. Bertrand Russell has told us, in his *Autobiography*, how he was drawn into epistemology and theory of mind as a teenager. He had reflected on the implications of attempting to build up a comprehensive world view using classical physics as its skeleton, and one consideration above all convinced him that this could not be done. Such an account (he believed) could not encompass the phenomenon of consciousness, and for him, "consciousness was an undeniable datum." (In this respect, the term "consciousness" served Russell in precisely the same way that the term *âme* had served Descartes 250 years before: specifically, as a name for "that which eludes the rigid laws of classical mechanics.") Similarly, as we well know, William James's ideas about the "buzzing booming confusion" of primitive sensory experience are customarily referred to as the "stream of consciousness" theory, and this same way of characterizing individual sensory experience has also been influential in 20th-century literature. (Virginia Woolf's novel, *The Waves*, in particular, uses this notion extensively.)

Today as much as ever, the idea of "consciousness" preserves its metaphysical charms. For instance, the neurophysiologist, Sir John Eccles, finds it impossible to believe that the electrical and biochemical science of brain processes that is his professional concern will ever succeed in bringing absolutely all of our mental life within its grasp, and he is accordingly tempted to reserve an independent realm for those aspects of mentality that elude the rigorous chains of neurophysiological causation. (This realm he associates with our possession of a nonmaterial "consciousness.") Meanwhile, philosophers of a more analytical inclination have done scarcely more than nibble at the edges of the debate about Consciousness. They have taken some first worthwhile steps in the course of elucidating Freud's three types of mental entity and process: conscious, preconscious, and unconscious. They have said helpful things, also, about self-knowledge and self-deception, both of which topics are tangentially related to the larger debate about consciousness. On the whole, however, most analytical philosophers seem to have been daunted by the issues involved. Discretion has proved the better part of valor, and they have turned their attentions elsewhere.

One can hardly blame them. Anyone who attacks the general issue of consciousness will quickly come to recognize what a tangled thicket(s) he is getting into. In addition to the traditional epistemological issues as raised by Russell and James, there are some highly technical matters of psychophysiology and neuroscience to be kept in mind: for instance, those connected with "rapid eye movement" sleep, and with the division of mental functions between the two hemispheres of the brain. Meanwhile, there is a well-developed body of sociological discussion having to do with, e.g., the so-called "cultural-historical conditioning" of consciousness. Even on the level of everyday life, the range and scope of "consciousness" idioms is vast, and has become vaster during the last few years. On top of the subtleties arising from recognition of the psychoanalytic "unconscious," we have been required to digest the "altered states of consciousness" attributed to drug use, as well as the ethnic and gender self-consciousness associated with "consciousness raising." Here, we can begin by picking out a few sample terms and idioms selected to serve both as *representative instances* of the whole, larger family of consciousness terms, and also as the basis for some tentative hypotheses about the *conceptual genealogy* of the notions involved.

II

The actual situation may, in fact, be somewhat less confused and intractable than it at first seems. Even if we include examples from neuroscience, sociology and psychoanalysis, hallucinogens, and minority group discussions, an underlying sense can still be made of these terms and idioms, and we can develop a first rough catalogue of the idioms in question—conscious, consciously, with conscious care, in full consciousness, unconsciously, preconscious, and so on—which classifies them under three broad headings:

(1) Some of them are concerned with our basic sensory responsiveness to, and awareness of, our situations, i.e., with what might alternatively be called "sensibility."

(2) Others have to do with knowing what we are doing, acting with due attention, and/or readiness to monitor some sequence of events in which we are involved.

(3) Still others focus in, more specifically, on our ability to give an explicit account of the character of our actions, the point of view and perceptions in the light of which they are performed, and the intentions associated with them.

Let us first look at some samples of each type (sensibility, attentiveness, and articulateness) in turn.

Sensibility

Somebody who falls asleep from exhaustion or intoxication "lapses into unconsciousness," while one who reawakens "regains consciousness." A man who is struck on the head may "fall unconscious" (which is of course quite different from "plunging into the unconscious" while, after a few minutes, he may become "painfully half conscious," though still unable to focus his attention on where he is or say exactly what is going on around him.

This family of usages and idioms expresses only a minimal notion of what it is to be "conscious," to live and act "consciously," or to have any serious and significant kind of "consciousness." In order to be "conscious" in this first, minimal sense, one need not be in any way attentive or articulate, still less capable of making one's intentions explicit. On this first level, a human infant is conscious or unconscious no differently from a human adult. Nor do you even have to be human. On this level, most higher animals lose and regain consciousness in the same ways, and in the same circumstances (e.g., when struck on the head) as human beings.

Furthermore, in speculating about the phenomena of losing and regaining consciousness, falling unconscious, and the like, we may reasonably assume that they call relatively simple and straightforward neural systems or pathways into operation. They may not be "simple" by any absolute standards, of course, nor do we, perhaps, yet understand fully what they in fact are. Still, the different sensory functions involved in this basic "consciousness" are evidently linked in a somewhat gross and undiscriminating manner: under a general anesthetic, hearing is marginally the last sense to go, but basically they all come and go together. This holds true equally for many other kinds of living things, and so, presumably, the regions of our brains implicated in these phenomena are neither the most recent in evolutionary terms, nor physiologically the most complex and subtle.

From the sociological and psychoanalytic standpoints, this first class of phenomena has no direct or special significance. If one is to manifest group consciousness, one must of course be "conscious" in this preliminary sense as well. Falling asleep does not rob you of ethnic, gender, or class consciousness, although it does leave you with little chance of manifesting that consciousness, so that the question of your group loyalties must remain in suspense until you wake up again. I say "little chance" rather than "no chance," because even in this case (as in the psychoanalytic case) the question might conceivably arise whether your dreams do not reveal something about your class, gender, or ethnic awareness. Nor can the Freudian "unconscious" itself be wholly dissociated from the phenomena of distractedness, daydreaming, hypnotic trance, and outright sleep. Accordingly, "unconsciousness" in this first sense, i.e., "lack of external sensibility," may certainly be *distinct from* "the unconscious" in its psychoanalytic sense, but they need not, on that account, be wholly *separable*.

Attentiveness

Somebody who pays close attention to the things going on around him is "conscious" of those happenings; while one who lets his attention wander or become diffuse may cease to be conscious of them. He may be quite "unconscious," for instance, that the people at the next table are dealing in hashish, or making rude remarks about him.

Correspondingly, somebody who drives down the road with an unusual attention, both to the actions of other road users and to his own actions as a driver, does so "consciously and carefully", while one who is distracted from the road and traffic conditions by external worries or fantasies may be "unconscious" of, say, the child playing ball on the sidewalk who suddenly runs out under his wheels. This does not, of course, imply that an inattentive driver "loses consciousness." Being distracted is quite different from falling asleep at the wheel: the driver was awake all right, but he let his mind wander.

Consciousness, in the first, "sensibility" sense, is thus a precondition for being *either* "conscious" *or* "unconscious," in this second sense, of the traffic, the pedestrians, and the effects of your own driving. (Somebody who is fast asleep is in no position to be either attentive *or* distracted.) In this second sense, to be "conscious" takes one far beyond the minimal condition of waking sensibility, and implies also a certain concentration, monitoring, and/or attention on the part of the agent concerned.

Can infants and animals be "conscious" in the second sense? The answer to that question is not obvious. When a wakeful dog starts up with its ears cocked, and "points" in the direction of a distant footfall, we may be tempted to conclude that it is conscious of its master's imminent arrival. But this second usage cannot be extended from humans to animals as unambiguously as the first, "sensibility" usage. The same is true for infants. A mother's eye of faith may very early perceive in her infant a "consciousness" of her identity, presence, and facial expressions, but the reliability of her perception is open to discussion, even though nobody was in any doubt whether the child was asleep or awake, i.e., "conscious" in the first sense. Neurophysiologically, again, this second mode of consciousness evidently calls into play mechanisms that are more complex and delicate than those involved in simple sleeping and waking. Furthermore, these mechanisms apparently operate with different degrees of discrimination, both at different stages in individual development, and with respect to different sensory modalities.

The sociological aspects of "consciousness" come into their own on this second level. The extent of someone's consciousness of class, gender, or ethnic origins can, in fact, be measured by the amount of attention and care that he or she pays to such considerations; while, correspondingly, "consciousness raising" is concerned with heightening the individual's attentiveness to precisely these issues. By contrast, the same is not so clearly true of the psychoanalytic "conscious" and "unconscious." Certain kinds of distractedness and defects of attention ("tunnel vision") do, of course, serve as familiar symptoms of neurotic disability. Exposed to situations that activate psychopathologically stereotyped responses, paranoids and obsessives are unable to pay realistic attention to the things that are going on around them, even to things in the center of their attention, where these do not square with their delusions. But the temporary "unconsciousness" of the realities of the external situation so induced is quite different from the essential "unconsciousness" of the psychoanalytic "unconscious" itself. If anything, the latter involves an inability to attend to the realities of the agent's own *inner* state, rather than inattention to the *external* situation.

Articulateness

> A businessman who knowingly arranges to obtain money from a client on false pretences is engaged in "conscious and deliberate" fraud, while one who fails through pardonable inadvertance to mention some material fact, and so by chance leads to the client's bankruptcy, "unconsciously" becomes the agent of the client's ruin.

This third group of idioms and usages marks off as "conscious" one subclass of courses of action: namely, those for which the agent can articulate an explicit motive, plan, or intention. To say that an agent acts in full consciousness of the nature and quality of the resulting actions implies a capacity (though not necessarily a willingness) to give a full account of the relevant aims and purposes. In this third sense, accordingly, consciousness is directly associated with the activity of planning. A conscious action, in this sense, is the outcome of a fully worked out plan; conversely, actions that are the outcome of no coherent plan may evoke the comment that the agent evidently does not "know" (i.e., is not "conscious" of) what he or she is doing.

Once again, "consciousness" in this third sense is distinct from— but also inseparable from—"consciousness" in the second sense. An agent may be attentive to his situation and watch his own responses and actions with care; nonetheless, he may be acting from no very explicit motives, as the outcome of no fully elaborated plan. On the other hand, he cannot act consciously and deliberately as the expression of a detailed plan without paying attention to what he is doing, and how it affects the current situation. Thus, things done designedly and deliberately ("consciously," in sense 3) cannot be inadvertent ("unconscious," in sense 2).

Nor can things done inadvertently, or with a wandering mind, be either fully or adequately thought out, well or badly planned; rather, they are done "thoughtlessly" or "without thinking."

Thus, the three kinds of consciousness—together with the associated idioms—have certain essential connections. They are not lumped together casually, through the chance use of a common set of words and phrases; on the contrary, they are related as *prerequisites* or *preconditions,* one of another. Consciousness of the first kind (basic sensory responsiveness) is a precondition for consciousness of the second kind (attentiveness); and consciousness of this second kind is, similarly, a precondition for consciousness of the third kind, i.e., the possession and pursuit of articulable intentions or plans.

The psychoanalytic notions of the "conscious," the "preconscious," and the "unconscious" are finally at home on this level. Somebody whose motives and actions are substantially "unconscious" will give a coherent account of his or her actions only with great difficulty; and the Freudian theory of "repression" helps to explain how infantile or juvenile experiences that were fraught with too much emotional conflict can diminish our ability to account for our actions. This third class of idioms also covers the use of the term "consciousness" by Marxists, social critics, and others for the special modes of interpretation peculiar to particular cultures or social groups. Differences in such "historically or culturally conditioned" consciousness manifest themselves through the assumptions that people from the relevant group or culture make, in the course of describing their situations, the events occurring around them, and their own roles in those events.

(Why is the word "consciousness" used in this context? Such usage seems to rest on a Kantian or Wittgensteinian assumption that the terms we use to speak of situations influence the manner in which we think about and even perceive them. This assumption also carries over into the use of "group consciousness" idioms: people with different kinds of gender, class, or ethnic "consciousness" supposedly end by *seeing* the same events differently.)

One final difference should be noted. In the first ("sensibility") sense, human infants, children, and adults all lose and regain consciousness in the same general ways, and a normal infant is undoubtedly *born with* the capacity for "consciousness," in this sense. In the third ("articulateness") sense, the ability to work out plans of action, for which one can give an account, is something that a newborn child—equally undoubtedly—lacks, and has to develop subsequently during childhood and adolescence. Correspondingly, the neurological regions and pathways implicated in articulate (sense 3) consciousness are more complex and plastic than those involved in sensible (sense 1) consciousness. Thus, in different respects, one can reasonably speak of consciousness as being *either* innate *or* developed, depending on what kinds of examples you have in mind: still, a failure to draw the necessary distinctions between different kinds of examples—and different senses of the term "consciousness"—can quickly land one in difficulties and inconsistencies.

III

So much for a first rough classification of consciousness idioms into three broad groups. We can now work our way back to the philosophical questions that arise out of that taxonomy. My first question has to do with the *conceptual genealogy* by which these three sets of ideas and idioms are related:

> Which of these three groups represents—in point of history—the primary, or original sense of the terms involved, and which of them are secondary, or derivative idioms?

If we attempt to answer the first question, the theoretical arguments of philosophical empiricism will pull us in one direction, the historical evidence about actual practice in the opposite direction.

Anyone with a sympathy for the arguments of Russell and James will naturally be inclined to assume that the original sense of "consciousness" is the first of our three senses, i.e., the sense in which—dreams apart—falling asleep involves having one's stream of consciousness suspended and waking up again means having it resumed. In that case, however, what are we to make of the other two groups of idioms? If the term "consciousness" primarily refers to basic sensibility, why should the same term have been extended to embrace, also, first attentiveness, and subsequently articulateness? Might it not have been extended—with equally good, or bad, reason—in a hundred other conceivable directions? Starting from this direction thus leaves the association between the three groups of idioms essentially arbitrary. Let us try reversing the sequence.

Suppose instead that the original sense in which an agent is called "conscious" refers to the capacity to articulate plans and projects, and that we think of attentiveness and sensibility as the derivative aspects of the notion. This alternative approach at least has the merit of making the association between the three groups of idioms intelligible, since, as we noted earlier, the primary aspect of articulateness presupposes the two derivative aspects of attentiveness and sensibility. An agent can be effectively articulate about his actions only if he is also attentive to them, to say nothing of his being awake, while he can be attentive to his actions only if he is not asleep, insensible, or "unconscious" (in sense 1).

In different practical contexts, we may consider an agent's "state of consciousness" (e.g., in assessing his or her responsibility for some particular action) on any of the three levels. In reply to the question, "Did the agent act in full consciousness of the situation, and of the character of his or her actions?" we may have occasion to reply in three different ways:

In sense 3—Richard Nixon covered up the Watergate affair *in full consciousness* of what was involved; but he deceived himself into thinking that, as President, he could claim sovereign immunity and so protect his associates from prosecution";

In sense 2—"The accused driver did not run the little girl down *consciously and premeditatedly*. On the contrary, his mind was not on the road, and he was quite unaware of (i.e., not conscious of) her running out from the sidewalk";

In sense 1—"At this point in the drama, Lady Macbeth wanders across the stage, apparently trying to rub blood off her hands: not in pursuit of any conscious intention, however, since she is *not truly conscious* at all, but sleepwalking."

Accordingly, if we take acting from (in deliberate conformity to) a fully worked out plan as our paradigm of individual consciousness, the practical interconnections between the three groups of idioms will immediately be apparent. The idioms covered by the second sense are concerned with the immediate preconditions for deliberate, planned action (specifically, attentiveness); those covered by the first sense, correspondingly, are concerned with the further, more basic preconditions for such attentiveness (specifically, sensibility).

Once the practical context of judgments about consciousness is made explicit, however, our argument can be carried one step further. As concerned with the question whether agents acted "deliberately and in full knowledge," judgments about consciousness need not be confined to cases involving *separate individuals acting alone*. That is why I spoke about acting from a fully worked out plan as the paradigm of "individual" consciousness, rather than consciousness *sans phrase*. So let me now take the next step and argue that individual consciousness (in *any* of these three senses) is not the original element in the whole family of ideas about "consciousness" at all. Historically speaking, on the contrary, threre are grounds for concluding that the original force of the term had to do less with the states of mind, plans, and actions of separate individuals than with the concerted, jointly coordinated states of mind, plans, and actions of *several agents at a time.*

Etymologically, of course, the term "consciousness" is a knowledge word. This is evidenced by the Latin form, *-sci-,* in the middle of the word. But what are we to make of the prefix *con-* that precedes it? Look at the usage of the term in Roman Law, and the answer will be easy enough. Two or more agents who act jointly—having formed a common intention, framed a shared plan, and concerted their actions—are as a result *conscientes.* They act as they do knowing one another's plans: they are *jointly knowing.* So long as their joint project or conspiracy is not yet perfected and agreed, each individual agent will no doubt be required to reveal his own personal ideas explicitly to his collaborators. But the *con-scientia* created as a result will, properly speaking, begin only when all those personal ideas have been pooled and used to frame a shared plan. In the law of conspiracy, correspondingly, the kind of responsibility attaching to *any single agent,* on account of consequences flowing from the actions of *two or more* persons, depends on the extent of their shared "consciousness," i.e., on how far each separate agent acted jointly with—or alternatively, in parallel with, independently of, or even under a misapprehension about the ideas and intentions of—the other agent or agents.

Looking back at our earlier taxonomy, we might now ask whether we should not have classified the idioms of consciousness into four groups rather than three. For, going beyond the sensibility, attentiveness, and articulateness of individuals, we should have recognized that the concerted plans of multiple agents manifest yet another, fourth aspect of consciousness. Agents who act as partners in a shared project, carried out jointly, with the intention of collaborating, and with each having full knowledge of the other's role in the project, are engaged in a "conscious" collaboration. They act as they do "consciously"—i.e., in the light of their mutual understandings—and they may thus be contrasted with "unconscious" collaborators, i.e., independent agents, neither of whom knows the other's intentions, but whose actions happen to produce together ("co-cause") results that might alternatively have been the outcome of joint planning. Think, for instance, of the motorists whose driving generates a traffic jam, and so "unconsciously" foil the escape of some jewel thieves whose getaway car is blocked by the traffic. The police would be proud to bring about the same result "consciously," i.e., as the outcome of joint forethought and planning.

The original sense of the term "consciousness" corresponds accordingly to *none* of the three groups of ideas and idioms included in the earlier taxonomy. Rather, their true historical ancestor appears to be the juridical sense of "conscious," "consciously," and "consciousness"—concerned with the pooled knowledge of several collaborating agents—and the whole family of terms derives originally from the Latin word *conscientia*, or "knowing together." Furthermore, if we label this usage "sense 4," the relationship between sense 3 and sense 4 is once again that of a prerequisite or precondition. Being able to articulate your own individual plans of action explicitly (being "conscious" in sense 3) is a precondition for concerting your intentions jointly with other agents. Thus, being able to collaborate or conspire presupposes articulateness, just as being able to articulate your plans presupposes attentiveness, and being able to pay attention presupposes basic sensibility.

Just how much do these historical or etymological connections prove? It might be objected in reply that, regardless of the historical origins of the term "conscientia" in Roman law, this fourth sense of the term "conscious" is, by now, archaic or technical, while all the current idioms of consciousness are concerned, nowadays, with the states of mind of separate individuals rather than multiple agents. When we talk of two agents as collaborating "consciously," all that we need be implying (on this alternative view) is that each of them individually knows about—is "conscious of"—the intentions of the other: each of the agents thus enters the collaboration "consciously" in sense 3, as part of *his/her own* deliberately chosen course of action. If that is the case, there is then no need to understand the phrase "conscious collaborators" as meaning collaborators who have concerted their plans; it need only mean collaborators each of whom, for his own part, enters the joint project consciously.

This objection is ingenious, but not conclusive. For suppose that the circumstances are slightly altered. Each of two agents knows what the other intends to do; each of them recognizes what consequences will follow if both of them carry our those plans; so one of them—without telling the other—refrains from acting as he or she had originally intended. (A trivial example: two people both want hot baths, but the storage tank does not hold enough hot water for them both, so one of them puts off taking a bath until later.) Here, each of the two agents may, for his own part, be quite "conscious" of what is at stake, and their independent actions may actually produce a result that might, alternatively, have been produced by concerting their actions; yet would we be happy, in the absence of any communication between the two agents, to speak of this result as flowing from the way in which "*they* consciously acted," i.e., from "*their* conscious collaboration"? Surely not, for they never even discussed the matter! Whatever we might say about an individual agent's "conscious involvement" in some course of events, we *do* still—even colloquially—understand the term "conscious" in such a sense that the phrase "*their* conscious decision or action" implies *more than* the sum of "the conscious decisions or actions" of each agent separately. And this *more* is precisely the implication that their knowledge was joint, pooled, and concerted.

Linking all four groups of ideas and idioms into a single conceptual genealogy, I thus conclude that the original sense of the term "conscious" is conscientia, i.e., the mutual knowledge possessed by joint agents in a shared plan. One immediate precondition for entering into such a jointly concerted plan is, no doubt, that the agents must be conscious in the third, derivative sense of "articulate," since only one who "knows his own mind" can be an effective collaborator; while that articulateness calls, in turn, for consciousness in the other two, still weaker and more derivative senses, of "attentiveness" and "basic sensibility." So, as against Russell and James, I would argue that the buzzing, booming, cognitively undifferentiated flux of personal sensory inputs—far from being the *root* of all our ideas about consciousness—can properly be spoken of as a "stream of consciousness" only as a courtesy matter. To take mere sensibility as the root idea is, in fact, to ignore the characteristic practical force of the term "conscious," whose full meaning has to do not with the sensory, but with the cognitive, not with the personal but with the shared—with the explicit and articulate rather than the undifferentiated and inchoate, i.e., with public "signals" rather than with private "noise."

IV

What has happened to the adjective and adverb, ''conscious'' and "consciously," in the philosophical usage of the last hundred years or so is, accordingly, just what happened earlier to such everyday colloquial verbs and adjectives as "think," "mind," and "experienced." Everyday terms having a familiar sense in the public domain of joint actions, pooled understandings, and interpersonal meanings have been projected into the private, individual domain of hidden thoughts, sensations, and feelings. In addition, the corresponding abstract nouns (consciousness, thought, mind, and experience) have been given a certain "false concreteness" as the supposed *names* for the content of basic sensibility. As a result, we must now do something to answer the further philosophical question:

Why have all the central abstractions of epistemology, from Descartes and Locke up to Russell and beyond, gone this same way?

How is it—i.e., *for what reason* is it—that familiar ideas and idioms concerned with public, interpersonal, and articulable knowledge have repeatedly been reinterpreted as referring to something essentially inner, personal, and inarticulate?

How are we to deal with this question? That is not wholly clear. This is one of those philosophical questions that are easier to state than to answer. (At the moment, indeed, I do not even fully see what *kind* of an answer the question really calls for.) We might start by tackling the problem in a straightforward manner, as an issue for historians of philosophy. We might, that is, simply catalogue the arguments for the epistemological primacy of the private realm, as advanced by writers from Descartes and Locke up to James and Russell, indicating why all of these writers have been obliged to look outside that "hidden" realm for the words needed to speak about it. But we surely cannot leave matters at that. For, by this time, it should be evident that this move has consistently diverted philosophers into an epistemological dead-end street. (Whatever we may get from wholly unstructured sensory inputs, it is not "knowledge," let alone "hard" or "indubitable" knowledge.) At this point, accordingly, we must go on and face two further issues: first, how one can avoid being tempted into further dead ends of the same kind in the future and, second, why this move proved so attractive around the year 1600, and has kept its charms for so long.

Taken on this alternative level, the question, on its face, once again raises issues of a historical character: specifically, questions about the broader framework of European thought from the early 17th up to the late 19th century, within which philosophers took this new epistemological course. All the same, the deeper issues involved here are surely of more than historical concern. Although the attempt to "sentimentalize," "personalize," or "individualize" epistemology has played a central part in philosophy only during the last 300 years, the considerations that have fueled it apparently represent one of those inbuilt tendencies through which (as Kant tells us) the human reason tends systematically to overreach its own proper limits—*an die Grenze der Vernunft anzurennen.*

Even though we may be convinced that this belief in the epistemological primacy of the personal is largely fallacious, we should recognize that we ourselves are still vulnerable to the charms of this belief, and that we may have our own reasons for exaggerating the claims of private sensations and sensory inputs to serve as bases for knowledge.

Here, let me merely open up two first lines of argument. To begin with: What was it that made the intellectual situation in Europe in the years following 1600 so favorable to the reconstruction of philosophy on an essentially personal, private, or individual foundation? As to this question, it is helpful (I believe) to view this move as only one aspect of a much larger shift: namely, the *rediscovery of the individual,* which had already played an important part in the development of 16th-century humanism. That shift was associated with the breakdown of the traditional social and intellectual consensus about "order" and "degree" in both human and natural affairs. Recall John Donne's long poem, *An Anatomie of the World,* which uses the death of a young girl as an occasion to reflect on "the frailty and decay of the whole world"—i.e., the decay of the whole *world picture.* Writing as a contemporary of Galileo in 1609 or 1610 (some 75 years before Newton's *Principia*), Donne refers passingly to current controversies about the astronomical system of the world:

> The Sun is lost and th'Earth, and no Man's wit
> Can well direct him where to look for it.
> And freely men confess that this World's spent
> When in the Heavens and the Firmament
> They seek so many new.

But, almost at once, he switches to questions of political authority and social degree, and records how his contemporaries have lost their implicit faith in the social and political order, have been driven in on themselves, and have as a result felt obliged to set themselves up, individually, as the measure of all things:

> 'Tis all in Pieces, all Cohaerance gone,
> All just Supply, and all Relation:
> Prince, Subject, Father, Son, 'tis all forgot
> And every man alone thinks he has got
> To be a Phoenix, and that there can be
> None other of that kind he is, but hee.

In France, the most influential spokesman for individuality and self-knowledge had been Michel de Montaigne; and it was Montaigne's cosmological skepticism that Descartes was in due course to react against, when he set about constructing his own mechanistic picture of the physical world. Whereas Descartes parted company with Montaigne over questions of astronomy, and insisted on developing a comprehensive "natural philosophy," or theory of physics, he did so (I would thus argue) from within the same general—and basically individualistic—attitude toward all intellectual problems. The external sources of assurance on which people had relied in earlier times—the traditional cosmology, and its associated beliefs about hierarchy in human affairs—might after all be reestablished; but this could be done only if some way were found of anchoring ideas *internally,* in the Self. The outer world, as represented in the medieval world picture, had failed us; the only recourse was therefore to look to the individual Ego. Given this one change in its ultimate point of attachment, much of the traditional scheme could otherwise be left unaltered. So, in the *Meditations,* we find Descartes happily repeating many of the traditional arguments that he had learned from the Jesuits at La Flèche, and adopting a conservative attitude toward all questions of practical philosophy, especially ethics. All the "originality" he was claiming was that he had given these familiar arguments and beliefs a new and more secure mooring, by anchoring them within an inner world of individual experience or mind, reason or "consciousness."

Am I arguing that, from the very start, the Cartesian program was essentially fallacious, even that it had something pathological and narcissistic built into it? Yes and no. Certainly, Descartes' agenda did involve some elements of real grandiosity. Thus, he would allow as "intelligible" only those things that he could appropriate to himself and bring within the scope of certainties guaranteed by the operations of his own mind. And this same restriction continued to shape the epistemological debate right down to the time of James and Russell. The locus of *meaning* and *certitude* was, characteristically, placed within the individual's own mind. That belief in the "inwardness" of meaning and certitude is, above all, what other, more recent philosophers—from Hegel to Wittgenstein—have taught us to question. The post-Kantian analysis of intersubjectivity, out of which Wittgenstein's own argument emerged, has thus brought to the surface the standing objections to basing epistemology on any purely individualistic program.

Still, fallacy or no, the temptation to look for epistemological assurances within our own individual "consciousness" remains a powerful one. It is well enough to criticize the idea that inward mental experience can be described in an essentially private language, but this argument can too easily lead one on to question the very *existence* of the "inner world of the mind." (People used, only half jokingly, to ask whether Gilbert Ryle actually had an "inner life"!) Faced with the wish to find a philosophical home for dreams and afterimages, private, unexpressed hopes, fears, and beliefs—not to mention stomach cramps and other idiosyncratic experiences—we still find it hard to be sure just how much weight epistemologists are entitled to place on such things, and just how little. In this respect, the tension between the "inward" character of at least some of our personal life, and the public character of the language in which those episodes have to be articulated continues to pose a challenge to philosophy.

Given the general nature of this challenge, it should not be particularly surprising that recent philosophers have chosen to give to the term "consciousness" some of the same uses and associations that were earlier given to "mind," "thought," and "experience," and to see it as embracing all those items of which we are individually sensible, to which we are equipped to pay attention as individuals, and which we alone can articulate on our own individual accounts. If there is any continuing fallacy here, we shall not escape it by denying a personal kind of "inwardness" or "privacy" to *any* experience. That would land us in throwing out the baby with the bathwater. We lapse into fallacy only when we are tempted to go further, and conclude that *all* perception and experience have this fundamentally inward or private character, and that the resulting, *internal* world of purely private data constitutes a "stream of consciousness" by appeal to which we can alone justify any claims to knowledge of the *external* world in which we live, and move, and have our being.

CHAPTER 4

Some Senses of Subjective

JOHN P. SABINI
MAURY SILVER

Seeing how the subjective and the objective fit is necessary to under-stand human action. The fitting, unfortunately, usually seems to require leaping deep, metaphysical canyons. But the appearance may be overly forbidding. We may be able to bring together objective and subjective, at least as they are of interest to students of the social life, by taking another path, albeit through a thicket. We shall see whether this path leads to a single use of "subjective" (and of "objective") or whether there are several different contrasts concealed by these words. Perhaps a patient untangling of brambles will save us leaping over a chasm.

Our plan is first to tease out several senses of subjective and objective, and see how they are related. Then we shall probe some ways in which human actions are subjective, or appear to be, and see what comes forth. Finally, we shall bring all this to the subjectivity (objectivity) of moral judgments.

Senses of Subjectivity

Sense 1: The Subjectivity of Points of View

To start with the concrete, consider a tree. We take it that common-sense actors believe, treat, and understand trees as objective, i.e., as something that not only they, but anyone can see, touch, smell, and so

AUTHORS' NOTE: A version of this chapter first appeared in *Moralities of Everyday Life* by John Sabini and Maury Silver. Copyright © 1982 by Oxford University Press, Inc. Used by permission.

forth. We assume that if a tree fancier were to call a friend's attention to the beauty of a white birch or the stench of a fruiting ginko, (s)he would take it for granted that the friend would see or smell the same tree. If not, how would "calling attention" make sense? Yet something about a tree is subjective: anyone's (everyone's) view of it.

What a person can see about a tree is tied to his or her vantage. Two people standing in different positions relative to the tree will see different parts of it. In this sense, views of a tree are subjective. The "subjective" here calls attention to the way the view is tied to the position of the person; someone standing somewhere else would have a different view of the tree. But the subjectivity of the views does not shake anyone's belief in the objectivity of the tree; rather, the subjectivity of the views supports our belief that the tree is objective. We would be astounded, shaken in our belief in the tree's objectivity, if it had the same appearance from every vantage—even a perfectly symmetrical tree would look different from an airplane than from any side.

Our belief in the reality of the tree is grounded in the fact that as points of view differ, so do appearances in an intelligible way; our belief in the objectivity of the world is sustained not so often by agreement as by an orchestration of difference. Thus, there is no inconsistency between the belief that there is an *object,* the tree, and that views of it are subjective, i.e., from a point of view. They are intertwined concepts. Subjectivity is neither a defect nor a virtue of a view, but part of what it means to have a view. Even God's point of view, if He or She can be said to have one, must be subjective.

Sense 2: The Objectivity of a Point of View

In the sense we have just discussed, all descriptions from points of view are subjective, but in another sense each is objective. When our tree fancier describes what can be seen from one point of view, (s)he takes it for granted that, were a friend to take the same position, the friend would see not only the same tree, but also the features that were described, e.g., that the branches cross at a certain height. Given our conception of objects in the world, then, we find it natural that descriptions will differ in intelligible ways with various points of view, and that descriptions from the same point of view will be the same. The notion of an object in the world, then, is sustained by both a subjectivity and an objectivity of description.

A visual illusion provides an interesting intermediate case in which a view is objective, in that anyone would have it, and yet this view does not fit with other views from different positions. For example, suppose a traveler in a desert sees a water hole and wishes to check his perception. The traveler calls to a friend, who also sees it. But as they approach, the appearance of water retreats. They now realize that they have seen a mirage, not an oasis. In our current sense, their claim to have seen a water hole *was* objective, in that anyone would have seen what they saw, but we and they, knowing that these views do not fit in the way views of a real water hole do, would not claim they had seen an object—a water hole. But neither had they suffered hallucinations. Because their descriptions fit the concept of an object in one way but not another, we have use for the distinction between hallucinations and mirages.

Sense 3: The Subjectivity of Distortion

There is a sense in which we say that some views of things are objective, in contrast to others which are subjective. In this sense, to call a view subjective ascribes a defect. To call a view subjective in this pejorative sense is, at least, to call it distorted. This use is brought out in an advertisement for a book on wine:

> Because sensory responses are easily influenced by various physiological, psychological, and cultural factors, wine evaluation can be a highly subjective process. *Wines: Their Sensory Evaluation* tells how to minimize these factors so that more consistent, objective evaluations can be made [1979].

Against this sense of subjective, but not the first, we are advised to be objective in our evaluations, descriptions, opinions, and the like. Note that although we may treat someone's claim as subjective in this sense, we still treat the person as making an objective claim in the second sense, i.e., as making a claim about what anyone would see—a claim which is wrong. The fact that we, too, take his claim to be objective (in sense 2) makes it sensible for us to correct the person and gives him/her a reason to pay attention to our correction. It gives a point to consulting wine books.

With these distinctions in mind, let us examine Nagel's (1979) introduction to his article on objectivity and subjectivity.

> The problem is one of opposition between subjective and objective points of view. There is a tendency to seek an objective account of everything before admitting its reality. But often what appears to a more subjective point of view cannot be accounted for in this way. So either the objective conception of the world is incomplete, or the subjective involves illusions that should be rejected [p. 196].

Here, Nagel appears to be opposing the subjectivity tied to points of view with some objectivity. If Nagel were using sense 1, we would understand what it means to have a *subjective* point of view, although we'd find the "subjective" redundant.[1] But, if so, we do not understand how there could be an objective point of view to *oppose* it. Then again, in sense 3 there *is* an opposition between subjective and objective, but this opposition is not much of a problem—no one treasures distortion. Of course we want an objective, undistorted account of something before admitting its reality. Nagel seems to slide between senses 1 and 3. This is easy. In both senses of "subjective," experiences are tied to individuals. But distortions are tied differently than points of view. As we shall see, our other senses of "subjective" also show a way experiences are attached to individuals.

Further on in his study, Nagel equates "more objective" with "more encompassing" (see pp. 206-207, passim). We are not sure why more encompassing should be more objective, although we can see how at times a more encompassing view can be more useful than a more limited view. But sometimes it is not. A view is better or worse depending on our purpose at hand. Near is clearly better, though more limited, than far, if we wish to make out the texture of a bark, but far is better if we are interested in the pattern of branching. Perhaps Nagel is not really urging us to adopt a more encompassing view, but to build a better, more extensive model, one that represents more of reality.

Consider a model of a tree. Imagine that we take photos of a tree from several different points of view and construct a plastic model. We might say that the model is more encompassing than any one picture. But notice that the model is not a point of view at all, and that to use the model one must take a point of view toward it. Our model should be objective, undistorted, but since it is not a point of view, it is not an objective one. Nor is it a subjective one. The problem of the opposition between "objective" and "subjective" views arises no more with models than trees.

Perhaps we are being too literal. Perhaps Nagel does not mean *objective point of view* in a specifically visual sense. But he does claim that as our view becomes more encompassing, it loses something, and this makes sense if we use a visual metaphor. If point of view means something like a model or system of beliefs, then it is clear why a more encompassing one is better—all other things being equal, it is better to know more than less, but why need there be a trade-off between the encompassing and the close? What do we lose as we know more? Perhaps as we unpack further senses of subjective and objective, Nagel's problem will become clear to us.

Senses 4 and 5: Subjectivity of Ends, and Objectivity of Means Suiting Ends

How can we extend our analysis of subjectivity to senses more interesting to a social psychologist than to a botanist? We shall do this by considering what Weber and those following him (see Schutz, 1962; Berger and Luckmann, 1967), at least sometimes, intend by the "subjective meaning" of something. What is the subjective meaning of a shoe? Weber's method is to discover the subjective meaning of something for someone, or some group, by seeing how it is related to a person's motives, i.e., goals, ends, purposes, and the like. Thus, the same shoe has different "subjective meanings" for two people if the shoe differs in how it will advance their distinct interests. The subjective meaning of a shoe to a person who wants to walk somewhere is distinct from the subjective meaning of the same shoe to the owner of a shoe factory, a shoe fetishist, or someone who has no other way to drive a nail. This sense of "subjective" shares features with the "subjectivity of point of view" (sense 1). In both senses, something is connected to an individual. In both, subjectivity is ubiquitous: All views or "meanings" are subjective. And, just as even God would have to have a subjective view of a tree, were He or She to have a view, so too, if He or She were to attach meaning to something, i.e., give it a place in His or Her plans, it would have to be a subjective meaning.

Just as *claims* about subjective views (in the first sense) are treated as objective, i.e., it is taken for granted that were others to take the same position they would see the same thing, so too is there a sense of objective, our fifth, in which claims about subjective meaning are treated as objective. To see this, consider the claim that the "subjective meaning" of a shoe to someone wishing to walk somewhere is to permit the walking without pain or danger. This claim is treated as objective, in that the person making it asserts that the shoe will in fact fit with that goal. Objective claims (senses 2 or 5) can be wrong, of course. The claim that a cubic centimeter of air has that same protective "subjective meaning" for the individual is equally objective (in this sense 5), but it is wrong. Thus, *ordinarily* a person who asserted that a cubic centimeter of air had that subjective meaning would simply be wrong about the shoe's subjective meaning to him or her.

Sense 6: The Subjectivity of Bias

To extend our visual analogy one step further, there is a sixth sense in which the meaning someone attaches to something can be subjective.

Parallel to our third sense, this one carries the force of distortion, and has as a contrast "objective." It is particularly relevant to judgments. To appreciate this sense, imagine a judge asked to hear a case in which the defendant is his wife's paramour. Assuming traditional sentiments on the judge's part, a defense counsel might search for a judge with a more objective view of the case—meaning a judge without a personal interest. Because of the judge's likely purpose—revenge—he is likely to err in his treatment of the defendant. There is a conflict between the subjective purposes the judge may have, and the interest he ought to have: procedural justice. An "objective" judge in this sense is not without an interest in the case—sleeping judges may be common, but they are not for that reason objective. Objective judges in sense 6 attach a subjective meaning to the proceedings (sense 4), but the subjective meaning is the one the proceedings ought to have. In this sixth sense, then, subjective judgments are distorted, biased, or confused because of the values or goals of the actor; objective judgments, on the other hand, are guided by the *appropriate* goals or values.[2] Just as an objective view of a tree in sense 3 (undistorted) is subjective in sense 1 (from a point of view), so is an objective view of guilt or innocence, in our present sense, subjective in sense 4 (subjectivity of ends).

Intermediate cases abound. Again, consider the hiker who chooses the cubic centimeter of air to protect his feet. We said that his claim that the "meaning of air" for him (sense 4) was to protect his feet was objective (sense 5) but wrong—that air did not have this subjective meaning for him. But this is too simple. Suppose that right after he puts on his socks, he searches for his cubic centimeter; he won't go out of the house until he finds it, and so forth. If this is part of his routine, we would have to say that he believes the cubic centimeter of air has the effect of protecting his feet, and would then say that it has this subjective meaning for him.

Consider this case in relation to hallucinations. Suppose someone stares at a blank wall and announces that he sees someone about to attack him with a meat axe. What we say about this will depend on what he now does. If he ignores it, we will not know what to say; we will not know how to take his utterance—perhaps he is just repeating a phrase he learned. But, if he runs away, then we might well say he had a hallucination of a killer, and we might call this perception "subjective." But the subjective, here, does double work. It both ties the "perception" to the individual in a way similar to the way "points of view" tie perceptions to individuals, *and* it points out the error being made. Similarly, the "subjective meaning" of the cubic centimeter is doubly subjective. It is used to show that the hiker believes the air protects, and at the same time, that he is mistaken.

There are cases analogous to our mirage, also. Consider a culture in which garlic is worn to ward off colds. Not only does the individual believe it, but it is something everyone in such a position (culture) believes. Thus, like a mirage, the belief meets *a* test of objectivity, but also like a mirage, it fails to articulate with other beliefs (or at least it can in principle be shown to).

To return to Nagel, he rightly sees that the perception of objects in the world from the point of view of an agent's plans, goals, and so forth is subjective, or as he puts it, "internal."[3] He looks for an objective point of view about, say, the meaning of life "in detachment from specific or general human purposes" (pp. 196-197). But just as "point of view" is intertwined with "subjective" in sense 1, so too is "meaning" intertwined with "subjective" in sense 4. Just as it is confusing to ask for an objective point of view (sense 1), so is it confusing to ask for objective meaning in sense 4.

Sense 7: Emotion

Another common use of subjective is in connection with emotion. This use is closely related to sense 4 (the subjectivity of ends), as Weber saw. To understand someone's emotional reaction to an event is to understand how the event relates to one's goals, purposes, and so forth. Crying at the death of a friend is understood because we understand the role of a friend in the life of an individual. But emotions are subjective, personal, in a further way.

We call emotions subjective not only to relate the actor's reaction to the actor's situation, but also to stress that for there to be an emotion, the actor must not only perceive the situation, but be affected by it. And being affected by something is more personal, is more a matter of individuality, than perceiving or understanding. Nonetheless, given the point of view, the goals, and the nature of the reaction, *which* emotion the actor is having *is* objective (sense 5—ends).

Sense 8: Cartesian Subjectivity

So far we have found a tidy heap of "subjectives" and "objectives" without intruding upon Cartesian privacy. But there is this eighth sense of subjective in which sensations are subjective. The experience I have when I look at a red patch is subjective in this way. In this sense, the question, "Is your experience of red the same as my experience of red?"

involves two subjectivities—yours and mine. As social psychologists, we have little to say about this sense, as troubling as it may be to metaphysicians; we suspect that common-sense actors have very little use for it (save, perhaps, pain reports). All the other senses of subjectivity are tied to social, corrigible claims about perspectives on objects, ways to goals, deviations from fair standards, and distortions of correct judgments. This sense of subjectivity is not. Fitting the other subjectivities to this sense would need a procrustean fitting indeed. As social psychologists interested in describing and exploring common-sense thought, we shall continue to steer a path around this eighth sense.

Evaluations

Colleagues and students sometimes tell us that evaluations are subjective. We want to see, using the various senses we have articulated, the ways they are subjective, and what would lead people to want to say they are "really" subjective.

People often use subjective and objective as if each had a single contrasting sense. As we have seen, they do not. Perhaps this is innocuous, perhaps subjective evaluations in one sense will happen to be subjective in all senses. Perhaps not. We shall be especially concerned to compare evaluations with descriptions, since descriptions, or at least good descriptions, are felt to be objective (see Jones and Nisbett, 1971, for an evaluation of the subjectivity of evaluations).

Let us take a specific case, the evaluation that a paper is "poorly typed," and see how the senses line up.

Well, in sense 1 (from a point of view), my judgment that this paper is poorly typed is subjective. I am looking at the paper from a certain angle, in good light, and so forth. But then, my judgment is objective in sense 2 (objectivity of a point of view); after all, I claim that you too will see what I see if you come here and look at the paper under the same light. In sense 3 (subjectivity as distortion), my judgment may be faulty, subjective; perhaps what I take to be uneven spacing is really my astigmatism. In terms of the subjective meaning of my criticizing my secretary (sense 4—subjectivity of ends), it is relevant to know that I am submitting the paper for publication to a fussy editor, and that I am judging the typing in light of this end. Since it is from the point of view of my particular motive, my evaluation is subjective. On the other hand, I claim that if you wanted to get published in that journal, you too would notice the typos. Thus, the poor typing is objective in sense 5 (objectivity of means suiting ends). I claim to have no axes to grind, I do not dislike my secretary, and insofar as

I do not, my judgment is objective in sense 6 (objectivity as unbiased). I am dispassionate at the moment, not overcome, so we shall let sense 7 be (subjectivity of emotion). And as neither the paper nor the quality of typing are sensations—sensations are not perceptions, not about things in the world—sense 8 (Cartesian subjectivity) is irrelevant. The sensations I have as I look at the paper are subjective. But then, all sensations are, so this makes my evaluations no more subjective than it makes all of my descriptions.

The senses of subjective, at least for the evaluation of a poorly typed paper, do not line up. Rather, the same evaluation is both subjective and objective in several different senses.

Further, the senses in which this evaluation is not objective have to do with either a failure of an attainable objectivity (subjective as distortion or bias), or call attention to a condition of all descriptions or evaluations (subjectivity and objectivity of points of view, and the subjectivity of goals and the objectivity of means suiting ends).

Our taxonomy leads us to say that evaluations are fundamentally objective; yet there are strong tugs to feel that they are "really" subjective. We shall diagnose these tugs by comparing a disagreement over the description, "The rock is hard," with a disagreement over the evaluation, "That is a poor chess move." We start by examining what we might say and do if we found ourselves in disagreement with someone about an obvious description. Then we shall compare and contrast this with the course of a disagreement over an obvious evaluation.

Imagine we meet a visitor from, say, the Trobriand Islands, who claims that a particular rock is not hard. Perhaps the person doesn't understand the use of the word "hard." But let us imagine the she is fluent in English, Oxford trained, and, by and large, calls the things we call hard "hard." Despite this, the visitor insists that this particular rock is not hard. So, to make sure, we bang on the rock, and note the pain in our hand; we notice that eggs shatter and windows break on impact with this "not hard" rock. We then arrange these same observations for our Trobriand colleague, who still insists the rock is not hard. What are we to do; what are we to say? There are limits to what we can do to convince such a person, and in the end we just have to say that she has missed something important about the rock.

Suppose someone said, "From the visitor's point of view, the rock isn't hard," or, "The rock may be hard to you, but clearly it isn't to the visitor" (attempting to use sense 1 of subjectivity). The usual case of talking about things from other points of view, the case in which such talk explains differences between people, uses the linked senses 1 and 2 (the subjectivity and objectivity of points of view). To see how this talk works, consider the following case:

A golfer gets off a very bad tee shot into the rough, onto a low hill. The second shot is equally errant, missing the green. We might explain the failure of the second shot by saying that from the golfer's point of view, one couldn't see the green, and that is why the second shot was so misguided. Why are we satisfied with this account? Because we take it for granted that people cannot see through trees and hills, and that people aim less well when they cannot see what they are aiming at. How does this compare with the "not hard rock"? The claim that the rock is not hard "from the visitor's point of view" does no explaining. Although we can understand, from what we know about humans, that golf balls aimed from behind obscuring trees and hills miss their mark, we cannot understand, from what we know about humans, how someone who bangs his or her hand on a rock can fail to notice that it is hard. Unless the point of view the person is said to have can, because of its concrete, relevant details, explain why an ordinary person equipped with sense and concepts gets the understanding wrong, then pointing to a point of view is otiose.

Now, in contrast to the hard rock disagreement, let us consider an argument over whether a chess move is good or bad. Suppose someone makes a move allowing one's opponent to fork one's king and queen, and we call that a bad move. Is this claim objective in the same way(s) as our claim that the rock is hard? Let us bring our Trobriander back. Suppose this person does not notice the badness of the move. This time we would be considerably less surprised, since they have rocks but not chess in the Trobriand Islands. So we teach the visitor chess; someone had to teach her "hard." Once we do, and we know she has mastered it — having even occasionally mated us — are we any less mystified by the visitor's not acknowledging the badness of the move than we would be by her failure to acknowledge the hardness of the rock?

Perhaps a good move, "from the visitor's point of view" makes more sense than in our rock example. One's view of a green can be obscured by trees; one's view of a particular move can be distorted by an obsession with a particular strategic line—the player with the forked queen may have had his/her eye on the mischief being planned for an opponent's rook. Saying that the player blundered into the loss of the queen because it looked like a good move from the player's point of view works if it articulates why the move was a blunder with why it looked good to the player; if it does not then it has no explanatory force. Hence, saying it was, or better, that it looked like a good move from his/her point of view, does not deny it was a bad move. Rather, it shows how the error came about while conceding the "bad move" evaluation.

We have so far shown how statements about hard rocks and evaluations are similar. Why, then, do we have tugs to feel that the evaluation and not the description is "really" subjective? Recall our hard rock and our Trobriander. It is conceivable that as Oxford found the visitor, she not only did not have the English word "hard," but even that her native tongue had no translation. Still, we would be astonished if she did not consistently respond to the hardness of some objects and the softness of others. Such a person might have no concept to capture the way in which some objects are similar and others different, but presumably would show us recognition of this feature by the ways in which she handled hard and soft objects. Recognizing bad chess moves is quite different. We would find it miraculous if someone who grew up in a culture that plays no chess recognized the chess move as bad or in some way responded to good and bad chess moves differently without having been tutored in the game. Hardness is the sort of thing anyone sentient in any culture would have to bump into; the badness of a chess move requires sapience and a certain sort of experience. The tug to call evaluations subjective may have its source in our understanding that while all people distinguish hard from soft, only some people, those having learned the rules of chess, can tell good from bad moves. Still, and this is what we want to hang on to, in sense 5 (the objectivity of means suiting ends), given that one purpose a person has in playing chess is the point of chess—winning—then claims about the badness of a move are objective, i.e., corrigible, the sort of thing anyone who knows chess could be led to see. Once the move has been made, if someone were to evaluate it, that person would have no more choice about which evaluation to give it than to say whether a rock were hard or soft. One could, of course, choose to talk nonsense, but nonsense is a defect of descriptions as well as evaluations (see Searle, 1969, on institutional and brute facts).

The hardness of rocks and the badness of chess moves, then, are quite different, but one way they are not different is in whether common-sense actors treat them (when they are being serious rather than theoretical) as properties of the external, objective world rather than like pain reports, where they have some sort of privileged perspective on an "internal matter."

We want to extend our chess story in two directions to see what problems confront us in applying the notions of objective and subjective to other human affairs in order to uncover more tugs toward subjectivity. We shall consider more slippery human actions. Does the objectivity of the characterization of a chess move tell us about chess or action? Once we address this, we will be in a position to consider in what sense moral judgments are objective. First to action.

One feature of our chess story is that losing one's queen is a move any chess player would find infelicitous. But notoriously, both descriptions and evaluations of an act collected from observers of the act differ. This lack of consensus seems to challenge the objectivity of all reports, seems to allow free reign to the notion that the act was an X to Y, or from Y's point of view, while it was a W to Z, or from Z's point of view. It would seem that noticing hardness is a matter of *recognition,* while perceiving what someone did is just a matter of *interpretation.* What exactly does the indisputable fact that people often give different accounts and interpretations, show?

First, we may have different accounts of the same act which are not inconsistent. The accounts of a play given by a set designer, the producer, a critic, a member of the audience, or a follower of the leading man may differ—as we would expect them to, given their different purposes, interests, and the like (subjectivity of ends). Yet each, once (s)he understands the interests and standards of the other, can assess the various accounts. This kind of difference reminds us of the subjectivity of ends, and the need to have common standards and commonly understood ends.

Second, disagreement may just show that people are sometimes, or often, wrong. But this is hardly a problem peculiar to discussions of actions. Let us image disagreement about something physical, say, the presence of TB, and see whether a belief in the subjectivity of diagnosis follows from this. One hundred radiologists are asked to examine a chest film for TB, and 50 say there is TB, and 50 say there is not. Would not everyone agree that there is nothing subjective about the matter, but that half are wrong? But perhaps this is because of a particular feature of TB: We have criteria for deciding whether a person has TB—the presence of the appropriate bacillus. Thus, we cannot only say that half are wrong, but we even know how to tell which half.

No doubt it is more difficult to find criteria for most human acts than for TB, and often there may not even be criteria. But nothing about an irreducible subjectivity of human action follows. Sometimes we cannot appeal to criteria in physical cases, either. Let us say that 50 people call a wall green and 50 call it red. What criteria could we use to settle this issue? Still, even without seeing the wall, are we not all convinced that one group is right and the other wrong? *So are they.* Hence, objectivity does not depend on criteria. Indeed, the fact that people do disagree with each other shows that they treat the focus of their disagreement as objective.

Then why is there this tug to take disagreement as implying subjectivity? Perhaps it is this: The senses of subjectivity we have examined, e.g., points of view, goals, and the like all involve personal differences—differences between what two people see (given their positions), differences between what two people want (given their values), and so on. "Subjective" is invoked to emphasize differences. But the use of subjective in these ways does not imply disagreement, the shared belief that if one claim is correct the other is wrong. We cannot understand how two claims, one that a person has TB or that a wall is green, the other that a person does not have TB or a wall is red, can both be true. The inability to imagine reconciliation shows that we don't have claims from different points of view, subjective claims, but disagreement about the nature of the object. Occasionally, we are shown how a disagreement we thought irreconcilable can be reconciled; here we would invoke "point of view" and say that the two positions were not really in disagreement. (Consider quantum mechanics and the light as particle, light as wave controversy.) Thus, although subjectivity arises from differences, not all differences imply subjectivity.[4]

Ambiguity

There is another source of our inclination to say that human action is subjective; it arises from a fact about many actions: They are ambiguous. Ambiguity leads to a failure of consensus, to differences. And differences pull us into subjectivity. So, although ambiguity presents its separate problems, problems we can't adequately cover here, we shall highlight a few features of ambiguity and how these features relate to subjectivity.

First, to say that something is ambiguous is often just to say that given the facts at hand, one is unwilling to commit oneself to a judgment—not out of whim, but because the facts are not adequate to the judgment. For instance, our radiologist might have said, after looking at the chest X-ray, that it was ambiguous whether the patient had TB. This would not be denying as a matter of fact that the person either had or didn't have TB; rather, it would mean that the evidence was inconclusive. Future lab tests might well allow a decision. And, Schrödinger's cat aside, we would not say that the patient caught or escaped TB at the moment the decisive test was done. This sense of ambiguity relates to the first sense of subjective;

we would call cases ambiguous just when we recognize that our point of view does not allow a decisive claim *about the object*. Yet *this* claim is objective in sense 2 (the objectivity of points of view), since it claims that anyone looking from this point of view would also see its indeterminacy. Contrast this with a first-year medical student's claim about the same X-ray: "I don't know whether it shows TB." The medical student might mean that the X-ray was ambiguous, that no one could tell, or just that (s)he lacked the experience to tell.

It is just when the objective facts are uncompelling, ambiguous, that wants, beliefs, and the like can most easily introduce bias. Objective ambiguity invites subjectivity in the senses of bias (senses 3 and 6). Nonetheless, they are distinct.

Reneé Richards furnishes another kind of ambiguity. The issue of whether Reneé Richards should be allowed to play in the Women's U.S. Open Tennis Championship arose because Reneé had been born a male, but had had a sex change operation. People found it difficult to decide. Why? Were they missing any facts? No. They found it ambiguous because our concepts of man and woman were not set up to cope with such a case.

The concepts were once clear; you could tell a man from a woman on many grounds—which sort of external genitalia the person had (at the moment), which sort he or she had had at birth, whether the person was a mother or father, and lately, which chromosome pattern the person had. Because the features never contradicted one another, there was no pressure to develop a convention about which feature(s) was criterial and which was symptomatic. But technology creates new instances: Austin's cat has delivered a philippic. In the Reneé Richards case, because concrete matters turned on it, the officials had to decide one way or another. Creating a third category would not work—with whom would she play tennis, herself?

Although we may not be able to resolve Reneé's sex, still, we can all see how the features we pointed to are relevant, and we also know that other facts about this person are irrelevant to whether Reneé is a man or a woman—e.g., the city in which she was born, or her skin color. The problem is that although this much is objective, which "criterion" is compelling is not clear. But our shared understanding of what is relevant structures our thinking about the case. Objectivity plays a role even in this ambiguous case; indeed, the objective relevance of genitalia and chromosomes creates the ambiguity.

It is also ambiguous, but in a different way, just where a forehead ends and a head begins. Border points are ambiguous; we cannot always say to which side they belong. Even the most precise and careful observations could not settle this issue, nor, in contrast to the TB case, could further information of any sort help. What is needed is not observation but legislation. If it mattered, some community could adopt a convention, sign a treaty, and create a rule of language to decide the matter, but until it does so, border cases remain border cases. Still, all of this scarcely denies that the concepts of forehead and head are objective or that there are points which are clearly one or the other.

Many human actions are ambiguous. Imagine that someone tells us after a talk we have given how much (s)he enjoyed it. Now, we all know that such comments are a part of academic courtesy, so it may not be clear what to make of it. The issue is not, as it might seem, one of sincerity but of what the actor was doing: We may have been the recipient of sincere compliments or sincere politeness. Of course, if the congratulations go on for a day and a half, then it is clear which they are. At the other extreme, a muttered "Nice talk," offered in the rush from the room, is clear. But there are cases in between where neither the recipient nor, perhaps, the host can say. Such cases are simply ambiguous.

Perhaps most, or even all, human actions are ambiguous. First, we are not often in a position to know everything that could be relevant to a judgment about a particular act, even our own, and we know it. Second, it may often pay us to act ambiguously. Consider flirting. Flirting depends on acting in a way that might be a sexual overture, but also might not. I might just be putting my hand on your shoulder to steady myself. In order to flirt, one must keep one's intentions ambiguous. Further, there is no reason to assume that an actor's intentions need be more articulate than his/her actions. Ambiguous acts may mask clear intentions, but then again they may reveal ambiguous intentions.

Suppose it were so that *all* human action was ambiguous. Then why make the claim that human action is objective? Because even if it were so, and we never had all the relevant information, we still know how to separate relevant from irrelevant in context. The objectivity of human action rests not on certainty about real cases, but rather on our shared understanding of what matters and how it matters. And, even if no information could resolve these actions (they are all on the borders of foreheads), not every *conceivable* action would be ambiguous were it to happen. If it turns out that people can be shown to purposely construct ambiguity, then presumably we would account for their doing so in terms of their understanding of what would not be ambiguous.

Morality

Having assembled our taxonomy, examined an evaluation or two, and considered some ambiguities of human action, we are prepared to think about the subjectivity and objectivity of moral matters. We shall consider separately two different kinds of moral claims. An example of the first is "Jim is an adulterer," which is a moral claim because "adulterer" is a piece of moral talk. (If the reader does not believe that adultery is a moral charge in this culture at this time, we ask him or her to imagine Ohio in 1953 and to imagine our discussion to be about that culture.) An example of the second is "Adultery is wrong," which explicitly addresses the moral status of adultery. These claims raise different issues with regard to subjectivity and objectivity, yet arguments about the subjectivity of one often intrude into arguments about the subjectivity of the other. We shall try to keep them separate, and touch on why they are so easily conflated.[5]

For this discussion, the most relevant sense of subjective is our sense 4, the subjectivity of ends—subjective meaning. It is relevant in the sense that someone might say, "For me, that wasn't adultery." How might we make sense of this? Well, the person might mean that (s)he was not trying to commit adultery, that it wasn't the goal; rather, the person was trying to impress a client to win a new account. But wouldn't we say, "So what? It's adultery anyway!" Indeed, people rarely have adultery per se as their goal.[6] Since committing adultery does not depend on the meaning of the act for the participant, the claim is not subjective in this sense. But this does not mean that everyone who has sex with someone other than his or her spouse is an adulterer. Perhaps there has been a confusion of identical twins. Some moral charges are not independent of the meaning of the act for the actor, but adultery is, and it is not unique. Lying is another. If you lied to an armed maniac to thwart a plan to bomb Hoboken, in praising you we would not deny that you had lied, but point to how your lie had saved a city.

"Murderer" is not like this; it takes account of the subjective meaning of the act for the actor—the actor's point of view—at least to a degree. Killing someone in self-defense, with the goal of preventing your own assassination, is not murder. Still, "murderer" does not specify the actor's intentions either. A murderer need not intend to kill; someone merely willing to accept the death of some bank guards regrettably near the vault that one must blow up to steal the bonds is still a murderer. Thus, "murderer" takes account of the subjective meaning of an act to a person—at least to a degree—but only the *objective* (sense 5) subjective (sense 4) meaning of the act to the person.

If someone wished to convince us that a "murder" was really self-defense, that person had better be prepared to show first that it was self-defense that was the goal, and second that the act was suitable to bring about self-defense, i.e., that it was called for. Just thinking that your goal is self-defense is not sufficient. One might hallucinate a threat, be sincerely afraid for one's life, kill a blameless other in fancied defense, and still not be a murderer, but not because one acted in self-defense; rather, because one is insane. Thus, even when the moral assessment depends on the meaning for the actor, and the offense is in this sense subjective, that meaning must still be sensibly related to the objective situation. Although, as we have seen, "Jim is an adulterer" is not subjective in sense 4—the subjectivity of ends—the claim that Jim is an adulterer could be subjective in a trivial way. Imagining an adulterous affair behind the most casual flirtation of one's enemy, Jim, is subjective in our sixth sense— biased. Just as we found for the evaluations we considered, we find for the moral claims (of this sort) that they are not fundamentally, irreducibly subjective. But now we turn to the second sort of claim in the moral domain: Adultery is wrong.

In what sense could this be subjective? What would convince us that someone was treating it as a subjective matter? First, what could someone mean who said, "It's wrong from my point of view"? One thing it could mean is that in our fourth sense (in relation to my goals), it would be wrong for me; it would make me feel bad or interfere with things I am trying to achieve, and so on, but here, "wrong" is being used in a pragmatic sense, and further the claim is objective in sense 5—I am asserting that as a matter of fact I will feel bad, or run into trouble. Or, to change examples, someone might mean that since I am a policeman, it is wrong for me to ignore your speeding. He means that it would be OK for a civilian to ignore the speeding, but the role creates an obligation. In sense 5, this is an objective obligation. And, in sense 6 it is an objective, unbiased assessment. Or someone might mean, to return to adultery, "My wife is hopelessly insane, and therefore I have a special exemption from the marriage vows." But insofar as the person offering this reason believes it to be a reason, he is acknowledging that adultery is wrong (otherwise, why would he need an exemption?) and his claiming an exemption rests on the implicit argument that anyone who had such a wife would be entitled to the dispensation.

Kovesi (1967) has called attention to another distinction between adultery and murder. It is queer to say, "This particular murder is not wrong." This is because, in calling something murder, the facts relevant to its being right or wrong have already been taken into account. There is no "justified murder," since if it is justified it is not murder. But as the above example suggests, this is not true of adultery. Because we may in a specific case, or perhaps in all cases, not want to say that adultery is wrong, and because it is an objective matter that adultery is pejorative, we feel a tug to deny that some cases of extramarital intercourse are "adultery"—thus treating adultery on the model of murder in order to neutralize its disparaging implication.

Another possible use of "X is wrong is a subjective matter" trades on ambiguity. Consider abortion. Everyone agrees that at some point after conception, say, 20 years after, destroying the upshot of the conception is wrong. But because specifying any point as *the point* at which destroying the upshot is murder seems arbitrary, the issue of the moral status of abortion is objectively ambiguous. Yet some people must act, regardless of the ambiguity. As a result, someone who did not have an abortion for moral reasons might say, "Having an abortion is wrong for me," meaning that she recognizes the arbitrariness of *her* boundary-drawing, and she recognizes that others might morally draw the line at a different point. But just as the ambiguity of border points does not call into question the objectivity of the concepts forehead and head, so the ambiguity of some questions of right and wrong does not call into question the objectivity or even clarity of all decisions about right and wrong.

A famous example of Sartre's leads some to say that morality is subjective. In his example, during the Nazi occupation of France a man is torn between joining the reistance and taking care of his mother. On Sartre's example, one cannot say which is right for him; whichever decision he reaches, he would realize it could not be "universalized," i.e., he (or we) could not say that everyone else ought to decide as he decided if they were in his place. He must make a decision about what is right, and yet he knows it isn't an objective one (sense 2 or 5). But this does not show that morality is not objective in general. It is another case of ambiguity, where the ambiguity itself is objective; it is ambiguous in a way similar to the way in which Reneé Richards's sex is ambiguous. In both cases we can see reasons for either decision. In both cases we can all understand that although there are reasons on both sides, a decision must be made one way or the other, and that the reasons do not compel either way. But taking Sartre's example to show that all moral decisions are subjective, or better, ambiguous would be akin to taking the Reneé Richards case to show that whether every person is a man or a woman is subjective or ambiguous. So Sartre's case does not threaten the objectivity of decisions of right and wrong, it merely highlights the ambiguity of some such decisions.

Another possible reason for saying, "The issue of whether adultery is wrong is subjective" is the fact of cross-cultural differences in the conception of what is right and what is wrong. Right and wrong are not qualities like the hardness of a rock—transcultural, physical. But neither is the right or wrong of, say, adultery like the goodness or badness of a chess move—"bad moves" are derived from the "point" of chess. Perhaps, Aristotle and Aquinas notwithstanding, there is no "point" of life, to derive right and wrong, and therefore good moves are not deducible. What instrument to use to get rice to the mouth is probably not deducible from a set of first principles, either; some would say it is an arbitrary convention. Yet this too is objective, something every member of a culture knows and expects others to know. Hence, even if the rightness or wrongness of adultery turns out to be more arbitrary convention than chess, cross-cultural variation gives us no reason to call its wrongness subjective, personal, or a matter of individual taste (sense 4). The rightness or wrongness of adultery is, at least, a cultural fact. Of course, the wrongness of adultery can change. Perhaps in 1953 adultery was wrong, and perhaps in 1995 it will clearly be right. And perhaps at the moment it is ambiguous, but none of this shows it is subjective, either. Even fashion has its objectivity.

Perhaps what people might mean by saying that the rightness or wrongness of adultery is subjective is that right and wrong come down to "feelings." There are at least three ways to take feelings. One way is to take them to be sensations. On this story, my feeling the wrongness of adultery is akin to my having sensations when I look at a red patch. In this sense, the subjectivity of morality would be just like the subjectivity of the redness of a patch, the size of a square, and everything else, since there are sensations involved when I perceive anything. Cartesian privacy, if it is a threat, is a threat to everything, not to morality in particular.

But a second sense of feeling has to do with feeling angry, grateful, proud, and so on. And, as has been argued extensively (see Meldon, 1961; Kenny, 1963; Bedford, 1962), while this sense of feeling includes some sensational element, it also includes something else, something objective. To know that one is angry one must know what anger is—what an angry reaction is, what a provocative act is, and so forth. If the rightness or wrongness of adultery were a matter of feeling in this sense, then deciding whether something feels "right" or "wrong" would depend on knowing right from wrong as an objective matter so that the feeling could be identified. So even if the claim that the wrongness of adultery depends on emotional feelings, on subjective facts (in the emotion sense of subjective), were correct, it would not deny that the rightness or wrongness of adultery is objective in the fifth sense (corrigible).

Of course, there is yet another sense of feeling, as in "I feel that the oil crisis is a hoax." But here, "feel" is used roughly as a substitute for "believe," and is an objective claim in sense 5. And in this sense, an anesthetic person could feel the wrongness of adultery or the chicanery of the oil companies. In any of these senses of feeling, the objectivity of rightness or wrongness is left standing against claims that morality depends on feelings.

There is one sense left in which someone might say that "Adultery is wrong" is subjective. Perhaps this is meant to deny that the claim is objective in senses 2 or 5 (corrigible). Putting sensations aside, could any claim be subjective in this way? How about, "I dreamt I was King of France"? This seems to be a claim. But unless it implies that you believe that "If you were in my position (or had my goals, beliefs, values, and so on) you also would have dreamt you were King of France," such a claim is subjective, lacks objectivity in sense 2 or 5. But even this claim depends on our understanding of what it would be like to be King of France. If we are to understand morality as being subjective in this way, then we must understand what it would be for adultery to be right or wrong as an objective matter. Only then could we understand what it would be for adultery to be right or wrong in this subjective, dream sense.

Working out from a simple case of a person looking at a tree, and exploring how the language of point of view or subjectivity does its job there, we find no reason to say that morality is fundamentally subjective. We do see reason to say that it is a cultural matter, and sometimes an ambiguous matter, but not a fundamentally subjective one. Yet the tugs remain. But if they do, they are not supported by the senses we have alluded to. Perhaps there are other clear senses of "subjective" that have eluded us. Or perhaps the tugs come from conflated uses, talk in which various incompatible senses are used at once. The empirical project remains to track down the actual uses of "subjective" or "point of view" by both common-sense actors and scientists. This should be a most interesting chase.

Notes

1. If one examines both the lay and social science literature closely, one finds that "subjective" is very often used in just this redundant way. It does provide emphasis.

2. Lysenko is an interesting case. Biologists forced to treat Lysenko's claims as sensible were thinking and acting in a biased, distorted way. Yet we would not call their bias subjective, nor would we call their judgment objective. Subjective, in this as in the other senses, carries the force of "personal," and while Russian biology was a distortion, it was not, for the most part, a personal one.

3. Just as there are a swarm of senses of "subjective" and "objective," which it pays us to keep distinct, so too are there distinct senses of internal and external—closely related to subjective and objective. Elsewhere we have made some effort to keep them distinct (Sabini & Silver, 1980).

4. Agreement doesn't imply objectivity either, at least agreement in the sense of having the same response as others. A colleague asked subjects to judge the *saltiness* of Rorschach cards! The judgments were, rumor has it, consistent, both over time and between subjects. But does this show that these willing (even heroic) subjects took it for granted that other people would (or should) judge the stimuli as they did? Or did they take their own responses to be akin to "I like chocolate ice cream"?—a matter of taste and a matter of coincidence if peoples' tastes coincide. They were not asked.

Presumably, none of the subjects would know how to show that any of their judgments were biased or distorted. Nor do senses 1 and 4 of subjectivity apply: What could count as a "point of view"? This particular judgment, and the semantic differential which it models, is neither objective nor subjective; it is meaningless. Of course, one could baptize another sense—subjective as meaningless—but what work would it have?

5. We stress the distinction between these two sorts of claims in part because Berger and Luckmann have argued that the first sort of claim arises as an issue in every culture, whereas the second sort arises only in special circumstances in specific cultures. On their view, dealing with the first sort of claim is essential to the regulation of a culture; fretting about the second is a frill.

6. It would be misleading, ordinarily, to say that a person's goal was adultery: As these things usually go, the person's goal is to have sex. If the person about to perform the act were to discover, at that moment, that his marriage wasn't actually a marriage (imagine that his wife was already married at the time of their wedding, unbeknownst to him), he would find that he could not (logically) commit adultery. But presumably this would not frustrate his immediate purpose, nor keep him from his goal. On the other hand, one might have adultery as a goal, say to get back at a spouse, or to set up the grounds for divorce.

References

Berger, P., & Luckmann, T. *The social construction of reality.* New York: Doubleday, 1967.

Bedford, E. Emotions. In V. C. Chappell (Ed.), *The philosophy of mind.* Englewood Cliffs, NJ: Prentice-Hall, 1962.

Gerth, H., & Mills, C. W. *From Max Weber: Essays in sociology.* New York: Oxford University Press, 1958.

Jones, E., & Nisbett, R. *The actor and observer: Divergent perceptions of the causes of behavior.* New York: General Learning Press, 1971.

Kenny, A. J. *Action, emotion and will.* London: Routledge & Kegan Paul, 1963.

Kovesi, J. *Moral notions.* London: Routledge & Kegan Paul, 1967.

Meldon, A. I. *Free action.* London: Routledge & Kegan Paul, 1961.

Nagel, T. *Mortal questions.* New York: Cambridge University Press, 1979.

Schutz, A. *Collected papers.* The Hague: Nijhogg, 1962.

Sabini, J., & Silver, M. Internal-External: Dimension or Congeries? Unpublished manuscript, 1980.

Searle, J. *Speech acts.* Cambridge, MA: Cambridge University Press, 1969.

Wines: Their sensory evaluation. Scientific American Advertising Blurb, 1979.

Wittgenstein, L. *Philosophical investigations.* New York: MacMillan, 1953.

CHAPTER 5

Psychological Dimensions

ROM HARRE

The Need for Psychological Dimensions

If we believe that the structure of ordinary language reflects and in part creates the psychology of the people who use that language, then we need an analytical scheme for understanding ordinary psychological concepts. On this view, the analysis of these concepts must be the starting point for any technical or scientific psychology. It is in terms of common-sense psychologies that everyday folk construct themselves as persons and criticize the psychological activities, the reasoning, emotional displays, and so on of others.

Dimensional and Componential Analysis of Concepts

A distinction presupposed, but not explicitly stated, in much analytical philosophy, is that between the legitimate field of application of a concept and the root ideas and implications which are its meaning. Positivistic theories of meaning would be unable to make this distinction. A field of applications can be presented as a space. Taking the metaphor a step further, I shall call the critical study of fields of application "dimensional analysis" and the teasing out of root ideas "componential analysis." In this chapter, I undertake a dimensional analysis of certain mentalistic concepts whose componential analysis I shall be merely sketching without out detailed argument.

The distinction can be illustrated with concepts from other systems, for instance, from medicine the concept of "disease." Consider a one-dimensional space representing a spectrum from physical to mental disorders. Traditionally, diseases were confined to the general category of physical disorders, but the concept was not used for war wounds nor injuries through accident. Recently, "disease" has been used for mental disorders, taking into this application its original system of root ideas and implications, such as the distinction between symptom and cause. From the traditional co-relativity of cure to disease, the idea of treatment has been imported into the sphere of mental disorder. And this has various moral implications. The middle ground of the one-dimensional space of disorders includes psychosomatic complaints. It remains interestingly clouded. Even members of the medical profession do not speak of psychosomatic diseases, but rather of conditions or complaints. A detailed analysis and discussion of the various matters here adumbrated would be a formidable undertaking. Such a project would issue in a full dimensional analysis of the concept of disease presupposing a componential analysis. The componential structure of the concept would need to be kept under constant review since it would be liable to be influenced by changes in the range of application, revealed by dimensional analysis.

One might object that talk of dimensional and componential analysis of a concept or concept cluster is just a pretentious way of reintroducing the traditional distinction between the extension and intension of a term. The similarity is evident. I have two reasons for taking an oblique approach via my neologisms.

(1) The extension of a term is rarely explicitly considered, nor is its structure analyzed in any detail. It is usually treated as given ("the members of such-and-such a set"), and more importantly, as unstructured. Philosophers should perhaps have drawn a moral from one aspect of the problems that arise with attempts to understand mentalistic concepts. Though we may have a clear account of the intention of a term (the root ideas it comprises, so to speak), the range of application of the term may be problematic. This point is evident in much of the discussion of mental concepts that has followed Ryle's treatment in the *Concept of Mind* (White, 1967). In this chapter I want to emphasize the way fields of application of a concept are structured, and to illustrate the importance of giving an account of that structure in elucidating the workings of a concept or concept cluster. Philosophers have tended to follow the way of thinking of taxonomists, for whom the extension of, say, *lepus caniculus* is just the undifferentiated collection of rabbits.

(2) To some extent, positivistic theories of meaning are still with us, theories in which meaning is elucidated through that to which a term refers. Sortal terms tend to be explicated extensionally. The extension of

a term can hardly be thought to be problematic unless one already has some idea of its meaning (or the root idea in the concept), the field of application of which one is trying to discuss. To pick out componential analysis independently of dimensional analysis is a way of insisting that the elucidation of the intention of a term is to be treated as a problem independent of the study of the structure of its field of application.

Folk Psychology and Scientific Psychology

There are many ways in which folk psychology is incomplete, and there are many psychological processes for which folk concepts provide an inadequate analytical scheme. Hence, as the empirical investigation of human life proceeds, new terms will need to be introduced to enable us to express novel hypotheses, new distinctions, and so on. The underlying reason for all this, which I shall argue in this chapter, is that although people do construct themselves in accordance with their theories of how people are supposed to be, they do not, as a rule, have explicit knowledge of a wide variety of psychological processes—those we could call automatic or habitual. Such processes involve causal chains, some of which are physiologically based and some perhaps more perceptively analyzed as the product of habits. The latter will in turn have been acquired by processes, some of which are conscious and all of which are social. An adult, accustomed to acting in accordance with unconsidered social habit, may not have an adequate conceptual system for describing, let alone understanding, the sources of the general features of his or her activity. It is clear, then, that new terms will be required as patterns of social action that are usually taken for granted come to the attention of detached observers. I can illustrate the point with Goffman's (1971, chap. 5) concept of the tie-sign. A tie-sign is something we do to indicate to others that we are with someone, even when we are awaiting their return. Introducing the concept enables us to identify a social psychological phenomenon that has never been part of anyone's direct consciousness, except perhaps an actor preparing to simulate life on the stage. To be acceptable as part of a conceptual system for analyzing and understanding social life, tie-sign will have to coordinate with adjacent concepts of the common-sense system, such as "marks of affection," "standoffishness," and so forth.

This chapter is based on the principle that psychological activities occurring in ordinary life ought to be generalized to control the introduction of technical terms for novel hypotheses and new distinctions. In the course of this discussion I shall be arguing for a particular set of dimensions upon which to represent psychological concepts. These dimensions are intended both to facilitate the analysis of ordinary language and its associated folk psychology and to control the introduction of neologisms.

But the growth of explicit knowledge of existing phenomena is not the only kind of change that needs to be dealt with. Social and psychological practices change, and some of these changes are wrought in the field of application of psychological concepts. As Wittgenstein (1953) pointed out, no conceptual system is prepared in advance for all possible applications, so that moments of choice are likely to arise. They seem to arise in two ways. Phenomena occur within an existing field of application that call in question the internal structure of a concept. For instance, the concept of disease, with its traditional root ideas and implications, is unprepared for the discovery of physical malfunctions that derive from a genetic defect. In calling sickle cell anemia a disease, we have decided a previously undetermined usage. By making the decision one way rather than another, the structure of the concept is changed. But it may be that some change occurs (perhaps a technical innovation) that suggests the application of the existing concept, with its existing structure of root ideas and implications, to a new field of phenomena. For instance, the appearance of organized, internationally linked terrorist gangs tempts one to apply the concept of war to conflict between these gangs and state security forces. But this application reflects back upon the internal structure of the concept which, let us suppose, once included the root idea of national conflict.

In the discussion to follow, I offer some tentative dimensional analyses of some commonplace psychological concepts. These will involve both of the above considerations. I proceed as follows:

(1) A development of a 3-space of dimensions appropriate for locating psychological concepts. This will lead to the examination of the consequent constraints on the introduction of neologisms, constraints which would explain how the range of a concept is coordinate with existing uses.

(2) The examination of contrasting cases. In one case, new applications have taken root, so to speak, without serious confusion. In another, despite technical innovations which might have led to conceptual relocation, none seems to have occurred.

Rejection of the Cartesian Dimensions

Despite the fame of Ryle's *Concept of Mind,* the criticism of the Cartesian way of understanding psychological concepts has not caught on in the thinking of psychologists, nor indeed of many philosophers, for that matter. Discussions are still carried on in terms of the traditional pair of dimensions, subjective-objective, and inner-outer. In most discussions these dimensions are mapped onto each other, so that the subjective and the inner are treated as co-extensive, while the outer coincides with the objective. I want to run over some familiar ground to reemphasize the necessity for abandoning these dimensions for graphing psychological concepts.

Though they are mapped onto each other, the distinctions embodied in the traditional dimensions depend upon radically different ways of dividing psychological reality. But the matter is not so simple. The subjective-objective distinction is, I think, a complex dimension, the product of two further distinctions. This inner complexity leads to a characteristic equivocation in the way the distinction is used. Sometimes it seems to be used to emphasize the difference between attributes which are person-dependent, such as thoughts and feelings; and those which are person-independent, such as physical properties. This distinction, I suspect, reflects the conceptual truth for an entity to have a subjective attribute—for example, to be able to entertain thoughts—it must necessarily be a person. But anything corporeal can have physical attributes, such as mass. This is not sufficient to account for the way the subjective-objective distinction has been taken. It also seems to depend in part on the difference between inter- and intrasubjectivity. If this is correct, the distinction is related to the way in which some items can be present to only one consciousness, such as sensations or memories, whereas others, such as material things and their physical properties, can be present to many consciousnesses at once. Or at least it is so arguable. To maintain the distinction in this form, one would have to resist a traditional philosophical argument against the propriety of accepting any intrasubjective objects of experience. There are arguments for sense-datum theory that, if viable, would have the effect of legitimating only the intersubjective pole. But for my purposes it is neither here nor there whether one accepts such an argument. Even to frame it one must admit, at least in thought, the conceptual distinction between inter- and intrasubjectivity. The distinction is required even if one of the poles represents an empty category. Sabini and Silver, in their contribution to this volume, discern a yet wider range of senses in the use of the subjective-objective distinction, among which are those I have emphasized in this argument.

The inner-outer distinction is treated, I argue, as co-extensive with some version of the subjective-objective distinction. Sabini and Silver demonstrate that the trouble with the subjective-objective distinction is worse than a mere equivocation, so the argument against the distinction could be strengthened still further. The distinction between inner and outer states is clearly related to the body. But without further argument, it seems to dissolve into a rather feeble metaphor, by which the surface appearances of the body are treated as nonmental, while the mentalistic attributes are supposed, somehow or other, to be inside the skin, behind these appearances. We speak of concealing our thoughts by the control of facial expressions, that is, of the outer surface of the body, that part which is visible to other people. To talk of the hidden thoughts, by contrast, as inner, is to slip into thinking that what is concealed is hidden within the body. Without investigating the muddles involved in this slippage in any detail, it is clear that the inner-outer distinction is a mess. Neither "subjective-objective" nor "inner-outer" are useful distinctions for categorizing psychological properties, and to treat them as co-extensive is only to confuse the issue still further.

Arguments which collapse the conjoint distinction by denying one of the poles are exemplified in a good deal of traditional philosophy. I have in mind, for example, the paradoxes of interactionism. If the extensional identity of inner with subjective properties and of outer with objective attributes is maintained, and the former are attributed to mental substance and the latter to corporeal substance, we have a classical Cartesian distinction. I note in passing the two extreme forms of solution to the problems engendered by that gloss on the distinctions. There is the proposition that interaction is ultimately an illusion (materialism), and then there is the proposition that it is miraculous (Leibniz's preestablished harmony). Neither seems to me to have much appeal if one starts by rejecting the distinction from which the problems of interaction arise.

More recently the argument has turned on a slightly different issue which has surfaced in the debate between Husserl (1960) and Schutz (Schutz & Luckmann, 1973, chap. 3). By indulging in a phenomenological reduction and experiencing the achievement of the first and second *epoché*, Husserl found himself firmly ensconced within his own subjectivity. In *Cartesian Meditations*, No. V, he began to brood on the problem of how one could return from the verge of solipsism to the intersubjectivity upon which the human relations characteristic of an ordinary life would depend. As he put it, "How could inter-subjectivity be transcendentally constituted?" "How could it be shown to be a necessary condition for the possibility of experience?" His argument turned out to be very weak. He seems to have thought that only by *assuming* that the bodily appearances of other people are animated can we return from a phenomenological reduction to inhabit an intersubjective world. In such a world we can presume that others see us as we see them; that is, as animated bodily appearances. Only within the joint domain of persons can there be agreed experiences of unitary material things. In his commentary on this problem, Schutz reverses the trend of the argument. He proposes that we should take intersubjectivity as given. We should then ask how is subjective activity—that is, personal experience, which is ours and ours alone—constituted from the given intersubjectivity? Put this way, the problem no longer seems to be philosophical. It could be treated, as indeed I think Merleau-Ponty (1965) treats it, as an issue in developmental psychology. Students of human development should be able to find out how as a matter of fact we learn to refrain from public display of our thoughts and to conceal them, as we say, from each other. How do we come to understand that the point of view from which we understand a public thing creates for us, as individuals, distinctive appearances from those experienced by people differently placed? Developmental psychologists have tried to build up an account of how individuals come to have the idea of experiences being theirs and theirs alone. Shotter (see Richards, 1974, chap. 11) and others have proposed the idea of psychological symbiosis. Mothers who continuously complement the psychological and social deficits of infants by talking to and of their child as if it had the full complement of psychological capacities, in particular as if it were a fully competent self, seeing and acting upon the world from its own standpoint, eventually create adult human beings. This story hints at other ways than the Cartesian of mapping mental concepts.

New Dimensions

The dimensions I propose to develop depend on a foundation of basic considerations for which I shall not provide detailed arguments. I hope they will be recommended by their utility.

Consideration 1. Human life is lived as one among many. Even when momentarily solitary and acting for oneself alone, an individual's linguistic capacities and knowledge of conventions ensure the presence of the many. Nevertheless, a human individual has some idiosyncratic attributes, for example, a unique biography, and often conceives and acts upon personal projects.

Consideration 2. Consider a list of attributes traditionally taken as characteristically the province of psychology: feelings, emotions, knowledge, intelligence, consciousness, and so forth. In different cultures, and indeed different moments in one's own life, these attributes may differ greatly in the degree to which they are displayed to others or kept to oneself. In some cultures, feelings may rarely be displayed. Schoolboy cultures generally require knowledge to be kept to oneself, knowledge which should be publicly displayed only to teachers. Even consciousness need not be displayed. In an emergency, one may pretend to be asleep.

Whatever may be the original of the human tendency to form groups, be it a genetically transmitted, physiological structure or a culturally maintained, adaptive device invented by human ingenuity, it is characteristic of human beings to form collectives of all sorts for a variety of purposes, both expressive and practical. Some human attributes have both an individual and a collective *realization*. For instance, agency can be realized in both individual and collective exercises of power. By taking these basic considerations together, we get the following dimensions:

(1) If we consider the possibilities for display of one's psychological attributes, it is clear that these can be undertaken with oneself as the only audience, e.g., mulling over one's plans to oneself, or one may go so far as to reveal a project publicly for the attention of anyone who cares to take notice. I shall call the poles of the dimension of display "private display" and "public display." Since displays range from revelations and productions for quite specific others to general and open performances, the poles of display encompass a dimension which we could imagine to be continuous.

(2) Certainly some apparently psychological attributes can be realized as a property of one or of many, and in differing degrees, provided the "many" are not a mere rabble (an aggregate) but a collective. For instance, one human being can impose his will upon a multitude of others. Groups of people as collectives, for instance, institutions, can be agents of a sort and can exercise power. A group may impose its will upon an individual. There is some middle ground, since individuals can act through collectives and vice versa, and that in differing degrees. I propose a second continuous dimension, the poles of which I shall label "individual realization" and "collective realization," against which a variety of psychological attributes can be considered.

(3) Further dimensions could be created aux choix. For the purposes of this chapter I shall construct a third dimension on the basis of the assumption of a pervasive human tendency to create order. The third dimension arises through observing that the urge to create order, if I may so speak, can be manifested in personal matters, for instance, in an individual living a well-planned life, or in various degrees in social matters, as in setting up an institution with well-defined chains of command. I shall call the poles of this dimension "personal order" and "social order."

To illustrate the application of this three-dimensional system, let me offer as a preliminary example a brief dimensional analysis of the common-sense concept of intelligence, as expressed in terms like "clever" or "smart." We ask, "Is intelligence a private attribute, or can it be publicly displayed?" I would be inclined to say that although the notion does have private applications, its essentially comparative nature suggests that it is fundamentally an attribute of public performances. Is it the exercise of a power that is individually located, or is intelligence a feature of actions or projects that stems from the activities of a group? I think the answer is clear. As it is ordinarily understood, intelligence is an attribute exemplified in individual exercises of competence or skill. Is it exemplified in the creation of order among the personal aspects of life, or among the social? I would be inclined to say that we regard the exercise of intelligence and the creation of order to be ubiquitous. In the dimension of order, intelligence would be represented by a line rather than a point in the three-space. It is a power to create a certain kind of intentional object, personal or social, e.g., personal belief system or social institution, and whose display is fundamentally public. Its dimensional analysis can be represented as in Figure 5.1.

In Figure 5.1, I have represented the axes of the three-space as orthogonal, that is, as independent of one another, so that display, realization, and order are features of human life which can vary independently relative to the "one-many" distinctions. At best, this is true of the relation of the private-public axis to each of the others. But the axes of realization and order in particular cases are not orthogonal. Consider the attribute of power or agency. Order may be imposed upon a group of people by the exercise of power by a single individual who achieves his plan for the

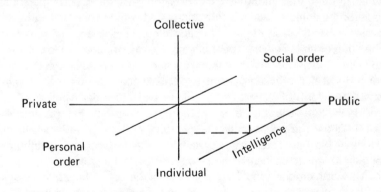

Figure 5.1

structuring of the activities of a group—the authoritarian scout master who sees to it that all the pup tents are neatly in line and that all lights go out together.

Each of eight cells offers possibilities for the use of psychological concepts. The location "private-collective-social" allows for the attribution of quasi-psychological concepts to such pseudo-entities as firms. For instance, the concept of "information" could be applied to this location in the three-space. We might speak of a firm concealing information from other firms.

A psychological attribute need not be forever fixed in a particular application. The development of a human being, as conceived, say, by Vigotsky (1962), would typically involve a time-dependent displacement of attributes through the three-space. For instance, small children have not learned to keep their intentions to themselves. The concept of "intention" for a two-year-old would be located in the region public-individual-personal. A year and a half earlier, at the stage of psychological symbiosis, when its mother was formulating the child's intentions for him or her, the concept would be located in the region public-collective-social.

However, the long history of the Cartesian distinction must reflect some important aspects of the psychological functioning of human beings. It can hardly have convinced so many if it were wholly without some empirical foundation. The nearest approximation to that distinction in the three-space would be a major conjoint axis running through the space from the cell private-individual-personal to public-collective-social. If I may remind the reader of the argument of the first section, I particularly want to deny that attributes located at the private-individual-personal pole of the conjoint axis are to be identified with inner states and processes, while those at the public-collective-social pole are thought of as the outer or visible events or conditions. This association would collapse the new dimensions back into the Cartesian distinction. Though the major conjoint axis represents an important distinction, the use of the three-space as a form of representation allows us to consider whether other cells in the three-space are also empirically realized. For example, important cells are the public-individual-personal and the private-collective-personal. I shall try to show that certain important psychological attibutes ought properly to be located in one or the other of these boxes.

It is worth emphasizing that I do not want the poles of my dimensions to be taken as distinctions, dichotomizing the conceptual structure of folk psychology, and by the covert rule of common-sense concepts in professional psychology determining the conceptual structure of that field as well. I am proposing that the dimensions are *continua*. A psychological concept can be considered as more or less privately displayed, and so on. The continuity of the dimensions I will propose are mediated by language and other symbolic systems which span the space between the poles. I offer the following three formulae by way of explication.

- In the private . . . public dimension: language is understood as a common *instrument of representation.*
- In the individual . . . collective dimension: language is understood as a common *instrument of action,* e.g., "I order . . ." by comparison with "It is required that . . ."
- In the personal . . . social dimension: language is understood as a common *instrument of representation and action.*

I have introduced these dimensions schematically and with a minimum of argument. In order to secure a measure of conviction, I will try to show how they would be employed in dealing with some particular cases.

Two Examples of Dimensional Analysis

This chapter is based upon the idea of a distinction between the problem of determining the location(s) of the application of a psychological concept and that of discovering the internal structure and implications of that concept. But the possibilities of application are partly determined by the semantic components of a concept which are themselves adjusted to presuppositions about the range of entities, properties, and processes to be covered in its extension. Thus, if "knowledge" is construed as "justified true belief," one is committed to a field of application carved out of whatever is the field of application of "belief." Arguably, however, the concept of "belief" covers a range of attributes, dispositions, or states which are individual-personal. Hence, construing knowledge as justified true belief would tend to confine the field of application of that concept to the individual-personal cells of the space.

The conceptual structure of psycholinguistics recommends itself as a nonbehaviorist format for any branch of psychology by virtue of the distinction between theories of competence and theories of performance, that is, between theories concerning the cognitive resources required for competent action and theories concerning the productive processes by which those resources are employed by particular actors to create coordinated action-sequences. To avoid too close identification with psycholinguistics, I shall refer to competence theories in general as "resource theories" and performance theories in general as "action theories." Referring these theory types to the analytical three-space, it is immediately evident that action theories are necessarily social. Acts as intentions must be matched by interactors' interpretations for an action of a specific sort to have occurred. Resource theory, it might be thought, ought to be person-centered and individual, since an actor uses his knowledge to form his intentions, and an interactor uses his to interpret what the actor is doing. Knowledge as a resource for action, it would seem, though socially deployed, is individually realized.

But this would be too simple. In many cooperative enterprises actors have to be prompted, controlled, or corrected by reference to a knowledge resource other than their own individual representations of locally correct means-ends principles. Cases can be found in the practical order of apprentices working under a master craftsman, and in the expressive order of participants in a ceremony who have to be taken through their contributions step by step by the officiating chief of protocol. Resource theory must, therefore, allow forms of knowledge which are collectively located and socially ordered.

Knowledge

These considerations suggest that in examining the extension of the concept of knowledge with respect to the above three-dimensional system, we may find ourselves required to accept a generic account of knowledge wider than, but including, that which emerges when knowledge is studied only relative to Cartesian limits. In particular, aspects of the use of the concept for some specific forms of knowledge which have, as it were, dropped from sight through the use of the Cartesian dimensions, may become visible.

Let us consider the location of knowledge as a psychological attribute on the three dimensions which I have proposed above.

(1) Private-public: while it can hardly be denied that there is private knowledge, it seems clear that some items of information are permanently and impersonally displayed. For example, wall maps of the layout of an underground railway could be said to represent knowledge which is neither private nor personal. Anyone who has the necessary skills to interpret these diagrams has access to that knowledge; it is, you might say, public knowledge. As Popper (1972) has pointed out, the invention of ways of recording discoveries makes it reasonable to speak of "objective knowledge"—information which has become detached from any particular knower. Zyman (1968) has made a somewhat similar point in arguing that a concept of "public knowledge" is needed to understand the epistemology of institutionalized science.

(2) Individual-collective: sociologists' complaints about philosophers' ways of treating knowledge have hinged on the way in which cognitive resources in the successful performance of some social practices are distributed through a collective. In such cases, no one individual knows everything that is required in order to perform a given practice successfully. A performer may have to be prompted by others, and sometimes everyone involved may have to consult a manual or script. This feature of a knowledge system, that it is distributed through a collective, can be found in all kinds of social activities. For example, the knowledge needed by the workers in constructing a building may be distributed through a collective so that a team is required to bring off the activity successfully. In the expressive order, it seems that very complicated informal rituals, such as football aggro, draw on a knowledge system distributed through the collective of fans. Particular individuals are known to have fragments of the knowledge.

(3) Personal-social: the introduction of the idea of a social order relative to social knowledge leads to a third dimension. The human collective through which a body of knowledge is distributed might be a structured society, the persons making it up being ordered in some way. We would expect, then, if a knowledge corpus was distributed through the collective and the collective was structured, that the knowledge corpus should be treated as having a structure dependent on that order. If knowledge is socially organized, then the possibility of differential access to knowledge has to be considered. Persons in different role positions might have very different degrees of access to the knowledge corpus. Perhaps by the very fact of belonging to the same social class as those who are the personal repositories of important fragments of the corpus, some people have access to knowledge which others cannot attain. Sociological studies show that this is true of many forms of professional knowledge, the most notorious being medicine (Schutz & Luckmann, 1973).

However, the representation of the concept of knowledge in the analytical three-space is historically based. Nothing could have preempted the way the concept developed. The decision to call the information stored in libraries or in computer memories "knowledge," even if qualified as public or impersonal, is strictly arbitrary. At best, Popper, in proposing the category "objective knowledge," is not making a philosophical point but reporting a fact of historical linguistics.

Memory

Philosophical controversy about memory has turned on whether memory is to be thought of as a certain continuous state representative of the matter remembered, or whether it should be thought of as a disposition to recall that matter. The argument for the latter position is based on a construal of the act of remembering as an achievement ("I've got it!") rather than as a task ("I'm looking for it"). An argument for the former position might concede all the points about dispositions and achievements, but insist that dispositions must be grounded in some continuous state of the being to whom they are attributed. To be in the state which is grounding the disposition to recall is the nub of what it is to have a memory. Despite the essentially personal location of the memory-grounding state, there are problems about the authoritativeness of memory which prompt one to consider whether perhaps memory might not have a public aspect, too. To claim to have remembered is prima facie evidence that the recollection is true or verisimilitudinous. But evidence from documents or from recollections of the events by others may cast doubt upon the claim. Thus, on the question of whether a recollection is a genuine memory, people, however certain of themselves, are not necessarily authoritative.

In the Cartesian one-dimensional space, remembering is a mental process, so memories as mental phenomena must be inner events or states. Neither the process nor the phenomena occur publicly on the outer surface of the body. The association of the subjective-objective cluster of distinctions with the inner-outer dichotomy is part, I think, of what has made memory puzzling. There is evidently no secure subjective criterion for definitely assigning an inner state to the favored epistemic category of memory, i.e., correct recollection of things past. So something seems wrong with making memory inner-subjective, yet the category inner-objective is ill-formed within the Cartesian scheme. Let us try mapping memory on the three-space of dimensional analysis instead.

Relative to the individual-collective dimension, it is clear that, as currently employed, items from the conceptual cluster around the notion of memory are applied to matters located at the individual pole. This reflects the conceptual truth that a remembering, when genuine and done by me, is my memory and not someone else's. But once we introduce considerations of authority, social structure appears. For instance, a mother's recollections are more authoritative as to the genuineness of the earliest recollections by her offspring, despite the feelings of conviction that may accompany their own recollections of their childhood. On these grounds we should say, while remembering is individual, memories are located in a social order, since their validation is not a personal matter. Although the signs of having remembered are often publicly displayed (the self-congratulatory tap on the forehead with the heel of the hand), the memorial experience seems essentially private.

Relative to the three-space, memory seems to be located in the private-individual-social sector.

In the first section, I remarked that technical innovations and changing social practices sometimes bring pressure on a conceptual system well adjusted to traditional concerns and ways. This can lead to moments of decision. The current rules for using a concept or concept cluster can run out, not being prepared for a novelty yet to be described. A community can institute new uses of existing concepts or introduce new concepts to deal with such moments. There is presently a certain amount of pressure on the memory-cluster in both the individual-collective and the private-public dimension.

Diaries, engagement books, chronicles, and so on have long been part of the equipment of civilized men. They are clearly devices for the extension of individual memory. But they have not influenced the concept. Most are actually, and all are potentially, public. Perhaps for that reason they have been conceptually set off as *aides memoires,* as mnemonic devices, and so on. Even the conceptual system for dealing with electromagnetic recording has followed the same trend, since tapes and discs are treated as the memory of the gadget, not as the memory of the person (or corporation) whose equipment it is. Tendencies to personify such gadgets have perhaps helped to direct the conceptual innovations to cope with such developments in the direction they have actually gone, but I can see no a priori reason why they should have gone that way.

On the other hand, record keeping, and particularly secret record keeping by institutions, such as government departments, firms, banks, and so on, has led to the use of terms in the memory cluster to talk about those records. Remarks like, "Some institutions have long memories" have begun to appear. Philosophical treatment of this kind of development must turn on whether "memory" is used here metaphorically, preserving its original sense, or whether the new domain of application reflects the appearance of a new specific term on all fours with traditional usage, requiring us to recognize the coordinate usages. The implications and potential misunderstandings deriving from the innovation will be very different in each case.

It seems that our present conceptual system preserves the range of application of the traditional concept cluster with which we deal with the ordinary human faculty of memory. But if all our psychologies are to be organized around the joint search for resource theories (competence) and action theories (performance) and, thanks to technical innovation, some of the resources we call upon for recollecting and correcting recollections are to be located in the public-collective-social cell, the psychology of memory is thereby transformed, since the resource theories component is transformed. It seems to me that if I routinely use a computer to assist my recall of past events, the faculty that is ordinarily called "memory" is not the same for me as for some country cousin not so equipped. In principle, the memory banks of a computer are public, limited only by the contingent rules governing access.

To sum up these considerations, it is quite clear that the conceptual system in which memory is embedded is not prepared for advances in modern technology. The tendency in our culture has been to confine memory to personal recollections without public help, the latter being treated as mnemonics, records, and so on. In order to give some motivation for extending the psychology of remembering under the pressure of contemporary innovations to include our relations with gadgets, I owe notice of an intermediate case to L. Heit (1979). He pointed out that even in the old conceptual system we admit the notion of a shared memory. This concept applies in the sort of case where two or more people contribute to a conversational reconstruction of events in which they both took part. Each contributes to and amplifies the recollections of the other. A psychological study of shared memory would require an investigation of the conditions under which a contribution from one served as a reminder for the other. Under what conditions did one allow his recollection of an experience to be corrected by the other, and so on?

These considerations could be extended to include a number of other important classes of psychological concepts, such as intentions and emotions. I have argued elsewhere that intentions are complex in just the way that we have seen knowledge to be complex. We need to use the whole three-space for the representation of the location of the concept. Similarly, Sabini and Silver (this volume) have given a convincing argument for the use of a similar analytical scheme for understanding some of our emotional concepts, such as "envy." It seems clear that traditional psychological theory as embedded in everyday English benefits in clarity of exposition from the use of the more elaborated scheme I have proposed as an alternative to simple Cartesianism. If the underlying metaphysical issue is resolved in such a way that we can take it that it is a necessary property of psychological concepts that they can be considered as possibly locatable somewhere in the three-space, then we have an a priori structure for controlling the introduction of new concepts. So, for example, the use of a concept like "attribution" to pick out the psychological phenomenon of giving praise and blame to others by the ascription of dispositions would have to be considered against its mapping onto the three-space. To what extent are attributions public rather than private? How far are they able to be composed by individuals or determined by the acceptance of the community? And in what way do they structure human interactions to give them social form?

Summary

It follows from the argument so far set out that knowledge is partly socially located and distributed. A general psychology of social action requires knowledge as a necessary component of competence; that is, of the cognitive resources of someone able to act adequately as occasion demands. If these are genuine features of the use of the concept as it is located in ordinary explanations and accounts of ordinary life, then the theory of action which is coordinate with ordinary understandings cannot be a wholly individual psychology. For the resources upon which an actor draws in forming intentions to act, which may be realized if the conditions are right, may be knowledge which is not his own personal possession. So, though action must be individual, and the performance-theory aspect of an action in psychology must deal with individual processes, the competence theory may not be individual at all.

It seems clear that knowledge is not necessarily a personal property, either philosophically or functionally. I have argued that, although in its ordinary usage the concept of memory seems to be closely tied to the personal and private capacity for recollection, technical innovation could lead us to modify it. The field of study of the psychology of memory may change in such a way that we should include a person depending on public-social and collective ways of storing and recollecting events of his own past. In this case, the individual personal component of memory would be reduced to two capacities—knowing where to look to find the impersonal storage of representations of one's past, and the capacity to understand the deliverances of machines, that is, knowing how to interpret the recording conventions.

Consciousness

Turning now to the consciousness, the psychological phenomenon central to our deliberations as reported in this volume, I want to offer a summary componential analysis setting out what I take to be the root ideas in our ordinary notion. I shall find connections here with earlier remarks by Toulmin and by Taylor. Using the componential analysis, I want to try some dimensional analysis, both to elucidate the field of application proper to consciousness concepts and to examine the propriety of an increasing trend to revive the suggestion of G. H. Mead (1934), that consciousness is *somehow* a social phenomenon (Coulter, 1979, chaps. 1, 2 and 6).

Componential analysis

I propose that we can understand contemporary uses of the notion of consciousness with the help of three root ideas: awareness, attention, and reflexiveness. I take awareness as an undefined root idea upon which to build the rest of the analysis, appealing to common experience as to what this phenomenon is taken to be. This set of root ideas is very close to the analysis offered by Toulmin. Indeed, I think it is identical, since his notion of "articulate accounting" clearly presupposes both reflexive awareness and reflexive attention. A person could not give an account of himself unless he were aware of some of his states and capable of selectively attending to some among them. In general, the personal states of which people are aware are their being aware of or attending to something.

The relation of the three root ideas seems to be as follows:

- Awareness is a necessary condition for attention. Attention is a necessary condition for reflexive consciousness.
- A person is aware of a range of objects, each of which is a possible object of attention.

Diagrammatically, the three root ideas of the concept of consciousness can each be represented as relational pencils from P, a person, to various intentional objects, represented as O_1, O_2, and so forth.

(1) Awareness

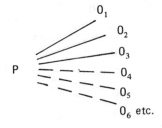

$O_1 \ldots O_3$ are actual objects of awareness. $O_4 \ldots O_6$ are objects of possible awareness.

(2) Attention

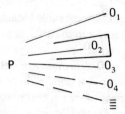

$O_1 \ldots O_3$ are objects of awareness. Only O_2 is an object of attention.

(3) Reflexivity

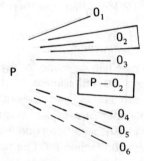

$P\text{-}O_2$ becomes an intentional object for P. In this representation, P as such has not yet become an intentional object for P. I am inclined to think that perhaps it never could. Hence, this treatment is in accordance with Kant's view that P must be a transcendental object, not given in experiences but known to exist as a necessary condition for experience.

I think the analysis sketched out here is coordinate with Taylor's view. Consciousness is a state relative to what he calls a significance feature, that is, a feature which is interest-relative to a being. The idea of picking out a feature as significant is close to the idea of attending to a matter of interest (danger, excitement, provocation, and so on) and so structuring a primitive field of awareness. I would be unwilling to accept this feature of experience as adequate to pick out human beings, since I am sure chimpanzees attend in just such an interest-relative way. But if we add reflexivity, so that one's own attention relations can become significance features, we have the beginnings of conditions significant for a moral world, the characteristic world of human beings, a world where shame becomes possible.

Dimensional Analysis

Dimensional analysis necessarily locates consciousness in the private-individual-personal sector in the analytical three-space of the last section, since the three root ideas I have identified as components of the cluster of ordinary notions of consciousness are variants of the basic pencil structure having its origin in P, a person. It immediately follows that the only states of consciousness of which any person can be aware are his own. We can share objects of consciousness with other persons, but not states of consciousness. To put this in another way, states of consciousness cannot become objects of consciousness for anyone, except the human being whose states they are. This follows necessarily from the structure of the concept of consciousness as I have set it out above, as a pencil of relations centred on P. How, then, can there be any sense in talk of social factors in consciousness?

Social aspects of consciousness

I believe that a case can be made for the need to recognize a social aspect at the second stage of refinement of consciousness—attention. Attention is relative to a capacity to pick out a delimited object of attention, with the remainder of a field of awareness becoming relatively unattended. But which aspects of an undifferentiated field of awareness can become objects of attention for a particular human being is determined by that person's system of categories. Even the most extreme innatist must concede that at least some of a person's categories have their origin in the society in which one is brought up. The range of possible objects of attention for an individual is socially influenced, if not determined. The point is readily illustrated. Cultural factors seem obviously required to explain the differences in the heavenly constellations picked out by Mediterranean people from those identified by meso-Americans. The Great Bear is not a possible object of attention for an Aztec. A case can also be made for the general point from the effect of training in the capacity to select kinds of objects of attention. Span of attention seems to be increased by practice. The institution and maintenance of programmes of training, say in identifying edible plants, are clearly social in origin.

At the third stage of the refinement of consciousness, reflexive or self-consciousness, the social element appears in a more complex way. It seems that one could hardly bring one's attending to an intentional object into one's field of awareness, and realize it for what it was, that is, as one's own attending to an intentional object, unless one had a working concept of oneself. We have already noticed that this concept could not have been acquired by immediate awareness of oneself. Hume's criticism of the idea of an empirical concept of the self seems well taken, but that argument does not warrant a general skeptical conclusion concerning the utility of a working concept of the self. It follows only that the self is not a possible object of awareness. It follows that the concept of self must be acquired in some way other than by direct experience. The most convincing theory I know of is that one acquires the concept of self through being treated as a self by others. This theory encompasses a thesis in philosophy. It explains how one can come to acquire a transcendental concept, a concept of something not given in experience, but a necessary condition for experience. It also involves a thesis in developmental psychology. It suggests that the conditions for the possibility of actually acquiring a concept of oneself involve an essentially social element.

References

Coulter, J. *The social construction of mind.* London: Macmillan, 1979.
Goffman, E. *Relations in public.* London: Penguin, 1971.
Heit, L. Personal communication, 1969.
Husserl, E. *Cartesian meditations.* The Hague: Nijhoff, 1973.
Mead, G. H. *Mind, self and society.* Chicago: University of Chicago Press, 1934.
Merleau-Ponty, M. *The structure of behaviour.* London: Methuen, 1965.
Popper, K. R. *Objective knowledge.* Oxford, Eng.: Clarendon Press, 1972.
Richards, M. P. M. (Ed.). *The integration of a child into a social world.* Cambridge, Eng.: Cambridge University Press, 1974.
Schutz, A. *Collected papers* (Vol. I). The Hague: Nijhoff, 1962.
Schutz, A., & Luckmann, T. *The structures of the life-world.* London: Heinemann, 1973.
Vigotsky, L. *Thought and language.* Cambridge, MA: MIT Press, 1962.
White, A. R. (Ed.). *The philosophy of mind.* New York: Random House, 1967.
Wittgenstein, L. *Philosophical investigations.* Oxford, Eng.: Blackwell, 1953.
Zyman, J. *Public knowledge.* Cambridge, Eng.: Cambridge University Press, 1968.

CHAPTER 6

Characteristics of Language

JUSTIN LEIBER

I start with three sets of issues that have bothered me and others recently. What I want to show is that if we keep in mind a distinction that comes to us from biology, we will then find our way toward sorting out these three sets of issues. The distinction from biology is that between analogy and homology.

For example, the antennae of insects might be said to be analogical to the whiskers of cats, the high-pitched squeaks of bats, or the hands of humans. All serve the function of figuring out what is in front of the organism, particularly when the organism's eyes are ineffective. Hence we have analogy. But we do not have what biology mostly trades in. We do not have homology. For insect antennae, cat's whiskers, bat's squeaks, and human hands do not have a common form of biological development; they are not the same organs; they lack a phylogenetic or genetic relationship. There is no branch of biology that studies *the organ for feeling out dark environments*. Homologically, there is no *organ for feeling out dark environments*.

I will now give a brief rendition of the three sets of issues. They are familiar, even notorious.

(1) The first might be put so: Does Washoe, the chimpanzee whom the Gardeners instructed in something like American Sign Language, really have language? The Gardeners say Yes and Obviously Yes. The linguist says No. Why the passion? What is the issue or issues that might decide the question? Is there a plausible resolution?

(2) Although the second set of issues might be put as the question: *Do computers think?* I would rather put it as: What is the normal form for

psychological descriptions? Some people, for example, have thought that we are universal Turing machines (UTM) and that the normal form for descriptions of our psychological states will be Turing machine tables. If you take this line, then you might say that computers think if they are UTMs and think the same as us insofar as they instantiate the same Turing machine tables. Particularly those who see a sharp distinction between physical and psychological description and explanation need to provide sense to the notion of the normal form of psychological description.

(3) If you think that my first two sets of issues are narrow, trivial, or unattractive, perhaps you may be happy with my third. What I have in mind is the old and confused issue of the objectivity or subjectivity of psychological and sociological description and explanation. As an example of the subjectivist's viewpoint, I quote Jonathan Culler's rendition of Trubetzkoy's structuralism:

> The methods of linguistics and the social sciences are different from those of the natural sciences. Whereas the phonetician is concerned with the properties of actual speech-sounds, the phonologist is interested in the differential features which are functional in a particular language, the relations between sounds which enable speakers of a language to distinguish between words. It is clear that these tasks cannot be accomplished by the methods of the natural sciences, which are concerned with the intrinsic properties of phenomena themselves and not with differential features which are the bearers of social significance. In other words, in the natural sciences there is nothing corresponding to the distinction between *langue* and *parole:* There is no institution or system to be studied. The social and psychological sciences, on the other hand, are concerned with the social use of material objects and must therefore distinguish between the objects themselves and the system of distinctive or differential features which give them meaning and value.

So we have our three sets of issues. Let us see how we may cleave them with the distinction between analogy and homology. By way of hinting where we are going, I will say now why I came to think that the analogical/homological distinction is important for the psychological sciences.

I have been impressed by work done within what has been called component, modular, subpersonal, or faculty psychology. That is, work that suggests we may be best understood as a collection of specialized competencies. Some who have thought about the problem of individuating such faculties have even talked, for example, of a language *organ.* A little reflection may in fact suggest that those who speak of components or faculties speak of them in the way we speak of organs.

Those who speak of faculties and components make free (if often ad hoc) reference to all of the following in individuating faculties and components: evolutionary arguments, species-wide generalizations, differential and biologically programmed rates of development for individuation, evolutionary and genetic appeals, lateralizationist and localizationist views about the brain, brain morphology, and brain damage, phylogenetic discriminations in brain structure, and so on. But to make these sorts of appeals is to regard components as biologists regard organs.

For example, those who believe that we learn language through our general intelligence and that we have no highly structured language acquisition faculty point to evidence that children who are left-brain-damaged in their early years can easily transfer and redevelop linguistic knowledge in the right brain. On the other hand, those who wish to defend the notion of an autonomous linguistic faculty point to more recent data that suggest that infants who experience a left hemispherectomy have a permanent syntactic deficiency. But both of these groups would be incoherent if they were not already thinking of a component or a faculty as an organ, that is, thinking of components or faculties as individuated in the manner that the biologist individuates organs. And what is basic to the biologist's mode of organ individuation and description are the notions of homology, of growth phylogeny, and of genetics. Analogy, free-wheeling similarity of function, is but the foil or counterfeit of homology.

Indeed, the maturation of biology might be said to be the replacement of analogical description and explanation by homological description and explanation. We have a visual organ, a visual faculty, because of our biological nature, not because we, and analogously any other organism or mechanism, happen to be frequently bathed by electromagnetic radiation that bounces off of our environment. We do not have an organ or component for feeling out dark environments because of our biological nature, not because we, and analogously other organisms and mechanisms, do not need to or cannot figure out dark environments.

I first consider the question about the normal form of psychological description.

It cannot be denied that the development of artificial computing devices has had the same sort of importance for human cognitive psychology as the development of pumps had for the understanding of the human circulatory system. We have been captivated by the view that we are in some sense universal Turing machines, and that in some sense the normal form for a description of a human mind (or a routine of a human mind) is a Turing machine table. Turing suggested in effect that any computer which could be said to have the same Turing machine table as a human would therefore bear the same cognitive predicates, the same psychological descriptions. E.g., if and only if the machine and I instantiate a Turing machine table for addition, both the machine and I can be said to know that $5 + 7 = 12$, that $2 + 2 = 4$, and so on.

Indeed, some people now suppose a view about cognitive psychology which I will call "universal Turing machine functionalism" for long, and "functionalism" for short. The fundamental thesis of UTM functionalism is just that a human mind is a universal Turing machine and that the normal form, or appropriate descriptive level for psychological description is that provided by Turing machine tables. Since it may seem reasonable to suppose that we, like most artificial computers, are essentially universal Turing machines, we can give a complete description of a human mind by indicating the routines or programs it currently has on hand. One might suppose that we are born with some of these routines, including program constructing routines, and that we construct others in learning. The vision seems to be that of a powerful universal computer— the mind—connected to sensory input and motor output channels at its peripheries. What goes on outside this central computer goes on outside psychology and is to be ignored on the principle of "methodological solipsism" that insists that mental states are what they are, irrespective of whether the external, nonmental environment is one way or quite another.

I suggest that the real strengths of functionalism, of the computer analogy, are coupled with real difficulties, and that the functionalist program seems hopeless on a straightforward construal and indeed curiously out of kilter with some of the most interesting recent work in cognitive psychology and linguistics. I want to suggest that we are *not* universal Turing machines at any detailed and significant level of psychological description and that while Turing machine tables may model some of our cognitive capacities, it is misleading to take these tables as the *normal form* for psychological descriptions.

After indicating what may be right about the computer analogy, I will try to indicate its weakness through analogizing the universal Turing machine to something I will call a "universal locomotive machine." I will then try to show how UTM functionalism seems out of kilter with significant recent advances in cognitive psychology and linguistics, and I will conclude by proposing a "modular" or "biological" view that is supposed to keep the strengths of the computer analogy while eliminating its weaknesses. I hope that what I will say here will neither seem shocking nor revolutionary. I intend it as a summary of what has struck many of us in recent years.

There is much that is helpful in the computer analogy. It supports and explains our sense that an appropriate and attainable cognitive psychology above all deals in mental states and capacities, not occurrences or processes, and ascribes these states and capacities to whole cognitive systems. When I say that the computer and I know that $5 + 7 = 12$, I am not saying that some sort of event has or is occurring. Nor am I saying that one can locate some bit of neurological writing, index card, or data chip, and say that *this* item *is* the knowledge or belief that $5 + 7 = 12$; the computer and I calculate by general routines. We have wholly discarded, as a viable and fruitful level of psychological description, the traditional notion of the mind as ever so many bits of knowledge and belief swimming in the neutral fluid of mind like myriad tin foil motes in a globular glass paper weight. In brief, mental states and capacities are the primary subject matter of a viable cognitive psychology. These states and capacities are to be described as systems of rules, of which a Turing machine table would be a sort. And these mental states and capacities are ascribed to the whole cognitive system—their location is mind-wide. (Some might deny that these mental states and capacities have any location at all. Such was traditional dualism. I have nothing to say to those who think so. But the modern mentalist, or UTM functionalist, takes it that all mental phenomena have physical tokens and that these tokens are brain states.)

To use the common picture, the human mind at the normal form level of psychological description is a black box, with observable input and output behavior. The normal form of psychological description is the simplest, most detailed, and most powerful characterization of the software, the functional innards, of what is located in the black box, although in no particular part of it more than another.

For the UTM functionalist, of course, Turing machine tables are the normal form for psychological description (perhaps one might rather say *sets* of Turing machine tables, since an infinity of Turing machine tables can each characterize the same computational capacity). The notion of a Turing machine seems to add content and precision to an otherwise vague functionalism. It seems to provide the normal form for psychological descriptions. We know what must go into a Turing machine table, what is to be left out, when such a table is complete, and how to compare tables.

I now introduce my Universal Locomotive Machine, Slinky. It is to

bear the same relationship to biology that the UTM functionalist supposes the universal Turing machine to bear to psychology: As a universal
Turing machine exhausts possible moves in "computative space," so the
ULM exhausts possible moves in "living space." For simplicity, I will talk
of Slinky navigating in two dimensions. The extrapolation of three dimensions is unproblematic. Just as Turing embellished his conception
with a clerk who read the tape and followed the machine table instruc-
tions, one may think of Slinky as the toy of that name, a coil of flexible
steel that will follow itself over one step in any direction in which you
invert its top, and indeed will wriggle down stairs step-by-step, once
started.

A machine table for our ULM would consist of quintuples somewhat in
the manner of a Turing machine. We have a table with five columns. In
each row we have a location state, a movement instruction, a location
state (a move, that is), an erase-rewrite instruction, and a tape-reading
instruction (right, left, stay). This is analogous to the Turing machine
quintuples of current state, symbol under reading head, new state, symbol to be written, and direction of tape movement. For example, the
following would be a fragment of a Slinky table specifying a move of three
squares to the north (N3).

Location State	Movement Instruction	Location State (new)	Erase-Rewrite Instruction	Tape-Reading Instruction
W	N	N	0	right
N	3	2	2	stay
2	2	1	1	stay
1	1	0	0	stay
0	0	0	0	stop

You can have either of two versions of Slinky. In the *solipsist* version,
the initial location state has nothing to do with the literal, physical location
of Slinky. We regard the "W," in effect, as the input of Slinky's sensors—
whether Slinky has an external west orientation does not matter. Similarly, when Slinky "moves," changing "W" to "N," this will be understood as a change in Slinky's sensors (the motor output and sense input
loop ignores the actual external environment). Animation, so to speak, is
but locomotive function deep.

In the naturalist version, we will have a Slinky who actually moves
around in the environment and has some means for determining that it
has so moved. We do not care how it manages these movements and
determinations, we just want some account of how these functions are
achieved.

In distinguishing the solipsist and the naturalist Slinky, I am alluding to the debate between the methodological solipsist Jerry Fodor and naturalist Hilary Putnam about the meaning of the terms in our cognitive states. I wish not so much to choose between them as to make it clear that my points are orthogonal to their debate. Whether or not there is a self-contained "language of thought" is orthogonal to the question as to whether there is a perspicuous, general, and systematic form for the description of psychological states—one mind-wide, mind deep, and mind illuminating, so to speak.

From my comparison between the UTM and ULM, it is obvious that I am skeptical about Turing machine tables as the normal form for psychological description. It is not that Turing machine tables are wrong as descriptions of psychological capacities or states; it is that such descriptions are vague and analogical.

Functionally speaking, animals locomote. Slinky, as a universal locomotive machine, can be understood as a pure instance of animation. We could then think of any biological organism as a ULM in generic character, and as a particular characterized by a set of ULM tables. Similarly, thinkers compute. The UTM is a pure instance of computation. Thus we may think of any general thinking thing as a UTM and, more particularly, as a set of Turing machine tables. This would be the normal form for psychological description, just as Slinky tables would be the normal form for animate description.

The objection to both of these characterizations is not that they are false but just that they are vague and analogical. It is too vague and analogical to say of two things that they locomote in the same way because they share universal locomotive machine tables. Similarly, there is not much to offer a viable psychology in a notion of "same thinking" that assumes that two things have the same minds or mental states because they share Turing machine tables.

Preevolutionary biology did trade in general functionalist theories of locomotion, respiration, and ingestion that were to apply to organized devices in general. Preevolutionary biology is notorious for its lack of a secure basis for individuating, describing, and explaining species of biological organisms, and kinds of organs and organ systems.

Functionalist psychology, of course, goes back just as far. Descartes, for example, writes:

If these were machines which bore a resemblance to our body and imitated our actions as far as it was morally possible to do so we should always have a very certain test by which to recognize that, for all that they were not real men. The test is that they could never use speech or other signs as we do when placing our thoughts on record for the benefit of others. For we can easily understand a machine's being constituted so that it can utter words, and even emit some responses of a corporeal kind, which brings about a change in its organs; for instance, if it is touched in a particular part it may ask what we wish to say to it, if in another part it may exclaim that it is being hurt, and so on. But it never happens that it arranges its speech in various ways in order to reply appropriately to everything that may be said in its presence. Although machines can perform certain things as well as or perhaps better than any of us can do, they infallibly fall short in others, by which means we may discover that they did not act from knowledge, but only from the disposition of their organs. It is morally impossible that there should be sufficient diversity in any machine to allow it to act in all the events of life in the same way as our reason causes us to act.

Were Descartes, as we, to concede that there is no "moral impossibility" here, his functionalist psychology would force him to conclude that machines or extraterrestrials who can be said to function as UTMs and who share our machine tables have the same mind and cognitive states as we. There is but one realm of thought, and all who think travel the same, whatever their species, origins, or organs.

Again, it is not that Descartes is wrong. We can and we will want on occasion to speak in such a functional and analogical fashion. We can and have adapted our vocabulary for mental states to the characterization of computers and extraterrestrial, nonhuman thinkers. People who work with computers or speculate about extraterrestrial intelligence do this all the time. It is evident that the attempt to avoid moral and political speciesism must embrace such talk. But a scientific psychology cannot hope to go far with such talk, any more than zoology would be wise to indulge in a general analogical theory of locomotive function.

A proper borderline case arises in the description and explanation of Washoe's training in American Sign Language. In a functional and analogical sense it is obviously reasonable to say that Washoe is something of a person, and a person with something comparable to the moral status of a human. And if all one means by saying that Washoe has language is just such a functional and analogical claim, then Washoe does have language. But Washoe does not have language in the homological sense. It is not natural to Washoe. There is no secure way of individuating, describing, and explaining Washoe's gestural activity in the developmental, phylogenetic, and genetic way that is open for us respecting our linguistic capacities. Washoe has no language organ, no linguistically lateralized brain or innate program for linguistic growth.

The point of the last two sentences is crucial. We simply cannot treat Washoe's capacity for gestural behavior as an "organ program" on a par with our linguistic capacities. Humans (as apes) can use *every* part of the sensory-motor-vascular systems in *the functional-analogical sense* of "reception" and "communicative"—blinking, hand movements, blushing, belching, head shaking, whistling, humming, snarling, dancing, nuzzling, stature, leg movements, facial expression, body odor, and so on. Implicitly, no linguistics, and explicitly, no homological linguistics, can be formed from such a hodge-podge. It is this way with Washoe's signing.

On the other hand, Washoe truly is a borderline case because Washoe's cognitive and emotional life does appear in other respects to be homologous with ours. In visual recognition of new individuals as dogs, cats, and birds, Washoe presents not only analogies but also, one suspects, homologies to our visual recognition of instances of such animals. Washoe's visual recognition faculty, among others, appears closely homologous to ours. It is to be individuated, described, and explained in terms of common embryonic and infantile development, common morphological, neurological, phylogenetic, and genetic features.

Homologically or biologically speaking, Washoe shares our visual faculty but lacks language, lacks a language organ. Analogously or functionally speaking, we may say that Washoe both sees and communicates, as we may say this of many computers and mechanical devices, or of countless imagined varieties of extraterrestrials.

The Gardeners have a right to say that Washoe has language analogically. And I think the linguist is right in maintaining that Washoe lacks language homologically. The passion that surrounds the issue is dispelled if one makes such an analogical/homological distinction, and if one realizes that the moral questions about Washoe may properly be decided on analogical grounds. Morality eschews phylogeny as biology embraces it. I may befriend and respect Washoe without insisting that all my faculties are one with hers.

But if I am skeptical about the viability of the functional notion of the normal form for psychological description of any species of thinker, I am also skeptical about the idea that there is a great deal more to the notion of the normal form for psychological description for any member of the species of human thinkers. My discussion of Washoe may suggest my skepticism on this latter point. I claimed that it made good homological sense to understand Washoe's visual recognition faculty as much like ours, while I denied that Washoe had a language organ. But that amounts to saying that we may share normal form descriptions for the functioning of our visual recognition faculties while lacking a common linguistic faculty. This is what one might expect, for homological reasoning above all trades in the comparison and individuation of organs, components, and faculties.

Indeed, the great recent progress in modular or component psychology in linguistics and vision, for example, already suggests that the way into the black box of the mind is to split it up into a number of black boxes, a number of separable levels of normal form description. What I am insisting on is that the basis for splitting up the mind into components has been and should be homological—species-wide, organ systematic, comparative, developmental, phylogenetic.

Examples are not hard to come by. Perhaps the most enduring feature of recent linguistics has been the realization that to describe a language is to give its generative grammar, that, is to specify a device for generating the sentences of the language. And this generative characterization wears its species-wide, developmental, organ systematic, and phylogenetic character on its sleeve.

Early in the 1960s Chomsky and others showed that a viable linguistics must insist that a description of a language should approach observational, descriptive, and explanatory adequacy. These goals are endemic to current linguistics of almost any ilk. Indeed, these goals have been implicit in previous linguistics. A good grammar will not only generate the observed features of the language but will also indicate what features belong to its sentences for the normal human speaker-hearer of the language. It will describe the sentences as understood by the normal human who has acquired the language in the normal way. It will describe the language in a way that explains how the normal human language learner develops a grasp of the language.

This means that one's choices in writing the description of a particular human language will be affected by data about other human languages and about human linguistic development. The language is not regarded as a tool, artifact, or arbitrary set of rituals *out there,* as something that may be learned or used willy-nilly by any species of thinker. Rather, we write into the description of the language its character as an outgrowth or realization of the human language organ in a particular social locale—just as, say, the elaborate tunnel-nest systems of Southwestern prairie dogs may be understood as the outgrowth of the prairie dog's developmental program as adapted to a particular environment.

The thesis of the autonomy of syntax is often taken to be equivalent to the claim that linguistics is a self-contained science. But this thesis would also seem equivalent to the claim that there is a language organ, the claim that homological considerations of development and phylogeny have a central place in motivating linguistic description and explanation.

When one bolsters autonomy of syntax with references of lateralization, species-wide language acquisition programs, and so on, one is clearly seeing the linguistic faculty as an organ, as, that is, something to be individuated and characterized homologically.

One can see the success of component and homological psychology in the study of visual recognition, facial recognition, and some other areas. When we section up the brain in a scientific and perspicuous psychology, we will slice phylogenetically. Indeed, in our crude first approximations this is what we already do. One is hardly eccentric in speaking of the "reptile brain," the "new brain," and so on. The only secure subdivisions of the brain that we now have are phylogenetic. Indeed, the only viable hope for any sort of mind state/brain state identity thesis will be in an insistence that brain states and components be individuated phylogenetically, and perhaps also an insistence that the most crucial mental states and components are woven with homological and developmental insight. That is to say that we may not capture all of the functional notions implicit in folk psychology in a satisfying way.

If functional and analogical explanations do fade into the background of our future psychology, the case of linguistics will seem typical, and our psychology will but have followed the pathway of biology. We will replace functional and behavioral notions and organic and phylogenetic ones. The question will be not what is *done* but what faculty, developing how, does it. Not, for example, language as something out there, but a language organ; not locomotion, but legs.

We may conclude with some insight into our third set of issues, the putative gulf between the subjectivity of the social and psychological sciences and the objectivity of the natural ones. Recall that Trubetzkoy maintained:

> The phonologist is interested in the differential features [of speech sound] which are functional in a particular language, the relations between sounds which enable speakers of a language to distinguish between words. It is clear that these tasks cannot be accomplished by the methods of the natural sciences, which are concerned with the intrinsic properties of phenomena themselves and not with the differential features which are bearers of social significance. In other words, in the natural sciences there is nothing corresponding to the distinction between *langue* and *parole:* there is no institution or system to be studied. The social and psychological sciences

are concerned with the social use of material objects and must therefore
distinguish between the objects themselves and the system of distinctive or
differential features which give them meaning and value.

In these claims of Trubetzkoy we see the view of a language, or any
sort of cultural artifact, as some local institution, some *langue,* that ante-
dates and shapes the arbitrary individual's performance. But this is misguided with respect to linguistics and many other studies of our cognitive
life. Even to talk of *a* language is less than accurate. The distinction
between languages and mere dialects is more political than anything else.
What exist are the systematic responses of particular humans' language
organs to their local environments. Similarly, there are no British and
Peruvian, for instance, visual worlds but rather the human visual faculty
and its developmental capacities as these are realized within various
environments.

Once one thinks of the biological sciences, one realizes what is wrong
with Trubetzkoy's dichotomy. When one claims that "the natural sciences
are concerned with the intrinsic properties of phenomena themselves
and not with the differential features which are bearers of social significance," one is obviously ignoring biology. For what is a biological cell, let
alone a multicellular, organ-bearing animal, but something whose character can only be understood in understanding how it spawns both internally and externally differential features which are bearers of biological
significance? Put the *langue/parole* distinction in biological terms and
you see how our view is altered. Think, for example, of a species of song
bird. There are dialectical variations, and the nestling does not acquire a
full song unless exposed to adult singers. The *langue* would be a dialect
perhaps, and *parole* would be the actions of an individual bird. But who
would think of describing and explaining the *langue* except as the characteristic development of the species' singing faculty, developing as a biological program in a particular locale?

The claim, then, is that there may be *distinctively* sociological and
arbitrarily cultural sciences, but that the biological mode of explanation
may often prove a bridge, a series of bridges, or a defiantly intermediate
mode of explanation, and may equally prove to be the homological
framework within which sociological generalizations will find their home,
and that in any case is the most immediately viable mode of progress for
cognitive psychology. Assuming that biology is a natural science, it would
seem clear that the "methods" of the natural sciences are wholly appropriate to what the cognitive psychologist investigates. There is no reason
why we should not look forward to the naturalization of our understanding of ourselves. We are not simply a species of animal, we are a collection
of cognitive organs, individuated, characterized, and explicable on developmental, comparative, and phylogenetic grounds.

CHAPTER 7

Explaining Human Conduct: Form and Function

KENNETH J. GERGEN
MARY M. GERGEN

Brisk competition among theoretical accounts has been a virtual hallmark of the social sciences since their inception. Parallels to the caustic clashes among radical behaviorists, neo-behaviorists, phenomenologists, and cognitivists within psychology may be located throughout the social science spectrum. Often the attempt is made to resolve such conflicts either through conceptual integration or incorporation. In the first instance, the theorist attempts to amalgamate domains, thereby multiplying strengths while cancelling weaknesses. This has been essentially the course taken by neo-behaviorists in psychology, who have capitalized on the radical behaviorist romance with observables, but who have simultaneously employed cognitive constructs to mediate between stimulus and response. Others have chosen to reduce conflict among competing accounts not through integration but through incorporation. Thus, for example, learning theorists have attempted to show how the major findings in the psychoanalytic domain can be subsumed by learning theory; dissonance theorists have incorporated data generated by mechanistic theories of attitude change; and self-observation theorists have attempted to incorporate dissonance theory results.

Although conflict among competing theoretical accounts is continuous, there are particular reasons for contemporary reconsideration. At present we appear to be facing a conflict of fundamental significance in the social sciences. Spurred by developments in analytic and hermeneu-

AUTHORS' NOTE: This chapter was facilitated by National Science Foundation Grant 7809393 to the senior author. Gratitude is expressed to Joseph Rychlak for his critical reading of an earlier draft.

tic philosophy, a variety of heterodox voices have become increasingly vocal in the social sciences. Proponents of ethogenics, ethnomethodology, dialectics, interpretive theory, phenomenology, and critical theory have all joined in trenchant attack of traditional behavioral theory and its associated methods. Further, one may discern conceptual affinities among these various dissidents. For example, the assumptions of a voluntaristic base for social action, the pivotal function of rules and plans, and the importance attached to the social construction of reality have all figured prominently in almost all of the various discordant groups. This "family of malcontents" is particularly worthy of attention, for unlike many earlier contenders for theoretical prominence, their implications pose fundamental problems for scientific metatheory. As argued elsewhere (Gergen, 1979), in the acceptance of scientific metatheory one also constrains the forms of scientific explanation. By the same token, the acceptance of certain theoretical forms may violate assumptions of traditional metatheory and stimulate consideration of alternative forms of science. It appears an auspicious juncture, then, for an analysis of theoretical conflict and integration within the sociobehavioral sciences, with special attention devoted to the problem of assessing explanatory superiority.

We shall address these issues by way of exploring forms of behavioral explanation along with their ostensible and latent functions within the sciences. We shall first attempt to examine various explanatory forms in ordinary discourse and the typical means by which such forms are granted justification within this domain. As will then be maintained, quotidian forms of explanation possess counterparts within the more formal theories of the sociobehavioral sciences. After examining contrasting forms of explanation in science and everyday life, we shall turn to the problem of function. In particular, we shall examine the traditional assumption that the validity, and thus the predictive capacity of competing explanatory forms, may be established empirically. This assumption will be found wanting, and the more general question will be raised concerning alternative criteria of evaluation. We shall then examine several recent theoretical attempts in psychology to reveal explanatory confusions, and conclude by developing a rationale for the valuational comparison of explanatory accounts.

Explanation in Everyday Life

Questions of why persons act as they do pervade the sphere of daily relations. One asks why some individuals succeed while others fail, why some are principled while others are profligate, why some are devoted while others are unfaithful, and so on. It also seems widely accepted that the answers to such questions can be correct or incorrect with respect to fact. It is legitimate to accept certain answers on the grounds of accuracy while rejecting others as biased or erroneous. One who gives an empirically dubious explanation may properly be asked for supporting evidence; an "accurate" explanation is believed to reflect the existing state of nature. We shall return to examine these assumptions more carefully in a later section. For now, however, they provide a basis for distinguishing among two important aspects of explanation. Specifically, we may delineate explanations on the basis of the evidential domains typically employed for purposes of enhancing intelligibility or justification.

Let us consider, then, the explanations that might be offered by Peter when he spies his neighbor, Patrick, running past his window early one morning. Without relevant information about his neighbor's life conditions, Peter might answer the question of why Patrick is running by pointing to characteristics or aspects of the individual himself. He might thus answer the question "why" in such terms as "Perhaps Patrick just feels like a run," "He just likes to run," or "Patrick must be a jogger." All such explanations may be termed *person-centered* inasmuch as the explanatory locus is embodied in the person whose actions are in question (specifically, his "feelings," "likes," "habits"). In effect, the explanation is accorded justification by reference to such characteristics. In general, when an action is cut away from its temporal context, the range of potential explanations may be constricted; explanations are favored that make reference to the character of the acting agent. In this sense, one might expect to find person-centered explanations across widely diverse cultures and historical periods. They make intelligible those actions for which antecedent and subsequent events are ambiguous or unavailable.[1]

Of course, for many actions one is informed about prior and subsequent events. As such information becomes available, one's grounds for explanation may be conveniently expanded. For example, suppose Peter learned that Patrick had read a health report that morning arguing that his life was endangered if a program of vigorous exercise were not launched. On this basis Peter might conclude that Patrick was running because "the health report convinced him he should obtain exercise," or that Patrick had "been frightened by the report" into beginning a program of running. Peter might also learn that, after running, Patrick was greeted by his lovely wife who praises him for his new regimen. Armed with this information, Peter might conclude that Patrick runs "in order to please his wife," or that he is "driven by his wife's praise" to continue his practice. All such explanations point to events surrounding the act of running itself. On this basis we may distinguish person-centered explanations from those which are *situation-centered.* In turn, situation-based explanations may be divided into those making reference to *antecedent* events (e.g., the morning's health report) and those referring to events *subsequent* to the action in question (e.g., wife's praise). Again, it would appear that such forms of explanation might be found in virtually all cultures. Temporally expanded contexts furnish a broad array of explanatory loci.

This initial distinction serves to place the *locus* of explanation; it specifies the generic source of the action. A second distinction may now be considered, one that denotes the *degree* of controlling force residing within the designated locus. In this case we may distinguish between explanations that grant inexorable power to the generic source versus those that grant the source only a facilitating role. An explanation granting full determinative power to the designated locus may be termed *empowered.* As explanations grant a lesser degree of force to the locus, they may be said to approach the *enabling* end of the explanatory dimension. An empowered locus demands the occurrence in question; an enabling locus merely aids or abets it.

It would appear that the one important ground commonly used to justify explanations along the empowered-enabling dimension resides in the repetition of occurrences. In particular, highly repetitive occurrences are often employed as grounds for empowered explanation. Thus, if Patrick is seen running every day without fail for ten years, his behavior might be explained in terms of a "chronic need to run," "a well-engrained habit," "a fixation," or even "an addiction." In each case the explanation suggests that the action is a necessary outcome. The need, habit, fixation, or addiction is empowered to force the occurrence. In contrast, if Patrick were seen running only on July 21st, and no other day, his behavior might be explained as "a whim." A whim does not demand the action of running; it merely facilitates or enables the action to occur. Or, if Patrick is running on a sunny day, one might say that the "sun put him in a good mood for running." Again, the explanation does not empower the sun; the weather merely serves as one among many possible contributors to action. That repetition serves as the justification for the degree of force granted the explanatory locus is clarified by the attempt to reverse such examples. To explain Patrick's repetitive running in terms of "daily whims" or his single venture as a "habit" would simply be cultural nonsense.

Thus far we have considered two major aspects of explanation, their specification of locus and the degree of controlling power granted the locus, along with the observational grounds typically used to justify such explanatory choices. It is particularly useful at this juncture to consider the dimensions of explanation in tandem, for in doing so a variety of basic explanatory forms are generated. To illustrate, in Figure 7.1 variations along the empowered-enabling dimension are arrayed against variations in the person versus situation directing dimension (both in the antecedent and subsequent context). As is apparent, both person- and situation-centered explanations may thus vary along the empowered-to enabling dimension. Thus, to explain Patrick's incessant running in terms of "addiction" would be to employ a highly empowered form of person-centered explanation. To explain the same activity as the result of his "being raised as a track star" would be to empower a situational locus. At the same time, one may also employ person-centered explanations that are enabling in character. To explain the running in terms of a personal decision, e.g., "He ran because he thought it over and decided," is to imply self-direction. However, in making personal "decisions" one is always free to curtail the action by the same means. In contrast, the explanation, "He ran because the health report informed him" would be enabling and situation-centered. One need not do as the health report directs. Additional exemplars of the various explanatory form are included in the figure.

Viewing this range of explanatory types from a broader perspective, a close connection can be discerned between them and central distinctions

	Empowered explanation	Enabling explanation
Situation-centered (Pre)	"he was required by his doctor" "he was raised as a track star"	"the health report informed him" "his wife suggested it"
Person-centered	"addiction" "it is habitual"	"he decided" "he was in the mood"
Situation-centered (Post)	"he is destined to . . . "	"good health is his goal"

Figure 7.1 Forms of behavioral explanation

within recent psychological and philosophical discussions. In the former case, inquiry into attributional psychology has focused heavily on the distinction between *internal,* as opposed to *external,* loci of causality. Theory and research have centered on factors that yield attributions of internal, as opposed to external, sources of action (see Frieze, Bar-Tal, & Carroll, 1979; Jones & Nisbett, 1972; Kelley & Michela, 1980; Ross, 1977), along with individual differences among people in the tendency to see themselves as controlled by external forces, as opposed to being in control of such forces (see Phares, 1976; Strickland, 1977). This distinction between internal versus external loci of causality is captured in the present analysis by the division between *person-* and *situation-*centered explanations. However, the present analysis also suggests that the psychological literature has been unduly restrictive in its concerns and misleading in important respects. In particular, attribution investigators have been almost wholly insensitive to what is here termed the empowered-enabling dimension of explanation.

Given the traditional concern in attribution research with the relationship between causal attribution and the allocation of responsibility (blame and praise), this distinction seems essential. Far more significance would seem attached to the difference between behavior that is empowered as opposed to enabled by its causal source than to the external versus internal attributions so focal in the traditional literature (Gergen & Gergen, 1980). If a person commits a crime because of a brain tumor (an empowered source of action), we may be far more lenient than if the same crime were the result of "personal decision" (an enabling source), even though both attributions are internal or personal (also see Buss, 1978).

Within philosophic analyses, a major distinction has been drawn between explanations relying on *reasons* as opposed to *causes* (see Peters, 1958; Taylor, 1964; Toulmin, 1970). The former often refer to voluntary or intentional choices, while the latter refer to behavior produced by antecedent conditions. Reasons on this account have been viewed as the equivalent to the Aristotelian concept of "final cause," while causes have often been compared to Aristotle's "efficient cause." As can be seen, this distinction is paralleled in the present analysis by the empowered-enabling dimension. However, the present analysis also suggests that the distinction between reasons and causes has often been too sharply drawn. There is a strong tendency in philosophic literature to treat reasons and causes as two distinct classes of explanation. One's fall through the air is caused; volition has no function in such an explanation. Yet one walks because one chooses to do so; cause is irrelevant. While this kind of distinction is useful for expository purposes, we see from the present analysis that it too is overly restrictive. Rather than falling into a dichotomy, we find ordinary language explanations falling along a continuum—with many explanatory loci granted an intermediate and negotiable degree of power over action. Thus, for example, to explain one's actions as the result of "intense passion" may be viewed by many as determinative (empowered), but by others as only contributing to the outcome (enabling). Presumably, the degree of "causal force" granted to passion would be open to negotiation. Virtually all explanatory loci, including the concept of intention itself, are open to such alterations in meaning.

Finally, it is important to note that these various distinctions are not intended as inclusive. Additional distinctions may be essential for other purposes. For example, the present analysis is limited wholly to a synchronic time dimension. It would be essential in a full treatment of explanatory types to take account of explanation in the diachronic sphere (see Harré, 1979; Rosnow, 1981). In the present case, this would necessitate an expansion from a two- to a three-dimensional schema, and would permit discussion of various forms of narrative. However challenging, such expansion is unnecessary for the central purpose of the present chapter.

Explanatory Forms in Psychological Science

By distinguishing among the loci of and the power granted to ordinary language explanations, we were able to derive a series of explanatory forms of broad generality. At this point it is useful to extend this analysis to the level of explanation in the sociobehavioral sciences. As a number of analysts have argued, in order for their accounts of human behavior to "make sense" within the culture more generally, such scientists are forced to link their formalizations to ordinary language conventions. Without such linguistic linkages, the scientific formalizations would remain obscure and remote. As others maintain, sociobehavioral scientists have not generally succeeded in transcending cultural conventions with respect to understanding human conduct.[2] As argued, scientific explanation too often seems a translation into a rarefied professional language of common, taken-for-granted accounts within the culture more generally. From both standpoints there is reason to suspect a close relationship between ordinary language explanation and explanatory accounts in the sciences.

To explore this possibility, we may attempt to match a variety of prominent scientific explanations with the two-dimensional grid developed above. We shall confine ourselves primarily to the field of psychology in this case, not only because of the particular investments of the writers, but because much explanation in sociology, anthropology, political science, economics, and history relies heavily on assumptions about the human psyche.

Within the psychological domain, it would first appear that radical behaviorism, in major degree, employs a form of situation-centered, empowered explanation. From Skinner's (1969, 1971) standpoint, behavior may be explained in terms of the reinforcement contingencies encountered by the organism (see Figure 7.2). People act, according to this analysis, because of the particular patterns of reward and punishment to which they are exposed. Events in the prebehavioral context (reinforcement contingencies) are viewed as the source of action (situation determination) and are essentially empowered (i.e., have determinate control over behavior). In contrast, the theories of Freud and Piaget are in large measure empowered theories of the person-centered variety. This is so to the extent that each views behavior as reliant on ontogenetic programming of psychological development.[3] Similarly, those theories of human cognition positing automatic processes of information storage and retrieval are person-centered and empowered. And, to the extent that trait theorists view human behavior as the result of internal, determining tendencies over which the individual has minimal control, they

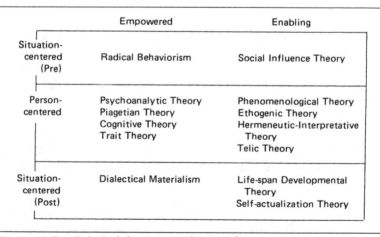

	Empowered	Enabling
Situation-centered (Pre)	Radical Behaviorism	Social Influence Theory
Person-centered	Psychoanalytic Theory Piagetian Theory Cognitive Theory Trait Theory	Phenomenological Theory Ethogenic Theory Hermeneutic-Interpretative Theory Telic Theory
Situation-centered (Post)	Dialectical Materialism	Life-span Developmental Theory Self-actualization Theory

Figure 7.2 Psychological theory as explanatory form

share the explanatory form favored by Freudians, Piagetians, and cognitive theorists.

It is difficult to locate theories within psychology that explain individual behavior in terms of goals that inexorably move the individual toward a singular end. Many would argue that both the Freudian concept of *Thanatos* and the Jungian concept of the *individuation process* are proper candidates, but in both cases the relevant theories are open to such wide-ranging interpretations that precise placement is hazardous. In an important sense, the dialectical materialist view of historical change falls within this sector. Insofar as a classless society is treated as an immutable endpoint to which all cultures inevitably evolve, the theory is post-situation-centered and empowered.

When we turn to the situation-centered and enabling form of explanation, perhaps the better candidates are to be drawn from traditional social psychology. In particular, various forms of social influence theory in social psychology tend to explain behavior in terms of the characteristics of the situation to which the individual is exposed. For example, in traditional attitude change research, such factors as source credibility, source attractiveness, message characteristics, and media factors (McGuire, 1968) all serve as predictors of attitude change. Yet few investigators in this realm would wish to argue that people could not, if they wished, choose to ignore such factors or to obfuscate their effects. Similarly, when conformity researchers trace behavior differences to variations in the size and composition of a group, and when obedience researchers explain subjects' conduct in terms of the characteristics of the experimenter or the victim, they are employing a situation-centered and enabling form of explanation. The cause of the action is traced to the environment, but the investigators typically view subjects as capable of resisting such influences.[4]

As we shift focus to the person-centered form of enabling explanation, we find phenomenological theory of the more humanistic variety to be an optimal candidate. To the extent that the theorist assumes that individual behavior is a result of the phenomenological field at the moment of action (Rogers, 1961), and that people are essentially free to choose their actions at any given moment (Bugenthal, 1965), such theories justifiably fall within this sector. Most important for present purposes, however, is the above-mentioned family of dissident theories inspired by philosophic accounts of human action (see Peters, 1958; Taylor, 1964; Winch, 1958). In particular, ethogenic theory (Harré & Secord, 1972), hermeneutic-interpretative theorists (Gauld & Shotter, 1977), constructivists

(Berger & Luckmann, 1966), and telic theorists (Rychlak, 1975) all tend to place major reliance on psychological constructs that permit the individual ultimate freedom of choice. Most such theorists are thus prepared to argue that internal rules, conceptions, interpretations, plans, and the like play an influential role in guiding human action. However, such theorists also maintain in the typical case that people can, if they wish, choose to disobey rules, create new conceptions or interpretations, or abandon plans once adopted. The central explanatory role frequently played by the concept of "intention" further solidifies the placement of such theories into this sector.

Theories of the post-situation-centered and enabling form are most difficult to locate in contemporary psychology. Certain lifespan developmental accounts isolate stages of the life course considered normative within age-cohorts, but generally eschew the conclusion that the stages are ontogenetic or ultimately determinative (Gergen, 1978). Maslow's (1962) concept of self-actualization has similar properties. The goal of self-actualization invites action but does not, within Maslow's system, require its occurrence. Again, however, such placements within the present structure are derived from central emphasis as opposed to unambiguous specification.

The Empirical Evaluation of Explanatory Forms

Having seen that the explanatory forms within the sociobehavioral sciences may largely parallel those forms discerned within the culture at large, we may now begin inquiry into the function of explanation within the sciences. Again, our aim is not to furnish a full account of explanatory function, but to focus on essential issues for the understanding of theoretical conflict and its resolution in the sociobehavioral sciences. Such issues are rendered all the more acute by the preceding analysis. Recent psychology has been marked by two significant "revolutions," each of which has essentially attempted to alter the central explanatory base within the science. Thus, the "cognitive revolution" has replaced a situation-centered, empowered form of explanation with a person-centered explanation of the empowered variety. And the aforementioned "action" revolution eschews person-centered, empowered explanations, attempting to replace them instead with person-centered, enabling forms of explanation. Significant questions are raised by such historical shifts. In what sense is one to view these revolutions as progressive? On what grounds is one to claim the superiority of one form of explanation over its competitors?

Let us consider, then, the chief function traditionally assigned to explanation within the sciences. Consistent with the common assumptions of daily life, along with a longstanding commitment to a correspondence theory of truth, sociobehavioral scientists have generally argued that explanation should augment the discipline's capacities for prediction and control. The inferior explanation can be located by its failure to make accurate predictions (i.e., to resist attempts at falsification). It is on just such justificationist (Weimer, 1979) grounds that theorists have laid claim to the superiority of cognitive theory over Skinnerian theory in accounting for language development and other complex activities of the organism (see Fodor, 1975; Neisser, 1976). It is on similar grounds that major battles have been fought in recent social psychology (specifically, dissonance versus self-observation and incentive theory explanations of attitude change; biological arousal versus evaluation apprehension explanations of social facilitation; and self-serving bias versus cognitive process explanations for causal attribution).[5] And it is on the same grounds that Taylor (1964, 1970) has laid claims to the superiority of teleological as opposed to mechanistic (situation-centered, empowered) explanations.[6]

Let us approach the problem by making two separate but related inquiries. In particular, we may ask whether explanations falling along either of the two dimensions thus far singled out are, with respect to their dependence on observation, essentially interchangeable. That is, can the explanatory form anchoring one end of each dimension posited above incorporate all evidence amassed by a competitor at the other end of the dimension? If this argument can be sustained, the conclusion is inescapable that observation cannot in principle serve as the benchmark for selection among competing explanatory forms. There may simply be no observations that would allow one to rule between or establish the enhanced validity of one as opposed to another explanatory form. In this light, we may first ask *whether it is possible in principle to locate a person-centered explanation for every situation-centered explanation of a given observation and vice versa.* Could one satisfactorily employ a personal locus of explanation for any competing explanation based on situational events (either anterior or posterior), and with equal plausibility locate a situational explanation that may satisfactorily serve in lieu of a person-based explanation? There would appear ample reason to argue for empirical equality in this instance.

At the outset, in examining ongoing experience one is confronted with a flow of what are usually taken to be separable events. One may observe Patrick, for example, reading the morning paper, donning his jogging outfit, bolting from the house, running for six kilometers, and returning to the loving smiles of his wife. Yet mere observation of the stream of events themselves reveals no causal locus; there are only events themselves occurring across time. From this standpoint, any placement of causal locus is quintessentially non-empirical. It is a verbal construction for designating and linking events within the flow, but the construction itself is not forged from observation of the events themselves. Thus, when asked to explain Patrick's running on a given day, one may intelligibly say that he was frightened by the story in the newspaper, he was moved by personal decision, or the vision of his wife's admiration compelled him to run. Each is an acceptable verbal rendering, and each connects the event of running with a different locus (either in the situation or person). There is no apparent standard of objectivity by which one may evaluate these various accounts. So long as an action is imbedded within an ongoing stream of events, the placement of explanatory locus would appear objectively arbitrary.

Yet this argument alone is insufficient, relying as it does on the controvertible presumption of independent events. As an alternative approach let us consider more carefully the dualism implied by the situation-person dichotomy. At the outset it seems apparent that this distinction itself lies beyond the possibility of empirical evaluation. One cannot furnish empirical justification for a world independent of personal experience if the arbiter of the case is personal experience itself. Thus, the grounds for determining what counts as an external (situational), as opposed to an internal (experiential), event would appear to rely on social conventions governing modes of communication (see Rorty, 1979). To illustrate, one is permitted to speak of "*that* aggressive action" in certain instances, thus granting the action an ontic status independent of the observer; however, in other instances one must speak of "my perception of aggression," thus placing the locus of aggression within the observer. In this light it becomes apparent that for any situational event or observation specified by the environmentally oriented theorist, one may locate an acceptable way of redefining the event in cognitive or experiential terms. The language of situation-centeredness may be fully convertible, then, to a language of person-centeredness. Let us apply this conclusion to explanatory conflicts in psychology.

The radical behaviorist often argues that all behavior can be understood in terms of the environmentally based reinforcement contingencies. No conception of mental apparatus is required to comprehend the individual's pattern of activity, and causality is exhausted in the tracing of systematic relationships between situation and behavior. Yet from the cognitive or phenomenological standpoint, "reinforcement contingencies" do not possess an existence independent of the constructs or meaning systems of individual perceivers. Physical stimuli do not come packaged in the form of "reinforcement contingencies"; the perceiver must essentially impose such meaning on stimuli. There are no reinforcement contingencies over and above those perceived, and given the proper perceptual set they may be perceived everywhere and nowhere.

To consider a second application, it is often argued by social attraction theorists that such factors as another's physical attractiveness and similarity to a perceiver are potent factors in generating attraction in the perceiver. In effect, this explanation of attraction places major emphasis on the driving power of external factors. Yet it may be argued with equal plausibility that physical attractiveness and similarity are not inherent properties of the stimulus world. Rather, they are creations of the perceiver; they lie within the "eye of the beholder." Thus, if interpersonal similarity is an important conceptual criterion for the perceiver, he or she may process the stimulus world in such a way as to generate its presence or absence. Similarly, the perceiver may carry with him or her standards of physical attractiveness and simply process available stimuli in such terms. In neither case does the causal source of the attraction lie within the stimulus world. In principle, for every external entity employed in the explanation of human conduct, the person-centered theorist may locate an internal mechanism or process that generates the resulting action. Every external event may be transformed into an internal representation.[7]

Yet, situation-centered theory is not removed from contention by the fact that all its empirical supports may be relocated in the subjective sphere. The person-centered theorist faces particular peril in attempting to furnish a satisfactory account of the genesis of the constructs, meanings, or representations of the perceiver. If such internal systems do not rely on environmental inputs, if empirical stimuli in themselves have no meaning, or there are no "unconstructed effects," then how do internal processes, representations, and the like spring to life? If not based on external impingements or "unstructured input," explanatory devices such as "concepts" or "meanings" must be dependent for their development on some other source. The latter source eludes convincing specification. Further, the situation-centered theorist is typically able to offer an account of the internal state, mechanism, or process by pointing to environmental events on which they and the resulting action appear to be based. Thus, for example, when the person-centered theorist argues that a given action resulted from a "purpose," the situationalist may counter by pointing to existing external conditions that are actually "producing" the purpose and the subsequent behavior. Jones may say that his purpose in crossing the street is to purchase tobacco. However, for the behaviorist, Jones is responding to the effects of previous reinforcement history. "Purpose" may be viewed as a mere hypothetical byproduct of reinforcement history. Or, if the internalist points to "rules for taking turns" as an explanation for patterns of conversation, the situationalist may argue that such rules are the result of cultural conditions.[8] In sum, neither the person- nor the situation-oriented theory may convincingly dispatch the opposition on empirical grounds.

Given arguments for the empirical incommensurability of person-versus situation-centered explanations, we may ask whether there are reasons for suspecting interchangeability along the empowered-enabling dimension. When the justificatory base for empowered versus enabling explanations is considered, the possibility of an in-principle argument begins to emerge. As we have seen, variations in the reliability of occurrences are typically employed to justify the degree of empowerment assigned to a causal locus. We must now examine more closely the manner in which the reliability of occurrences is identified. On what grounds can one determine whether an observation made at t_2 is a member of the same class as an observation confronted at t_1? This question has hardly been an inconsequential one in the history of philosophy. Indeed, it was the basis of Heraclitian thought and served as a major stimulus to both the Platonic and Aristotelian systems. It is a problem that continues to be pursued today under the rubric of identity theory (Perry, 1975). Although a review of this history is beyond the scope of this chapter, it is sufficient for the present to note that no empirical solution to the identity problem has been sustained. It may be ventured, on the contrary, that whether two events represent instantiations of the same abstract class remains primarily a matter of the judgmental criteria brought to bear. Whether the configuration called "Patrick" at t_1 is the same or different from the configuration at t_2 depends on the particular criteria one selects for judging same or different. Patrick's voice, for example, may change its quality from moment to moment, and whether one views it as the same voice depends upon which particular qualities are selected. In this sense, the attribution of same versus different is not driven by empirical inputs, but rather represents a form of discriminatory imposition.

From this standpoint, the extent of phenomenal reliability is fundamentally a matter of personal construction. Faced with a stream of experience one may, as the Zen priest, be delighted with the immense novelty furnished by each passing moment, or, like the author of Ecclesiastes, encounter nothing new under the sun. There would appear no objective means of ruling between these two conclusions. In similar manner, the means by which one would empirically justify an empowered as opposed to an enabling explanation remains unclear. If reliance cannot be placed on the objective reliability of events, how is empirical commensurability to be achieved in this instance?

In summary, we find that in terms of empirical justification, there are no apparent means by which one could rule between the situation- and the person-centered locus, nor between an empowered and an enabling force. As a result, there is reason to argue that with respect to matters of prediction and control, no one of the explanatory forms derived above can achieve superiority.[9] Before inquiring into alternative functions for explanation in the sociobehavioral sciences, it will prove instructive to examine the conceptual impasse resulting from the failure to take account of differential explanatory bases.

The Confounding of Explanatory Bases in Psychological Theory

It follows from the above analysis that each of the explanatory forms isolated above can be elaborated in such a way that an intelligible account can be rendered of virtually all aspects of human conduct. That is, with sufficient conceptual skill, one should be able to extend any explanatory form to the point that it becomes a fully general theory of human activity. Such attempts may occur without fear of empirical threat from an opposing explanatory base. In effect, the constraints on theoretical imperialism are not empirical. However, this conclusion further indicates that theorists weaving more than a single explanatory form into the same nomothetic net are doing conceptual mischief. At a minimum, such confounding is unparsimonious: the theorist employs a greater number of explanatory forms than is necessary to generate understanding. If any single form is subject to infinite extension, any conflation of forms creates an unnecessary burden to comprehension. More importantly, the use of multiple explanatory forms fosters conceptual incoherence. To place the locus of explanation external to the individual logically precludes a commitment to person-centered explanation; to argue that a locus of explanation is empowered (determinative) precludes a theory of freely selected action. It will prove useful to illustrate these arguments.

Let us consider perhaps the most widely credited attempt at theoretical integration in contemporary psychology, namely, social learning theory (Bandura, 1973, 1977). With compelling clarity, social learning theory appears to furnish a solution to the long-standing antinomies between behaviorism and cognitive theory, and between determinism and humanism. With respect to the behaviorist tradition, social learning theory places strong emphasis on empirical data, the importance of response contingencies, and the centrality of behavioral responses. Simultaneously, however, Bandura wishes to emphasize the role of cognitive processes, learning through observation, and self-regulating devices, all of central interest within the cognitive tradition. An array of cognitive devices are thus said to mediate between stimulus and response. To share in the advantages of the determinist tradition, Bandura proposes to furnish a precise and systematic account of human behavior that rests on a broad spectrum of evidence, and that promises predictive validity. Yet the attempt is further made to achieve immunity to the humanist criticism of traditional behaviorism, to whit, that people are viewed as helpless pawns in the hands of uncontrolled contingencies. Bandura thus argues that people are "self-regulating" organisms who employ and manipulate symbols to direct themselves along useful paths, and who effectively shape their environment.

From the present standpoint, this integrative synthesis represents a full confounding of explanatory bases. First, consider the distinction between situation- versus person-centered explanations. In his 1977 volume, Bandura's initial discussion deals with the effects of response consequences or reinforcement on behavior. In effect, a heavy emphasis is placed on the effects of external events on the activity of the individual. As Bandura maintains, reinforcement has a strong "regulatory" effect on behavior. In the case of aggressive behavior, for example, he argues, "The influential role of antecedent events in regulating aggressive behavior is most clearly revealed in experiments that arrange the necessary learning conditions. When aggression is rewarded in certain contexts but not in others, the level of aggressive responding can be altered simply by changing the contextual events that signal probable outcomes" (p. 63). As we have seen, this situational form of explanation, when extended, may account for virtually all human activity in its terms.

Yet, as the theory is progressively elaborated, the power of reinforcement is pushed into the background. For, as we later find, it is not the power of external impingements that regulates behavior but the cognitive apparatus that is to be credited. As Bandura argues, people use symbolic codes to understand their environment; they attend, remember, and organize at the symbolic level. As he argues in this instance, "People do not respond to each momentary item of feedback as an isolated experience. Rather, they proceed and synthesize feedback information from sequences of events over long periods of time regarding the conditions necessary for reinforcement, and the pattern and rate with which actions produce the outcomes. It is for this reason that vast amounts of behavior can be maintained with only infrequent immediate reinforcement. Because outcomes affect behavior through integrative thought, knowledge about schedules of reinforcement can exert greater influence upon behavior than does the reinforcement itself" (p. 97). In effect, a shift has been made to an internal or person-centered locus of explanation. As the shift is made, external reinforcement is obviated as an explanatory device.

One plausible rebuttal to such an argument is to maintain that the two systems, internal and external, operate in concert. Behavior is thus a joint consequence of two causal resources, just as the operation of an engine depends both on the input of fuel and the characteristics of the combustion chamber. Although compelling at the outset, closer scrutiny reveals the shortcomings of this line of rebuttal. In principle, statements about the effects of external events on the organism operate as surrogates for propositions about internal events; and all that is said about internal functioning may be viewed as a recasting of propositions about the external world. In the former instance, we have already seen that all description of reinforcement contingencies can be viewed as a misplaced account of what the individual privately constructs as meaningful reward and punishment. And in the second case, if one is attempting to account for the effects of external events on observed behavior, it must be realized that statements about internal functioning do not add new information. They constitute linguistic edifices that stand as simulacra for, and can tell us nothing about, that which we already know by observation.[10]

Although to a lesser degree, social learning theory seems similarly obscure with respect to its commitment to empowered as opposed to enabling forms of explanation. In major respects the theory is an empowered one. It attempts to make a systematic account of how various external and internal mechanisms operate within the prototypical human being. The theory attempts, then, to describe "human nature" and treats its generalizations as holding across time and circumstance. Bandura's concept of "reciprocal determinism" is revealing in this instance. As he points out, the environment has a deterministic effect on individual functioning, but the individual also has effects on the environment. This latter emendation does not alter the deterministic character of the theory, as any effects of the individual on the environment can be viewed as the systematic result of prior effects of the environment on the individual.

Yet Bandura himself is not wholly sanguine about the strong form of empowerment represented in this analysis, and in numerous instances shifts to a language of enablement. For example, in speaking of the process of social modeling, it is noted that, "When exposed to diverse models, observers rarely pattern their behavior exclusively after a single source, nor do they adopt all the attributes even of preferred models. Rather, observers combine aspects of various models into new amalgams that differ from the individual sources . . . different observers adopt different combinations of characteristics" (Bandura, 1977, p. 48). In effect, the individual is left free to select patterns of modeling—thus cutting the process away from the empowerment of stimulus inputs. As further illustration, we find that "by manipulating symbols that convey relevant information, one can gain understanding of causal relationships, create new forms of knowledge, solve problems, and deduce consequences, without actually performing any activities . . . (people) can formulate alternative solutions and evaluate the probable immediate, and long-range consequences of different courses of action" (Bandura, 1977, pp. 172-173). Again, no determinative account is furnished for the basis of such activities as symbol manipulation, creation, problem-solving, deduction, the formulation of alternatives, or the evaluation of consequences. They appear to remain as enabling sources of action, thus countermanding the deterministic roots of the theory. And, as we have seen, were this enabling analysis extended, it could account for all observations for which the empowered explanations were otherwise employed.[11]

Other behavioral accounts are also rendered problematic in their reliance on both empowered and enabling forms of explanation. Marxist theory is perhaps the most obvious example. In certain respects, the theory is empowered; it argues for the inevitability of a certain form of society. Yet in its orientation toward praxis it is essentially enabling; in its exhortation of workers to join in the overthrow of the ruling class it implies that the individual is free to do other than achieve that which is destined. To some degree, Freudian theory shares in the same dilemma. In several instances Freud argued for the overdetermination of human behavior: Any given action serves as the final common pathway for multiple determining factors. Internal dynamic processes are empowered in this sense. Yet, as Habermas (1971) demonstrates in his analysis of Freud, it is also assumed that through psychoanalysis the individual may achieve emancipation from determinative dynamics. The individual gains freedom over empowerment, and is thus presumably operating on a psychologically enabling basis. George Kelly's (1955) theory of personal constructs is similarly problematic. While Kelly frequently argues for the determining constraints placed upon the individual by his or her construct system, he is also prepared to view human beings as scientists in miniature. In the latter guise they possess the freedom to alter their constructing tendencies and to freely adopt alternatives. They are empowered by constructs, and yet enabled by the capacity for choice to escape them. Without closer attention directed toward fundamental differentiation in explanatory form, theoretical work may continue to fall prey to such compelling but obfuscating syntheses.

Toward Valuational and Generative Criteria in Explanatory Assessment

Thus far we have differentiated among a limited but essential range of explanatory forms in the sociobehavioral sciences and have demonstrated that choices among such forms cannot be made on empirical grounds. We may now confront the complex question of criteria for explanatory choice. Faced with a range of empirically incommensurable explanatory forms, by what standards might one select, develop, or sustain a particular form of explanation? Traditional criteria of parsimony, internal coherence, and aesthetics do not easily serve as guides in this case, as there is no obvious reason to suppose that any particular form of explanation is uniquely deficient in such respects. The criterion of intelligibility also fails to solve the dilemma. Although the content of a given explanation may be more or less intelligible across historical periods, such alterations fail to threaten the viability of the underlying form. Thus, to explain behavior in terms of "fate" is less acceptable today than in former times. However, this particular explanation is but one exemplar of the class of situation-centered explanations. Although this exemplar may be currently unacceptable, the genre is not thus thrown into question. In the present era, "dialectical materialism" is an explanation of relatively wide appeal and is of the same generic form as the concept of fate. Similarly, "inherent evil" is a person-centered, empowered explanation of little contemporary appeal, but is parallel in form with Chomsky's concept of "deep structure." The form remains viable as the content varies in accord with taste and understanding.

Let us turn our attention, then, to two potentially viable candidates for evaluating explanatory competitors. The first is the criterion of valuational implication. In their capacity to influence common conceptions of the social world, along with relevant patterns of human activity, most forms of explanation are inherently valuational. They favor certain patterns of action and discourage others. For example, a link has long been sustained in Western culture between the empowered and enabling forms of explanation and the allocation of praise and blame. A crime may yield punishment in the degree to which it is attributed to an enabling (voluntary) as opposed to an empowered (involuntary) locus. Thus, in the manner in which explanations for various forms of conduct are framed, the scientist enters a case for or against the activity in question. To explain aggressive behavior in terms of the inexorable force of environmental influences (empowered explanation) is to abandon the right to hold people responsible for aggressive action; to explain the same action in terms of rules or plans (enabling explanation) is to encourage the process of moral sanctioning. Or, to explain altruism in terms of ontogenetic changes in the cognitive system (empowered explanation) is to reduce the social credit earned by the charitable; to argue that the same actions result from insight and intention (enabling explanation) is to augment the esteem awarded for such actions.

Although a full unpacking of the valuational implications of competing explanatory forms is beyond present ambitions, it will prove illustrative to examine several potential linkages between the present schema and a range of valuational positions. We may first consider the distinction between empowered and enabling forms of explanation. At least one highly significant valuational dimension corresponding to this distinction is that holding between *control* and *freedom*. Empowered forms of explanation might serve as commodious expressions of one's investment in a reliable, predictable world of human affairs. Should one fear the potentially chaotic implications of human nature without fundamental direction, the empowered explanation might serve as a psychological palliative. Should one desire assurance that nature is not capricious, that human activity is safe and reliable, or that one's spontaneous impulses will not thrust one into a state of incongruence with the moral order, the empowered or involuntary explanation might serve as a substantial implement of support. In contrast, for one who values unencumbered self-expression, who responds bitterly to reductions in freedom, who possesses trust in others' spontaneous action along with his or her own momentary impulses, the enabling or voluntary form of explanation is much to be preferred. In sustaining such an explanation of human activity, one may derive a challenging sense of personal potential.

Paralleling this correspondence between empowered versus enabling explanations and the values of freedom versus control, it is possible to locate a basis for internal versus external explanation in the values of *aggregate as opposed to individualized benefit.* If one's ideological investment rests within the larger community, broader social institutions, or the state, the situation-centered explanation is a fortifying one. If one distrusts singular self-expression or the efficacy of individuals acting alone, if one fears social isolation, or if one suffers from feelings of fundamental social disconnection, then the situational form of explanation may have substantial utility. In contrast, for one with a major commitment to self-expression, personal control of one's destiny, or the power of individual thought or action, personal forms of explanation may be of paramount interest. When one possesses an abundance of self-confidence, values his or her actions, distrusts dependence on others, or fears social engulfment, there is much to be gained through person-centered forms of explanation. [12]

Forms of explanation may also serve as grounding supports for broad social institutions. Differing political, religious, and economic bodies, for example, may be fortified by particular forms of explanation and hold an ideological stake in their continuance (see Figure 7.3). In the case of governance, for example, many would be prepared to argue that supporters of totalitarianism have special reason to favor situation-centered, empowered forms of explanation. Monarchy, oligarchy, fascism, and dictatorship might all be sustained as systems of governance by forms of explanation that assume both a fundamental lawfulness in human activity and that place the key to such activity in the hands of those controlling the environment (Argyris, 1980). In effect, such explanation might furnish the necessary confidence to sustain such forms of governance, and the form of knowledge thereby generated might lend itself to use by those in control of situational factors. [13] In contrast, various forms of republicanism might be favored by person-centered forms of empowered explanation. If one assumes a uniformity in human nature, i.e., that all people are moved to action by the same internal mechanisms, and that such basic mechanisms operate in relative autonomy from environmental input, then a form of governance might be favored in which the state is properly viewed as a product of the multiplicity of individual agreement. Those with strong interests in community autonomy, states' rights, or regional solidarity might thus retain a strong investment in person-centered, empowered explanation.

With respect to the situational form of enabling explanation, a congenial connection might be made with various forms of liberalism. In its traditional argument that rule of law sustains social order, that people

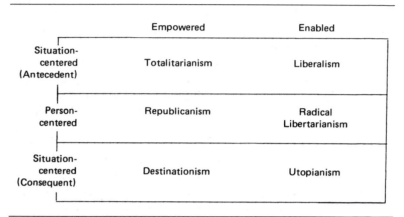

	Empowered	Enabled
Situation-centered (Antecedent)	Totalitarianism	Liberalism
Person-centered	Republicanism	Radical Libertarianism
Situation-centered (Consequent)	Destinationism	Utopianism

Figure 7.3 Explanatory forms and potential links to political ideology

must be held responsible for their actions vis à vis the rules of law, and that enlightenment of the masses enhances responsible action, explanations of human behavior stressing voluntary processes responsive to environmental stimuli might be particularly serviceable. A psychology that spoke less in terms of deterministic mechanisms than rational decision making and effective communication might find strong support in a liberal establishment. In contrast, powers favoring revolution against existing forms of governance, laissez-faire social policies, or radical libertarianism might derive greater sustenance from a person-centered form of enabling explanation. When prevailing explanations grant the individual powers of creative and autonomous decision making, centralized controlling bodies are rendered suspect.

Having glimpsed a number of ways in which valuational commitments may serve as criteria for explanatory preference, we may consider a second potentially viable criterion, namely that of intellectual generativity. Elsewhere it has been argued that competing interpretations of human action may legitimately be compared by virtue of their capacity to unsettle or challenge common assumptions within the culture (Gergen, 1978). The criterion of comparison in this case has been termed *generative* inasmuch as challenges to existing assumptions serve as premises for alternative courses of human conduct. Theoretical univocality in society serves to constrain options; as prevailing theories are challenged, new options for action may emerge. Such arguments apply equally to explanatory forms. As any given explanation gains hegemony, certain forms of conduct are discredited or discouraged. The generative explanatory form would challenge the plausibility of the prevailing form, render an alternative account plausible, and in doing so reduce the force of existing constraints on action.

This line of argument may be illustrated within the context of the recent history of psychology. The rise and recession of behaviorist psychology, along with the "cognitive revolution," is well documented and broadly acknowledged. In addition, behaviorism represents a situation-centered form of the empowered polarity of explanation; the cognitive revolution primarily served to recenter the explanatory fulcrum within the individual. The previously described explanatory confusions built into the neo-behaviorist models, such as social learning theory, may thus be viewed as a normal outcome of the transition between differing forms of explanation. In any case, throughout the century the dominant form of explanation within psychology has remained empowered.

It is of further importance to realize the close connection between favored forms of explanation and the metatheoretical bases of scientific activity. With its emphasis on documenting systematic relationships among discrete observables, and its search for the necessary and sufficient antecedents for various behavior patterns, the behaviorist paradigm was well appointed to serve as a handmaiden to early logical positivist philosophy. With the tempering of early positivist tenets, including the admission of hypothetical constructs and the demise of inductivism, the stage was properly set for the cognitive revolution in psychology. In effect, the selection of theoretical explanation in psychology may reflect in important measure the assumptions made by scientists themselves as to the character of scientific conduct (Gergen, 1979). In this light, one must take very seriously the more recent withering away of the traditional empiricist roots within the philosophy of science. Attacks on the traditional beliefs in value-free observation, cumulative knowledge, the ideal of unified science, and the like essentially leave the scientist without contemporary philosophic justification. It may fairly be said that there is currently no corpus of philosophic ideas to which the scientist qua scientist may confidently turn for either comfort or guidance. And, by extension, there is little in the way of philosophic support for the empowered form of explanation now prevailing within psychology.

Adopting the generative strategy, it may be ventured that the most significant theoretical undertaking at the present juncture should be enabling in form. Required for the unsettling of widely accepted assumptions in psychology are voluntarist theories of human action. Such forms are to be particularly valued in light of the relative state of bankruptcy in metatheoretical support for empowered forms of explanation—both behaviorist and cognitive. In effect, by using generative criteria much may be gained in the sustained theoretical efforts of rule-role theorists, hermeneutic-interpretavists, ethogenecists, and telic theorists. With the elaboration of such work a contribution may also be made to the development of an alternative metatheory for the sociobehavioral sciences (Gergen and Morawski, 1980).

Implications for Integration

We may conclude by returning to the initial concern with problems of theoretical conflict and integration in psychology. Four major conclusions may be ventured on the basis of the present analysis:

(1) Virtually all explanatory forms may be satisfactorily sustained within the sociobehavioral sciences. As we have seen, there is no obvious way of dislodging any given explanatory form through empirical means. With respect to the particulars of human activity, no given explanatory form wears a mantle of objective superiority. In light of this conclusion, reasons for theoretical integration should derive from analytic or valuational as opposed to empirical concerns.

(2) Many forms of theoretical integration are precluded by the present account. In particular, the employment of multiple explanatory bases within the same theoretical account would appear both unwarranted and obfuscating. Social learning theory proved to be a case in point. On the same grounds, it would appear inauspicious for theorists in the rule-role domain to adopt or import mechanisms or processes from other explanatory domains. To "enrich" rule-role theory with concepts of drive, habit, reinforcement effects, ontogenetic evolution, or social-structural context would appear to undermine its fundamental coherence.

(3) There is nothing in the present arguments that would preclude the continued development of various behaviorist, cognitive, or fatalist forms of scientific explanation. Theorists in these domains may continue to formulate intelligible and compelling accounts of human activity. The major challenge posed by the present analysis to theorists of such persuasions is on valuational and generative grounds. Such theories are highly vulnerable to attack on moral and ideological grounds. If such theories are to be sustained, it is important that justification be furnished on these grounds. Further, these forms of explanation are losing intellectual vitality; metatheoretical support for their sustenance is additionally problematic. If such explanations are to be nurtured by the discipline, attention is needed to the restoration of their generative potential.

(4) Theoretical integration would appear well worth pursuing in those domains sharing an explanatory base. In this respect, substantial benefits may be garnered from a thoroughgoing integration of the rule-role, the hermeneutic-interpretative, the ethogenic, the telic, and the phenomenological orientations to social action. By virtue of central emphasis, each is an enabling form of person-centered explanation, and integration would pose no special problems of coherence. Further, such integration would appear particularly auspicious as it would stand as a unified contrast to the forms of empowered explanation that have so long dominated the sociobehavioral sciences. And too, should such an integration prove successful, it would offer a compelling base from which to establish an alternative metatheory for the science.

Notes

1. Research with Carrie Cornsweet and Beth Albrecht into explanatory accounts employed in early Greek drama, early Buddhist philosophy, and 10th-century Japanese courtly writing lends strong support to the broad applicability of the framework developed in the present chapter.

2. Influenced by Weber, Winch, and Collingwood, among others, many argue that the social sciences should *ideally* reflect the culturally shared conventions—that so-called *etic* theoretical approaches are artificially imposed on culture and thus misleading, while *emic* theory furnishes "inside," and thus valid, understanding of the culture. The problems encountered by such a view are conveniently summarized by Thomas (1979).

3. Unambiguous categorization of these and other theories in terms of an explanatory locus is problematic. Theoretical accounts are themselves open to alternative interpretations, and depending on interpretive emphasis could be differentially classified. However, the present decisions would appear to reflect common opinion concerning the explanatory metacenter of the systems in question.

4. The extent to which these accounts rely on enabling explanations is fully revealed in the moral stance adopted by both Asch (1956) and Milgram (1974) in their classic works on conformity and obedience. In both cases the investigators hold subjects as personally responsible for their actions, and thus morally culpable. In effect, they champion the individual who would *choose* not to conform to the crowd or capitulate to authority.

5. Relevant is Harold Kelley's (1971) analysis of causal attribution, in which it is maintained that the search for cause in daily life is undertaken for the same purposes (although less systematically) as in the behavioral sciences. Specifically, Kelley argues, "The attributor [of causality] is not simply a seeker after knowledge; his latent goal in gaining knowledge [about causes] is that of effective management of himself and his environment" (p. 22).

6. As Taylor (1970) says, "Now it seems to be a widespread belief among researchers in the field of academic psychology that [teleological] explanation is inherently non-empirical, that is, contestable. . . . But a little reflection should show that this view is ill founded" (p. 55). Support for Taylor's view may be found in Wright (1972).

7. It is this argument that frustrates the aims of neo-Humeans to exhaust the concept of causality in the tracing of the constant conjunction of observables. To argue that environmental event X "causes" behavioral event Y on grounds that each Y is preceded by X, and Y's absences are always preceded by X's absence, demands a specification of X. Yet such specification must necessarily rely on the individual's internal representation of X. The result

is that the representation (which may or may not reflect the "actual" properties of X) can properly be viewed as the causal source, and not X in itself.

8. As Boden (1973) has argued, for example, intentions (reasons) may be the result of prior causes. Or, as argued by others, external events may stand in a contingent relationship with reasons, and reasons may be only contingently related to action. Thus, reasons may be viewed as but integers in a Humean account of explanation by constant conjunction (see Ayer, 1967; Davidson, 1963; MacIntyre, 1970).

9. One may continue to resist this conclusion on the grounds that for all practical purposes, broad agreement can be reached on whether certain observable events (an auto crash, a fire, a given conversation) preceded an action or not, and to the extent that such events serve as the explanatory fulcrum (e.g., "The auto crash is the reason he did not report to work today"), one may legitimately conclude that certain explanations are empirically correct and others false. Yet this attempt to salvage the argument for empirical criteria is ultimately without substance. The argument being made in the present chapter is not whether a given event preceded a given action, but whether the specified antecedent *brought about* the action. In the case above, the entirety of cultural history preceded the failure to report to work, and yet the auto accident is singled out as the causal agent. It is not the existence of events in cultural history that is being challenged in the present thesis, but the basis for singling out or designating one event as opposed to another as the causal agent. The grounds for such designation would appear to lie within given systems of culturally shared rules for legitimate explanation; they are in no way to be derived logically from observation.

10. In effect, in the case of fuel and the combustion chamber we have two isolable events. In the case of stimulus and experience we have only one event but two languages (a situational and a personal).

11. An unpublished paper by Joseph Critelli, William Smith, and Carol Ansted furnishes arguments bearing a close affinity to those presented here. As they maintain, in the case of social learning theory, "while a semblance of the behavioral metaphor has been retained at the linguistic level, terms have been redefined to convey mentalistic meanings, with the resulting double message leading to confusions in the logical integrity of the theory" (p. 1). And, with respect to the ambivalence between empowered and enabled forms of theorizing, they note, "Bandura's position on free choice and agency seems no more scientific than that of humanistic ... theorists. ... In various explications of self system functioning, Bandura repeatedly employs a descriptive language that hints at a personal freedom bordering on free will" (p. 57).

12. Relevant is Sampson's (1981) critique of cognitive theory for its failure to take account of collective processes.

13. Each of these arguments connecting explanatory forms with forms of governance may be countered in a variety of ways. However, the point of this analysis is not to suggest a point-to-point congruence but simply to demonstrate the broad social significance of theoretical choice within the sciences.

References

Argyris, C. *Inner contradictions of rigorous research.* New York: Academic Press, 1980.

Asch, S. E. Studies of independence and conformity: A minority of one against a unanimous majority. *Psychological Monographs,* 1956, *70,* (Whole No. 416).

Ayer, A. J. Man as a subject for science. In P. Laslett & W. R. Runciman (Eds.), *Philosophy, politics and society.* Oxford, Eng.: Oxford University Press, 1967.

Bandura, A. *Aggression: A social learning analysis.* Englewood Cliffs, NJ: Prentice-Hall, 1973.

Bandura, A. *Social learning theory*. Englewood Cliffs, NJ: Prentice-Hall, 1977.

Berger, P., & Luckmann, T. *The social construction of reality*. Garden City, NY: Doubleday, 1966.

Boden, M. A. The structure of intentions. *Journal for the Theory of Social Behaviour*, 1973, *3*, 23-46.

Bugenthal, J. F. T. *The search for authenticity*. New York: Holt, Rinehart & Winston, 1965.

Buss, A. R. Causes and reasons in attribution theory: A conceptual critique. *Journal of Personality and Social Psychology*, 1978, *36*, 1311-1321.

Chomsky, N. *Language and mind*. New York: Harcourt Brace Jovanovich, 1968.

Critelli, J. W., Smith, W. C., & Austad, C. S. Social learning theory and the metaphor of mind as behavior. Unpublished manuscript, 1980.

Davidson, D. Actions, reasons and causes, *Journal of Philosophy*, 1963, *60*, 685-700.

Fodor, J. A. *The language of thought*. New York: Crowell, 1975.

Frieze, I. H., Bar-Tal, D., & Carroll, J. S. (Eds.). *New approaches to social problems*. San Francisco: Jossey-Bass, 1979.

Gauld, A., & Shotter, J. *Human action and its psychological investigation*. London: Routledge & Kegan Paul, 1977.

Gergen, K. J. Toward generative theory. *Journal of Personality and Social Psychology*, 1978, *36*, 1344-1360.

Gergen, K. J. The positivist image in social psychology. In A. R. Buss (Ed.), *The social context of psychological knowledge*. New York: Irvington Press, 1979.

Gergen, K J., & Morawski, J. The emergence of an alternative metatheory for social psychology. In L. Wheeler (Ed.), *Review of personality and social psychology*. Beverly Hills, CA: Sage, 1980.

Gergen, K. J., & Gergen, M. M. Causal attribution in the context of social explanation. In D. Görlitz (Ed.), *Perspectives on attribution theory* (David Antal, trans.). Cambridge, MA: Ballinger, 1980.

Habermas, J. *Knowledge and human interests*. Boston: Beacon Press, 1971.

Harré, R. *On social being*. Oxford, Eng.: Basil, Blackwell & Mott, 1979.

Harré, R., & Secord, P. F. The explanation of social behaviour. Oxford, Eng.: Basil, Blackwell & Mott, 1972.

Jones, E. E., & Nisbett, R. E. *The actor and the observer: Divergent perceptions of the causes of behavior*. Morristown, NJ: General Learning Press, 1972.

Kelley, H. H. *Attribution in social interaction*. Morristown, NJ: General Learning Press, 1971.

Kelley, H. H. *Causal schemata and the attribution process*. Morristown, NJ: General Learning Press, 1972.

Kelley, H. H., & Michela, S. L. Attribution theory and research. *Annual Review of Psychology*, 1980, *31*, 457-502.

Kelly, G. *The psychology of personal constructs*. New York: Norton, 1955.

MacIntyre, A. The idea of a social science. In B. R. Wilson (Ed.), *Rationality*. Oxford, Eng.: Oxford University Press, 1970.

Maslow, A. H. *Toward a psychology of being*. Princeton, NJ: Van Nostrand, 1962.

McGuire, W. J. The nature of attitudes and attitude change. In G. Lindzey & E. Aronson (Eds.), *Handbook of social psychology* (Vol. 3). Reading, MA: Addison-Wesley, 1968.

Milgram, S. *Obedience to authority*. New York: Harper & Row, 1974.

Neisser, U. *Cognition and reality*. San Francisco: W. H. Freedman, 1976.

Perry, J. (Ed.). *Personal identity*. Berkeley: University of California Press, 1975.

Peters, R. S. *The concept of motivation*. London: Routledge & Kegan Paul, 1958.

Phares, E. J. *Locus of control in personality*. Morristown, NJ: General Learning Press, 1976.

Ringen, J. D. Explanation, teleology, and operant behaviorism: A study of the experimental analysis of purposive behavior. *Philosophy of Science*, 1976, *43*, 223-253.

Rogers, C. R. *On becoming a person*. Boston: Houghton Mifflin, 1961.

Rorty, R. *Philosophy and the mirror of nature*. Princeton, NJ: Princeton University Press, 1979.

Rosnow, R. L. *Paradigms in transition*. New York: Oxford University Press, 1981.

Ross, L. The intuitive psychologist and his shortcomings: Distortions in the attribution process. In L. Berkowitz (Ed.), *Advances in experimental social psychology*. New York: Academic Press, 1977.

Rychlak, J. F. Psychological science as a humanist views it. In W. J. Arnold (Ed.), *Nebraska Symposium on Motivation*, 1975, *23*, 205-280.

Sampson, E. E. Psychology and the American ideal. *Journal of Personality and Social Psychology*, 1977, *35*, 767-782.

Sampson, E. E. Cognitive psychology as ideology. *American Psychologist*, 1981, *36*, 730-743.

Skinner, B. F. *Contingencies of reinforcement*. New York: Appleton-Century-Crofts, 1969.

Skinner, B. F. *Beyond freedom and dignity*. New York: Alfred A. Knopf, 1971.

Strickland, B. R. Internal-external control of reinforcement. In T. Blass (Ed.), *Personality variables in social behavior*. Hillsdale, NJ: Lawrence Erlbaum, 1977.

Taylor, C. *The explanation of behavior*. London: Routledge & Kegan Paul, 1964.

Taylor, C. The explanation of purposive behavior. In R. Borger & F. Cioffi (Eds.), *Explanation in the behavioral sciences*. Cambridge, Eng. Cambridge University Press, 1970.

Thomas, D. *Naturalism and social science: A post-empirical philosophy of social science*. Cambridge, Eng. Cambridge University Press, 1979.

Toulmin, S. Reasons and causes. In R. Borger and F. Cioffi (Eds.), *Explanation in the behavioral sciences*. Cambridge, Eng.: Cambridge University Press, 1970.

Weimer, W. B. *Notes on the methodology of scientific research*. Hillsdale, NJ: Lawrence Erlbaum, 1979.

Winch, P. *The idea of a social science*. London: Routledge & Kegan Paul, 1958. (Originally published in 1946.)

Wright, L. Explanation and teleology. *Philosophy of Science*, 1972, *39*, 204-218.

CHAPTER 8

The Human Sciences: A Radical Separation of Psychology and the Social Sciences

PETER T. MANICAS

There are a number of good reasons for sharply distinguishing psychology and the social sciences. The argument depends, of course, on clear and defensible conceptions of both psychology and the social sciences and, in turn, these depend on the very conception of science which is to be assumed. Unfortunately, there is no easy consensus on these issues. On the other hand, the time may be ripe for a gathering together of some of the strands bearing on the problems. Behaviorism and behavioral social science are surely on the run, as is the orthodox, neo-positivist social science which has undergirded and propelled these positions. What follows, then, is an attempt at overview, an effort at joining some of these strands and refocusing the debate. The leading idea is rejection of the belief that the sciences of man are aimed at explaining behavior, whereby I mean not only "movements" or "responses," but "actions" as well. The idea that the explanation of motivated behavior is not the task of either psychology or the social sciences may seem bizarre on its face; nevertheless, once we see what this means, many of those diverse strands bearing on the problems of the human sciences fall coherently into place.

It may be best to begin with a brief characterization of psychology as it is here conceived. In the course of developing this characterization, we may begin to join some of the strands.

On the view urged here, psychology is neuropsychology and is a discipline continuous with the biological sciences. It has as its special tasks the study of psychological processes and structures, e.g., learning, perception, cognition, and motivation and their explanation via appeal to their generative mechanisms. Wundt, James, Koffa, Kohler, Goldstein, Lashley, Vygotsky, Luria, Hebb, and Pribram come to mind, although as we shall suggest, a wide variety of experimental work in nonphysiological orientations, e.g., in cognitive and developmental psychology, is both illustrative and important. Thus, to cite but two well-known examples, Piaget's studies of the stages of child development and Chomsky's transformational grammar are concerned with the structure of our competences, with an effort to grasp the kinds of underlying operations which give us the capacities which we have as humans. This suggests an alternative formulation: A scientific psychology aims at knowledge of those mechanisms and structures which give humans the special powers which they have (acquire and develop), and which they exercise in acting in the world.[1]

But this is not to explain behavior, neither the particular acts of particular individuals, nor kinds or classes of actions characterized in general terms. Thus, such a psychology would not seek to discover why John ate meatloaf for his breakfast on Sunday last, nor would it seek knowledge of the lawful relations obtaining between something called "eating behavior" and its constantly conjoined antecedents. On the other hand, a scientific psychology would, were it successful, be in a position to give an account of the complex story of those mechanisms which constitute human nutritive capacities and which underlie the characteristic patterns of human ways of eating. This story would no doubt involve a number of complex structures and processes: metabolic, perceptual, cognitive, and so forth. More generally, then, psychology would aim at understanding *how* it is that humans are able to do the things they do: How do they learn? What are the mechanisms of human motivation? How do these relate to the mechanisms of cognition?

It may be objected that there is nothing interesting in these remarks, or more seriously that it is by no means clear how the position they represent differs from those which do not explicitly disavow the explanation of behavior, at least as the *ultimate* task of psychological science. But there is much confusion on this score, perhaps even on the part of psychologists whose own work the present writer would take as exemplary. The confusion may be explained: On the one hand and, as it turns out, fortunately, the actual practice of science is not always identical with its reconstruction by logicians (whose work is then read by scientists); on the other hand and unfortunately, that reconstruction, until recently, has been at bottom fundamentally mistaken. Accordingly, the most direct way to clarify the foregoing is to offer a few brief comments about the philosophy of science being rejected and, correlatively, the one being assumed. This is evidently not the place for a full-dress account or defense.[2]

Most crucial in the present context is rejection of the orthodox assumption that "the world is so constituted that there are descriptions such that for every event the simple formula, 'whenever this, then that' applies" (Bhaskar, 1975, 1978, p. 69). This regulative ideal, Laplacean in origin, in turn supports the thesis, derived from Hume, that scientific laws are statements of constant conjunctions between events. On this view, developed systematically in "classical" 20th-century philosophy of science, by saying that science seeks knowledge of laws, it is easily assumed that science seeks to "explain" events by subsuming them under laws. Finally, then, when the events to be explained are behaviors (however construed), it is easy to suppose that the explanation of behavior is the (ultimate) aim of scientific psychology. At the same time, it is not so easily seen that if the explanation of behavior *is* the ultimate aim of science, then something like the foregoing orthodox beliefs must be assumed for science to be possible.

It should be emphasized here that while behaviorisms have been especially explicit in *constructing* a "scientific" psychology modeled on these key themes (and thus have made the effort to have their practice conform to their "theory"), the whole of psychology has been seriously affected by these ideas.

But with the conception of science assumed in this essay, there may be no description such that for some events (at least), the formula "whenever this, then that" applies. On this view, the world is radically *open*. This does not, however, make science impossible. It means rather that science must aim at knowledge of something other than laws construed as constant conjunctions of events. As Bhaskar (1975, 1978) writes, science aims at producing knowledge of "real structures which endure and operate independently of our knowledge, our experience and the conditions which allow us access to them" (p. 25). For psychology, this means that we may come to understand the generative mechanisms which constitute human powers without being able to explain or predict (better than we now do) the flux and plethora of acts which constitute the lives of actors in the everyday world. (The parenthetical material is important: see below.)

Suppose, then, that it is conceded that psychology ought to aim at an understanding of what persons can do and not what they will do. Nevertheless, it may be argued that when psychologists study such processes as perception or learning, "they do so by observing certain behaviors under various conditions; to the extent that they are successful in identifying and describing certain processes, they are also explaining behavior."

This objection is surely pertinent. Responding to it should advance clarification of the position being developed here. On the conception of science here assumed, the objection fails to grasp the full significance and rationale of experiment, or more seriously, the reason why, in our world, natural science *is* experimental.

As we have said, science seeks knowledge of the mechanisms which produce the phenomena of the world, but, and this is the crucial difference between the present position and the dominant paradigm of science, the structures and mechanisms of those things which operate in the world are, leaving aside astronomy, *never* operating under conditions of closure. That is, the formula, "whenever this, then that," applies only in the exceptional case, when the system or structure is either isolated from external influences or when those influences are (relatively) constant. Since these structures are "open," acquiring knowledge of them requires work: One must develop a theory which, if its postulated entities and processes exist as postulated, would explain the production of phenomena. And since the systems are open, we can test the theory by experiment. We experiment precisely because in the everyday world, there are *patterns* and *not* constant conjunctions. In an experiment, we intervene precisely in order to create a closure, and thus to get access to those enduring structures which operate willy-nilly in the world.[3]

Accordingly, in psychology, there is a sense in which *in the experimental situation,* we explain behavior. But that is exactly because in the experimental situation, led by our theory of the relevant generative mechanisms, we have intervened to create (an approximate) closure. We do this not because we aim at *explaining* the result, but because in experimental science, it is the way we *test* the theory which postulates the generative mechanism. The knowledge we obtain (when we do) is not knowledge of constant conjunctions by which we "explain," in Deductive-Nomological fashion, "behavior," but is instead knowledge of those enduring mechanisms which constitute human powers and which operate outside the artificial strictures of the experimental situation where, not surprisingly, there are few, if any, constant conjunctions "given" in experience.

These remarks are admittedly incomplete. With them in the background, we may proceed to the next strand in the connected fabric.

Ryle's (1949) *The Concept of Mind* and the later writings of Wittgenstein inspired what is called the "philosophy of mind." The concept of *action* came quickly to the forefront of the debate. Philosophers of action, responding to both behaviorism and to materialism (physicalism) in psychology and philosophy, argued against the very possibility of "causal" explanations of behavior, and usually on those grounds against the very possibility of a scientific psychology. In general, these philosophers contended that our ordinary explanations of behavior, expressed in the concepts our ordinary language, were not reducible or replaceable, logically or empirically, by "causal" explanations.[4]

It is not the present intention to assess the many arguments for the conclusions which they drew or to argue that in the last analysis, either the "new dualists" or their opponents were correct. From the present point of view, *both* sides of the argument were infected by the assumption that it was the aim of a scientific psychology to explain behavior. Indeed, once this assumption is dropped and psychology's tasks are properly understood, the key insight of action theory may be properly located. At the same time, their antiscientific animus is deflated.

The fundamental insight of action theory, an insight shared by others (e.g., Scriven, 1964; Joynson, 1974), is this: There is absolutely no reason to suppose that our ordinary explanations of behavior, expressed in our ordinary language, could be replaced or improved upon, no matter how successful some future psychology might be.

There are two main reasons for this, and Scriven (1964) has identified them both: First, a "colossal quantity" of psychological knowledge "has already long since been snapped up and incorporated in our ordinary language" (p. 167).

We know a great deal about one another; otherwise, it would be hard to imagine how we could get along at all. What therefore might be surprising to a Martian investigator—some real discovery about human motivation or desire—will *not* be a discovery to us. This knowledge is reflected in human languages, whose concepts and distinctions are the product of a long evolutionary and historical experience, an experience in which, as Scriven notes, "the easy material" regarding human behavior has been "winnowed out" and where much of the "nonsense" has not survived the press of continued experience. Of course, our concepts and distinctions are still revisable; some could be abandoned and others could be added, through incorporating insights (and discoveries) made by remarkable individuals: poets, philosophers—even psychologists. But there is no reason to believe that our ordinary understandings are generally in error, that our modes of explanation—as schematized by action theorists—are wrong, or that they could be even marginally improved by alternative concepts and alternative modes of explanation.[5]

Second, as was already noted, acting agents—including lower animals—are themselves radically "open systems," in the sense that they are continually being affected, not only by a changing genetic constitution, but by random (and largely uncontrollable) "stimuli" in a subjective environment, an environment which *is* only as it is *seen* or *taken* by the agent. But if so, the idea that we could improve on our explanations (and predictions) of behavior by a better psychology is utterly misconceived.

This is not to say that agents have "free will," if that means that actions are not "determined" or that there is some ghost in the machine which acts independently of "causes." It means, rather, that orthodox conceptions of "determined" and "caused" do not apply, that a scientific psychology does not require that actions be tied univocally to "stimuli" (under whatever nontautologous description), or indeed that they be tied to anything which can usefully be described as the constantly conjoined antecedent of behavior.[6]

Of course, as we have noted, there are *patterns* and *tendencies.* These make possible our human transactions as ordinarily understood (and predicted) and give rise to the belief that for actions, there are underlying generative mechanisms which operate as open systems in the world. But lacking closure, why should anyone suppose that a scientific psychology could improve upon the skills in explaining (and predicting) behavior which humans gain in becoming socialized human beings?

Related to the foregoing point is the fact that as regards the explanation (or prediction) of behaviors about which we would like especially to have a more systematic and rigorous account, e.g., why some couples are continually hostile, why some persons turn to crime or suicide, why some people get the right answers more of the time than others, many (most?) of the relevant determinants are *biographical* and *social* and necessarily involve appealing to specific individual biographies and specific situational factors. That is, even if we had an adequate, integrated psychological theory, the idiosyncratic nature of individual life trajectories would put extensive limits on our ability to go beyond the crude generalizations and correlations which we now have.

A great deal of what today goes under the heading of "psychology" is specifically engaged in confronting biographical and social factors in an effort to explain criminal behavior, failure in marriage, and so forth. Consider, for example, any issue of *Psychology Today.* In doing this, it in effect crosses into social science, but does so by centering the account on the individual and the personal. Several comments are pertinent to this move.

First, insofar as such inquiry is supposed to explain behavior, the considerations adduced above still hold. The embarrassing lack of well-founded "theory" or of practical results is hardly surprising. Second, this style of social science encourages the idea that we convert, when possible, social problems and political issues into personal and psychological problems and thus shift the burden of "maladaptive," "misadjusted," "deviant," and otherwise troublesome behaviors from the social context in which they arise and are played out to the individual. This is much too large a topic to deal with here, but it seems clear that, as with the liberal and illiberal practicality noted later, there are historical and structural causes for this "age of psychological man" (see Mills, 1959; and Rieff, 1959, chap. 10).

Finally, when such inquiry is genuinely able to advance our understanding of the social, situational (structural), and historical factors implicated in the analysis of such problems, such inquiry is good social science and ought to be identified as such. Although we may disagree on particular examples, many of the inquiries of Freud, or of more recent writers (Erickson, Ernest Becker, R. D. Laing, Kenniston, Lifton, Coles, and many others) are best construed as social science rather than psychology. But if psychology should abandon the idea that its task is to explain behavior, it is perhaps less clear that it should be understood as continuous with biology.

The current vigorous interest in "cognitive psychology" has much to commend it insofar as it represents a clean rejection of the narrow problem definition and methodological strictures of behavioristic psychologies. But for a number of reasons, not to be examined here, the effort at machine simulation models seems to be misguided (see Leiber, this volume).

On the other hand, no one is ready to deny that while "the human being is a system of a different order than any existing systems, natural or artificial" (Harré & Secord, 1972, p. 87), the human organism is a natural organism with an evolutionary history. Presumably, it is therefore possible for a scientific psychology to grasp an understanding of the generative mechanisms and processes which make the *human* organism what it is. We might then understand how the linguistic, intellectual, and social powers are developed and "represented" in the maturing nervous system.[7]

Such a psychology is not "reductionistic." It does not seek to ignore or bury the "subjective" and "phenomenological." For it is the phenomenological from which it must begin, which it must take for granted, and which it seeks to understand. Thus, as Köhler (1964) has pointed out: "to build a science of psychology one must begin with the phenomenal world, but then one must transcend it."[8]

Nevertheless, there are sure to be doubts about the meaning of a nonreductionist neuropsychology. Thus, Joynson (1974), who concurs that "the layman's understanding is both extensive and reliable" (p. 16), and who rejects behaviorism in psychology, raises critical questions regarding neuropsychology on grounds which center "on the role which the psychologist is supposed to play" (p. 68). He points out that "if the only valid principles derive from neurology, it is not clear what the psychologist has to contribute, or what the word 'psychology' stands for in the term 'neuropsychology'" (p. 69). Apart from the institutional problems of turf preservation (a real problem given the number of people earning a living in the fields of the human sciences!) there are some genuine methodological and philosophical difficulties here. However, on the present view, they have been both misconstrued and exaggerated.

The misconstrual stems from the idea, already discussed, that because physiological mechanisms are implicated in all human behaviors, a physiological psychology would explain behavior by providing a physiological account of the causes of behavior. Such accounts would either *replace* ordinary (mentalistic) explanations, or else ordinary explanations (if true) would *reduce* via "identity theory" to the physiological accounts. Once, however, we abandon the idea that neuropsychology explains behavior, the problem dissolves. Surely humans would not be what they are without the brain and central nervous system they have, and surely these are "generative"—in the appropriate sense—of the things we can do. The biological sciences in general have as their tasks the detailing of such mechanisms and the explanation of such powers.

These remarks will not satisfy Joynson, since he will object that psychological constructs are still necessary and that these require psychological—in contrast to neurological—investigation. In his criticism of Hebb, he argued that Hebb "makes free use of mentalistic terms such as sensation and perception," and he objects that Hebb is actually a "crypto-dualist" whose attempts to introduce physiological definitions "conceal from Hebb himself the fact that he really is thinking in mentalistic terms" (Joynson, 1974, p. 76).

The present problem is not to assess Hebb's substantive theory (which, as was noted, is but one of the candidates). Moreover, Hebb is surely mistaken if he does suppose that his use of such terms does not crucially presuppose and depend upon their ordinary meaning. Finally,

Joynson is correct in contending that Hebb is "thinking in mentalistic terms." But that is precisely the sense in which the effort is *not* reductionistic. For how else could Hebb think if he were interested in discovering the mechanisms of perception? Perception is just that which is the phenomenological presupposition of the inquiry and which, if eliminated, would eliminate the problem *as* psychological.

Moreover, the question of whether Hebb (or other physiologically oriented researchers) is a crypto-dualist, an out-of-the-closet dualist, or a materialistic monist is largely red herring as regards the present problem. For on any of these "theories," the ontological status of the phenomenon of consciousness is not the issue; *if*, that is, it is agreed that these phenomena are not *sui generis* and independent of the brain and central nervous system (see Brandt & Kim, 1967; and Armstrong, 1968).

Perhaps the problem which bothers Joynson is the same which bothered Scriven (1964) when he wrote, "to argue that the true future of psychology lies elsewhere, e.g., in neurophysiology" is to argue for "a future which exists after the grave, since that stage is no longer psychology" (p. 168).

There is a sense in which this is true, but it matters a great deal on the construal of the key terms. Scriven writes:

> We are constrained by the definition of the subjects here to deny the term "psychology" or "psychological explanation" to explanations which simply use variables from other subjects as they are commonly recognized; although they may in fact explain molar behavior that can be regarded as psychological behavior [p. 169].

If we assume here that "psychological behavior" is *action* as that is generally used, then, as we have argued—indeed, using Scriven's own arguments—there is no reason to suppose that molar behavior could be explained by appeals to physiology (or chemistry). We may, however, amend Scriven's claim (and come perhaps closer to what Scriven himself intended) so that we rule out as psychological explanations of psychological *phenomena* (perception, learning, and so forth) in physiological terms.

It is by no means clear why we should do this (except again for the sake of the vested interests of those psychologists who have no interest in physiology). To be sure, an inquiry which restricted itself to the physiological (to anatomy, morphology, histology, cellular chemistry, and the like) without making the effort to *explain* human powers, especially the complex cognitive powers, would not be a neuro*psychology* at all. Nor is it clear what kind or amount of specifically "psychological"—phenomenological, introspective, (yes, even) behavioral—inquiry is demanded as part of the theoretical and experimental program.

On this score, Fodor's (1968) account (following Deutsch, 1960) of two phases in explanation is helpful, but perhaps misleading. It is extremely helpful to think of psychological explanation as exhibiting two phases, a "functional characterization" in psychological terms of the phenomenon to be explained (e.g., perception) and in the second phase, a specification of physiological structures that embody the functional characteristics of the phase-one characterization. (This way of viewing the matter also shows the sense in which neuropsychology is not reductionistic.)

But we should not suppose (as Deutsch did) that there is therefore a division of labor between physiology and psychology such that psychologists are engaged in phase-one inquiry and physiologists are engaged in phase-two inquiry. As Fodor (1968) rightly noted, the two phases "may be simultaneous in point of history" (p. 207) and more importantly, the two phases *must* be understood as conditioning one another. The problem, thus, is one of "mutual fit and adjustment." Indeed, it is at this experimental "moment" where neuropsychology is distinguished from neurology.[9]

But these considerations will still not satisfy psychologists like Joynson (or Maslow, Rogers, and many others) since for these writers, construing psychology as a *biological* science only makes matters worse. For them, experimental psychology "misses many of the essentially human aspects of life" (P. Warr, cited in Joynson, 1974, p. 92). For these writers, "psychology has been too exclusively mechanistic, pure and individual in its orientation; it should give greater weight to the experential, the applied, and the social" (Joynson, 1974, p. 92).

As we shall suggest in what follows, the "challenge" of humanistic psychology provides another good reason for insisting on a clear division between the provinces of psychology and the social sciences. Joynson's charges provide a useful point of departure.

No doubt the main thrust of humanist criticisms of experimental psychology was aimed at behaviorisms, and therefore there is somewhat of an irony in Joynson's claims. Behaviorisms have denied the relevance of the "experiential"—at least as that has been construed by many humanist writers—but behaviorisms have not balked at being *applied*. Indeed, from the present perspective, and though the story is too complex to tell here, one should be struck with the ease by which the applied human disciplines have overwhelmed the quest for *understanding* as such: We can still identify a difference between physics and engineering. But applied psychology, as liberal or illiberal practicality, has become the tail which wags the dog.[10]

Yet, however much we may feel the need for expert advice and opinion as regards our human problems, a scientific psychology would not be an applied psychology. This is not to say that having gained an understanding of the mechanisms of learning, motivation, and so forth that we might not be in a better position than we now are to generate ameliorative technologies. At present, our technologies (e.g., learning machines, drug therapies, conditioning programs) are largely grounded inductively— when they are grounded at all. Indeed, most clinical practices, it must be admitted, have neither a theoretical nor an experimental basis, even if practitioners lay claim to "scientific" authority and have "credentials" which "prove" their expertise.

In this regard, Szasz (1961) is correct in insisting on a distinction between "problems in living" and "pathology," and he would seem to be correct in holding that most of the genuine practical problems confronting individuals are not amenable to resolution by some psychological *science*.[11] This is not to deny, as before, that there are remedies for such problems or that there might be persons specifically qualified to deal with them. Sometimes the problem is social in the sense that amelioration requires changes in the social context. Sometimes help can be provided through participation in self-knowledge, or in building confidence, and so on. But the therapist/social worker is not a psychologist, however much people need the help of the other people.

The criticism that experimental psychology is *individualist* and omits altogether considerations of the *social* is also serious, but from the present perspective, it too rests on a misconception.

It is surely true that people as we ordinarily think of them and know them are social beings in the important sense that human powers are socially realized. Accordingly, what we call "mind" is a social product, insofar as neither "mind" nor "person" can be reduced to a neuropsychology. This is, indeed, the crucial error of reductionist philosophies of mind.[12] But one must be careful about what this means and what it does not mean. It does not mean, if the foregoing is correct, that inquiry into the generative mechanisms, which in the maturing nervous system are the basis of human powers, is impossible. It *does* mean that since mind is social, neuropsychology cannot explain the *contents* of mind—what persons think or feel, what are their goals or attitudes, *why* they think what they think, and why they have the goals and attitudes which they have. And, of course, that is why it would be foolhardy to set the task of psychology to be the explanation of behavior. But that point has been insisted upon right along.

Moreover, since "mind" is social, what has been called social psychology is best construed as a transitionary discipline, in the sense that it links our knowledge of human powers as physiologically explained and as they are realized socially. This is very close to G. H. Mead's (1934) definition: "Social psychology ... presupposes an approach to experience from the standpoint of the individual, but undertakes to determine *in particular* that which belongs to this experience because the individual himself *belongs to a social structure*."[13] In this regard, Mead's theory of "mind," "self," and "society" *is* the underlying rationale for the bridge between people as human *organisms* and people as *social* beings.

And there is no problem in this distinction if *for methodological reasons* we keep squarely in mind what we are doing in inquiry. As Solomon (1974) has argued in his explication of Freud, "A nervous system is not a person, nor is a psyche a person" (see also Sellars, 1965). What neuropsychology needs is not the *person* as understood in our ordinary thinking about one another, but rather a being which is, as Solomon (1974) notes, something which "is at once the subject of both neurological and psychological predicates ... a nervous system and the psychic apparatus" (p. 51). Such a being is a person when its powers are exercised socially, for then its *mind* has specific content and it *acts* in the world (Margolis, 1976).

Social psychology, then, is itself a *social* science, for like the other social sciences, it begins with the concept of people as we know and understand them in our everyday lives.[14] So conceived, social psychology is historical and engaged in the effort to comprehend the historically specific meanings and "the rules governing the mobilization of resources by agents in their interaction with each other and nature" (Bhaskar, this volume). Accordingly, social psychology is not an experimental science in the way that experimental psychology is, but is an investigation which must look to actual "life situations" (Harré & Secord, 1972, chap. 3).

But one should not suppose that the task of social science is to explain the actions of persons *sociologically,* for as with psychology, the territory of social science is also restricted by common sense. Indeed, in regard to the actions of persons, it is the *same* territory.

It is not therefore surprising that the idea that action is *meaningful* and *intentional* is shared by "interpretive sociologies," phenomenological sociology, hermeneutics, and by action theory, for as we have noted, it is in precisely such terms that our ordinary explanations of behavior are couched. Thus, some of the reasons which militate against replacing or improving ordinary explanations of behavior by explanations from a scientific *psychology* also militate against their improvement or replacement by a scientific *sociology*. The person remains, from either point of view, an "open system." While some of the determinants of social behavior (action) lie outside the range of psychology, others, e.g., genetic and biological factors, lie outside the range of social science. But if psychology's proper aim is an understanding of the generative mechanisms of human powers, what is the task of social science?

Following Anthony Giddens (1976) and Roy Bhaskar (1978, 1979), we must first make a categorical distinction between *human action* and *social structure*. Just as "people" and "society" are radically different kinds of things, so too are human action and social structure radically different—however dependent social structure is on human action.

Human action is most usefully characterized as an "ongoing reflexive monitoring of conduct" (Giddens, 1976, p. 156; see also Harré & Secord, 1972, chap. 5). Human action, as motivated, is explained by appeal to reasons, beliefs, desires, and interests. But the distinct theoretical interest of social science is an understanding of social structures—the relatively enduring *products* and *media* of all human action. That is, social structures such as language preexist for individuals; they thus *enable* persons to become persons and to act; and at the same time they are "coercive," limiting the ways we *can* act. Yet social structures are *constituted* by actions which either reproduce or transform those very structures.

The idea that social structures preexist for individuals, are relatively enduring, and are constituted, reproduced, and transformed by action is absolutely crucial for grasping the task of social science. As Giddens (1976) has argued, the fundamental aim of social science is to grasp structures and to discover "the conditions which govern the continuity and dissolution of structures" (p. 156).

This way of viewing the matter confronts exactly the final strand in the fabric we have been developing, for with it we may see exactly both the strengths and limitations of the several warring parties in the philosophy of the social sciences. As Giddens (1976) writes, "the characteristic error of the philosophy of action [and one must add here, of phenomenology and of interpretative sociologies in general] is to treat the problem of 'production' only, thus not developing any concept of structural analysis at all; the limitation of both structuralism and functionalism, on the other hand, is to regard 'reproduction' as a mechanical outcome, rather than as an active constituting process accomplished by, and consisting in, the doings of active subjects" (p. 121). Thus, the one makes social *science* impossible and issues in voluntarism and idealism; the other makes a social science possible, but in so doing denies the efficacy of human agency.[15]

Social science does aim at understanding society, and while society consists only of individuals acting and relating to one another and with nature, it is not essentially concerned with explaining behavior, even if, as with experimental psychology, it must confirm or reject the theories which it formulates about social structure by seeing what people do and why they do it.

On the view urged here, society is best understood as "an articulated ensemble of . . . relatively enduring structures; that is, as a complex totality subject to change in both its components and their interrelations" (Bhaskar, 1978, p. 14). But since social structures do not exist independently of the activities which constitute them, and since the agents of a society do not necessarily comprehend the structural properties of their activities and interactions, an adequate social science would also have a *critical* component.

That is, by identifying particular structures and explaining the conditions for their constitution, social science becomes an instrument for the expansion of "the rational autonomy of action" (Giddens, 1976, p. 159). Thus, while it is true that human activity is conscious and intentional, it is by no means true that the social structures, which are the medium and product of conscious activity, are themselves self-consciously, intentionally, or indeed, rationally produced. But in order to move in the direction of making them so, one must know *what* they are and *how* we reproduce them.[16]

It may not be inappropriate to conclude this effort at overview with some brief comments on the relation of "nature" and "culture."

It is essential to emphasize that *because* persons are biological *and* cultural, the idea that the human sciences will be able to explain the acts of humans is bound to remain unfulfilled. There can be no doubt that individuals are the joint product of genetic determination and specific socialization, and that their actions are the joint product of what they are and of the social structures through and by means of which they act. But to explain behavior, we would need to be able to distinguish the mix, to weight it, to identify the mutual effects and reciprocal contributions—and to do this diachronically.[17]

On the other hand, if we aim to understand ourselves and our societies better than we now do, then for methodological reasons we ought to think of ourselves as *people* for purposes of inquiry into the social structures through and by means of which we live our lives, and as organisms, albeit with special powers, for purposes of inquiry into the generative mechanisms of those powers.

On the present view, psychology is not, however, simply a biological science since, as we have noted, the distinctive human powers are realized only socially. That means that the *psychological* starting place of inquiry into the generative mechanisms is always culturally loaded. Moreover, it is then an empirical question of whether and how cultural factors relate to the biological infrastructures.

It may be that there is a basic species universality as regards human powers, but variation in the structures as a function of cultural factors. Or it may be that there are no significant cultural differences and that all differences are purely idiosyncratic. From this point of view, evolutionary biology, anthropology, ethology, comparative psychology, and related disciplines are surely pertinent.

By contrast, social science is *thoroughly* cultural. Inquiry into social structures is socially specific and historical. But this is not a contrast between traditional *Geisteswissenschaften* and *Naturwissenschaften,* since we reject the positivist conception of science on which this dichotomy rests.[18] There is no contrast here between idiographic and nomothetic science. Indeed, as we noted, once we reject the assumption that the *natural* world is constituted so that for every event, the simple formula, "whenever this, then that" applies, any radical disjunction of the natural and human sciences fails. People are different than stones, and thus there are differences in the *methods* of the human and natural sciences. On the other hand, once science is properly understood and the tasks of the human sciences are rightly defined, the duality of nature and culture should constitute no obstacle in the way of the advance of the human sciences.

Notes

1. In an excellent article which was brought to my attention after the present essay was written, Charles Taylor (1973) has suggested a three-fold division within psychological practice: the study of "infrastructural conditions for the exercise of (human) capacities," the study of "the structures of these capacities, our competences," and finally, the "explanation of motivated behavior," our performances. Essentially, I am denying the last as a reasonable task for psychology. Moreover, from my point of view, the study of the structures of our

capacities and their infrastructural conditions, e.g., in the central nervous system, cannot profitably be disjoined.

2. Especially to be recommended, however, are Stephen Toulmin, *The Philosophy of Science* (1953) and *Human Understanding,* Vol. 1 (1973); Rom Harré, *Principles of Scientific Thinking* (1970) and *Philosophies of Science* (1972); and Roy Bhaskar, *A Realist Theory of Science* (1975, 1978).

3. This owes much to Bhaskar's (1975, 1978) discussion, especially Chapter 2.

4. There is, of course, a vast literature. Two good examples are A. I. Melden, *Free Action* (1961); and Norman Malcolm, "The Conceivability of Mechanism" (1968). Charles Landesman's "The New Dualism in the Philosophy of Mind" (1965) is a sound early rejoinder. See also J. A. Fodor's excellent *Psychological Explanation* (1968), especially Chapter 1.

5. The status of psychoanalysis remains a problem. Toulmin (1948) and more lately, Taylor (1973), have pointed out that psychoanalysis is partly a hermeneutic science, since it involves discerning interpretations of an agent of which a subject might not be aware, and indeed "against whose disclosure he fights vigorously." The analyst then relates these interpretations "in terms of underlying mechanisms of a quite different sort," e.g., mechanisms of repression or displacement.

If so, a psychoanalytic explanation of some act might be incompatible with a lay account even though, like the lay account, it demands a hermeneutical model or schema. But then, a hermeneutical *science* which would explain behavior better than we ordinarily do is not to be ruled out.

Although the issues relating to psychoanalysis are complex, three observations might be made here. First, insofar as the idea of unconscious motivation is the lynchpin of such an explanation, it is by no means clear that its psychoanalytic use is so far removed from our ordinary pre-Freudian concepts. (On this point, see especially A. C. MacIntyre, *The Unconscious* (1958). For two illuminating accounts of the notion of consciousness, see Toulmin (this volume) and Taylor (this volume).

Second, because they are interpretations, our ordinary accounts are always amendable, and in particular cases may be altogether withdrawn in favor of, perhaps, a causal account, or alternatively a psychoanalytic explanation. But this presupposes (at least) that we have a well-confirmed scientific theory of the mechanisms involved and how they are implicated in the case at hand. There is an analogy to discovering post hoc that someone ran a red light not because the person was in a hurry, but because (s)he is red-green color-blind. Evidently, in the case of the psychoanalytic mechanisms in question, we lack the needed well-confirmed theory even if, of course, there are many who would defend something like unconscious motivation. As MacIntyre (1958) points out, we do not *need* to postulate an unconscious to provide explanatory background for anomalies in the conscious mental life. The central nervous system is "at once obvious and legitimate." This move would undermine (or transform) psychoanalysis as it is presently understood. In this regard, one should look at Charles Rycroft's (1979) interesting review of Sebastiano Timpanaro's *The Freudian Slip.*

Third, and following Toulmin, although it is a mistake to argue that Freudian accounts are "causal" and thus deny agency, it nevertheless seems true that explanations of actions in terms of unconsciousness motivations will not always or even generally replace more straightforward accounts, for if this were to obtain, our taken-for-granted abilities to transact with one another would be greatly upset. It is for these reasons that we can accept a version of Ryle's (1949) point that "the classification and diagnoses of exhibitions of our mental impotences require specialized research methods. The explanation of the exhibition of our mental competences often requires nothing but ordinary good sense" (p. 326).

On the present view, if for example, someone eats because he seems hungry and he confirms this, we can be quite satisfied with the explanation even though we lack an understanding of the complex generative mechanisms underlying such action. The predication "feels hungry" is a promissory note which does not demand cashing. On the other hand, if that person eats perpetually and tells us with evident sincerity that he wished he could stop, we would like a better understanding of the relevant mechanisms (psychoanalytic or otherwise). Because our usual explanations of such behavior break down, we are left with guesses about *real* motivations or questions about "weakness of will" and the like. Of course, if we had an adequate integrated psychological theory, we might be in a position to say why the more obvious ordinary account breaks down when it does!

Compare here also Bhaskar's compressed discussion of "depth-rationality" in Chapter 14 of this volume. As he points out, there is always "the possibility of self-deception, rationalization, deception of others, and systemic mystification." But he also notes (crucially, as regards the present problem) that the nature of the cognitive unfreedom and thus the constraints upon "cognitive emancipation" are very different in the domains of psychoanalysis, social phenomenology, and historical materialism. And it may be that we are only occasionally self-deceived, more often deceived by others, and perpetually mystified!

6. See Taylor (1973) and Fodor (1968). But neither of these writers goes to the root of the problem, that "regularity determinism" is a dogma of the philosophy of science and that therefore the explanation of behavior is a misconceived ideal for psychology. On the thesis of regularity determinism—that there is some description for every event such that "whenever this, then that" applies—see Bhaskar (1975, 1978), especially pp. 69ff.

7. There are, of course, a number of theories in the current literature. One might mention here the publications of Hebb, Pribram, Vygotsky, and Luria, as well as the unpublished writings of my colleague, Eugene Sachs.

8. Cited by MacLeod (1964). MacLeod's sometimes misleading essay is also very useful.

9. The "two-phase" characterization is, of course, a logical abstraction, but it is not at all alien to the work of the "classic" experimentalists, from Wundt to the Gestaltists. Moreover, a good case can be made for Freud in its terms. See R. C. Solomon's (1974) excellent essay, "Freud's Neurological Theory of Mind."

10. A full-scale treatment explaining this phenomena remains to be written. It would need at least to raise important questions regarding the nature of science and its *mis*conception in the human sciences, the relation of this misconception to technology, and the development of the bureaucratic ethos and of the whole business to the development of corporate capitalism. C. W. Mills (1959) got a bit of it in his *Sociological Imagination*. Goran Therborn's *Science, Class and Society* (1976) did not explicitly examine this phenomenon. Nevertheless, it failed in its effort to join some of these themes.

11. For example, T. Szasz, *The Myth of Mental Illness* (1961) and *Ideology and Insanity* (1970). On the relation of "theory" to "practice" in psychotherapy, see Perry London, *The Modes and Morals of Psychotherapy* (1964).

12. An excellent formulation is Joseph Margolis's "Countering Physicalistic Reduction" (1976). Margolis argues that "Persons are . . . *culturally* emergent entities whose existence . . . is to be admitted when . . . certain specimens of *Homo Sapiens* . . . are so trained that they exhibit a mastery of language and a capacity for self-reference" (p. 14). He argues that his view is "hospitable to materialism (though not to reductionism)" (ibid.).

13. Compare also Dewey, "All psychology that isn't physiological is social." Quoted in C. W. Mills, *The Sociological Imagination* (1959).

14. The formulation by Harré and Secord (1972, p. 87) is marvelous: "It is the heart of radical proposal of this book, that we should treat people, for scientific purposes, *as if they were human beings,* as we know and understand them in everyday life."

This may be as good a place as any to acknowledge my debt to Paul Secord.

15. Bhaskar's (1978) article in *The Journal for Theory of Social Behavior* maps the current furor with insight and brevity. In addition to Gidden's extremely penetrating book, referred to in the foregoing, one should see also Richard J. Bernstein, *The Restructuring of Social and Political Theory* (1976).

16. Again, see Bhaskar (1978, p. 22) "On the Possibilities of Social Scientific Knowledge . . . " (p. 22ff.) for a crisp formulation of the critical component of social science, as well as Chapter 14 of this volume.

17. Another notable effort at bridging the nature/culture dichotomy is sociobiology. One may suspect that insofar as it aims to explain behavior, indeed, by *bypassing* psychology altogether, it will continue to be the object of acrimonious and unproductive debate.

18. This is *another* long story. With classical political economy came the idea that there were *laws* of society. Comte then gave the first clear articulation for the new philosophy of science and gave us as well its name, "positivism." As he wrote, a "true science" studies "the laws of Phenomena," their "invariable relations of succession and resemblance." *Geisteswissenschaften*, born of Romanticism, were a response to this. Marx is the crucial figure. It is fair to say, I believe, that Marx saw his task as providing an alternative to the positivist social science of his day and, at the same time, he rejected the antiscientific, speculative, and religious aspects of the idealist, antipositivist criticism. Unfortunately, the positivist strains in Marx came to dominate later Marxism, and it has taken a century to get back to where Marx was.

Bhaskar (1978) has argued persuasively that both naturalists and antinaturalists have accepted an essentially positivist account of natural science, especially the underlying empiricist ontology. And he has also pointed out that within Marxism, an exactly parallel dispute has occurred.

References

Armstrong, D. M. *A materialist theory of mind.* London: Routledge & Kegan Paul, 1968.

Bernstein, R. J. *The restructuring of social and political theory.* New York: Harcourt Brace Jovanovich, 1976.

Bhaskar, R. *A realist theory of science.* Sussex: Harvester, 1975, 1978.

Bhaskar, R. On the possibilities of social scientific knowledge and the limits of naturalism. *Journal for the Theory of Social Behavior,* 1978, *8.*

Bhaskar, R. *The possiblity of naturalism.* Atlantic Highlands, NJ: Humanities Press, 1979.

Brandt, R., & Kim, J. The logic of the identity theory. *The Journal of Philosophy,* 1967, *64.*

Deutsch, J. A. *The structural basis of behavior.* Chicago: University of Chicago Press, 1960.

Fodor, J. A. *Psychological explanation.* New York: Random House, 1968.

Giddens, A. *New rules of sociological method.* London: Hutchinson, 1976.

Harré, R. *Principles of scientific thinking.* London: Macmillan, 1970.

Harré, R. *Philosophies of science.* Oxford: Oxford University Press, 1972.

Harré, R., & Secord, P. F. *The explanation of social behaviour.* Oxford: Basil, Blackwell & Mott, 1972.

Joynson, R. B. *Psychology and common sense.* London: Routledge & Kegan Paul.

Köhler, W. Cited in T. W. Wann (Ed.), *Behaviorism and phenomenology.* Chicago: University of Chicago Press, 1964.

Landesman, C. The new dualism in the philosophy of mind. the *Review of Metaphysics,* 1965, *19.*

London, P. *The modes and morals of psychotherapy.* New York: Holt, Rinehart & Winston, 1964.

MacIntyre, A. C. *The unconscious.* London: Routledge & Kegan Paul, 1958.

MacLeod, R. B. Phenomenology: A challenge to experimental psychology. In T. W. Wann (Ed.), *Behaviorism and phenomenology.* Chicago: University of Chicago Press, 1964.

Malcolm, N. The conceivability of mechanism. *The Philosophical Review,* 1968, *77.*

Margolis, J. Countering physicalistic reduction. *Journal for the Theory of Social Behavior,* 1976, *6.*

Mead, G. H. *Mind, self and society.* Chicago: University of Chicago Press, 1934.

Melden, A. I. *Free action.* London: Routledge & Kegan Paul, 1961.

Mills, C. W. *The sociological imagination.* Oxford: Oxford University Press, 1959.

Rieff, P. *Freud: The mind of the moralist.* New York: Doubleday, 1959.

Rycroft, C. Review of S. Timpanaro's *The Freudian slip*. *New Left Review*, 1979, *118*.

Ryle, G. *The concept of mind*. New York: Barnes & Noble, 1949.

Scriven, M. Views of human nature. In T. W. Wann (Ed.), *Behaviorism and phenomenology*. Chicago: University of Chicago Press, 1964.

Sellars, W. The identity approach to the mind-body problem. *Review of Metaphysics*, 1965, *18*.

Solomon, R. C. Freud's neurological theory of mind. In R. Wollheim (Ed.), *Freud: A collection of critical essays*. New York: Doubleday, 1974.

Szasz, T. *The myth of mental illness*. Delta, 1961.

Szasz, T. *Ideology and insanity*. New York: Doubleday, 1970.

Taylor, C. Peaceful coexistence in psychology. *Social Research*, 1973, *40*.

Therborn, G. *Science, class and society*. London: New Left Books, 1976.

Toulmin, S. The logical status of psycho-analysis. *Analysis*, 1948, *9*.

Toulmin, S. *The philosophy of science*. London: Hutchinson, 1953.

Toulmin, S. *Human understanding* (Vol. 1). Oxford: Clarendon, 1973.

CHAPTER 9

On the Relation of Sociology to Philosophy

ANTHONY GIDDENS

I do not intend in this chapter to discuss the connections between sociology and philosophy on a general level. My view, for what it is worth, is that a clear separation between sociology and philosophy could only be sustained so long as each subject were dominated by positivistic standpoints. That is to say, it is plausible only so long as one believes that empirical social research can be kept wholly free from, or "uncontaminated by, metaphysical issues" on the one hand, and that on the other the tasks of philosophy are limited to those of the "underlaborer" sort, secondary to and parasitic upon the work of science. If one rejects such conceptions of both sociology and philosophy, one is led to the conclusion that both empirical social analysis and sociological theorizing involve inherently philosophical endeavors. When I began the work which eventuated in my book *New Rules of Sociological Method* and some of the sections in *Studies in Social and Political Theory,* I was struck by the fact that many sociologists and philosophers have over the past two or three decades been working on a common range of problems, but with very little cross-referencing between the two bodies of literature. Anyway, I would take as a motto the well-known statement of Merleau-Ponty:

> Philosophy and sociology have long lived under a segregated system which has succeeded in concealing their rivalry only by refusing them any meeting-ground, impeding their growth, making them incomprehensible to one another, and thus placing culture in a situation of permanent crisis.

In order to demonstrate the overlap of the literatures of sociology and philosophy, I want to consider three related sets of issues which I wrote about in a preliminary way in the two books mentioned above, and which I have attempted to elaborate in considerably more detail in *Central Problems in Social Theory:*

(1) What should a theory of action involve in the social sciences—how should we best conceptualize "human action" in sociology?
(2) How should we best conceptualize the notion of "structure" in sociology?
(3) What conceptual connections should be supposed to exist between these two—between the ideas of action and structure—in sociological explanation?

Approaches to the Theory of Action

I think it rather obvious that an important dualism runs through the literature of both sociology and philosophy in respect of problems of human actions. There exists, of course, a great deal of philosophical literature devoted to the explication or analysis of action, much of it influenced by the writings of the later Wittgenstein. Some of this early literature, in some part following leads suggested by Wittgenstein himself, was preoccupied with the critique of behaviorism in philosophy and in psychology, although it would be safe to say that subsequent work has tended to become emancipated from such a polemical target. Much of the literature concerned with the philosophy of action remains quite unknown to most sociologists, including many whose primary interests lie in the field of social theory. I would say that this is particularly true in the United States, where controversies such as that stimulated by Winch's *Idea of a Social Science* have not become as well-known as they have in Britain. I do want to make the claims in this chapter that sociologists must pay attention to philosophical writings on action, and that the philosophical literature on action theory embodies ideas that are of basic interest to social theory.

However, there are major limitations to the bulk of the writing produced by philosophers of action, and it is here we encounter the dualism I mentioned above. The action philosophers have given a great deal of attention to the concept of action itself, and to intentions, reasons, and so on. But they have given very little attention indeed to the *unintended consequences* of action, the manner in which consequences are of concern to social theory. Thus Davidson, in a very well-known article, discusses the following issue: I move a switch, turn on the light, illuminate the room, and at the same time alert a prowler. Davidson's concern, as that of other philosophers who have discussed this and many other similar examples, is confined to questions of action description: Do I do four things, or only one that can be described in four different ways? Without wishing to deny the interest and significance of problems of action description, it can be pointed out that Davidson's discussion is characteristic of the vast majority of philosophical analyses of action which limit their concerns to what might be called "the production of action" on the part of actors. They have not been concerned either with the consequences of acts that escape actors' intentions or purposes, or with what I shall call the *unacknowledged conditions* of action. Partly for these reasons, issues which have always rightly brooked large in the work of social analysts—problems of the nature of institutions, of social change, conflict, and power—barely appear at all in the writings of the philosophers of action.

Much of the same is found with those schools of thought within the social sciences which have given prominence to human action in some sense akin to that employed by most of the action philosophers. A good case in point is symbolic interactionism, as drawn upon, for example, by Goffman. Goffman—in contrast to many sociologists—treats human beings as reasoning, intentional agents, aware of and capable within the social environment which they help to constitute through their action. Although it is by now a banal observation, it still seems to me true to say that Goffman's sociology lacks any sustained treatment of the phenomena mentioned above, especially of overall processes of institutional transformation. Symbolic interactionism, in the hands of Blumer, Goffman, and others has not successfully developed modes of institutional analysis.

Strong on action, weak on institutional analysis, this theorem can be reversed when we look at the other side of the theoretical dualism that has tended to prevail in the social sciences and philosophy. Those traditions of thought which have placed the unacknowledged conditions and unintended consequences of action in the forefront, and which have emphasized problems of institutional organization and change, have by and large failed to develop theories of action at all. They have stressed the primacy of object over subject, of social structure or social system over the purposeful, capable social actor. Such is the case, I would argue, with the majority of writings associated both with structuralism in France and with the varieties of functionalist thought which have been so influential in the social sciences in the English-speaking world.

The latter claim might at first appear difficult to defend in light of the fact that perhaps the leading functionalist thinker in sociology in recent times, Talcott Parsons, has expressly couched his ideas in terms of what he called the "action frame of reference." I should want to maintain, however, that Parsons's sociology lacks a concept of action—in the sense in which I want to use the term in this chapter, at any rate. A conception of action in the social sciences, I want to argue, has to place at the center of everyday fact that social actors are *knowledgeable* about the conditions of social reproduction in which their day-to-day activities are inter-meshed. The reasons people have for their actions—or what I prefer to call the "rationalization of action," as involved with the chronic reflexive monitoring of conduct that social actors routinely carry on—are crucially involved with how those actions are sustained.

In *The Structure of Social Action,* Parsons tried to integrate what he called a "voluntarist" viewpoint of human conduct with a resolution of the "problem of order" in society. Although he claimed to have synthe-sized the ideas of several prominent 19th-century thinkers, the basic outline of the conception he ended up with is, in my opinion, a heavily Durkheimian one. Parsons connected "voluntarism" with a recognition of the "emergent properties" of collectivities via the notion of the inter-nalization of values: Core social values are simultaneously the source of motivational components of personality and the source of social cohe-sion. What "voluntarism" comes down to here is an emphasis upon incorporating an account of motivation within a scheme of analysis of social systems—that the psychological study of the personality system must complement, via normative values, the study of social systems. The behavior of social actors is regarded as the outcome of the conjunction of psychological and social determinants, with priority attributed to the latter because of the preeminent role played by normative elements. The actor does not appear here as a capable, knowledgeable agent: Parsons's social actors are, in Garfinkel's phrase, "cultural dopes."

How, then, are we to conceptualize the knowledgeability of social agents? How are we to incorporate our own knowledgeability of this knowledgeability within a broad treatment of action in social theory? I propose to answer these questions—although only relatively cursorily given the current context of the chapter—in terms of Figure 9.1.

In Figure 9.1, I outline what I call a "stratification model" of action. The implications of this model, I want to claim, however, cannot be fully elaborated without reference to my subsequent discussion of the concept of "structure" in sociology. By using the phrases "reflexive monitoring of action" and "rationalization of action," I want to refer to the intentional or purposive character of everyday human behavior. But I want to refer to intentional behavior as *process,* as involved in the *duree* of day-to-day

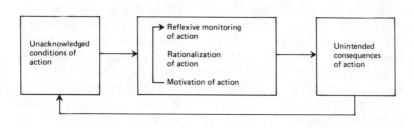

Figure 9.1

life. Too often philosophers treat "intentions" and "reasons" as discrete forms, somehow aggregated together in action. They ignore, or take for granted, what Schutz calls the "reflexive moment of attention" which breaks into the continuing flow of action. Unlike many action philosophers, who often use "motive" as causally synonymous with "reason," I distinguish the two, regarding motivation as referring to the desires that prompt action, and treating "motivation" also as a processual term. I do not limit motivation to promptings available to consciousness, but wish to allocate considerable conceptual space to unconscious impulses—again, I think, unlike most action philosophers who have either simply left the unconscious aside, or following Wittgenstein's lead, have been suspicious of the logical status of concepts relating to unconscious processes.

The knowledgeability of social actors refers to their mobilization of the rationalization of action, in relation to its reflexive monitoring and motivation, in ongoing contexts of social interaction. In conceptualizing knowledgeability, it is not enough merely to distinguish between conscious and unconscious. It is also important to differentiate two senses or levels in which agents are knowledgeable about the social environments they constitute in and through their action. I want to make a distinction that seems to me to be of fundamental importance, between what I shall call *discursive consciousness* and *practical consciousness*.

The distinctive feature of human action, as compared to the conduct of animals, I take to concern what Garfinkel labels the "accountability" of human action. I take the notion of accountability to be a highly important one, and mean by it that the accounts which actors are able to offer of their conduct draw upon the same stocks of knowledge that are drawn upon in the very production and reproduction of their action. The "giving of accounts"—or supplying of reasons—for action refers to the *discursive* capabilities and inclinations of actors and by no means exhausts the connections between "stocks of knowledge" and action. What actors are "able to say" about their activities is by no means all that they know about them. Practical consciousness refers to tacit knowledge that is skillfully employed in the enactment of courses of conduct, but which the actor is not able to formulate discursively. The knowledgeability involved in practical consciousness conforms generally to the Wittgensteinian notion of "knowing a rule" or "knowing how to go on." To "know" English is to know an enormously complicated set of rules or principles, and the contexts of their application. But to know English is not to be able to discursively formulate those rules or principles. Indeed, linguists have devoted a great deal of labor to formulating what we all already "know."

The knowledgeability of human agents in given historical circumstances is always *bounded,* by the unacknowledged conditions of an action on one side, and by its unintended consequences on the other. This is, as I have previously indicated, crucial to social theory, for if writers who have produced objectivist theories of social life, especially the functionalists, have been unable to develop adequate treatments of the knowledgeability of social actors, they have nevertheless quite correctly stressed the escape of activity from actors' intentions. History is not an intentional project, and all intentional activity takes place in the context of institutions sedimented over long-term periods of time. The unintended consequences of action are of fundamental importance to social theory, especially insofar as they are systematically incorporated within the processes of the reproduction of institutions. This is why I have drawn the dotted line linking each side of the diagram. Insofar as unintended consequences are systematically involved in social reproduction, they become conditions of action also. In recognizing the importance of this, however, I wish to avoid the teleological connotations of functionalism, which substitutes "society's reasons" for the reasons of actors. In the terminology I shall suggest below, societies have no "reasons" or "needs" whatsoever; only the actors do, whose activities constantly constitute and reconstitute those societies. Stripping the teleology from functionalism does not entail, as I shall try to show, abandoning the distinctively institutional emphases of functionalism in favor of some kind of subjectivism."

Concepts of Structure

In contemporary sociology, the term "structure" characteristically appears in each of the traditions of "objectivist" social thought I have mentioned earlier—structuralism, which has taken its name from it, and functionalism (which in its modern versions is often referred to in a rather cumbersome way as "structural-functionalism"). Structuralist thought still remains fairly alien to most English-speaking sociologists and philosophers, I would say, as do the poststructuralist writings of authors such as Foucault, Barthes, Derrida, and others. Although I think that structuralism has to be radically criticized in definite ways, I shall want to argue in what follows that certain ideas prominent in the structuralist tradition, to do with the notion of structure itself, are of some considerable importance to social theory.

A curious feature of the functionalist literature is the vast amount of ink expended on the concept of "function" as compared to the virtually complete absence of discussions of the notion of "structure," a notion which is nevertheless continually used by functionalist authors. Consequently, the idea of structure typically figures in Anglo-American sociology as a received one, used in unexamined fashion. Most English-speaking sociologists, when they use the terms "structure" or "social structure," have in mind some kind of connotation of structure as a "visible pattern" of social relations, as something akin to the girders of a building or to the anatomy of a body. In this kind of imagery, structure tends to be conceived as equivalent to *constraint*—a notion to which Durkheim perhaps gave the classic formulation, but which constantly crops up in the subsequent writings of sociologists.

The concept of structure which appears in structuralist writings is quite different from this—and, of course, in contrast to the fate of the notion in English-speaking sociology, has been much debated. To identify the differences, it is perhaps best to turn to the principal origin of structuralist thought in Saussure's linguistics, although somewhat confusingly Saussure did not employ the term "structure" but that of "system," a matter to which I shall return shortly. Saussure's thought turns upon a relation between moment and totality quite distinct from that involved in functionalist writings, a dialectical relation between presence and absence. The relation between a sentence or an utterance and a language is not like that between an organ of the body and the totality which is the organism. When I utter a sentence, or make sense of an utterance by somebody else, I draw upon an "absent corpus" of synthetic and semantic rules in order to do so. The syntagmatic relations between the words uttered exist in a temporal-spatial context, but the "structure properties" of the language, as characteristic of a community of language-speakers, do not. These properties have a "virtual existence" only.

I want to suggest a concept of structure in social theory which has affinities with this. I do not propose to abandon the notion that it is useful to conceive of social relations between individuals and collectivities—insofar as they are stably reproduced over time and space—as forming something like "patterns." But I wish to argue that this can most aptly be covered by the notion of "system," freeing that of "structure." In the subsequent structuralist literature where the term "system" appears, it is characteristically used as more or less synonymous with structure—or, as in Levi-Strauss, as one among other defining elements of structure. The concept of system here is largely a redundant one. But the same is true of functionalist writings. If one looks at the writings of the leading functionalist authors, it is readily apparent that they either tend to opt mainly for one term at the expense of the other or use the two interchangeably. This might initially appear odd, because there may seem to be a basis for sustaining a structure system distinction in functionalism. Employing the organic analogy, which is rarely far from the surface in most forms of functionalism, it might be supposed that the structure of society is like the anatomy of the organism; when the structure is working, we have a system. A system here is, as it were, a "functioning structure": structure plus function = system. If this equation is scrutinized more closely, however, it is apparent that the analogy does not hold for society. There is a sense in which the structure of a body can exist independently of its functioning. The anatomy of a body can be studied, its morphology described, even though it has ceased to function, to live. But this is not the case with society, with the patterning of social interaction reproduced across time and space. A society ceases to exist if it ceases to function. This is why even those functionalist authors who recognize some sort of distinction between structure and system tend in practice to collapse the two into one.

I propose to reserve the term "social system" to refer to reproduced patterns of social relations. There is a great deal that can be said about the notion of system in sociology. I do not think, for example, that we can rest content with the idea of system which usually appears in functionalist thought, which often equates it simply with homeostasis. But I shall not attempt to discuss such issues here, limiting myself to the concept of structure. The three basic notions I want to work with are the following:

STRUCTURE:	Recursively organized rules and resources. Structure only exists as "structural properties."
SYSTEM:	Reproduced relations between actors and collectivities, organized as regular social practices.
STRUCTURATION:	Conditions governing the continuity or transformation of structures, and therefore the reproduction of systems.

Social systems, in this scheme, are regarded as relations of interdependence, involving the situated activities of human subjects, and existing "syntagmatically" in the flow of time. According to the view I wish to develop (sketched in only a relatively cursory way here), social systems are not structures; they have structures or, more accurately, exhibit structural properties. Structures are, in a logical sense, properties of social systems or collectivities, not of the situated activities of subjects. Social systems only exist in and through structuration, as always and everywhere the outcome of the contingent acts of a multiplicity of human beings.

The connotation of "structure" that I am suggesting here is much closer to that employed by Levi-Strauss than it is to that which figures in functionalist sociologies. Levi-Strauss's approach is ambiguous in a certain sense, insofar as it is not clear whether he regards structure as relations between a set of inferred elements or oppositions, or as rules of transformation that produce equivalences across sets. It seems that a similar ambiguity crops up in mathematical notions of structure, where structure is usually thought of as a matrix of admissable transformations of a set: structure could be seen either as the matrix, or as the principles or rules of transformation. However that may be, I shall treat structure in social theory as concerning in its most basic sense the rules (and, as I shall elaborate upon later, the resources) which, in social reproduction, "bind" time and space, rather than the form of sets as such. Hence, "structure" as understood here is a generic term; structures can be identified as sets or matrices of rule-resource properties governing transformations.

An essential limitation of Levi-Strauss's use of structure (there are, I think, others) is that it has no notion of structuration, or at any rate a quite inadequate one. Levi-Strauss treats processes of structuration as combinatory forms produced by an external agent (the unconscious, in his sense of that concept). A theory of structuration, however, which is concerned with all types of social processes, although admitting the importance of the unconscious, must allocate a central role to discursive and practical consciousness—in the context of unintended consequences—in the reproduction of social practices. "Structural analysis" in the social sciences, in my sense, then, involves examining the structuration of social systems: A social system is a "structured totality" consisting of reproduced practices. Structural properties exist in time-space only as moments of the constitution of social systems. Nonetheless, we can analyze how "deeply layered" structures are in terms of the historical duration of the practices they recursively organize and the spatial "breadth" of those practices. The most deeply layered practices in this sense are *insti-*

tutions. To give an example: Some key structural relations instantiated in the capitalist economic system can be represented as the following set of transformations:

       private property → money → capital → labor contract → profit

The movement from left to right represents a series of transformations crucial to the production and reproduction of a capitalistic economy. Money, the medium of "pure exchange value," provides for the convertibility of property rights into capital. The universalization of money capital in turn is the condition of the commodification of labor power, and hence to the nature of the labor contract in capitalist production. The existence of property/money as capital in turn provides for the convertibility of capital into profit via the extraction of surplus value.

The Duality of Structure

In the first section of this chapter I posed as my third question: How should we understand the relation between action and structure? I argued that social theory and philosophy have suffered from a persistent dualism between those approaches which have developed concepts of action, which have tended in some sense to give primacy to the "subject," and those which have concentrated upon institutions and history, which have tended to give primacy to the "object," or society. According to the theory of structuration I am proposing in this chapter, this dualism should cede to recognition of a *duality* that is implicated in all social reproduction, the *duality of structure.* By the duality of structure I refer to the essentially recursive character of social life. The structural properties of social systems are both medium and outcome of the practices that constitute those systems.

The best way to illustrate this is by reverting to the Saussurian conception of the production of an utterance. When I utter a sentence, I draw upon various synthetic rules (sedimented in my practical consciousness of the language) in order to do so. These structural features of the language are the medium whereby I generate the utterance. But in producing a syntactically correct utterance, I simultaneously contribute to the reproduction of the language as a whole. This view rejects the identification of structure with constraint: structure is both enabling and constraining. The most revolutionary forms of social change, like the most fixed forms of social reproduction, in this conception, involve structuration. There is therefore no place for a notion of destructuration, such as is proposed by Gurvitch, among others. The idea of destructuration is required only if we continue to counterpose structure and freedom—

which, in my opinion, both Gurvitch and Sartre do. Although Sartre has been strongly influenced by Heidegger, he does not seem to have incorporated one of the most basic elements of the latter's *Being and Time* into his own work. The counterposition of past and present in Sartre is what I seek to escape from here. For Sartre, the past is "given and necessary," while the present is a realm of free, spontaneous creation.

To summarize: The differences that constitute structures, and that are constituted structurally, relate part to whole in the sense in which the utterance of a grammatical sentence presupposes an absent corpus of syntactical rules that constitute the language as a totality. The importance of this relation between moment and totality for social theory can hardly be exaggerated, involving as it does a dialectic of presence and absence which ties the most minor or trivial forms of social action to structural properties of the overall society, and to the coalescence of institutions over long stretches of historical time.

In case my overall emphases are not fully clear, let me at this point bring the discussion back to the knowledgeability of social actors. I intend it to be a major emphasis of the ideas developed here that institutions do not just work "behind the backs" of the social actors who produce and reproduce them. Every competent member of every society knows (in the sense of both discursive and practical consciousness) a great deal about the institutions of that society. Such knowledge is not *incidental* to the operation of society, but is necessarily involved in it. A common tendency of many otherwise divergent schools of sociological thought—but especially functionalism—is to adopt the methodological tactic of beginning their analyses by discounting agents' reasons for their action, in order to discover the "real" stimuli to their activity, of which they are ignorant. Such a stance is not only defective from the point of view of social theory, it has strongly defined and potentially offensive political implications. It implies a *derogation of the lay actor*. From this flow various important considerations—which again I do not have space to discuss here—about the status of social sciences as critical theory, and as implicated in practical social reform.

In conclusion, I want briefly to revert to a consideration I deferred: the notion that the structural properties of social systems can be regarded as involving rules and "resources." By referring to resources, I mean to stress the centrality of *power* to social theory. This helps us to return to the theme by means of which I introduced the chapter—the discrete treatments of common problems by philosophers and sociologists. I should want to maintain that the concept of action is logically linked to that of power, if the latter term is interpreted in a broad sense as the capability of achieving outcomes. Philosophers have talked about this under the headings of "powers" or the "can" of human activity, but so far as I know they have not tried to connect these notions to concepts of power developed in social and political theory.

Philosophical discussions of powers are concerned with the capabilities of individual subjects. Many analyses of power in the social sciences are also "subjectivist" in the sense that they seek to define power as the capacity of an acting subject to intervene in the course of events in the world so as to influence or alter those events. I would include Weber's famous definition of power in this category, although the "events" involved are the acts of others. Power is the capability of an individual to secure his or her own ends even against the will of others. Quite distinct from this idea of power are those concepts, such as that formulated by Parsons, which see power above all as a phenomenon of the collectivity. What we see here, I think, is a dualism comparable to and related to the dualism of action and structure noted earlier. The same methodological tactic is appropriate: We should replace this dualism with a conception of duality, acknowledging and connecting each of these two aspects of power. This I try to do by means of the notion of resources. Resources are drawn upon by actors in the production of interaction, but are constituted as structures of domination. Resources are the media whereby power is employed in the routine course of social action, but they are at the same time structural elements of social systems, reconstituted in social interaction. Social systems are constituted as regularized practices, reproduced across time and space. Power in social systems can thus be treated as involving reproduced relations of *autonomy and dependence* in social interaction.

This leads me to one final concept that I want to talk about briefly, a concept that is very important in the scheme of social theory I am trying to develop. This is the notion of what I call the *dialectic of control* in social systems. It is one of the main areas in which the theorem that social actors know, and must know (in practical and discursive consciousness) a great deal about the circumstances of their action, can be most readily related to questions of power and domination. By the dialectic of control I mean the capability of the weak, in the regularized relations of autonomy and dependence that constitute social systems, to turn their weakness against the powerful. My argument is that, just as action is intrinsically related to power, so the dialectic of control is built into the very nature of social systems. An agent who does not participate in the dialectic of control in a minimal fashion ceases to be an agent. All relations of autonomy and dependence are reciprocal. However wide the asymmetrical distribution of resources involved, all power relations express autonomy and dependence "in both directions." Only a person who is kept totally confined and controlled—perhaps someone in a strait-jacket—does not participate in the dialectic of control. But such a person is then no longer an agent.

I do not want to make the dialectic of control into a metaphysical principle, a contemporary variant of Hegel's master-slave dialectic. The dialectic of control is simply an intrinsic feature of regularized relations of power within social systems. As such, it provides a conceptual mode of investigating the conditions under which social systems remain stable or are transformed "from below." We may perhaps regard the early origins of the labor movement as a type case of the operation of the dialectic of control. The "free" labor contract introduced with the advent of capitalism, as Marx showed in his critique of classical political economy, served to consolidate the power of employers over workers. But the workers succeeded in turning this position of disadvantage into a new resource of their own through the collective withdrawal of labor, and from this the labor movement was born.

CHAPTER 10

The Concept of Social Realty

D. W. HAMLYN

There may be various reasons for prefixing the word "reality" with a qualifier such as "social," "physical," or "psychological." To speak of physical reality is normally to make reference to that part of reality which is determinable by physics (and some thinkers of course will maintain that that is all of it). It would be hard to give the same kind of connotation to "psychological reality," although it is not perhaps entirely out of the question. On the other hand, to speak of, say, some feeling as "psychologically real" may be to say simply that the feeling has a genuine role or part to play within an intelligible psyche. The phenomenon is real enough, one might say, as far as a given psyche goes. One might, I suppose, refer to certain social institutions as "socially real" for analogous reasons: they play a genuine role among and for those for whom they exist. But to speak in this way is not to commit oneself to any full-blooded concept of a social reality. There is a physical reality; there is no such thing, I suggest, as a social reality. Why is that?

The concept of reality is a tricky one. I shall not try to approach it directly, though I hope that things about it will emerge along the way. If we feel confident that it is right to speak of a physical reality, it is presumably because we think that at least most of the world in which we find ourselves is specifiable and determinable in physical terms. I say "most" because it does not really matter for our purposes whether that represents an all-pervasive ideology or not. On the other hand, no one really believes that the world in which we find ourselves is even for the most part specifiable or determinable in psychological terms. Certain things may be psychologically real to us, but there is not a psychological reality

189

in the way that there is a physical reality. Not enough of the world in which we find ourselves is so specifiable, despite the fact that the world contains so many other people. It happens to be the case that most of those people find themselves in societies, and many things about them are likely to be dependent on that fact, but just as we do not generally think of a psychological reality, so we do not think *in those terms* of a social reality.

Or do we? If it were thought that reality is in a genuine and firm sense a social construction and nothing more than that, there might be a case for saying that reality is in a genuine sense social—and hence that there is a social reality. That way of thinking is, for example, espoused in the now classic work on the sociology of knowledge by P. L. Berger and T. Luckmann, *The Social Construction of Reality*. They certainly use the term "social reality" (e.g., p. 29), but that is because they think of reality as a social construction. Berger and Luckmann's thinking, one might say, is by Alfred Schutz out of George Herbert Mead. Philosophically, I suggest that it is a somewhat unholy liaison (between phenomenology and social behaviorism), and given that, it is not surprising if its offspring is monstrous, as I think it indeed is. That it is monstrous is shown by the fact that there is no genuine sense in which reality is constructed, let alone socially constructed.[1]

Schutz speaks of the problem, or at any rate, one of the problems of the sociology of knowledge as that of the determination of the social distribution of knowledge (and Berger and Luckmann speak in the same way). What could be meant by the problem of the social distribution of knowledge? There are obvious sociological questions about why certain classes of people have certain kinds of beliefs, but belief is not knowledge. There are also obvious sociological questions about why certain kinds of knowledge are restricted to certain classes of people, where it is not sufficient simply to say that those people do not know whatever it is because they have not learned it or because they do not have the abilities requisite for learning it. But the problem of the distribution of knowledge in that sense is not the same as the problem of how and why knowledge exists at all. Even if the distribution of knowledge is, in part at least, a social product in some sense, it does not follow that knowledge itself is a social product in the same sense. Nor does it follow that that of which we have knowledge—reality itself—is in any illuminating sense a social construction.

What I wish to do is first to set out the senses, if any, in which knowledge of reality is a social matter. I shall then try to indicate that the "monstrous offspring" to which I referred above has nothing to do with any of those senses, while at the same time trying to diagnose the reasons which lead some people to think that it has. I want finally to try to say something about the role of consciousness in connection with knowledge of reality, and how this too impinges upon and is impinged upon by the social scene.

The Social Nature of Knowledge

There is a boring sense in which knowledge, including knowledge of reality, need not be social. I may know things that you do not, and vice versa. There must be a great many facts which only one person knows, although many of them will be extremely trivial—facts about one's everyday life, for example, and personal circumstances. It is, however, an essential feature of knowledge that it must be sharable in principle. There is nothing that someone else could not know in principle, whether or not they could know it in fact. The reason for this is that truth itself, that which makes fact fact, cannot be subjective, private, or merely personal. There may be personal truths in the sense that only one person knows them in fact, or that they constitute truths about that person alone, but there cannot be a truth which is private in the more fundamental sense that no one else could (logically) know it. Objectivity itself—the possibility of truth—presupposes intersubjectivity, or does so at least in the sense that truth is in principle sharable, as are also the methods for attaining and assessing truth.

To leave matters there, however, would give no adequate sense of the relation between the concepts of knowledge and reality. All that what I have said amounts to is that, whatever knowledge is of, then, given that the content of that knowledge constitutes truth, it must in principle be accessible to others apart from any individual knower. That, however, is consistent with the suggestion that agreement when it comes might be a happy accident, a preestablished harmony, or something of that kind. There is, however, a clear relationship between the concept of reality and the concept of a method or methods of gaining knowledge of it and of gaining access to it. What conception of reality should we have if that were not so? It is not as if the concept of reality constitutes, so to speak, a given, and that the question remains open whether there are any ways of access to it and if so, which. We should have no concept of reality were we not the sort of creatures we are, with senses and other capacities for the attainment of truth.

It is important not to confuse that remark with the claim that all that is meant by "reality" is to be found in the means of attaining whatever we call by that name. The latter claim would constitute a verificationism which is by no means implied by the assertion that we should have no concept of reality did we not have those means. The conditions under which we should have a given concept are not to be confused with the sense to be given to that concept. For our purposes, this point will be of increased importance when we come to the social aspects of the matter. For if it is true that we should have no concept of reality were we not social creatures (and that is not something that I have yet argued for), it does not by any means follow that the sense of the concept of reality is itself to be specified in social terms; it does not follow, that is, that reality is a social reality, or at least not in any illuminating sense.

All that I have said so far about the social aspects of knowledge and reality is that truth and objectivity (which are essential characteristics of knowledge) must be in principle sharable. That does not entail in any way that the concepts of knowledge and reality are dependent either for their existence or their sense on social conditions. Just as, to repeat what I said earlier, the agreement on what reality consists of, when it comes, might, if that were all there was to it, be a happy accident, so the sharability in principle of truth and objectivity is consistent with a situation where no social conditions in any genuine sense exist. An example of such a situation might be one in which individuals existed from the beginning and grew both physically and cognitively in isolation from each other, without even the possibility of relations with each other. Even in such a situation, truth would be sharable *in principle,* though not in fact. There are good reasons, however, for thinking that the supposition that such a situation is possible is absurd. I do not have in mind the physiological objections to the suggestion that a human baby could not survive, let alone grow up under such conditions. (There have been reported cases of "wolf-boys," after all, and whatever one thinks of that, the science fiction example of a child left alone with physiological needs serviced by machines does not seem obviously incoherent.) The real problem lies in whether cognitive growth of any kind would be possible in such circumstances—whether, that is, anything deserving the name of knowledge and understanding could ever begin.

There are, I believe, good reasons for supposing that it could not, reasons which I have set out and discussed elsewhere (Hamlyn, 1978a, chaps. 6 & 7).[2] The central and crucial argument can be set out in abstract form as follows:

(1) To know something is to know it as true. (Or, to avoid the implication and possible objection that this limits knowledge to language users, which I do not believe to be the case, to have knowledge of whatever kind is to know something as correct or right.)

(2) To know something as true, correct, or right presupposes knowing what it is for something to be true, correct, or right. (Or, in other words, knowledge of anything presupposes possession of the concepts of truth, correctness, or the like to some degree or another; and that this admits of degrees is very important.)

(3) The possession of the concepts of truth, correctness, and the like involves in effect an appreciation of the force of a norm; it involves seeing that there are or can be standards of correctness and the like. That is possible only in creatures who have been brought to see the force of a norm, by being brought to see certain ways of doing or thinking as right and others wrong.

(4) To be brought to see certain ways of doing or thinking as right or wrong implies something like correction by others, and more importantly, the seeing of this as correction.

(5) To see something as correction implies seeing the source of whatever is done as a corrector, and thus as something with desires, interests, and the like. This in turn implies standing in something like personal relations to that, and thus in that sense having something of a social existence. (This would be true even if the correction were carried out by proxy, e.g., by a suitably programmed machine; the corrections would have to be seen as motivated by appropriate desires.)

It is worth noting that this argument makes no appeal to the nature of human beings or to any other kind of creature; it turns solely on what is involved in the concepts in question. It would thus have application to any kind of creature to which the concepts in question could also be applied; and conversely, the concepts in question would be applicable to a given kind of creature only if the presuppositions spelled out in the argument had a place in that connection.

The social existence to which the argument leads is such that those that share in it must have enough in common to give a requisite sense to the concepts and forms of understanding that emerge from it (which is one thing, as I take it, that Wittgenstein was getting at in referring to the necessity of agreement in forms of life and to the idea that such forms of life constitute in some sense a "given"). Without it there could be no appreciation of the difference between correct and incorrect, true and false, and a fortiori reality and appearance, no understanding of such concepts at all. It may be thought that I have slipped in the concepts of appearance and reality rather easily here. But once given the idea that those sharing the social existence in question are conscious beings, there immediately follows the question which of the objects of their consciousness constitute (or are represented as) things as they are, and which do not. That question is equivalent to one about the distinction between reality and appearance. What is real and what is not has to be learned, but the way in which such a distinction gets applied through learning is dependent upon, although it may go along with, an appreciation of the conceptual distinction in general.

It follows from all this that we should have no conception of reality if we were not both conscious and social creatures, and equally, our consciousness of reality goes along with our consciousness of other people and is inseparable from it. It is in that sense, but not that sense alone, that the concept of reality is a social concept. It is that, however, in a more fundamental way than that in which, by the same token, all concepts are social. Any conceptual form of understanding presupposes the social existence of which I have spoken, since to have a conceptual form of understanding is to have knowledge—a knowledge of what it is for something to be X. It is for that very reason subject to the conditions which I have spelled out. But if such a form of understanding is to be more than merely abstract (and how could it be just that under the conditions mentioned?) it must involve an application to objects as instances. (Thus a full understanding of the concept X must involve not only what is formally involved in being an X, but also what sort of things actually count as Xs.) This application to instances is possible only within a conception of reality. Hence, the concept of reality is fundamental to conceptual understanding in general.

I have thus distinguished two senses in which knowledge of reality can be said to be a social matter. The first is the more obvious one—that anything we can be said to know must be sharable in principle if not in fact. But the second, on which I have spent considerably more time, is that only a social being can be said to have knowledge in general and knowledge of reality in particular. None of this, however, provides any legitimate sense in which reality itself can be said to be social. It might be thought, however, that there is a thin line between what I have said about the social presuppositions of the possibility of knowledge of reality and the suggestion that the conception of reality that we have is a social construction. It may be worthwhile, therefore, to say a little more about that.

In the argument that I spelled out earlier, each stage involves the invocation of some epistemic item—knowing, seeing as, or appreciating something. Hence, although I claimed that appreciating the force of a norm presupposes correction by others, it remains true that I conceived that as functioning only in the context of a further item of seeing as: seeing others as correctors. Thus the whole structure remains within the area of the epistemic and merely brings out the way in which some of it must also be social. There is no implication in this that anything is constructed by the individual, since whether he at any point has knowledge is not something that is up to him. But it might be said that whether or not anything is constructed by the individual is not in point; the question is whether anything is a *social* construction. In a sense, however, the same considerations still apply to that issue.

If something is to be a social construction, there must be a sense in which social factors, such as interpersonal agreement or convention, are a sufficient condition of its existence. In that sense various social institutions, such as perhaps the law or the state, are social constructions. It is a sufficient condition of their existence that people should agree to bring them into existence. That is not the case with knowledge or the concept of reality, let alone reality itself. Reality indeed puts a limit upon what can be constructed. The question of how great a limit that is is equivalent to the ancient question which exercised the 5th-century B.C. Greeks: How much is to be attributed to nature and how much to convention? (The relativism that is to be found in the views of many sociologists of knowledge is in many ways similar to that of Protagoras.)

Nevertheless, it might be argued, even granted that the concept of reality is a limiting concept, in that it brings with it the idea of a limit upon what is constructible by human beings, whether individually or socially (just as the concept of a thing-in-itself is a limiting concept for transcendental idealism, such as that of Kant), the content of that reality might nevertheless be a human construction. (Kant's so-called "Copernican revolution" is sometimes presented in that way, as the view that what we ordinarily think of as reality is in fact a product of the human mind, though subject to whatever constraint is imposed by things-in-themselves, the true reality, the concept of which is, however, a limiting one only.) There can be no logical objection to that as a possibility; it is just that there is no good reason to think it true. Nothing in the considerations that I have so far brought forward gives any warrant for thinking it so, since I have adduced social considerations only as necessary conditions for a conception of reality. To go beyond that we should need additional considerations.

The same moral is to be extracted from the thought of Wittgenstein, which some sociologists and philosophers have seen as involving a constructivism, or conventionalism, which might make him an ally in their cause. It is true that Wittgenstein puts great weight on agreement in judgments as a condition of the possibility of language being a means of communication, and therefore of publicity and objectivity generally. Such agreement in judgments amounts to agreements in forms of life, and these constitute in some sense a "given." Forms of life therefore comprise the limit within which and against which other forms of agreement are to be seen. But, it might be said, we are presented here only with a limiting concept. Whatever forms of life are (and this is not the place for an attempt to elucidate that notion), they determine little or nothing about the content of our judgments about the world. To appeal to them is simply to presuppose that there is an ultimate limit to human convention, but it is to say nothing about the nature of that limit as far as it affects the content of those judgments. To so interpret Wittgenstein would be to make of him a social transcendental idealist, for whom forms of life and agreement in them perform the same role as things-in-themselves play for Kant. Within the limits imposed by forms of life, there would still be a vast room for the part played by convention in determining the content of our judgments about the world.

I do not think that this would be a correct interpretation of Wittgenstein, since he does not say that all judgments or judgments in general depend on agreement, only that there has to be agreement in judgments *if* the possibility of common, public, objective understanding is to exist. The places at which such agreement in judgments has to exist may be determined by the sort of creatures we are, with common natures, sensibilities, and intellectual powers, as well as common needs, desires, and feelings to some extent, if not in every detail. None of these factors by itself determines what is real and objective. To suppose otherwise is to make the same mistake as supposing that whether or not a thing is seen as having a certain color, and if so, which, is dependent on our having a certain visual equipment (so that we can imagine creatures for whom there are no colors or very different systems of color), and that it thereby follows that it is not an objective matter whether things have colors, and if so, which. It is perfectly true that what is so and not so is something that can be determined only within a concept of reality, and furthermore, that that conception of reality may depend upon factors that have to do with us as human beings. But it does not follow from that that reality itself is what we make it or a purely subjective or conventional matter. To reach that conclusion we need additional arguments, and for a consideration of some instances of these, I shall now turn to my second main topic and look at the positions of Mead and Schutz, which, as I said earlier, have much to do with at least one prominent version of the sociology of knowledge and thereby with an emphasis on the concept of social reality.

Mead and Schutz

It may seem very odd that I put these two thinkers together, the first, one who called himself a social behaviorist, the second, one who was a phenomenologist, acknowledging a considerable debt to Husserl, for whom therefore the notion of consciousness has to play a very considerable role.[3] On the face of it the two thinkers belong to very different philosophical traditions, acknowledged or unacknowledged, and some good reason is therefore required for putting them together, apart from the fact or apparent fact that Berger and Luckmann acknowledge their influences. I think, however, that despite the obvious, but perhaps more superficial, differences between them, they do have something in common and that their joint influence is not just accidental.

Neither Mead nor Schutz had as his primary concern the setting out of a general epistemology which would provide an account, and perhaps justification, of our claims to knowledge of the world in general. They were both primarily interested in what Schutz called the "social world," i.e., the interrelationships of people and the way in which those interrelationships determine our understanding of others and of ourselves. They both saw the key to that understanding in human behavior or action. So for Schutz, for example, it is from lived action that we derive our understanding of others and through them of ourselves. So it is for Mead too, perhaps in an even more explicit way, since for Mead the self is a construction out of the attitudes of others, a social thing, so that there is no question of an understanding of ourselves except through our understanding of others and our reflection in them.[4]

What are crucial for Mead, the basic notions in this scheme, so to speak, are actions and reactions in relation to others. That is what makes him in a real sense a behaviorist. Consciousness, whatever it is, has no reality except in that context, so that while Mead is not a behaviorist in a Watsonian sense (he did not want to deny the existence of consciousness), he was so in putting a fundamental emphasis on behavior, without which consciousness would have, as far as psychology is concerned, no being. The content of that consciousness is provided by the way in which one's own behavior interacts with behavior on the part of others. If that is so, so it must be too for knowledge and consciousness of things in general. The sense which we attach to the world in general must come about via interactions with others; it is the world of a common experience so determined. In a footnote to *Mind, Self and Society* (p. xix, n. 9), Charles W. Morris, the editor, says that "it is clear that this conception challenges the individualistic basis of the traditionally conceived epistemology." And so it does, in a way, for there would be no knowledge proper without a publicity brought about through interaction between people.

That, however, is, as we have already seen, capable of more than one interpretation, and it is clear that Mead is committed to more than the view that it is a necessary condition of our being said to have knowledge and a concept of reality that we stand in relation to others. He is committed to the view that the sense which we attach to that reality and perhaps to the notion of reality itself is determined by interactions with others. It does not seem to me that it is very clear what that means, since unless the interaction with others is to be construed at the level of brute reaction or reflex (and how could that provide a sense of anything for the person so reacting, at least by itself?) one would have thought that the interaction already presupposes some sense of a world independent of oneself. Indeed, I am inclined to think that there is a muddle in this whole way of thought, to the extent that there is an attempt to reduce our understanding of things to the way in which they impinge on us, *via* the way in which different members of the "us" impinge on one another. The conception challenges the individualistic basis of traditionally conceived epistemology, not by saying that we cannot give sense to the kind of traditional epistemological problem initiated by Descartes without presupposing the "we" that that epistemological framework finds problematic (which, as a challenge, takes the form of a reductio ad absurdum), but by attempting to show how all that we have in mind in speaking of a public, objective world can be built up from interactions between persons. Such a view, it is true, does rule out the idea of one person building up a conception of a world by oneself, but it provides no explanation of how the "building up" can take place at all. I have spoken of interaction between persons as its foundation, but strictly speaking there are no persons at this stage, no "we," no "us." All that, too, has to be constructed, but how and by whom?

The idea that certain things can, and perhaps only in this way, gain a sense in relation to the part that they play in our actions and interactions is a perfectly sensible idea *once given that* we have a general understanding of the world and our place in it. But it cannot provide a foundation for that very understanding, for in order to see things as having this kind of sense, we should have to have that understanding already. In effect, Mead is charting a route to an understanding of the world—"I-we-them" (where "them" refers to everything else)—and it is the interposition of that "we" that constitutes the challenge to the "individualistic basis of traditionally conceived epistemology." But it is a challenge which misfires if, as far as understanding is concerned, the "I" already presupposes that "we"—and that is the implication, in effect, of what I set out in the previous section, and is something that we ought to learn from Wittgenstein (and perhaps, though I am less sure of this, from Merleau-Ponty).

Although Schutz is far from being a behaviorist, and qua phenomenologist bases himself firmly on the idea of consciousness, his general conception of what he is doing is not very far from that of Mead. Indeed, in one passage in *The Phenomenology of the Social World,* Schutz applauds Scheler, saying that he is right when he says that the experience of the We in the world of immediate social reality is the basis of the Ego's experience of the world in general (p. 165), although that is something that he does not elaborate there. The use of the phrase "social reality" in that context is indicative. If our experience of the world in general has to have a basis in the experience of relations with others, that world of others might well be said to have a reality in a more profound sense than the rest of the world. There is no good reason for thinking that it does have this kind of basis in the way that Schutz supposes.

In a way, the cardinal idea that Shutz derives from phenomenology is that our consciousness of many aspects of the world is one that relates them to our lives—it constitutes a lived experience or consciousness. It is a familiar idea among phenomenologists; indeed, one notion that is common among phenomenologists is that the way in which we conceive of the world is to be given sense in terms of lived experiences, in terms of the way in which that conception is, so to speak, cashed in our lives. But for Schutz this means that it is to be cashed in terms of a common-sense understanding of our own actions and behavior as they appear to our consciousness. The consciousness of others, in which the "social world" is based, depends on our ability to see through the behavioral and other bodily manifestations of others into their consciousness, which works on similar principles and simultaneously with that of others. Through this again, we can see into the past social world which is the subject matter of history. Schutz (1972, p. 106) says, "If I look at my whole stock of knowledge of your lived experience, and ask about the structure of this knowledge, one thing becomes clear: *This is that everything I know about your conscious life is really based on my knowledge of my own lived experiences.*" This is, I think, not so much a claim that our knowledge of other minds is based upon analogy with knowledge of our own, nor that we are justified in assuming the existence of other minds because of an analogy between our own expressed mental states and the expression that we see in others (something that has been much discussed by philosophers), but that, given that we do have knowledge of others, the sense that we attach to the consciousness of others is based on the sense that we have of our own consciousness.

That view, however, assumes that we *can* have a sense of what is available to our own consciousness without and prior to any contact with others. It therefore goes against the kind of considerations that I reviewed in the previous section. Hindess (1977, p. 67) speaks of the true foundation of Schutz's thought as "the unexamined basic project of reducing the world of objective mind to the behavior of individuals," something that Shutz derived approvingly from Weber. But there is really more to it than that, as Schutz's criticisms of Weber indicate, and as Hindess also admits. For the reduction is in terms of the sense that individuals attach to their own actions, and this is the primary notion in the account offered. Through this it is supposed that we can attach sense to the behavior of others, they being centers of consciousness just as we are, and occupying a common world. It is this last way of thinking that underpins the talk of a social world and social reality (although I am not saying that the notion of a social reality always receives just that underpinning). In fact, the so-called social world is in fact the most immediate point of application outside of ourselves of the understanding that we have of our own behavior through "lived experience." If the primary form of understanding is that which we have of our lived experiences, the only obvious application for that same understanding is the lived experiences of others *via* their expression in ways akin to that which our own behavior constitutes. Our understanding of the rest of the world must be derivative, and so dependent on what is social. Thus there is, it is supposed, a genuine sense to the notion of social reality, which makes that social reality more than the relatively small part of reality which has to do with social matters, more than the reality about what is social.

Thus, in Schutz too there is the progression of "I-we-them" (where "them" has the same sense as before). As opposed to Mead, there is perhaps a greater emphasis on the "I," for in Mead the "I" plays a rather shadowy role, as opposed to the "me," which is a social construction like everything else. But in both cases, the "I" has to be there at the beginning, not simply, as with Kant, as a presupposed correlate of a world of objects as a precondition of the possibility of objective experience, but as the possessor of that private, personal point of view on which knowledge of everything else, indeed the very conception of an everything else, depends and from which it is derived. If there is a further difference between the two thinkers it is, as indeed might be expected, in the role that they attach to consciousness itself. For Schutz it is fundamental; for Mead it is, as befits a behaviorist, subsidiary to behavior itself. Or, as one might put it, for Schutz behavior's role is to make the experience that consciousness provides "lived," to give it that "intentional" character (where "intentional" has the sense that it has for phenomenology as concerned with directedness towards an object or objects of a certain kind). For Mead behavior has a much more important role in his thinking.

"Psychology," he says (1934, pp. 40-41), "is not something that deals with consciousness; psychology deals with the experience of the individual in relation to the conditions under which the experience goes on. It is social psychology where the conditions are social ones. It is behavioristic where the approach to experience is made through conduct."

His approach to consciousness is through a modified parallelism; experiences or consciousness go along with the conditions which make them possible, but the main concern for Mead is those conditions, not the experiences or consciousness itself. Hence, although he sometimes appeals to the importance of attention, he is not concerned with the "intentional" character of consciousness; he simply acknowledges its existence without suggesting that it need be of concern for him. There is no recognition, as there is with Schutz, that action itself involves, through the intention with which it is or may be performed, some reference to consciousness. I shall in my next section say more about these attitudes toward the notion of consciousness before I return finally to the notion of social reality. It may be thought, however, that I have somewhat softened my attitude to what I earlier described as the "monstrous offspring" of the liaison between Mead and Schutz. That is not so. I think that the account that they offer of the relation between social considerations and knowledge and understanding of reality is seriously wrong, for reasons that I have indicated. For them, social considerations as part of the progression from "I" to "them" constitute far more than the necessary conditions for the possibility of knowledge that I spelled out earlier. But their main concern remains that of underpinning a science of society, in explaining how it is possible. The claim that reality as such is social remains at best muted. It is the full-blooded version of that in those whom they have influenced, such as Berger and Luckmann, that is "monstrous."

Consciousness

For one who like Mead puts all the emphasis on the physical or behavioral conditions under which experience goes on (provided that "behavioral" refers to bodily manifestations only), it may seem a natural question why consciousness exists at all. It is a natural question too for most modern forms of materialism, and it is sometimes suggested that consciousness is a notion that we shall live to do without and that a fully spelled out functionalism can take its place. Such views strike me as incredible. Mere expressions of incredulity, however, are not enough. The rejection of them must go by way of an attempt to show that what is essential to an understanding of human beings is lost when reference to consciousness is omitted. I can do little enough of that here. I shall content myself with trying to show that as far as concerns our present general concern—reality and knowledge of it—a notion of consciousness is required that lies somewhere between the two extremes provided in rough form by Schutz and Mead. That is to say that we need something less than the notion of a consciousness replete with a content as rich as that involved in an awareness of one's lived experiences, but something more than the mere accompaniment to behavior that Mead presupposes.

This point is not unconnected with the point that I have made before about not construing the story about conventions, social agreement, and social interactions as providing sufficient conditions for having a concept of reality, so that reality might be conceived as a construct from such matters. It is not unconnected with that, since if such a story is to have even the beginnings of plausibility, those who are a party to it must be conscious in some way. The Schutz story makes them conscious of aspects of their lives and actions at the very beginning; the Mead story, if taken seriously, implies that a consciousness of all that emerges only out of previous interactions with others, for self-consciousness, given Mead's view of the self, can only be a consciousness of the kind of interaction one has with others. Hence, on the Mead view consciousness plays no essential role until late on in the proceedings. What sort of interactions with others are these, however, if they involve no essential consciousness of what is involved on the part of those concerned? Does one need to go to the other extreme, however, and build in an elaborate form of consciousness of action and interaction at the very beginning, à la Schutz?

The schema that I presented in the section on the social nature of knowledge argued for the view that a condition (i.e., a necessary condition) of knowing anything and thereby having any sort of concept of reality is that one should stand in relation to others and thereby have some sort of knowledge of others. That is unobjectionable, provided that it is accepted that one can never know one thing and that any knowledge will be complex to the extent that whatever else he knows, the knower must know something of other people. I also said, however, that knowledge is a matter of degree, and it therefore follows that the knowledge of others of which I have spoken could be minimal. To the extent that it is knowledge proper, involving knowledge of the object as such and such, it must involve bringing the object in question under that form of knowledge which we call having a concept; it must thus involve more than a mere consciousness of the object simply as an object—a formal awareness of it, without an awareness of it as a such and such. But the more complex form of awareness must surely presuppose the simpler, arising from it either through learning or through being brought to see the object as such and such by causal conditions, whichever is the more appropriate.

It follows that the most basic form of consciousness will be this awareness of an object (and by "object" I have in mind only the formal notion of an object, without implying any material kind). Whether it ever occurs just like that is neither here nor there, although I have argued elsewhere (Hamlyn, 1978a) that in the case of feelings it is logically possible that there should be what I have described as "feelings toward," relating to objects in such a way as to involve no beliefs about them, even if it is inconceivable that all our feelings should be like that. Such feelings would be, or would involve, such formal awareness of objects. But our normal forms of consciousness involve elaborations of that in two ways. First, there is the elaboration through concepts that I have already mentioned, and through the connections with other things that that mediates. Second, there is the elaboration, not of course unconnected with that mediated by concepts, provided by the circumstances of our life in which the consciousness comes about. The form of consciousness involved in action, for example, is quite different from that involved in the use of our senses, as has frequently been pointed out, if only because actions are in some sense initiated by us in a way that sense perceptions cannot be. This gives a different character to the consciousness involved, just because the context is different. In an analogous way, the forms of consciousness of objects mediated by different senses have a different character or "flavor" because of the differing circumstances of that mediation. These circumstances of course furnish differing possibilities for the further elaboration of the consciousness in the ways that I mentioned earlier.

It remains true that this elaboration presupposes the basic, formal awareness of which I have spoken. The elaboration itself will involve interaction with objects (Hamlyn, 1978c) in causal ways, this being itself a condition for learning ever getting a foothold. But learning, presupposing as it does knowledge, has as a further condition the kind of interaction with other people that enables an understanding of the notion of truth or its like to emerge. These forms of interaction, however, rely on the fact that there is a world of varying aspects which constitutes the individual's environment. While only learning can bring about the possession of a conception of what reality is, and while certain aspects of the ways in which that conception becomes filled in for each of us depend upon the sort of creatures that we are and the kind of life that we lead, as well as upon the local circumstances in which we find ourselves, none of that gives any reason for supposing that reality is in any valid sense constructed by us. What reality is for us is something that we learn under these complex conditions, which involve a basic, minimal consciousness at one end and a peopled world at the other.

Nevertheless, consciousness does play an essential role in this process, and not just an incidental one, for unless even the basic form of consciousness were present there would be no room for speaking of knowledge, learning, or even a concept of reality at all. There would simply be causal interactions, and while some of those interactions might be with what are in fact people, there would be no reason for calling them *social* interactions proper, for these imply ways of seeing other people, ways that involve taking them, in however minimal a sense, *as* people. Without consciousness, none of this would be possible; and it becomes possible not because there is something creative in it, but because from it, through our interactions with a peopled world, learning takes place. We thus learn what reality is.

"Social Reality"

To one who has read Berger and Luckmann's *The Social Construction of Reality,* there may seem things in what I have said which are echoes of what they say, except of course that I have repudiated the idea of a construction of reality. They differentiate, for example, between primary and secondary socialization, the first coming to an end with the establishment of what Mead called the concept of the generalized other (Berger & Luckmann, 1967, p. 157). Berger and Luckmann think of knowledge as possible at this level, but merely that which is generally relevant, without reference to the differences brought about by social differences, where secondary socialization has its effect. I shall return to that point directly. Another point is their emphasis on the idea of "legitimation," which brings in the ideas of right and wrong, correct and incorrect, something I have also connected with social considerations. Given these echoes and similarities, why am I unrepentant about the "monstrous offspring"?

The idea of primary socialization gives no warrant for speaking of a "construction" of reality, whether social or not. It is merely that to learn about the world at all (for the conceptual reasons that I have noted), something of the character of primary socialization has to take place. Secondary socialization, however, is not just another step in the same direction. Differences in it clearly affect what Berger and Luckmann, following Schutz, call the distribution of knowledge, as long as that phrase is given a literal sense—some may know things that others do not—but they do not affect the very possibility of knowledge. Similar caveats are called for concerning legitimation. The ideas of right and wrong, correct and incorrect, are not extrinsic to the idea of knowledge; there is no knowledge where a sense of these things is lacking. Hence, legitimation cannot be construed as a process of elaboration or modification of preexisting knowledge.

One of the real troubles with Berger and Luckmann's thought, perhaps the central trouble, derives indeed from their conception of knowledge itself, since they use it in such a way as to cover a number of different ideas. When they speak of the distribution of knowledge, they do not have in mind simply what I mentioned earlier in speaking of the idea that some may know things that others do not. Instead, they think of all the different modes of consciousness that may be produced by social differences—different beliefs for example—as forms of *knowledge*. There is thus in this a straightforward confusion between knowledge and belief. Knowledge, one might say, is simply a legitimized belief, one approved of by the society in question. That, however, is not what legitimation came to as I interpreted it just now, for although the idea of right and wrong must be social in its origins, that does not mean that what is right is simply what society says is so. There is a difference, that is, between the conditions for the possession of the concept and what counts as a proper application of the concept. It is likely that in the process of knowledge acquisition, both things are learned or acquired together through the influences of an interaction with those of the immediate society in which the individual finds himself. That, however, does not mean that there is no distinction between them. Quite the contrary; it is vitally important to distinguish between them.

In their account of the end stage of the process of socialization, therefore, there is a confusion in their thought between knowledge proper and a variety of modes of consciousness, including belief (and by modes of consciousness I mean simply the various cognitive states that a conscious being can have because he is conscious). This enables them to think, like Mead, that knowledge is simply brought about by social interactions of varying kinds. At what might be thought of as the other end, there is the tendency to think, à la Schutz, of the form of consciousness on which social factors work as not essentially different from the socialized product. Socialization merely produces agreement in consciousness and legitimation (which can, in these circumstances, mean only uniformity). Putting together the two ways of thinking about consciousness simply produces the idea of a continually developing consciousness, where the process of development is really simply socialization. Given this, there is really no room for the idea of a reality which is independent of such a process of socialization and which indeed might provide a check on it. What is counted as real is merely what society brings about as an appropriate object of belief, and there is no distinction to be made between reality and what is so brought about as believed. Reality is social in that sense.

It is, however, nothing of the kind. A concept of reality, like all other concepts, may be social in the sense that the possession of it depends upon a social existence. Even here, however, it is necessary to be careful. The possession of the concept does not depend upon a social existence in the sense that society determines its character; it is merely that we should have no concept of reality, and no place for a distinction between reality and appearance, did we not have the sense of what it is for some things to be so and others not so. It is *that* which is made possible by social interaction. "Made possible" is, however, the right way of putting it. The social existence and interaction is a necessary condition of the possession of a concept of reality; it is not a sufficient condition. I said that this was so of a concept of reality, like all other concepts. But the concept of reality has a more fundamental place than other concepts have in this respect. To have a concept of X, to know what it is for something to be an X, involves knowing something at least about which things count as X and which do not. That, however, is not possible without a knowledge of what is so and not so, of what counts as a real instance of X and what does not. What is involved in our concept of reality is all that is involved in knowing this for a great variety of Xs.

In light of this, the best thing to say about the notion of social reality is that there is no such thing. That is certainly the least misleading thing to say. There is still, of course, that part of reality which consists of social relations and the like. There are indeed some things about society that are real and some that are not. But, as I said at the beginning, taking reality as a whole, that which is social does not characterize it sufficiently widely to justify the use of "social reality" as parallel with "physical reality." (Nor does it presuppose the same sort of contrast as "physical reality" does, to the extent that physical reality is contrasted with, say, mere appearances — illusions, hallucinations, and the like.) All in all, it would be better if the phrase "social reality" were dropped from the theoretical language of sociology.

Epilogue

It may be thought that my criticisms miss their target because of an overliteral interpretation of it on my part, in two particular ways.

First, whether or not Berger and Luckmann are interested at all in the idea of a construction of reality in general, it cannot be denied that they are mainly interested in that part of reality which has to do with human beings. That is evident too in the fact that Mead and Schutz, even on my own diagnosis, were primarily interested in what I have called the "I = we = they" transition, where all the terms denote persons. Have I not had to add that the "they" covers everything else but ourselves, and does that not involve a stretching of their intentions?

My answer is that while perhaps it may seem that it does involve that, it is unavoidable. For the idea of a social construction of the so-called social world—the "they"—is part and parcel of the idea of a social construction of reality in general. The social world is constructed, or thought to be, because everything is. The *epistemological* framework (and that is what I have primarily been concerned with) must include everything, whether or not those whom I have been criticizing are interested, as sociologists, in more than the part of it which is human. From the epistemological point of view, that distinction between the human and nonhuman is irrelevant. Hence, if any part of reality is "constructed" the whole of it is, and if the idea of a social construction of reality is one that is to be rejected, so must that of a social construction of that part of reality which is social.

The second point follows from this. It might be objected that I have made too much of the notion of "reality." Is there not a sense in which the social—the social world—must be a social construction? What else could the social be but a social construction?

That may seem a rhetorical question, but I believe that it is not. That the social is the social is of course a tautology. That it is the product of interrelationships between human beings, although in what may sometimes seem a recalcitrant world, is only a little less a tautology. But to say that it is a construction is to claim more; it is in effect to say, with the Greek Sophists, that it is entirely a product of *nomos* (convention), not *physis* (nature). Perhaps the most obvious example of a theory according to which something social is constructed is that to be found in a very literal interpretation of the social contract, according to which the state is constructed out of human agreements. There is little, if anything, of our more obvious social arrangements which is like that. On the other hand, convention may be very prevalent and much more may be due to that than is sometimes thought. It would be impossible, however, to accept that *everything* social is due to that. For one thing, an appeal to convention is an appeal to beliefs; to emphasize how much is due to convention is to emphasize how much is due to beliefs of a certain kind and with a certain sort of origin. There is, however, much in social relationships which is not cognitive in that sense, or need not be, but depends by contrast on natural feelings and reactions. Indeed, there would not be conventional responses to others if that were not so. There is no good sense in which all that is social is a construction. The division between nomos and physis is not the division between the social and nonsocial; the division falls across the social, as it does the human.

To repeat what I said earlier, if something is to be a social construction there must be a sense in which social factors, such as interpersonal agreement or convention, are a sufficient condition of its existence. Not everything in human, social relationships is such that social factors *in this sense* are a sufficient condition of its existence. Some of it depends on what is natural to human beings. Hence, not all the so-called "social world" is a social product through and through, and it is a matter of some importance for various reasons to determine how much of it is just that.

The notion of a social construction of reality, whether social or not, remains one that ought to be rejected. The offspring of the liaison between Schutz and Mead is unsatisfactory not just because of the disparateness of the parents (although that has no doubt accentuated the problem), but because the parents themselves share, despite first appearances, a common defect—a false epistemology.

Notes

1. It may not need to be pointed out, but perhaps it should be all the same, that my metaphor is taken from race-horse breeding! I use the term "monstrous" as it appears in the phrase "monstrous birth," to denote something that does not run true because it is derived from things that do not properly go together.

2. The matter is discussed further in "Exactly What is Social About the Origins of Understanding?" to appear in *The Individual and Social in Cognitive Development*, P. Light and G. Butterworth, (Eds.), Brighton: Harvester Press.

3. Hindess, 1977, claims that Schutz misunderstood Husserl, but I am not competent to pass judgment on that claim.

4. I shall have nothing else to say about that here; there are a few remarks on it in my "Self-knowledge," in Mischel, 1977.

References

Berger, P. L., & Luckmann, T. *The social construction of reality*. London: Allen Lane, 1967.

Hamlyn, D. W. The phenomena of love and hate. *Philosophy*, 1978, *53*, 5-20. (a)

Hamlyn, D. W. *Experience and the growth of understanding*. London: Routledge & Kegan Paul, 1978. (b)

Hamlyn, D. W. Perception and agency. *Monist*, 1978, *61*.

Hindess, B. *Philosophy and methodology in the social sciences*. Sussex: Harvester Press, 1977.

Kant, I. *Critique of pure reason*. N. Kemp Smith, trans. London: Macmillan, 1929.

Mead, G. H. *Mind, self and society*. Chicago: Chicago University Press, 1934.

Merleau-Ponty, M. *The phenomenology of perception*. C. Smith, trans. London: Routledge & Kegan Paul, 1962.

Mischel, T. (Ed.). *The self*. Oxford: Blackwell, 1977.

Schutz, A. *Collected papers I: The problem of social reality*. The Hague: Nijhoff, 1962.

Schutz, A. The phenomenology of the social world. G. Walsh & F. Lennert, trans. London: Heinemann, 1972.

Wittgenstein, L. Philosophical investigations. Oxford: Blackwell, 1953.

CHAPTER 11

On the Sociology of Mind

CHARLES W. SMITH

The thesis of this chapter is that many of the more troubling questions confronting the behavior/social sciences are due to a tendency to ignore, or at least minimize, the mind's social roots and the mental pluralism which these roots produce. By "mind" I mean the faculty and process of generating meanings and relating these meanings to each other;[1] by "troubling questions" I refer to among other things the intentionality of behavior, the role of consciousness, the social versus the individual component of human behavior, similarities and differences between social and physical behavior, as well as the very possibility of a social science.

The notion that mind has "roots," which in turn affect its structure, entails conceiving of mind as a specific life form which has attained its present state through a process of evolution. Though some may wish to reject this vision, I shall treat it for the purposes of this chapter as a given. So defined, mind is not a pure knowing machine; rather, it serves, consciously and/or unconsciously, human ends. It similarly has a material basis and a specific history.[2] Unfortunately, this vision of mind does not tell us what these ends are, nor does it explain how they are related to the general processes of generating and relating meanings. It similarly tells us little or nothing about its pluralistic structure or, for that matter, its social origins.

These questions can be approached in various ways: phenomenologically, anthropologically, developmentally, philosophically, and so forth. Whatever choice is made, however, the results are much the same; that is, one would end up with a very similar, if not identical, underlying structure. I cannot prove this within the scope of this chapter. I think I can demonstrate it, however, by quite arbitrarily presenting what I believe to be this underlying structure. I shall begin by elaborating upon the general concept of mind with which I started the chapter.

The concept of mind I am using is derived, as pointed out in Note 1, primarily from George Herbert Mead. According to Mead, the human mind is based upon man's ability to use meanings, i.e., meaningful symbols, which are themselves defined as significant signs, i.e., signs which signify in some way some other thing not inherent in the sign itself. To say that A is meaningful requires that A indicate or subsume some B which, in turn, requires some sort of nonrandom relationship between A and B. A meaningful world, consequently, is necessarily an ordered world. (I am here admittedly attempting to gloss over a very complex and important issue, namely the meaning of meaning. I emphasize here, with Mead, the gesture/response character of meaning because the focus of concern is the emergence of meanings rather than the character of meanings within a meaningful world per se, where signs may be said to *be* meaningful rather than to *have* meaning.)

The "miracle" of the human mind is that man was able to grasp these ordered relationships experientially. Man was able to do this, according to Mead, because of the coming together of three things: man's heavy reliance upon verbal gestures; his highly developed nervous system; and his social nature. Without reviewing Mead's argument in detail, these factors in combination enable us to see how certain things are significant to other things, i.e., they enable us to make the world meaningful. The specific meaning attributed to anything, however, does not reside in individuals, but in social collectivities.[3]

In slightly different form, this same general view—it could be called the social-intentional model of mind—has been forwarded by such otherwise different thinkers as Marx, Durkheim, Weber, Mannheim, Freud, Wittgenstein, and Collingwood, to name a few of its more influential proponents. They and others have made such a compelling case for this social-intentional view of mind that the burden of proof clearly lies upon anyone who would wish to deny either the social or intentional nature of mind.

If such a broad consensus exists—a consensus, I might add, which is capable of accounting for both mind's social nature and its ability to generate and relate meanings—it might legitimately be asked why we are still confronted with the sorts of questions presented in the first paragraph of this chapter. The answer, also noted in the first paragraph, is that there has been a failure to recognize within this social-intentional context mind's inherent pluralism.[4] Showing that mind is intentional and social is

no longer the problem; it is now necessary to show how different significance contexts generate different social-intentional mental modalities.[5]
Mind has evolved serving analytically distinct human/social needs and is,
consequently, inherently multilevel. In order to understand mind, it is
necessary to understand these different mental modalities.

What then are these different significance contexts and in what ways
do they generate different cognitive modalities? To answer the first part of
the question first, I would argue that there are four basic significance
contexts: (1) the organism/libido context; (2) the other people/social
relationship/power context; (3) the physical objects/spatial-temporal
world context; and (4) the symbolic meaning/ordered world context. To
answer the second part of the question, they generate different mental
styles or modalities by among other things: (a) having different foci of
concern; (b) employing meanings for different ends; (c) stressing different aspects or dimensions of things; (d) favoring different notions of
ordering and relating; (e) relying upon different sorts of conceptual criteria of "truth" and "falsity"; (f) entailing differing degrees of reflectivity;
and (g) assuming in very general terms differing views of "reality." To give
a quick and very partial summary of how contexts and modalities fit
together, we could say that in the first case mind functions primarily to
protect the organism qua organism; in the second to define and maintain
zones of jurisdiction; in the third to order, clarify, and make pragmatically
coherent the external physical world; and in the fourth to circumvent
symbolic contradictions and inconsistencies and impose clarity and
order.[6]

Mind is admittedly often engaged in all of these processes simultaneously. Nevertheless, I would argue that each modality deserves to be
analyzed separately. My reasons for making such a claim are four: first,
there are theoretical and empirical reasons for assuming that each modality has followed its own evolutionary path; second, and probably as a
result of the first point, each modality exhibits its own identity, whether it
be approached phenomenologically, anthropologically, developmentally, or philosophically; third, and no doubt because of points one and
two, the great majority of existing social theory reflects the analytical
identity of each modality; and finally and most importantly, the clear
juxtapositioning of the four modalities allows us to explain better many of
the most perplexing aspects of mind. I would offer basically the same four
reasons for adopting these particular modalities rather than any others, or
for adding or subtracting from the four.

It is beyond the scope of this chapter to support in a rigorous way any
of the first three reasons.[7] By analyzing each of these modalities of mind
in some detail, however, I hope to be able to lend some support to the

fourth reason. In short, my objective will be to analyze mind as a complex life form engaged in the related but analytically distinct activities of structuring (1) organic experiences and responses; (2) interpersonal relationships; (3) the external physical world; and (4) meanings themselves. Once this has been done, I will be in a position to indicate the social aspects of each modality, as well as some of the general implications of such a pluralistic view of mind.

In the significance context of the organism qua organism, mind is interested primarily in the biological and ecological viability of the organism and those things which are significant to it. It reflects this concern in two analytically distinct ways. First, it attempts to distinguish between conditions and factors which are beneficial to the organism's biological viability from those which are detrimental. It does this primarily through the use of the categories of pain and pleasure in conjunction with an approach/avoidance guidance system associated with a mnemonic monitoring faculty. Second, it establishes patterns of activities—habits— which serve to conserve the physical energies of the organism by limiting random activity. To summarize in terms of the first four parameters of mental modalities given above, the focus of concern is the organism, the objective is biological viability, the primary dimension is gratification, and the primary form of ordering is binomial classification coupled with negation.[8]

When it is the primary focus of concern, the organism, not surprisingly, exerts considerable control over mind. It is often difficult, in fact, to determine where and when the physical, chemical, and biological demands of the organism end and those of mind begin. As a result, in this modality self-awareness, reflectivity, and consciousness are generally limited.[9] Truth and falsity have at best a shadowy existence; what matters is the intensity and vividness of experience. One is hard put, in fact, to distinguish between the "external world" and "empirical experiences." Whatever reality there is becomes rather caught up and reflected in the experience itself. Mind itself often appears to be lost in the ongoing experience. Acts in response to even the most simplistic binomial pleasure/pain category system and—either in conjunction or separately—to the most behaviorally oriented directives—habits and approach/ avoidance rules—indicate, however, the presense of mind.

Some possible examples of this sort of mental activity would be getting dressed, telephoning/dialing one's home number, eating, or other often repeated behavior; other examples could be dropping a burning pan, shading one's eyes from a bright light, or unreflectively salting unsalted food. Such activities are clearly not genetically governed, although there may well be genetic input. Some form of mental activity is required. We may end up, however, doing things which we had no conscious intention of doing, such as calling home when we meant to call another number, getting into our pajamas when we meant to change for dinner, or eating food meant for another. We are similarly apt to drop a pan handed to us if, simultaneously, someone yells out that it is red hot, even if it is not hot. The explanation for such apparently inappropriate behaviors is that mind is not focused in these cases upon the external physical world; it is focused upon the organism and is concerned with the external world only insofar as this world appears to bear directly on the well-being of the organism qua organism. Though such activities may appear quite mindless, it follows that insofar as such activities require some sort of definition of the situation, mind is operative.[10] (A corollary of this is that habits are generally established within the organism/libido context.)

When mind's primary focus of concern is the external world, it also engages in categorizing and behavior patterning; in such situations, however, both processes are quite different. (For presentational continuity I have elected to deal with what was earlier presented as the third modality before what was presented as the second modality.) When confronting the physical world, mind's primary objective is to limit what William James referred to as the "blooming, buzzing confusion."[11] This objective is related to the conservation of organic energies discussed above, yet it is qualitatively different. Here, mind is concerned with discovering orderly relationships among objects in the world in order to enable man to adapt better to this world. Categorization and ordering in these cases, consequently, have evolved in conjunction with "discoverable" patterns in the external physical world itself. Central to these processes are our notions of space and time, objects, and causality, especially efficient causality.[12] This mental modality also fosters self-reflectivity and consciousness insofar as it includes human action and the actor as part of the external physical world and thereby makes them objects of possible study. It relies primarily upon a pragmatic criterion of truth, with heavy emphasis on the ability to predict. Finally, it accepts as "real" the same world of spatial-temporal objects that we in our everyday lives normally accept as "reality."[13]

In addition to the organism qua organism and the external physical world, mind has been and is also concerned with other people and social relationships. Moreover, it exhibits a distinct modality when other people and social relationships are its primary focus of concern. This third modality, however, is somewhat more difficult to isolate because other people are, among other things, physical objects and often experienced as such;[14] they are also quite likely to be experienced primarily in what might be called the "organic" mode, i.e., as sources of pleasure and pain. (I am here thinking of the role others may play in providing infants with care and nurturing. It is true that nonhuman physical objects too can be and are experienced as sources of pain and pleasure, but with rare exception—perhaps fire—few physical objects acquire gratificational attributes to the degree common for people.) I would suggest, however, that other people qua "others" are experienced primarily as other wills, i.e., as sources of power and influence; it is when they are experienced as such that mind exhibits its other people/social relationship modality.[15]

When other people/wills are the primary focus of concern, the primary objective of mind is to maximize and/or protect one's "zones of jurisdiction." The primary dimension utilized is power; the basic ordering principle is the notion of greater than/less than, often embodied in some sort of vector field. This generates not only the notion of zones of jurisdiction but also the notions of dominance and submissiveness. Not unsurprisingly, there is a very real sense in which "might makes right" in this modality; "truth" belongs to the strong, whether this strength be defined in terms of available physical resources or of conflicting arguments.

In terms of reflectivity and self-awareness, this modality often appears to be more like the organism/libido modality than the physical object/pragmatic modality. It seems to be less calculating and more experiential in character. One can talk about a "gut" reaction in this mode. On the other hand, there are times when this modality entails a greater degree of self-reflectivity and self-reflexivity than the physical world modality, in that it is often a necessary condition to grasp how others are grasping what is going on, which in turn requires understanding how oneself is grasping what is going on. That is, this modality often requires understanding others, which requires a high degree of self-understanding. This variability in reflectivity is one of the most enigmatic aspects of this modality.[16]

Reality in this modality, finally, is generally conceived in terms of wills and the zones over which they exert control. Whereas "reality" in the organic/libido modality is defined primarily in terms of pleasurable and painful experiences, in the external physical objects modality of spatial-temporal objects governed by efficient causality, this modality projects a reality of force fields. Here, relationships are defined in terms of the relative powers of the units involved, much as spatial structure is defined by masses, according to Einstein.

This brings us to our fourth modality, the symbolic meaning modality, which is more complex than any of the other three so far presented. This complexity is due in part to the inherently self-reflective character of this modality-mind's concern with itself. It is equally due, however, to the contradictory objectives which mind exhibits in this modality. To make some sense of all this, it is necessary that we understand what could be called the accidental nature of this modality, which in effect means the accidental nature of mind as we know it. This in turn requires some "evolutionary speculation," which I beg to be allowed to pursue if only for heuristic purposes.[17]

The notion that mind is social, as noted earlier, is based on the reasoning that mind deals in symbolic meanings which are themselves a product of social interaction (normally verbal) occurring in social settings.[18] This same set of factors—social setting, exchange of verbal gestures, and so on—is used quite explicitly by Mead to explain how mind emerged in the first place. I would argue, however, that these factors, even when they are combined with the organic, pragmatic, and social uses of mind outlined above, do not account for the evolution of the human mind.[19] Knowing how mind could have evolved and some of the uses it has had since it has evolved is not the same as accounting for why it should have survived in the first place. Other species have done quite well in adapting to their own organisms, and establishing working social orders without mind as we normally understand it. Man himself, in fact, often seems to do better in these endeavors by *not* thinking.[20] The question, "Why mind?" consequently still remains unanswered.[21]

To answer in brief what is probably an unanswerable question, I would argue with Durkheim that the primary survival value of mind was that it generated a new form of social solidarity. That is, what turned out to be the "evolutionary kicker" was that symbolic meanings made it possible for men to share a common worldview, which in turn provided a basis for a completely new type of social bonding and solidarity. We might say that Mead's meanings and mind made possible Durkheim's (1954, 1956) Collective Conscience and moral order.

It should be stressed that the type of social solidarity being discussed here is quite different from that associated with the other people/social relationship modality. In the other people/social relationship modality, mind serves to promote solidarity by establishing hierarchical social orders. In the present case, mind contributes to social solidarity by providing a symbolic universe which men can hold in common. Such shared worldviews need not even be concerned with social relationships per se, although in actuality such relationships are often a focus of concern.

Nevertheless, they can just as well be concerned with physical objects and/or organic experiences.[22] Insofar as mind's primary objective is to foster social solidarity by providing a worldview which can be shared, the *primary* focus of concern is, however, neither other people, physical objects, nor experiences per se, but rather symbolic meanings themselves.

In this fourth modality, mind no longer exists merely as a means for focusing on and setting significance boundaries for other things. Mind is interested in itself, i.e., mind as ordering/relating process is focused upon mind as symbolic meanings. Its basic objective is to produce symbolic meaning systems capable of being shared and, consequently, of promoting social solidarity. This in turn generates a predilection for conceptual order, since it is generally easier to establish a consensus around an internally consistent and ordered view than around a disordered view.[23] There is, however, a latent paradox in this which deserves brief comment.

Despite various differences among the four mental modalities, mind in all cases appears to be engaged in a process of simplifying the world by showing how different things are related to each other. What is paradoxical about this is that mind itself, by making the world meaningful in a very real sense, serves to complicate our world rather than to simplify it. Meanings obliterate the simple spatial/temporal boundaries which exist for other creatures and things; mind and meanings thrust man into what George Herbert Mead called the "undifferentiated here and now," which is infinitely more complex than the here and now of "pure sense" experience, insofar as meanings involve things and events which are distanced from us in both time and place.

When the primary focus of concern is the organism, the external physical world, and/or other people/wills, the danger of mind increasing our sense of disorder is counteracted by the specific objectives of each of these modalities. That is, the process of relating A to B and B to C is limited and constrained by the specific objectives of each modality. When mind turns in upon itself, however, the potential for generating disorder by attempting to relate everything to everything else becomes very real. Therefore, for mind to fulfill its prime objective of providing a basis for social solidarity (by providing an ordered worldview around which a consensus can be built), it must counteract its own tendency to search out further relationships between this and that, and attempt instead to achieve some sort of closure.[24] In this modality, consequently, the ordering tendency favors closure rather than relating. Given that it is specifically in this modality that we confront mind in its purest form, we could conclude—to put the matter somewhat crudely—that there is a strong element of "rubbing where it hurts" in what is generally considered to be pure mental activity.

The full implications of this notion of rubbing where it hurts cannot be dealt with here. The bottom line, however, is that pure thought in and of itself, i.e., stripped of ideology, stripped of sublimation, stripped of its instrumental objectives, is still reactive in character. It is not a reaching out process, but rather a means for handling the anxiety and confusion which are generated by meanings themselves. Put slightly differently, much so-called "pure" thought is concerned with resolving the ambiguity generated by mind itself and with tying up the threads of ongoing relationships spun by mind. In a very real sense, consequently, thinking as the ordering of meanings and attempts to avoid thinking, be it through the use of alcohol, television, sex, work, drugs, sports, and so forth have a very similar objective, namely, mental peace. The main threat to this peace—the thought which introduces the most discord—is man's recognition of his own mortality, since it indicates the final meaninglessness of man's efforts, unless some means can be found for giving life meaning, although it ends in death. It is not surprising, therefore, to find that this task has absorbed so much mental effort.

In terms of the attributes presented earlier, this fourth modality can be described as follows: its primary focus of concern is symbolic meanings; its basic objective is to promote social solidarity based upon a shared worldview; it stresses what could be called an ordering dimension—it is interested in the degree of order or disorder a thing contributes to our view of the world; and it utilizes whatever notion of relationship is likely to produce closure. It is a highly self-reflexive modality interested not only in the meaning of meanings, but also in the meaning of the meaning of meanings; it is therefore capable of extreme self-reflectivity. Concerned as it is with consensus, it favors what could be called a hermeneutic conception of truth, i.e., truth is defined in terms of degrees of explanatory power. Finally, its focus upon meanings themselves generates what would normally be considered an idealistic vision of reality.

Although the description of the four mental modalities presented above is brief, perhaps to the point of being cryptic, it indicates how such a pluralistic conception of mind can clarify, if not resolve, the types of questions presented in the first paragraph of this chapter. The task is not to specify the exact degree to which human behavior in general is intentional, egotistical, self-conscious, rule-governed, and so forth or the exact mix of organic, interpersonal, and collective factors, but rather to determine the relative significance of these factors in different situations. Our task, in short, is not to describe *the* intentional-social character of human action, but rather the multifaceted nature of this intentional-social character. This does not prohibit one from focusing upon a specific facet at any given time; it only requires that we recognize the limitations of any single modality. Like the old adage about the four blind men and the elephant, each may be correct in what he is describing, but none is able to picture the whole beast because each is limited to a specific part.

The key question, of course, is to know when one modality dominates and when another. We know, for example, that an established consensus may override common sense-experiences sometimes; at other times, however, such common sense-experiences may force an established consensus to be modified. Sometimes men act reflectively, and at other times they don't; sometimes they act with apparent purpose and at other times purely reactively. Men are capable of both theoretical and practical thoughts; they are also capable of both selfish and altruistic acts. Although these elements tend to cluster along the lines outlined above, the question of how specific people think and act in specific situations remains an empirical question. If the general thesis of this chapter is correct, however, it is an empirical question with a very decidedly sociological bent, i.e., how specific people think and act in specific situations is influenced more by sociological factors than traditional psychological factors. This brings us to the question of the social aspects of each of our four modalities and what could be considered the justification of the notion of a sociology of mind.

At one level, of course, all four modalities are social insofar as meanings are social products requiring both a social consensus and an understructure of social interaction.[25] Two modalities, the other people/social relationship modality and the symbolic meanings/ordered world modality, can be considered doubly social since, in addition, the focus of concern and the primary objective of each is explicitly social. A good case, however, can be made for the other two modalities on similar grounds, although in both cases the reasons are less apparent.

In the organism/libido modality, mind was described as being concerned primarily with the organism qua organism and gratification. In our everyday lives, however, this concern is reflected primarily in what could be called libidinal interests. Although there is interest in such things as a full stomach, proper body warmth, and the like, the main emphasis is upon discovering, maintaining, and generating supportive and pleasurable libidinal/interpersonal ties.[26] The sense of organic well-being and pleasure central to this modality is, consequently, defined and determined in what can only be called a social context. Put slightly differently, pain and pleasure are more normally defined in terms of our sense of being loved, cared for, and of interpersonal anxiety, loneliness, and so forth than vice versa. This assertion may seem to contradict our common-sense notion that many of our most pleasurable and painful experiences are nonpersonal in nature, e.g., a hot bath, a good meal, a physical shock. I would suggest, however, that the pleasure and pain of many of these apparently nonpersonal experiences are based upon a particular personal association with these experiences: the hot bath, perhaps, with being held; the food with being nursed, literally and figuratively; the shock with being disciplined abruptly; and so on. In short, it is the personal which conditions the nonpersonal rather than vice versa which, I might add, can explain how a masochist can obtain pleasure from physical pain.

The inherently social quality of the external physical world modality requires somewhat more explanation. As noted earlier, this modality gives us what passes most of the time as the "real" world," i.e., the world of objects in space and time. It must be remembered, however, that even this modality is intentional; the world is defined in terms of and in response to human interests and concerns. More specifically, the external physical world is defined in response to man's attempts to adapt to it which, in the case of man, also entail attempts to mold it to fit human interests. The external physical world is experienced as an instrumental challenge which requires an instrumental solution. The solution is human labor.[27] It is through our grasp of means/ends relationships that the external physical world is not only manipulated, but also defined and understood. This is not to deny the use of pure sense data in defining the external physical world, but only to assert that what could be called utility characteristics play an even more important role.[28] Often, of course, these types of characteristics work together, as in such notions as "hard." We call something hard because of its feel to our touch, because of the effort that it would take to break it or scratch it, and because it can break and scratch other things.

If the external physical world is defined primarily in terms of what may be called utility/labor characteristics, it follows that it is also socially defined insofar as labor itself is social in character. This may not be obvious, since labor is often treated as if it were individual and personal in origin. As we have seen above, however, labor/utility entails a means/end relationship; A is done to achieve B. What might be called the labor/utility value of anything lies in the labor required to create or maintain the thing. (It could be argued that it rather lies in the labor potential of the thing, but such potential is either a reflection of the inherent "cost" of the thing or a reflection of some sort of inherent "power" rather than utility/labor value.) The external physical world to which this utility/labor dimension applies is, moreover, a shared world. To talk about the utility/labor value of a thing, consequently, means to talk about the "average" value of the thing, i.e., the labor required of an "average" person. This requires locating utility/labor values within a social context of some sort, i.e., a context of joint labor, where it is possible to generate notions of average utility/labor value. This is often done by placing labor within the context of the division of labor, but even highly unspecialized labor is inherently social along the lines presented above.

Although the social nature of each of the four modalities deserves to be elaborated upon in greater detail, I hope sufficient substantiation has been presented to support minimally the idea of a sociology of mind. That is, I hope that I have been able to indicate how the very structure of mind, i.e., the nature of meanings and the way meanings are themselves interrelated, is tied into and reflects social factors.[29] Recognizing what I have called the doubly social nature of each of the four modalities of mind does not, in and of itself, however, constitute a sociology of mind. It is further necessary to examine the actual relationships between different social factors and the various mental modalities. Without such empirical grounding, the sociology of mind would degenerate into a purely speculative form of idealism.

The main problem in doing any empirical research, of course, is to know what to look for. In my *Critique of Sociological Reasoning,* I made some general suggestions bearing on this problem. I argued that how the world is defined in any given society is greatly influenced by the relative importance of cultural structures, class structures, and system structures. I similarly indicated some of the differences which might result from emphasizing particular dimensions. In my *Mind of the Market,* I attempted to analyze in much greater detail the impact of different mental modalities within a specific context. There are all sorts of important questions, however, yet to be pursued. Many of the most important of these could be classified under Giddens's notion of structuration and are related to his associated notion of duality of structures.[30] To be somewhat more specific, the problem is to show how different social factors favor specific mental modalities, which in turn reproduce specific types of social structures, and so on. There seems to be some evidence to the effect, for example, that differences in economic scarcity and surpluses influence economic consciousness per se.[31] Similar switches of consciousness often follow perceived physical threats,[32] dramatic changes in numbers and density,[33] and or periods of social change.[34]

These sorts of questions, of course, have been pursued by social theorists for some time. The sociology of mind could be of particular value in pursuing these questions insofar as it would suggest that the process of structuration may vary significantly from one mental modality to another. Different types of ideational structures may be influenced by and embodied in different types of social structures. The organic/libidinal modality, for example, may be very sensitive to numbers and social distances, but quite immune to differences in the distribution of physical resources. Just the opposite may be true of the external physical world modality. In short, not only are there different types of societies and not only do people look at the world differently, but the interrelationship between different societies and different worldviews may itself vary. This of course in no way undermines the importance placed by Giddens upon the process of structuration; it merely provides an added word of caution.

Given the number of issues I have raised and raced over, I am hesitant to introduce yet another. There remains one issue, however, which follows directly from the above and which has such significance for the social sciences themselves, including, I might add, the sociology of mind, that I feel compelled to mention it. I refer to the modality biases of the various social sciences themselves. To be more specific, and at the risk of oversimplifying matters, I would suggest that economists tend to utilize the external physical world/pragmatic modality with its means/ends notion of rationality and its bias for predictability; political scientists tend to define the world in terms of the social relationships/power modality and consequently to weight heavily the powers of argumentation; social psychologists, anthropologists, and others interested primarily in the day-to-day, face-to-face activities of people tend to adopt the organism/libido modality and to rely heavily upon the vividness of their examples for support; and sociologists, finally, tend to define the world in terms of the symbolic meaning modality and to rely upon "established opinion" as in "see Marx, Weber, Durkheim, and others." There are, of course, all sorts of mixes and overlaps. The general relationship between forms of thought and subject matter, however, holds in most instances. Moreover, these modalities influence the "findings" of these disciplines.[35]

The sociology of mind as a subdiscipline of sociology tends to have a hermeneutic objective, i.e., it tends to rely on interpretive consensus for revealing meanings. The reason for this is that sociology tends to focus on normative orders which themselves have such hermeneutic objectives, i.e., meaning systems of the fourth modality. There is nothing wrong in such a bias; in fact, given the character of the meaning systems under investigation, such a bias is the only correct approach.[36] It would be wrong, however, to assume that such hermeneutic objectives are always appropriate. The primary task of mind may be to promote social solidarity through shared meaning systems, but it is clearly not its only task. As we have seen above, it is also concerned with the external physical world, the biological and ecological viability of the organism, and zones of jurisdiction. Furthermore, as Durkheim himself recognized, social solidarity itself is not solely dependent upon a "Collective Conscience," especially not in modern society. There are economic ties, libidinal ties, and political hierarchies. These meaning systems cannot be judged in terms of hermeneutic criteria alone. Libidinal, economic, political, and religious "definitions of the situation" reflect different underlying processes; consequently, they require different forms of evaluation.

In summary, although the primary task of the sociology of mind may be hermeneutic, there is still room within the sociology of mind for such notions as "false consciousness," "social pathology," "economic inefficiency," and so forth. Certain meanings and the behaviors they generate may be understandable only in terms of the governing consensus of that group; other meanings and the behavior they generate, however, may be equally dependent upon the distribution of physical resources, political hierarchies, and/or social density.

So defined, the sociology of mind takes a position on the possibility of a social science almost identical to that put forward by Mannheim in his *Ideology and Utopia* (see also Bhaskar, 1979). In substance, it rejects both the absolutist's position and the relativist's position. The first insofar as it rejects the very possibility of an Archimedian point; the second insofar as it rejects the relativist's implicitly absolutist notion of truth. Truth is itself a contextual concept, i.e., in any given context there is a contextually relevant notion of truth. To complain that there is no universal, eternal truth is simply to misunderstand what the world and meaning are all about. This is admittedly a very difficult notion to accept, because it goes against mind's theoretical bias for closure.[37] It is a fact of life, however, which social scientists and sociologists in particular cannot ignore if they have any hope of doing what they claim to do.[38]

In concluding, I should like to make one final point. I entitled this chapter "On the Sociology of Mind." My purpose in doing this was to indicate my firm belief that sociology has much to contribute to our understanding of mind. In this I am again echoing Mannheim, who felt that sociology, and the sociology of knowledge in particular, should be seen as continuing the general pursuit of man's self-knowledge through an understanding of mind, a pursuit begun by philosophy and continued by psychology. Such a sociology of mind would also fulfill Simmel's (1964) conception of philosophical sociology insofar as it would contribute to our understanding of the "totality of mind, life and being in general" (p. 23).

Notes

1. Although the definition given is similar to that of numerous theorists, my own conception of mind has probably been most influenced by George Herbert Mead (see especially Parts I and II of his *Mind, Self and Society* (1934).

In stressing the social character of mind, I am again indebted to Mead, although, as will become clear in what follows, my own conception of this social character owes as much to Durkheim, Marx, Freud, and Weber as to Mead. My vision of mind's pluralistic nature probably owes most to Weber, although many of the original seeds were probably planted by Paul Weiss's *Modes of Being* (1958). I might just add here that an added problem has been a general tendency to ignore mind altogether and concentrate rather on such things as language, myths, logic, the brain, behavior, and the like. Fortunately, this trend seems lately to have been somewhat reversed with the increased interest in cognitive psychology, sociology of knowledge, rational choice theory, and the philosophy of mind itself.

2. I feel that there is really very little to be gained here by my arguing for either the intentional or evolutionary conception of mind, since it has been done already by others much better than I could do it. See, for example, Stephen Toulmin's *Human Understanding* (1973); Stuart Hampshire's *Thought and Action* (1959); Jürgen Habermas's *Knowledge and Human Interests* (1971).

I am here admittedly glossing over a number of very important issues, including perhaps what could be called the ontological status of mind itself. In this regard, I would highly recommend Roy Bhaskar's *The Possibility of Naturalism* (1979), with whose notion of transcendental realism I am most sympathetic.

3. For a more detailed presentation of Mead's position, see *A Critique of Sociological Reasoning* by Charles W. Smith (1979), pp. 11ff.

4. One major exception to this general rule has been Jürgen Habermas and his notion of cognitive interests. While there is a great deal of overlap between his overview and that being presented in this chapter, there are sufficient differences such that I have elected not to try to maintain an ongoing dialogue in the chapter itself. For a general overview to Habermas, I would still recommend the appendix of his *Knowledge and Human Interests*, also entitled "Knowledge and Human Interests."

5. Although the notion of significance contexts is clearly in Mead—Mead, in effect, defines mind as a significance determining faculty—I am indebted to Charles Taylor for resensitizing me to the inherent power of the notion of significance as it relates to our conception of mind and consciousness. Whereas Taylor has recently tried to use this significance feature as a means for distinguishing human consciousness from artificial intelligence processes, I am more interested in using it to distinguish among different forms of human thought.

6. I have previously presented this same fourfold schema in a slightly different form in my *Critique of Sociological Reasoning* (1979). I have also used a modified form of this

schema in analyzing stock market philosophies in my *The Mind of the Market* (1981). Persons interested in a more detailed discussion of the roots of these modalities would find the *Critique* of interest; those more interested in seeing the modalities applied would be interested in *The Mind of the Market.*

7. For a brief discussion of some of these issues, see my *Critique of Sociological Reasoning,* op. cit.

8. To say that I am here summarizing a great deal of material would be an understatement. For a more detailed discussion of the general issues, see my *Critique of Sociological Reasoning,* Part I. For a nice general discussion of the role of habits, see *The Social Construction of Reality* by P. Berger and T. Luckmann (1967); use the index. On binomial classification, see Claude Levi-Strauss, *The Savage Mind* (1968). For more general background on what I would call the gratificational/experiential modality, see Piaget, *The Child's Conception of the World* (1960); Erik Erikson's *Childhood and Society* (1950); and H. Sullivan, *An Interpersonal Theory of Psychiatry* (1968).

9. See Toulmin's discussion of consciousness as sensibility, this volume.

10. The implicit criticism of "behaviorism" is intended. Even at this apparently nonreflective behavioral mode, it is quite silly to deny man's mental life. For a more detailed discussion, see pp. 1-17 in my *Critique,* op. cit.

11. The actual reference for this oft quoted phrase is *Principles of Psychology,* Vol. I (1890), p. 488.

12. Here, I am drawing primarily upon Kant and his *Critique of Pure Reason* and the neo-Kantian pragmatic tradition, especially C. I. Lewis and his *Mind and the World Order* (1956). The question of whether or not these patterns are in the world or not is not an issue I wish to debate here. Let it suffice that in keeping with the basic ontology of Bhaskar, op. cit., I believe these patterns to be more than idealistic constructions of mind.

13. I am quite deliberately avoiding here any detailed discussion regarding the primary dimension of this modality. At a superficial level, it could be said that this modality simply relies on sensory dimensions, but as will be explained later it is more accurate to describe this modality as emphasizing a utility dimension.

14. This is the reason that I elected to analyze the external physical world modality first, although from a developmental point of view the other people modality probably has priority.

15. For a general discussion, see again Part I of my *Critique;* Erikson, op. cit.; Piaget, *The Moral Judgement of the Child* (1932); and Fritz Heider, *The Psychology of Interpersonal Relations* (1958).

16. Though all four modalities exhibit different degrees of reflectivity at different times, all but the power modality have a decided preference for a specific degree of reflectivity. For a more detailed discussion, see my *Critique,* op. cit.

17. For a discussion of the sense in which I use the term "evolution" in regards to mind, see Toulmin's *Human Understanding,* op. cit.

18. This is the view not only of Mead, but also of Mannheim and Wittgenstein, to choose two thinkers who have influenced a great many. The implication of this social product view of mind is among other things, that no human, no matter how marvellously endowed, would or could evolve a mind if reared in isolation. Similarly, the external physical world, no matter how well ordered, no matter how rewarding to those capable of ordering it, could stimulate man to think by himself.

19. It could be argued that Mead makes such a case by showing the survival value of communication. My personal feelings are that Mead's pragmatic bias prohibited him from grasping the "we" character of meaningful communication which was so central to Durkheim.

20. I am thinking here of various situations such as athletic activity, confronting new experiences, and so forth where we are often told explicitly not to "think." In actuality, of course, we are expected to do some sort of thinking, as most animals are required to "think" if they hope to survive. The issue, consequently, is one of degree, i.e., how complex a chain

of meanings we are supposed to use. The notion that one is not to think means that as one moves from one state of consciousness—meaning—to another, one should leave behind the meaning which led to this "new" meaning, and so on. In short, one can behave in a meaningful manner—one can even do so as the results of a mental process—but one is not supposed to maintain any awareness of this process or the possibility of reversing it.

21. I could argue that this question is irrelevant to the primary purpose of this chapter, which is to articulate in a programmatic manner the pluralistic character of man. I could also argue that the question is spurious insofar as it is impossible to do more than speculate on the evolutionary history of mind. To do so, however, would in my opinion be illegitimate, since my whole vision of mind, including its sociological nature, is based minimally on an evolutionary metaphor. Rather than attempting to sneak by the issue, therefore, I think it best to confront it directly, keeping in mind the primarily heuristic objectives of the effort.

22. I might just note that Durkheim felt that social relationships played a more important role in the structuring of shared worldviews than either physical objects or organic experiences per se. In this regard, Levi-Strauss is clearly a Durkheimian. In contrast, Marx, Weber, and Mead give more weight to man's interest in his physical environment.

23. Although I think this is intuitively quite evident, I am aware that it can be questioned. Despite work done in the area of brain damage, memory, consensus formation, and hermeneutics, further research would seem to be required to support this generalization.

24. This explains, I feel, why mind tends to become more dogmatic as it becomes more abstract. Mind comes on the scene as a process for relating meanings to each other; it is only when it turns in upon itself that it evidences its now inherent tendency for closure. This notion that various mental patterns may be the result of evolutionary developments is analyzed in some detail by Lionel Tiger in his book, *Optimism: The Biology of Hope* (1979).

25. This point was made earlier and could be considered straight Mead.

26. In effect I am underscoring what could be called the psychoanalytic view of the organism qua organism. Although the key figure here is obviously Freud, I think my own thinking has more in common with Erikson. See his *Childhood and Society* (1950).

27. I am here, in effect, giving the external physical world modality a Marxist definition, though I might add that it is also a view held by most American pragmatists, including Mead. For two excellent discussions of the Marxist view, see Habermas, op. cit. and Bhaskar, op. cit.

28. See Note 16. For a more detailed discussion of the relationship between the external physical world modality and the utility/labor dimension, see Part I of my *Critique of Sociological Reasoning* (1979).

29. Specifically insofar as it is concerned with the ways meanings are generated and related, the sociology of mind differs from the sociology of knowledge, which tends—primarily as a result of Mannheim's views—to focus upon the content of ideas. The sociology of mind is not willing to assume that the ways meanings can be related constitute either a psychological or logical/philosophical question. These processes, insofar as they are governed and influenced by social factors, are sociological as well. See Mannheim's *Ideology and Utopia* (1955).

30. See Anthony Giddens's *New Rules of Sociological Method* (1976). I would also recommend here Bhaskar's discussion of this issue in his *The Possibility of Naturalism*, op. cit.

31. For an excellent supportive example of this, see *The Shantung Compound* by Langdon Gilkey (1975).

32. A very good supportive example of this phenomenon—pointed out to me by John Courtney—was the positive public response to Trudeau's imposition of "marshal law" after the FLQ actions in Quebec in 1970.

33. This point has been made by various observers, but for a general overview with excellent references, I would recommend Robert Merton's *Social Theory and Social Structure* (1957), especially his chapters on reference groups.

34. This issue has also been wrestled with by many. For one of the more classic discussions with some very interesting empirical data, see *When Prophesy Fails* by Festinger et al. (1956).

35. I cannot help but note that associated with these different "methodological" approaches, one finds specific forms of criticism. Accusations of personal or class/ethnic bias, complaints about materials being "dull and boring," criticisms of data selection, and questions regarding the "meaning" of a piece of work are, in my opinion, highly correlated with the type of research being scrutinized.

36. For a defense of this position, see Giddens, op. cit.

37. I might simply note here that in keeping with points made in the text, it is usually the more theoretically oriented who are troubled by this sort of openness, rather than the more practical or pragmatically oriented. Ambivalence, of course, is the norm with the libidinally oriented.

38. The question of how one actually goes about doing such research is another question which can really only be answered in the context of some actual research. I tried to incorporate such observations where possible in my *Mind of the Market,* since it is basically a piece of empirical research. A great deal more on this, however, is required.

References

Berger, P., & Luckmann, T. *The social construction of reality.* London: Allen Lane, 1967.
Bhaskar, R. *The possibility of naturalism.* Atlantic Highlands, NJ: Humanities Press, 1979.
Durkheim, E. *The elementary forms of religious life.* New York: Free Press, 1954.
Durkheim, E. *The division of labor in society.* New York: Free Press, 1956.
Erikson, E. *Childhood and society.* New York: Norton, 1950.
Festinger, L. et al. *When prophesy fails.* New York: Harper & Row, 1956.
Giddens, A. *New rules of sociological method.* London: Hutchinson, 1976.
Gilkey, L. *The Shantung compound.* New York: Harper & Row, 1975.
Habermas, J. *Knowledge and human interests.* Boston: Beacon Press, 1971. Appendix published 1972.
Hampshire, S. *Thought and action.* London: Chatto & Windus, 1959.
Heider, F. *The psychology of interpersonal relations.* New York: John Wiley, 1958.
James, W. *Principles of psychology,* Vol. 1. New York: Holt, 1890.
Levi-Strauss, C. *The savage mind.* Chicago: University of Chicago Press, 1968.
Lewis, C. I. *Mind and the world order.* New York: Dover, 1956 (1929).
Mannheim, K. *Ideology and utopia.* New York: Harcourt Brace Jovanovich, 1955.
Mead, G. H. *Mind, self and society.* Chicago: University of Chicago Press, 1934.
Merton, R. *Social theory and social structure.* New York: Free Press, 1968.
Piaget, J. *The moral judgement of the child.* New York: Free Press, 1932.
Piaget, J. *The child's conception of the world.* Totowa, NJ: Litterfield, 1960.
Simmel, G. *The sociology of Georg Simmel.* New York: Free Press, 1964.
Smith, C. W. *A critique of sociological reasoning.* Oxford: Basil Blackwell, 1979.
Smith, C. W. *The mind of the market.* Totowa, NJ: Litterfield, 1981.
Sullivan, H. *An interpersonal theory of psychiatry.* New York: Norton, 1968.
Tiger, L. *Optimism: The biology of hope.* New York: Simon & Schuster, 1979.
Toulmin, S. *Human understanding.* Oxford: Clarendon, 1973.
Weiss, P. *Modes of being.* Carbondale: Southern Illinois University Press, 1958.

CHAPTER 12

Models and Language

KURT W. BACK

Cognitive Chasms and Linguistic Bridges

This chapter addresses itself to the widening gap between practice and theory in the field of individuals and society. The way in which scientists, especially social psychologists, work when dealing with this topic, has little to do with theoretical or metatheoretical concerns of general humanists and professional philosophers. The mainline approach to social psychology is restricted in content as well as in method. Content in more individual, psychologically oriented social psychology is concentrated on social perceptions and attribution, attitude formation and change, motivation, power and influence, communication, and allied topics; in sociologically oriented social psychology, there is more stress on social movements, socialization, processes of interaction, and other topics more integrated into the larger society. The methods in both fields are primarily those of experiment, social survey, and systematic observation. This mainstream approach respects some self-imposed limits, dealing for instance neither with definitions of human elements (even in social setting) nor with the constitutional elements of social experience.

Communication across this gap is difficult; social psychologists engaged in standard research, who can no longer see the wide implications dealt with by many theorists and philosophers, are inclined to push aside the current research work as trivial and restricted. This situation has led

AUTHOR'S NOTE: The research for this chapter was partially supported by NIE Grant NIE-G-78-0089 and by a grant from the Duke University Research Council.

members of both sides to seek a common ground. As a result, some novel and unusual branches of social psychology have sprung up (see Gergen, this volume). This chapter will concentrate on the link itself by dealing with the language used in describing the individual in society. Theories can be seen as systems or codes which organize experience and methods to produce the appropriate language. Different languages can be discriminated to a greater and smaller degree; for the present purpose, comprehensive schemes are needed which combine the activities of researchers and analysts. Thus, the first part of the chapter will deal with a classification that we can call model and research activity and the explication of the personal and social worlds.

Structures and Other Models

In many ways, the concept of structure transmits best the common and joint elements of the individual and social realms. However, even if the structural model can be used as the principal model, it needs to be supplemented by two other models or alternative ways of exploring the field as a whole. These three models correspond to some degree to the "three faces of social psychology" (House, 1974).

A similar argument can be made for a particular type of language, namely mathematics. Science, and especially social science, has had an ambivalent relation with mathematics, sometimes exalting it as the reality behind scientific fact, sometimes attacking it, and sometimes drawing back from certain mathematical models as mysticism, a charge which has been used since Pythagoras. If we consider mathematics as a type of language, more appropriate to some models than to others, we can advocate a more relevant and safer use of the metaphors of this language. The last section of the chapter will discuss some previously neglected kinds of mathematics which are of potential use in the social sciences.

Structural Model

Structuralists take seriously only theoretical concepts which are not directly observable. They do this by looking for realities specific to the human, interpersonal level. Thus, the model for human reality is language, the supreme human achievement, and structuralism started with the analysis of language (Jacobson, 1963). The structure of language is important by itself and provides a good starting point for a system encompassing the essentially human, interpersonal world. In discussing language as a system, we define something basic to our relation to the world and independent of specific words and context. This feature of language, the "deep structure" of linguists, defines a basic reality. In contexts other than language, particularly in social relations and cultural products, the structuralist tries to determine a similar deep structure.

The structuralist believes in the existence of this deep structure as the ultimate reality. It is a reality of which individuals who are acting in it may or may not be conscious. Observables are a reflection of a deeper reality which we can understand only by inference.

The structuralist does not reduce a given experience to its elements or to a simple level as an ultimate reality. Instead, human action can only be understood in terms of human achievement, such as language and culture. Hence, a personal relationship can be defined by the structure relating to the norms of the relationship, whereas larger societies can be understood as entities by themselves. Methodologically, the structuralist ideally looks for arrangements which will explain all the data under consideration, without exception. Each case which does not fit into the scheme is an indication of a wrong construction, or at least of an insufficient one in need of additional categories. This is an ideal. In practice, unexplained cases will remain. The ingenuity of the structuralist lies in getting perfect explanations for all cases, just as the biologically oriented researcher tries to find an experiment which will show the effect of independent variables. Anyone who has looked at Levi-Strauss's (1964-1974) five volumes of analyzing a set of South American myths is aware of the lengths to which this research can go.

These two characteristics, the need for variables at the same systematic level as observables and the ultimate aim for perfect validity, lead to a special methodology and logic of research: The researcher seeks to classify into a complete network of categories a means to determine the existence of all the structural variables which could possibly be important. Finally, the researcher wants to stay on the same human level, both for measures as well as for results. The favorite source of data for the structuralist, therefore, is language, for the analysis of language can give the structural categories. Two methods of data collection prominent in social psychology are used for the production and analysis of linguistic data: the interview, and content analysis. The interview is the method most specific to social psychology; it has practically been developed for the needs of the structuralist approach. Structural variables found here are not the profound ones that French structuralists, for instance, would use, but include demographic background variables and some basic attitudes, opinions, or behavioral dispositions. In practice, of course, even a large number of these variables cannot account for all the phenomena in a discussion, and only the extreme ingenuity of the researcher can some-times explain away discrepancies and exceptions (Leach, 1970). In addi-tion, the methods of research themselves might influence the results. Some of the categories found may really be functions of the data collec-tion process. However, they may be important structural variables as well, for interview response tendencies may be due to personality traits, just as inaccuracies may be structural variables in their own right (Berg, 1967). Thus, the abilities of the interviewer, as well as the individual relationships to the subject, may have to be categorized to explain the data.

Whatever the approximation to the ideal in practice, the logic of anal-ysis and data presentation is nevertheless specific to the structural model. The structuralist does not try to stress a priori real variables at the expense of others. The structural logic is more like class logic, i.e., looking at the data as intersections of defined classes to which the phenomena belong. Thus, a political point of view might be defined as an intersection of race, sex, economic status, and some ideological variable such as liberalism, conservatism, or interest in the environment, in addition to party identifi-cation. The intersections of all these classes will then be the logical anal-ysis of the data presented. The basic analysis for survey data is tabular presentation, where ideally some of the possible combinations are miss-ing and where others show the structure of the condition to be explained. Guttman scaling, which tries to arrange the data in a logical order and in such a way that certain combinations become impossible, is one example of this approach. The language of analysis is therefore an exposition of the different conditions which may affect the outcome, sometimes put into a hierarchical structure from the deepest structure to the most super-ficial.

Biological Model

While the structural model relies on purely human achievements, the biological model is an attempt to extend the perspective of the physical and biological sciences. It derives social relations from individual relation-ships just as it derives individual psychological behavior from physiologi-cal or physical facts. It does not see a unit larger than the individual organism and uses only those variables which have proven themselves to be important in biology. Its corresponding models are closest to the methods of natural science.

Reduction to biological variables is not an activity primarily concerned with observable events. Thus, in observing the presentations of a ritual, proponents of the biological model would say that what we are really seeing are relations between certain stimuli and responses, or certain narrow events, or actions leading to survival, or even further, certain molecular actions. We do not really observe these events; rather, we attempt to link some observable events to nervous phenomena, to genetic factors, or to evolutionary processes. This has been possible to establish in some cases. In effect, however, reductionism relies on the belief that observable human behavior can be reduced to biological or physical variables. This is a program, not a result of empirical research. The biological model of human nature is a rational system, beginning with a theory and trying to find observable facts to fit it. Within the topic of social psychology, it is an individualist system, trying to build up society from the individual, and trying to build up the individual from his/her own parts.

As the biological model tries to reduce the wealth of human behavior to what it considers essential, it has to discard many of the facts which impinge upon our senses in order to extract a few decisive variables. The model favors a particular method of research where the important variables are predetermined. Thus, for the behaviorist using this model, the important variable might be the reinforcement value of the response that the organism emits. In the early psychoanalytic version, as represented by Freud's "project" (Pribram, 1976), it might be the way in which behavior expresses the displacement of the libido, or in a more physiologically oriented version, it would be a search for hormones or nervous connections.

The sociobiologist would look at the conditions which have survival value for the species. The investigator is, of course, not restricted to natural situations to display the significant variables. He can create situations in which these variables can become overwhelmingly important and, ideally, exclusive of other conditions. This is the definition of an experiment. In experiments, basic variables can be introduced as independent variables, and made crucial in a contrived manner. Everything else can be subordinated or randomized, considered simply as errors in the discussion of the experiment. The experimental method is clearly the one designed to use with the biological model. It helps in introducing variables corresponding to the basic units, and in distinguishing those events which depend on the underlying and supposedly real, physical factors from the more ephemeral errors introduced by those matters which we cannot control.

Similar considerations lead us from methods of analysis to the kind of language the investigator uses to transmit the research results. The appropriate language consists of logic and techniques of inferential statistics. These procedures distinguish between the results of true variables and error. The term "error" includes everything else that one is not investigating at the present time, and that can therefore be discarded. The method of inferential statistics, including especially analysis of variance and correlations, is used to analyze and discuss data obtained by experiment. There are also methods familiar to us from the physical and biological sciences. The mathematics developed from both of them can be transferred to the study of social behavior, based on the biological model.

This model complements the structural model by stressing the continuity of human life with its biological sources. Some human actions and experiences can be understood as an extension of these biological factors and are reducible to this simpler level.

Interactionist Model

Although the two models of structuralism and biologism have many differences, they also have a basic commonality, namely, the belief that observable phenomena are not real but merely stand for the real truth. If one denies any preconception of reality behind the appearances of human life, then everything observable is equally real. The task of the scientist then becomes a detailed description of events, eliminating as far as possible any other presuppositions. The topic of study then becomes the events of interaction, their regularity, and their sequence. This model can be called the interactionist approach, as represented for instance in symbolic interactionism or ethnomethodology. In this model, human nature is the sum total of observable human interaction.

Followers of the interactionist point of view do not make any commitment to the basic nature of man and society. No presuppositions by the investigator are allowed. This approach is similar to the concept of bracketing by the phenomenalist, and in fact this model is close to the phenomenalist approach to social science. It is easier to state what is not considered in this approach than what is. What remains after presuppositions have been subtracted is the immediate picture. "Persons in a social setting" are the only facts given. From this point of view, individuals, as well as society, are abstractions. Reality is immediately given, hardly expressible; thus, even poetic language may be useful. Reality is organized by the acting individuals themselves, and this action is the proper subject matter for social scientists. In the terminology of the field, reality is constructed through negotiations. The appropriate method to employ for this model is observation, especially the observation of natural situations. Indeed, investigators with an inclination toward this theory of human nature prefer to employ observation, especially participant observation, as their method of research. One favorite occupation is observing the research process from different points of view, criticizing the suppositions made by other researchers in the course of their work. Just as the ideal of the biologist is complete control of a subject in the performance of a crucial experiment, and the ideal of the structuralist the complete disentanglement of a complicated situation by very surprising inferences, the ideal of the interactionist is to be an invisible observer who succeeds in finding an unusual and never-discussed situation. As the interactionist's idea of method is so close to that of literature, it is only fitting that a technical criticism of this method should have been put into novelistic form (Lurie, 1967).

The preferred type of analysis is also different from that found in the other two models. These models, whatever their differences, propose a simple reality beyond the phenomena. Their analysis consists of a translation of the facts into a clear, abstract language, preferably that of mathematics. In the interactional model, however, the facts are mainly transmitted through natural language. Interactional research reports and describes situations and arranges facts in sensible sequences. This is the only reality recognized. The interactionist uses logic to prove that a certain fact exists, and that a certain interaction did take place as an important reality in itself. Logically, the only quantifier is its existence. The data may also serve to reveal exceptions that do not fit into the schemes which the other kinds of investigators have prepared. Beyond this, no translation into other schemes is possible. The model of the interactionist is analogous to the procedure of the writer, the preparation of the representative anecdote, or the felicitous incident. In contrast to the abstract, logical way of presenting data in the other models, the interactionist does so in a dramatic way. The interactionists thus prefer to use natural language in looking at the use of mathematical and logical symbols as scientific and representative of the models which they reject. In the whole scheme of research, they add a valuable corrective by forcing a new look at the facts whenever clever abstractions threaten to dominate.

This classification of the models of human nature illuminates some of the difficulties that social psychologists have in appreciating each other's work. Even if few social psychologists adhere exclusively to a single model or accept all of its extremes, deep tendencies indicate irreconcilable ideals. The ideal of the biologist is to find a few variables which are measurable and which will turn out to be prominent. This ideal is open to the charge that an experiment should be a search for measurable variables and controllable conditions, whatever their importance in social life. Thus, they frequently trivialize experience for experiment's sake. Programs may lead to dead ends, resulting in the demonstration of the statistical significance of minute differences among irrelevant variables. Structuralists are sometimes overly clever in analysis while being unconcerned about the source of their data (Leach, 1970). Interactionists are charged with being purely descriptive, of producing literature rather than science. Even the strength of the interactionist perspective, namely that it is superior in style, may be a drawback in this connection. Each of the models of human nature and its associated research technique seems to be valuable from its own point of view for certain limited purposes. In the extreme, the models transcend the field of science. The biological model leads to the experiment as a game, structuralism to a myth, and the interactionist report to the drama or novel. Each of the models is frequently incomprehensible to proponents of the other perspectives. A possible textbook ideal of using the techniques in rotation, of starting with the interactional approach to get new facts, of refining these facts in an experiment, and then looking for distribution in society by a survey may look good on paper, but it has practical problems. Each scientist is so committed to his own approach that communication between them in constructing a composite science becomes unlikely in practical terms.

The Role of Mathematics

Basically, the disagreement lies in the views on the nature of language. In the biological model, language is reduced to physical production and to the coding and decoding of a signal. This act can be traced through different communication acts down the evolutionary scale, and so language is not exclusively human. As far as analysis of language is concerned, the biologist will probably be most confident with the mathematical theory of communication, dividing each language into signal and noise, corresponding to the use of general probability logic in describing experiments. The biologist's language tends toward the transmission of simple, clearly defined concepts. The structuralist, on the other hand, sees in language a characteristically human production, the result of an intensely human effort to classify and organize the world. Thus, structural language, too, will tend to abstract terms, but in a different way. The abstraction looks in units of meaning for traces of the effort to organize the world, which in turn leads to new subdivisions, new insights, and unexpected patterns. For the interactionist, language is only one observable, yet one of the most important, in actual human situations. However, it is exactly the function of the observation to find out how the meaning of language is established. No language has natural meaning; rather, it is negotiated as part of the interactional process. Thus, for the interactionist, one of the most important parts of the research is to determine how meaning and understanding arise from language in certain situations. And we may also suspect that writing the scientific report itself is also an attempt to establish meaning between the researcher and the reader.

Part of the conflict over mathematics is rooted in a circumstance which many philosophers of science have pointed to as a paradox of positivism, especially since Hume. The result has been that advocates of empirical knowledge work on an abstract model based on mathematically perfect figures and relations. While nominally the empirical approach has won in science, theorists have accepted the Platonic approach to perfect mathematical relations over the empirical, Aristotelian one. Thus, the so-called hard scientists, especially those using the biological model in the field, believe in the truth which is mathematically beautiful and perfect but which cannot be seen in the real world. The "soft" scientists, such as the interactionists, accept facts as given, and all the social sciences would stay away from the computer if they were trying to reproduce the world that we see with all its irregularities and unpredictable events.

Mathematics is not the high road to truth, but it can be usefully considered as a language or a metaphor. For certain intellectual tasks which we associate with science, mathematics is the ideal language system. Each term has a unique meaning: A number is a number and an operator is an operator. A mathematical system includes definite rules which combine symbols leading from one symbol to another and reaching a definite conclusion, given certain premises. Thus, if we can represent a set of phenomena by a mathematical system, we know how to handle the interrelations, and we know how to formulate laws and processes, deductions and theorems. In contrast, systems which depend mainly on common language depend on the force of argument, the manner of persuasion, or the empathy of the reader to come to the same conclusions which the scientist has reached.

It has become commonplace, however, to point out that even the best mathematical system cannot fulfill its own requirements. Despite much misinterpretation, such achievements as Gödel's Proof or Heisenberg's Principle of Indeterminacy show that even the simplest mathematical system of the hardest science will end up with an uncertainty, returning to the relation of the observer to the subject. The relations between mathematical systems and the scientific systems enacted upon them will never be as definite as we would like to believe. Natural language, with its inconsistency and lack of clarity, will always be necessary for human communication, even among scientists.

At many points in our discussion of the role of language in social research, we have touched upon the question of mathematics. Social scientists have long maintained an extreme attitude one way or the other toward mathematics. As a topic of research it has claimed central place, as in psychiatrist Warren McCullough's (1965) assertion that the answer to the question "What is a number that a man may know it and a man that he may know a number?" could solve the basic problems of psychology and philosophy. On the other hand, many neglect numerical and spatial relations as topics of research. The contrast is even stronger in scientific language itself, because some workers are consciously numbers users, while others are antimathematical. This corresponds to a general conflict over whether mathematics will save us or whether it constitutes the main evil of the social sciences.

Like any language, mathematics can be endowed with magical properties, but a somewhat more detached attitude may be more useful. Analysis of the different models will show the importance of current extensions of mathematics as they are adapted for the special needs in this field.

Biological Model

The biological model is most hospitable to the use of mathematics, but its use is mainly devoted to data collection and analysis. Computational techniques are developed to distinguish truth from error, and to assess the importance of accepted variables.

We may note a few peculiarities in this approach. Fault for the indeterminacy in social events is here pushed completely on to the data collection process. It is only the fallibility of the research which makes the data so unclear. Looking beyond the research and measurement techniques, the ideal is the clarity and exactness of the so-called exact sciences. However, most research in the social sciences, especially in social psychology, does not try to approximate this exactitude. Results are frequently given in functions and curves, but the empirical data usually show only two or three points. Of course, many curves would fit these empirical relationships. What really comes out of this type of study is the realization that under some conditions we find one outcome larger or smaller than another, or that some set of conditions falls between two others. The effort in the natural sciences to calibrate whole curves, which is also true for some branches of psychology, is avoided, partly because it would be prohibitive. The other reason is that most of the variables are not mathematically calibrated and are really only ordinal variables (Isnard and Zeeman, 1976). The data themselves do not lead to any analytic functional relationships; the shape of the curves is important, but frequently the research is not openly directed to this aim, and therefore exact qualitative mathematical analysis becomes unfeasible.

Structural Language

The aim of the structuralist is also a resultant mathematical, or at least logical, language. The different elements of structuralist exposition can be expressed in symbols, and the symbolic relationships can be expressed in mathematic metaphor: Levi-Strauss's "Introduction to a Science of Mythology" is a massive work using analogies between elements of nature and culture and the manner of cooking, the combination of different elements—hot, moist, cold, dry—in a way of preparing food. Thus, culture is to nature as cooked is to raw, a proposition which can be expressed in symbols. Frequently, structuralists will stay with complete verbal content in their writing, but their aim is a more formal system, signified by graphs and logical symbolism.

The difference in the use of mathematics in the biological and structural models is shown in the controversy over the use of significance tests in survey analysis (Selvin, 1957; Kish, 1959; McGinnis, 1958). Selvin suggests that the experimental model on which significance tests are based is not suited for survey research. Random assignment for the variables of the survey researcher is not possible. One cannot assign neutral respondents to such conditions as sex, residence, race, or age for the purposes of a study in the way an experiment would. Thus, the assumptions of experimental statistics are violated and the tests are useless. Selvin suggests that a number of classifications should be employed whose effect or lack of it on the original relationships would test their importance. McGinnis and Kish acknowledge the violation, but insist on the value of significance tests as against excessive purism. From the point of view adopted here, both sides in the controversy defend their favorite language: Selvin says that only structuralist mathematical language is applicable in a survey, while Kish and McGinnis are more comfortable with the style of the biological model, although strictly speaking, it is not proper.

Interactionist Language

By contrast, the interactionist's point of view tries to dispense with mathematical language because mathematics relies on a reality below the visible structures. Here, the interactionists are equally distinct from both other types, and their approach is opposed to mathematical methods for these data. Natural language has, of course, many advantages, but its disadvantages include a lack of codifiable procedure, generalizations, and even any easily transmissible method for organizing facts. The strength of the interactionist's rejection of mathematics ties in with the vivid description of single incidents which proves the existence of certain phenomena that might be discarded as error in the other systems. If a scientist has sufficient skill in narrating, the story may convince the reader more than the formulas of the other models. Also, the interactionist points to the inapplicability of many current mathematical techniques.

Language Conflict

The contrast of scientific language, like any language conflict in society, can easily become emotional and irreconcilable. If we accept that the kind of use of mathematics is really just a choice of language, which does not in itself guarantee a high order of truth, we may be on the first step to reconciliation. It is more practical to discuss the adaptation which any language must have to handle the facts and procedures at hand than to see this difference as a conflict in fundamental philosophies.

The nature of the data may be partly responsible for the conflict. It is an understatement to say that by their nature they are not very clear. In fact, physical and biological scientists have kept the clarity of their fields inviolate by relegating everything which might obscure their data to the fields of behavioral science and psychology. Thus, astronomers define the variability of the position of stars as due to different observers and/or to personal equation, and physiologists call the sensations which do not correspond to nervous channels, illusions.

As social scientists, we have the question of whether the data's lack of clarity comes from faulty techniques or measurement, or whether the facts of social relations are inherently vague and any definite analysis of doubtful value. The use of traditional mathematics and algebra commits the social scientist to the first alternative, eliminating the error of research, either through better design and control of the circumstances or by mathematical manipulation of the data to lead us to simple, unique relationships. This is the point on which the traditional or positivist social scientists are most vulnerable. After all, language has been developed to take care of social relationships, and it would be reasonable to think that everyday language, with all its faults, mirrors the reality of human relations. But can we accept everyday language without losing completely the advantages of mathematical discourse? If nothing else, the mental discipline of forcing oneself to state the relationship between concept and symbols and the possible method of procedure from one symbol to another makes for clarity of reasoning. This question has been faced in the development of new mathematical procedures, emphasizing qualitative differences but being exact nonetheless.

New Mathematical Languages

Historically, mathematics, especially algebra and analysis, has been developed in response to the needs of physical scientists. It is only recently that methods have been developed which may represent the conditions of the social and human sciences. These methods are more geometrical; they admit that there is a point soon reached beyond which precision cannot go, and therefore they are frequently mathematical without being numerical. The remaining part of the chapter will discuss these techniques in combining the different types of language of the social scientist.

The mathematical language needed should be adapted to the nature of the topic, namely the position of the individual within society. Two aspects are distinctive: The differentiation of concepts is not clear in nature, but at some point there are abrupt changes. These two conditions are interdependent. While in the physical world we find continuous or stepwise change, in the subjective and social world we find commitment. People belong to a state in society to a certain degree: rich or poor, working class or middle class, liberal or conservative, for or against abortion. They will be in this position only to a certain degree; this is the nature of the social world. Each of the models that we have discussed functions in the same way: Adherence of individual actions to a particular model is a question of degree. We are all rather biologically conditioned, mostly following a verbal structure, and mostly determined by interactions. By analyzing actions, we may follow a model as far as we can; it has weaker and weaker relevance. Suddenly it does not work at all and a complete reevaluation must take place.

Mathematical languages which present these peculiarities of the human mind have been constructed when mathematicians turned their interest to human problems. The procedure of degrees of membership in a set—the basic indeterminacy—has been dealt with in the theory of fuzzy subsets. Precise analysis of the immense qualitative changes of sudden breaks has been developed in catastrophe theory, and we can now turn to these languages as helpful for human models.

Fuzzy Subsets

The definition of fuzzy subsets can best be contrasted with the definition of regular subsets, or as we may call them by contrast, crisp subsets. In a crisp subset, each element can be assigned definitely to one or more subsets. In fuzzy subsets, we associate each membership with a number between zero and one which will characterize the degree of membership. In the extreme, zero and one signify nonmembership and membership in crisp subsets. This definition seems similar to probability. However, probability is only one of the interpretations which we may give to fuzziness; there are other interpretations possible. Fuzziness is not a fault of measurement but represents the fact that some events in nature, and especially some terms in language, cannot be defined exactly (Kaufman, 1975; Zadeh, 1965).

An example is preference for people: In classifying people into those whom I like and those whom I do not like, there would be many to whom I could just assign a certain degree of membership to one or the other set. This is not a probability statement but a recognition of the fact that sociometric links are not really very clear. Another example is medical diagnosis. We may define pneumonia by six diagnostic signs. If a certain case has all six signs, we would say it is a textbook case, assigning it a weight of one. If the case has only four signs, a physician might not put it in the set of pneumonia and give it a lower weight, or call it nonsymptomatic pneumonia. This does not mean that the diagnosis has a lower probability, but rather that the disease is not very well defined (Smets, 1978; Woodbury and Clive, 1974). Another difference between fuzziness and probability is that probabilities are combined and computed according to very definite rules which can be given in terms of arithmetic. In fuzzy sets, however, different rules are possible and there are a number of rules for modifying which are useful for certain purposes. Thus, addition (as logical sum) can be defined as taking the larger of the two weights, and multiplication (as logical product) as taking the smaller. From this fundamental definition, a whole set of operations can be defined which centers somewhat between arithmetic and the logic of classes.

Among other advantages, fuzzy subsets are adapted to the conventions of everyday language. If we want to divide the population into young, middle-aged, and old or poor, well-to-do, and rich, we know that we cannot assign every individual to one of the classes, not because of measurement errors, but because the terms themselves are so vague. We can, however, draw curves with different weights assigned to different ages or different incomes. A child of three, for instance, will have a weight of one for young and zero for middle and old age. At thirty, the weight for young might be a little lower and it may have a considerable weight for middle age, but not for old. At sixty, the situation would again be different. A similar arrangement could be made for describing incomes in terms of weights assigned to the terms poor, well-to-do, and rich. These curves of weights against age and income will give us some understanding of the meaning of the terms themselves. We might even find that the curves are different for different people and proceed to analyze the communications patterns, or difficulty in communication, between them.

Two other combinations of these curves may be noted. First, we can justify the method of combination of fuzzy sets that we have noted before. Thus the intersections of young and rich would have the weight of the lower one, through multiplication as logical product. A fifty-year-old has a low membership in the class of being young and rich, whatever the actual income, and a millionaire will have a higher weight for being young or rich, independent of actual age. This kind of combination can be extended and makes it possible for us to analyze complicated expressions to determine their weight.

Another extension may be used in the use of qualifiers. Thus we can use "very" to give us an approximation that corresponds to the square of the original weight. We can see what that means in the example of "old." If we use the weight of old at .2 for age 50, .4 at age 60, .6 at age 70, .8 at age 80, and 1 at age 90, the meaning of very old would be the square of those weights, which then is .04 at 50, .16 at 60, .36 at 70, .64 at 80, and 1 at 90. This curve represents what we mean by "very." "Very" is a linguistic modifier which can be represented as the square, a mathematical operator of weight. It depresses the meaning at a younger age and has a steeper slope at old age. In a similar way, "not so old" might correspond to the square root. Again, we can roughly qualify judgment processes, such as medical diagnoses, or emotions, such as personal preference (Zadeh, 1972).

Fuzzy set theory might also give us a way of manipulating meaning in a mathematical sense. We traditionally use mathematics as language by first stripping the terms of meaning. Numbers would refer then to formal properties but not to the concrete content of words. Fuzzy sets could allow us to include the meanings of words and discuss the different distribution of fuzzy coefficients, depending on the kinds of words we were talking about. We would still be using some abstraction from the wealth of information which is given in an ordinary sentence, but we would be trying to capture at least part of the richness which our use of common everyday language gives us. No gain of this kind, of course, could be bought without a corresponding loss. What we would be losing is the precision of arithmetic and ordinary algebra. We could not compute differences to the third decimal, but we could make rough and valid comparisons. This drawback, however, might be a real advantage if the roughness of distinctions corresponded to the actual state of affairs. The weakness of conventional mathematical models might be just that; they look for spurious exactitude where no exactness of terms can exist. The advantage of the interactional model and its verbal expression is that it uses vague verbal terms for situations which are by nature vague. The theory of fuzzy sets may give us a way of analyzing this condition in a rigorous way.

Catastrophe Theory

Fuzzy set theory is useful in representing the degree of assignment of individuals to conditions. Grade of membership becomes lower and lower until it is questionable whether membership could be meaningfully asserted or whether another membership would be more appropriate. There are situations in which certain conditions can lead to more than one consequence, depending on tradition or the sequence of previous events. With the same experiences and consistent beliefs, one person may well call himself liberal or conservative, depending on the original commitment. There is a range of degree of belief which would be compatible with both self-identifications. But the longer one persists in the identification on the side of a weak membership, the more abrupt will be the change when the original membership cannot be maintained. The analysis of these breaks is the topic of catastrophe theory.

In general, human perception translates the virtually infinite conditions of the world into a limited number of concepts; the degree of fit can be maintained up to a degree of fuzziness and leads to points where the identification cannot be maintained. Mathematically, this relation becomes a mapping process of the infinite universe into a small number of point sets. The mapping consists of taking the original, virtually infinite set of mental events and taking out a subset which consists of units of language and which is localized in space and time. This subset consists roughly of two parts. One part is an open field of regular points, that is, points which are qualitatively similar to all the points in the neighborhood. In calculus, this would be the differentiable points. The second set is a closed set of discontinuous points, or as they are called in the theory, the catastrophic points. The stability of the regular points is aided by the existence of attractors. The point set becomes a vector field, where all points are directed more toward the center. Its stability can be compared to a topographic map where water in a large area will run off to the same river system, and where the watersheds correspond to the catastrophic points. Linguistically, the attractor is the main idea in the word or sentence, which keeps its meaning and therefore guarantees the stability of the set of points, ideas, or of the nouns and sentences which represent them. In effect, the vector field could compare to a fuzzy set where the degree of fuzziness is measured by the distance of the vector from the attracting point. The part outside the regular points and spaces can represent abrupt changes from one term to another; in effect, much as verbs showing the relationship between different nouns (Thom, 1972, 1977, 1978).

Catastrophe theory defines an exact qualitative classification of the possible kinds of continuities or discontinuities in a space of up to six dimensions. Thom's fundamental theorem of catastrophe theory says that only seven qualitatively different catastrophes can exist under those conditions, with the quality being defined by the distribution of the extreme and unstable points. Thus, the simplest catastrophe is a parabola which has one minimum, one unstable point, and only one dimension. Each of these catastrophes' discontinuities is defined by an equation such as the one for the parabola; they can go up to power senses of six degrees, and each of them gives a typical shape from which they have derived the popular name, such as fold or butterfly. These shapes can lend meaning to the verbs which show the relation between stable points to the noun. To take the two simplest ones, a one-dimensional parabola will employ verbs representing continuing states, existing, or being. The next complication is fold or cusp, leading to a line which has one end and signifies the end of being, such as dying or ending. In sum, the theory leads to a thematic interpretation of different types of equations.

These same equations have been used to describe catastrophes or sudden changes in biological development, which gives the linguistic interpretation at least some degree of plausibility. By subdividing some of the catastrophes by the nature of some of the constants or parameters, and by including the combination of the simplest catastrophes, Thom ends up with sixteen types of some degree of catastrophes or discontinuities which he claims account for all relations and verbs representing them between nouns up to relations between four nouns, such as in the sentence, "John changes direction from North to South."

Conclusion

These two theories can transform purely verbal descriptions into mathematical relationships while keeping the meaning and ambiguity of natural language. They form a bridge between the different models of human nature. The analysis of different models has shown that we need some way of integrating the languages of mathematics, logic, and everyday language in order to accommodate the richness of the sum of all three of these models of human nature. We cannot deceive ourselves into believing that this task will be simple. We do deal with phenomena which are fuzzy in nature. The pretense of accuracy of exact arithmetic may deceive us into believing that we know more than we do. The immense complications of the human mind and of human society cannot be mapped into manipulable, visible units in a simple way. This is possibly one of the most difficult problems scientific theory has attempted. We certainly will need a new type of mathematics, an exact qualitative procedure, showing degrees of belongingness, critical points, and characters of curves.

The aim of developing a new branch of theory of human behavior can only be reached by making possible communications and understanding between advocates of different models, and by showing how the different models fit together. Constructing a new language which would encompass all these models may be a difficult task and lead to radical solutions, just as the program in the reconciliation of physical theories led to intricate, esoteric theories which are still not quite fully developed. Before they develop the evidence which is becoming more and more convincing, simple solutions will not be possible. The future will lie in the acceptance of techniques which seem hopelessly complicated at the present time.

References

Berg, I. A. Response set in personality assesssment. Chicago: Aldine, 1967.

House, J. S. The three faces of social psychology. Sociometry, 1974, 40, 161-177.

Isnard, C. A. & Zeeman, E. G. Some models of catastrophe theory in the social sciences. In L. Collins (Ed.), The Use of Models in the Social Sciences. London: Tavistock, 1976.

Jacobson, R. Essais de linguistique générale. Paris: Les Editions de Minuit, 1963.

Kaufman, A. Introduction à la théorie des sous-ensembles flous (Vol. 1). Applications à la linguistique, à la logique et à la semantique (Vol. 2). Paris: Masson, 1975. Translated and published by Academic Press.

Kish, L. Some statistical problems in research design. American Sociological Review, 1959, 24, 328-338.

Leach, E. Levi-Strauss. London: Fontana, 1970.

Levi-Strauss, C. Mythologiques, 5 vols. Paris: Plem, 1964-1974.

Lurie, A. *Imaginary friends.* New York: Coward-McCann, 1967.

McCullough, W. S. What is a number that a man may know it and a man that he may know a number? In W. S. McCullough (Ed.), *Embodiments of mind.* Cambridge, MA: MIT Press, 1965.

McGinnis, R. Randomization and inference in sociological research. *American Sociological Review,* 1958, 23, 409-414.

Pribram, K. *Freud's project reassessed.* New York: Basic Books, 1976.

Selvin, H. A critique of tests of significance in survey research. *American Sociological Review,* 1957, 22, 522-523.

Smets, P. *Un modèle mathematic-statistique simulant le processus du diagnostique medical.* Presses Universitaires de Bruxelles, 1978.

Thom, R. *Stabilité structurelle et morphogenèse.* Reading, MA., Benjamin, 1972 (English edition, 1974).

Thom, R. Language et catastrophe: Elements pour une semantique topologique. In M. M. Peixotto (Ed.), *Dynamical systems.* New York: Academic Press, 1977.

Thom, R. Topologie et linguistique. In Haefliger and Narasimhan (Eds.), *Essays on topology and related topics.* New York: Springer, 1978.

Woodbury, M. A. and Clive, J. Clinical pure types in a fuzzy partition. *Journal of Cybernetics,* 1974, 4, 111-121.

Zadeh, L. A. Fuzzy sets. *Information and Control,* 1965, 12, 99-102.

Zadeh, L. A. A fuzzy set theoretic interpretation of linguistic hedges. ERL Memo M335, University of California, Berkeley, 1972.

CHAPTER 13

Reflexivity in Field Work

IVAN KARP
MARTHA B. KENDALL

> In the social sciences subject and object belong to
> the same category and interact reciprocally on
> each other. Human beings are not only the most
> complex and variable of natural entities, but they
> have to be studied by other human beings, not by
> independent observers of another species.
> **E. H. Carr, *What is History?***

> An anthropologist of all people ought to be
> conscious of the extent to which his intellectual life
> is a product of his interaction with other minds.
> **M. Crick, *Explorations in Language and Meaning***

Field work occupies a central position in most anthropologists' conceptions of themselves and their discipline. Despite this, there is no real consensus about the meaning or nature of field work. Fledgling anthropologists often find that their initial months in the field include periods of intense psychological discomfort if not absolute despair, and they are likely to feel great confusion about how to proceed with the business at hand.[1]

Field-seasoned members of the profession are either rendered mute by questions about the nature of their field experience, or else they offer unconvincing analogies comparing field work to all manner of ordinary

AUTHOR'S NOTE: The authors would like to thank Charles Bird, W. Arens, Dan F. Bauer, Sandra Barnes, Ronald Royce, Bonnie Wright, Barbara Babcock, Kent Maynard, Pamela Bunte, Susan Diduk, and Alan Goldberg for their comments on earlier drafts.

varieties of social participation. In effect, one camp argues that each person's field experiences are unique and noncomparable, and the other camp argues that all human beings are ethnographers by virtue of their common humanity.

When conceptual polarities arise in this fashion, it may be because issues have been wrongly stated and questions incorrectly asked. The uncertainty that lies at the very heart of the field work experience is not a disease, but one of the conditions of existence of anthropological investigation.

We explore in this chapter some of the practical and theoretical problems posed by field work for anthropologists, and the reasons that it holds such fascination for them. We will argue that difficulties often result from anthropologists' inability to reconcile their actual field experiences with implicitly or explicitly held assumptions about the object of their inquiry. We will argue further that the fascination field work holds arises from its profoundly ambiguous nature.

Good field work, we maintain, is concerned with meanings as well as causes. It depends crucially upon discovering the meaning of social relations, and not just those characterizing the "natives'" relations with each other. It depends equally upon discovering the meanings of anthropologists' relations with the people they study, and their relationship to a community of scholars as well. It requires turning the anthropological lens back upon the self and coming to understand that one's own social realities are simply one society's construction rather than a given in nature. This reflexivity means that good field work does not just enlarge the field worker's conceptual field, but reorganizes it. It poses challenges to the field worker's most fundamental beliefs about truth and objectivity. It generates understandings and at the same time casts doubts on the validity of those understandings as it makes clear that self-awareness is a continuing process. To the extent that field work is reflexive, it is ambiguous.

To the extent that it is *not* reflexive, it is also ambiguous. Even the field worker who denies the essentially semantic nature of field work and who strives for "scientific objectivity" occasionally catches glimmers of the positivist observer's paradox: One sees other peoples' behavior and expression of intentions as being caused or determined by factors remote from their consciousness, and this implies that one's own behavior is the same. One can attempt to resolve this puzzle or one can try to ignore it, but either way, thoughts on the issue of objectivity will produce some unsettling moments.

The Practical Activity of Field Work
and the Myth of Field Work Methods

Probably the most shocking realization that novice anthropologists experience in their initial field situations is that they have to learn to draw boundaries. Students are trained by having them read highly schematicized accounts of other peoples' ways, but in these accounts the boundaries are already drawn and the structures laid bare. That, after all, is a major goal of ethnography. In rendering structural concepts apparent, however, ethnographic descriptions lend a concreteness to social facts that can create false expectations about what one will find in the field.

Students engage in field work, see people involved in practical everyday activities such as marketing and child-care, and ponder how they might abstract from such behavior the forms of social existence: lineages, alliances, classes, and so on. Confronted with this dilemma, and believing all the while in their own structure as fact, they often feel that their training was somehow inadequate. They fall victim to the myth of field work methods.[2]

They believe that there is such a thing as "good training" and that it incorporates "discovery procedures"; they convince themselves that there are operations which, when applied to a body of data, identify any systematic features characterizing that corpus and make them apparent. With time and experience, they either come to realize that the "recipes" they have for doing field work do not contribute directly to discovery, or they perpetuate the myth of field work methods by passing on improved methodologies to their own students. They turn to "field work manuals."

The success and popularity of such student manuals as Perti Pelto's *Anthropological Research* (1970) and Brim and Spain's *Research Design in Anthropology* (1974) are probably due to their implicit claims to present discovery procedures in the form of methodological rigor and research design. Pelto's suggestions for improving field work all follow from behaviorist, reductionist, and naturalist premises, namely, that the object of anthropological inquiry is the "stuff out there" and that that "stuff" has as two of its primary attributes *stability* and *observability*. His appeal is to those who believe that a finite set of determinate variables govern human behavior, and that isolating all the relevant variables will explain human action.

He argues for a "scientific" stance in anthropology rather than a humanistic one, but his view of science deserves closer attention. The following passage, with its pinings for the tests and measures available to "friends in other sciences," reveals a curious lack of interest in whether such devices are adaptable to, or even appropriate for anthropological research aims. On the contrary, he asserts that anthropology's traditional questions should be recast in an idiom more conducive to quantification.

> Much of the lore about field research that we picked up informally in our graduate student days was concerned with the gentle arts of rapport building and role-playing in field situations. We were not so much concerned, nor were our mentors, with rules of evidence, questions of representativeness, reliability, and the many other related elements of social inquiry with which our friends in other sciences seemed to be preoccupied. I can recall no discussion or even mention of the idea of "operationalizing variables" in those halcyon days [1970: xi-xii].

Pelto's conception of "science" promotes method over conceptual clarity. As a result, he blurs the important distinction between human action and human behavior. He fails to recognize that field workers do not observe subjects behaving; they *interpret human actions*. To recognize that field work consists of inferring the meanings of human activity is to acknowledge the role that the observers play in their own analyses, which is of course to deny that the behavior can be seen as *brute data* (see Bhaskar, Giddens, or Manicas, this volume).

We shall return to the question of "recipes" for field work in the next section, and argue that field methodologies are no more than devices for organizing and validating inferences. They are useful in that they help field workers frame questions and construct accounts in anthropologically acceptable forms, but they do not in themselves reveal much about social facts. Neither the great distrust of field work methods nor the extravagant claims for their efficacy are warranted. Coherent research procedures are necessary, but not sufficient preconditions for anthropological interpretations.

Field Work as Unique Experience: The Myth That No Advice is Good Advice

There are convincing reasons for arguing that every anthropologist's field experiences are unique. After all, each field worker does take a singular mixture of presuppositions, personal penchants, and past histories into the field, and these factors cannot help but color interpretations made there. They influence interpretations both because they predispose individual field workers toward particular ideological or theoretical positions, and because they figure in the manner in which field workers present themselves to the populations they study. This in turn has its effect on how those populations interact with them. Needless to say, the quality and depth of these human interactions have everything to do with the success or failure of the field trip as a research enterprise.[3]

In acknowledging the individuality of each persons's field experience, however, we should not be tempted to treat questions about the practical conduct of field research lightly. Some very eminent members of the profession seem to have taken the position that if we cannot tell our students what to expect in the field, we should confine our advice to them to matters of hygiene and personal comportment:

> The charming and intelligent Austrian-American anthropologist Paul Radin has said that no one quite knows how one goes about fieldwork. Perhaps we should leave the question with that sort of answer. But when I was a serious young student in London I thought that I would get a few tips from experienced fieldworkers before setting out for Central America. I first sought advice from Westermarck. All I got from him was "don't converse with an informant for more than 20 minutes because if you aren't bored by that time he will be." Very good advice even if somewhat inadequate. I sought instruction from Haddon, a man foremost in field research. He told me that it was really all quite simple; one should always behave as a gentleman. Also very good advice. My teacher, Seligman, told me to take ten grains of quinine every night and to keep off women. The famous egyptologist, Sir Flinders Petri, just told me not to bother about drinking dirty water as one soon became immune to it. Finally I asked Malinowski and was told not to be a bloody fool. So there is no clear answer, much will depend on the man, on the society he is studying, and the conditions in which he is to make it [Evans-Pritchard, 1976: 240].

Evans-Pritchard's conclusion that there is "no clear answer" may be cold comfort to novice anthropologists on the eve of their maiden voyages to the field, but there is no reason why this should be the only advice they get. There are established practices for gathering anthropologically relevant information in the field, and particular ways to address particular issues. A significant justification for having students write research proposals before they leave for their communities is to get them to think coherently about research questions and the strategies for answering them. The requirement that evidence in field reports be systematically presented is designed to guarantee that each person's field experience does not remain unique but is translated into an idiom that others can appreciate. Since the discipline requires certain standards of planning and forethought in field work and canons of evidence and intelligibility in field reports, it follows that there is a level on which anthropologists take the operations of data gathering very seriously.

What we often fail to make clear to our students and ourselves is the relationship between the operations they perform in the field and the accounts they subsequently construct about their field work. As we maintained earlier, *field techniques are not discovery procedures.* They do not contribute directly to analyses, although they aid field workers in organizing and rationalizing their experiences. They do not reveal "social facts"; they simply allow the researcher to proceed systematically toward inferring what those facts could be. This very important point raises the issue of the effect of disciplinary requirements on the actual conduct of field work. Whatever ethnographers may find in the field, they are obligated to frame their reports of it in certain ways and not others; that is, if they wish other anthropologists to view them as adherents of the discipline. What they do find in the field, of course, is already influenced to some extent by the values they carry as part of their anthropological training, including values attached to conduct, their own and others.[4] Field work is more than a simple two-way relationship between natives and ethnographers. The whole anthropological community has a stake in how these kinds of relationships work themselves out, if for no other reason than to guard its claim to being a serious intellectual discipline. If the importance of methodology is a recurrent but unresolved issue in discussions of field work, it is probably because anthropologists have failed to reflect upon the requirements for "seriousness" that they impose on themselves.

If we take the influence of the profession as a whole as having a bearing on the conduct of research, the methodology issue becomes clearer. Research procedures can be viewed as framing devices for translating one set of experiences into another—i.e., they allow the individual to converse with the discipline at large, which therefore makes them valuable in both the conduct and the presentation of research. By the same token, if professional values are attached so closely to research procedures, there cannot be a rigid separation between "objectivity" and "belief." This means that methodologies are not valuable because they are "objective" and "scientific," but rather that they are valuable because they allow us to communicate with each other. The scholarly community is the third party in field work. The danger for field workers is that they will confuse the requirements that field workers' accounts be systematic and consistent with the invitation to treat as privileged the influence of the scholarly community on the account itself; that is, as not subject to the same standards of critical evaluation. Anthropological research is as value-impregnated as any other form of human conduct.

Theoretical Perspectives on Field Work: The Myth of Social Homologies

Anthropologists are fond of presenting themselves to others by making analogies with taking different roles, not only in their accounts of themselves to the people they study, but in accounts of anthropology written for students and colleagues as well. The literature on field work is replete with descriptions in which field workers are likened to a spectrum of social types: children undergoing socialization, second-language learners, quasi-kinsmen, natural historians, strangers, helpful and concerned friends, and so forth.

These analogies try to grapple with the issue of how ethnographers discover the meaning of an alien people's action by situating the process of discovery in the capacities of all social beings. To the extent that they stress our common humanity and demonstrate that even Western modes of thought are based in these capacities, such analogies are interesting; but they may be misleading if they neglect the differences between the social situation of the anthropologist and the social types or roles with which ethnographers are compared.

Childhood socialization is a popular and frequently invoked comparison. The argument is made that anthropologists learn about social relationships in a given society in the same way that children growing up there do. Of course, they admit that they do not know what that process is, but they regard this as irrelevant: Anthropologists presumably already have whatever skills children use to acquire meanings, because anthropologists were once children themselves.

As Burnett (1976) shows, the analogy between childhood socialization and ethnographic method yields only partial insights. Both anthropologists and children undergoing socialization must learn sets of appropriateness conditions for acting. That is, they must learn how to relate rules to contexts, the degrees to which rules for behavior are negotiable, and they must learn about the limiting conditions of negotiation: power, self-interest (long-range versus short-range), and structure. But anthropologists, in common with other adults, are *not* like children, because they already possess established routines for rendering the world intelligible. They do not have to "learn how to learn" (deutero-learning, in Bateson's [1970] terminology); they have to learn content, substance, the "rule of conduct."

To see the faults in the childhood socialization analogy, it is only necessary to recall that while the final product of ethnographic endeavor should be logical, coherent, organized and clear, native cognition does not exist in this fashion. Hence, the comparison between ethnographer and child cannot make reference to the end result of the learning process, but only to the assumed antecedent state of the learner (naive about particulars versus informed about them), or to the unknown but assumed process of discovery. This is hardly enlightening. To compare one unknown process to another gets us nowhere. That anthropologists require their claims to knowledge to be explicit and testable suggests that there are significant differences between anthropological forms of consciousness and other, mundane forms.

In any case, social scientists have come increasingly to realize that socialization is a lifelong process and does not have any end point. The parallel may be drawn, then, between anthropological field work and adult socialization, as has sometimes been done. There are difficulties here as well.[5] Adult socialization is essentially segmental and discontinuous. Preparation for role-taking occurs both before and simultaneously with the assumption of social roles. Socialization for one role may be isolated from learning another role. Furthermore, any given adult's repertoire of roles is neither comprehensive nor does it conform to the requirements of an anthropological account.

A major difference between a field worker's experience of the social order and the native adult's is that the field worker continually refers back to his or her communities of origin, both scientific and natural. In this way the field worker is often compared with the role of the stranger or friend. The stranger analogy is interesting because of the qualities that the stranger role exhibits and what the stranger experiences. Strangers, according to Simmel (1950), combine the paradoxical qualities of nearness and farness. They are spatially near and culturally far. They exist betwixt and between, neither in one society nor the other. This has led Schutz (1964) to suggest that from the subjective perspective, the problem of the stranger lies in his inability to assume the "natural stance," to take intersubjectivity as a given in his social situation. Thus, the parallel between the stranger and the field worker rests on two qualities that they have in common. On the one hand, the stranger cannot be treated as either an insider or an outsider, but paradoxically is both; and on the other hand, the stranger is placed in the situation of having to discover what the natives take for granted. This double analogy seizes on the problem of the stranger in terms of the field worker's interaction with the subjects of his or her research and with the requirement that the field worker turn the implicit and practical knowledge of the socially committed actor into a discursive form.[6]

Fortes (1975) concurs, arguing that strangers, from the point of view of the indigenous peoples, are potentially dangerous individuals. Because they are unknown, they may bring either great misfortune or great opportunity; but in either case, it is the wise and prudent person who treats a stranger hospitably and with marked deference. In kinship-based societies, sojourners who settle in for extended periods may be reclassified as kinsmen or quasi-kinsmen, a symbolic acknowledgment of their being known, and therefore safe.

Fortes's analogy has the merit of pointing to the dynamic element in the field work experience. Field work does not entail the static assumption of a role or a single-stranded relationship, any more than does any other type of social activity. The field work experience is developmental and changing.

There are difficulties with the stranger analogy, however. Field work does not take place in a power vacuum, and the field worker is often placed in the position of being a representative of a colonial regime or a metropolitan culture (Maquet, 1964; Asad, 1973). These are part of the conditions of existence of the field worker, and they pose important ethical and analytical problems that the stranger analogy neglects.

One difference between the stranger and the field worker arises out of the different interest situation of the two. While the stranger may not be knowledgeable about or accepted in the social context in which he acts, he frequently maintains the social interaction out of necessity. Thus, the natives' conditions of existence affect him as much as them. Field workers, on the other hand, are not subject to the same constraints, and this must inevitably affect the quality of their experience. Rosemary Firth (1972) recounts a nightmare she had shortly before leaving the field. She dreamt that she really was a Malay woman, "squatting in front of a smokey fire." The participation that the field worker gives is neither as committed nor as constrained as the native's.[7]

In this respect, the field worker is less the native acting in the context of everyday life and more the performer in a ritual or the participant in a game. The same analogy is drawn by Firth in her essay and is apt in a number of ways. First, the game is "only a game" and can be terminated at any time the player chooses. Second, the goal of a game is not necessarily to win. Only some games are specifically competitive. The game may contain its own end rather than lead to an end, rather like Simmel's account of sociability (1950). In this case, the end may be the display of skill that is contained in many games. Games, in any case, have an amoral quality about them that catches an aspect of the field work experi-

ence. Both field worker and native recognize that the field worker's manipulation of the forms of native social life have a "not-for-real" quality
about them that allows the participants in the field work "games" to focus
on the quality of the doing rather than the consequence. Field workers
often remark that their display of knowledge has frequently led to a sort of
"How do you know that?" response that presaged a deeper penetration
into the forms of native life.

This attitude is aesthetic. Skill becomes an end in itself and leads to
further elaboration of form. In a sense, both the native and the field
worker know that it does not count in the same way as life-in-society.

The various analogies that have been drawn between field work and
different social roles are enlightening. Taken as a whole, however, they
show a general failure to stress an element of the field work experience
that differentiates it from the repertoire of roles that an adult may take on
as part of his or her life-in-society. Ethnographic analysis requires the field
worker to penetrate beneath the surface forms of social life in order to
produce a form of knowledge that is not found in association with ordinary social roles. In the case of friendship, for example, ethnographers
may indeed become friends with the people whose cultures they investi-
gate, and they may indeed perform the ritual or nonritual activities of the
kinsman. Yet an ethnographer's relationship to these people is not primarily one of friendship or kinship. As Richardson (1975, p. 521) observes: "The ethnographer must ask probing questions; he cannot, as
one does with friends, accept the informant as the person he is, but the
ethnographer must find out, he has to find out, why the informant believes what he does." Ethnographers cannot always act as friends, nor as
kinsmen either, since the goals of ethnographic description require them
to take an analytic stance with respect to the actions kinsmen and friends
perform in that social group. Ethnographers who do not maintain an
analytic disaffection from social roles—those who "go native" or who
take everything at face value—relinquish in the eyes of the profession
their claim to be involved in serious anthropological research.

This cannot be overemphasized. Anthropological assertions must be
couched in rhetorical form, i.e., they must be able to be tested and found
wanting by the audience to which they are addressed—the anthropological community. If anthropological arguments make reference to the
meanings native actors assign to their own action, they may also make
reference to factors beyond native comprehension. This is so because the
anthropological community itself requires ethnographers to deal with the
problem of native false consciousness. Responsibility to the profession,

i.e., to a community of scholars outside the community studied, affects the kinds of explanatory accounts ethnographers can offer, and this in turn affects the kinds of social interactions ethnographers in the field can have. Adult socialization within a community does not require the extreme analytic and skeptical stance required of ethnographers, and thus is in many ways an inappropriate analogy. Ethnographers are first socialized in their own community, and then again in their scientific community, and the latter in a way that places severe constraints on socialization in a native community.

There is a final analogy for ethnographic field work we wish to consider here, and that is the one likening it to second language acquisition. This comparison is an attempt to account for the presumed fact that a native actor's knowledge of his or her culture is implicit and unarticulated, while the ethnographer's formulation of this knowledge is explicit and coherent. Anthropologists learning about social relations in alien societies are said to be like adults learning alien languages, in that both groups consciously try to learn what natives assimilate unconsciously.

People pursuing this linguistic analogy generally make a distinction between native language learning and second language acquisition. For example, in first language learning, says the Soviet semiotician Yuri Lotman (cited in Eco, 1976, p. 138), a native speaker is "trained through exposure to a continuous textual performance of pre-fabricated strings of . . . language, and he is expected to absorb his competence even though not completely conscious of the underlying rules." Adults, on the other hand, "are introduced to an unknown language by means of rules; they receive a set of units along with combinatorial laws and they learn to combine these units in order to speak."

Lotman's characterization applies only to adults learning second languages in relatively formal classroom circumstances however. In informal language learning situations (which is where most second language acquisition takes place), the process is far more complex, interesting, and creative than Lotman seems to have realized. Adults picking up new languages "in the streets" try to abstract, infer, or construct rules characterizing the alien tongues at points where its grammatical processes differ from their own language. They almost never think consciously about grammar when their native idiom is structurally similar to the language they are trying to learn. For example, if a person's native language puts subjects before verbs and verbs before objects, and the second language does the same, the adult language learner will get a "free ride" on the implicit grammatical rules he or she already knows. In other words, the

learner will not have to learn any new rules, consciously or unconsciously. If a person's first language puts verbs before objects and the
language to be acquired puts verbs after objects, the learner may have to
formulate a new rule, but he could also continue to follow the word order
of the native languages and do things "wrong" from the point of view of
speakers of the other language. If there is no impediment to communication, this is a fairly practical strategy (Kendall, in press; Schumann, 1974,
1976). While adult language learners typically do look for organizing
principles for acquiring new tongues, they also involve themselves in
much creative trial and blunder. That is, they use a blend of unconscious
analogy, conscious analogy, conscious reformulation of analogy, and
imaginative projection to construct an abstract system (i.e., a grammar)
out of the unbounded evidence of speech forms.[8]

The real senses in which a field worker is like a second language
learner are these: (1) both try to infer and organize kinds of social knowledge that may not be part of the conscious apparatus of the people from
whom they are trying to learn, and both have to use their wit and imagination to accomplish this; (2) both measure their success in terms of
public acceptance of the products of these cognitive exercises.

It is important to note here that the abstractions a language learner or
ethnographer formulates are extremely difficult, if not impossible, to
confirm in certain circumstances, e.g., the non-native's "rules" may correctly project the behavior which natives manifest, without being the
same "rules" as those that the natives are following (indeed, they almost
certainly cannot be the same rules where the native's knowledge is implicit and the non-native's explicit), or the non-native's rules may project
incorrect behaviors which the natives accept out of politeness or respect
for the non-native. As long as the abstractions or rules generate expected
or acceptable behaviors, then they may be said to be in some sense
"correct," following a proof-of-the-pudding logic, whether or not they
are the "true" rules. On the other hand, when the non-native's abstracted
principles generate behaviors evoking puzzlement, consternation, cen-
sure, reproof, and the like from the native, then these formulations can be
said more clearly to be incorrect. The irony of this situation has not
escaped the attention of either linguists or ethnographers: We are certain
of our formulations only when they meet disconfirmation—only when
the people violate our expectations. When our rules are predictive, we
can never be sure they are the same as the natives' (Collett, 1978), or
even whether they really project "correct" behaviors from a native point
of view.

The stranger, the game, the second language learner, and the quasi-kinsman all confront the field worker in terms of a series of analogies that strive to capture a feature of the field work experience that is essential to an understanding of the process of interpretation that leads to discovery. All of these roles or situations attempt to present the paradox of field work, that it exhibits a peculiar combination of engrossment and distance. As an activity, field work often succeeds best where it is least aware of itself; that is, where the engrossment of the field worker is such that he or she brackets the difference between field work and life-in-society. This is a necessary step in the interpretation process that is so essential to field work as a methodology. In this way, interpretation and participation come together as a means of discovery. But discovery does not proceed solely through immersion in a form of life. The discovery of crucial facets of a form of life occurs only when the immersion of engrossment is broken by the experience of the unexpected and the unanticipated. This experience has been glossed by Zaner as "shock." Shock breaks the "natural attitude" and forces the actors to consider that there are possibilities other than the ones they have taken for granted or as given. *"Our attention shifts from that of engagement in to that of focal concern for the sense and strata of the very engagement itself"* (1970, p. 51, emphasis in the original).

It may help to explicate this experience in the context of field work through a description of an incident from Karp's (1978, 1980) field work journal. Karp customarily spent the late afternoon at a compound of a prominent elder who was both a friend and an informant. In the early evening, the people who had congregated around the elder's house would invariably be invited to share the evening meal. The food would be served by the elder's wife to the assembled men in front of the door of the elder's sleeping hut. On one such occasion, Karp brought an anthropologist friend who was visiting him. The friend was engaged in field work among an ethnic group some 50 miles away from Karp's field site. The guest was taken aback by the experience of eating outdoors. "The Tuken," he said, "regard eating outside as a disgusting act." Suddenly, what had seemed an unremarkable feature of Iteso social life became problematic. The anthropologists and the natives discussed the puzzle of these cultural differences. The natives saw nothing unusual about their culinary habits, but they did point out that one crucial way in which the person is evaluated was with whom and where he ate. A man who consistently eats inside his house without visibly demonstrating the evidence that he is willing to share his food with his neighbors is termed *epog,* a term the

Iteso translate as "selfish," and a considerable insult. In the context of Karp's investigation of neighborhood organization, the major focus of his research, this event led him to associate the display of sociability with the custom of eating outdoors and the sharing of food and drink with ideals of neighborliness and the terms by which persons are evaluated.

The experience of "shock" is one facet of the situation and experience of field work to which the analogies draw attention. Anthropologists have considered this form of *learning by contrast* in their discussions of field work. A. J. Köbben (1967), for example, argues that subjective experience is objectified through errors made by ethnographers and corrected by natives. From this viewpoint, the idiot might provide a better analogy than the stranger. The ethnographer's interaction with the natives provides a confrontation in which metacommunicative rules and devices are made manifest and explicit. The anthropological presence, as well, may produce questions about fundamental categories. In the same volume, de Josselin de Jong (1967) argues that "participants' views are made clearer by contrast and . . . ideals are sharply defined by conflicts." Thus these two essays draw a parallel between the experience of shock in association with contradiction and conflict in society, and the particular form it takes in the field work experience. Once again we see support for the position that field work as a research activity is based in fundamental and universal human capacities, and that while the organization of the experience may differ from context to context, the mechanism of learning by contrast is a basic feature of the process of discovery in field work.

Field workers experience "shock" through the medium of the social relationships they establish with the objects of their investigation, the natives. The learning process often works both ways, and the field worker uncovers that which is usually implicit or hidden through a process of mutual guesswork that is the "work" of the social relationship established between field worker and native. The recourse to analogy between field work and different social roles may be part of attempts by both the field worker and the natives to make sense out of the unusual situation of the field worker. In this sense, field work institutionalizes "shock." The field work relationship differs from other social relationships available to the actors in a society but also shares features of those relationships. Making sense out of social relationships, including field work relationships, entails semantic activity. In their relationships with the subjects of their investigation and with the scientific community of which they are a part, field workers use their semantic capacity in semantic activity to produce social relationships and as a research tool.

Field Work as Semantic Activity:
The Search for Meanings and Causes

Social relationships arise out of actors' definitions of situations and their interpretations of circumstances. Actors communicate their interpretations to others by means of shared symbol systems, and together the parties to an interaction negotiate a common definition of their circumstance. In this view of the nature of social relations, acts of interpretation are central. They allow actors to impute intentionality to other actors, and at the same time assume that like imputations will be made in turn.

In any social relationship, including the anthropologist/informant one, actors constantly test the accuracy of their inferences and imputations, and the process by which they do this is extraordinarily complex. They read other people's behavior as meaningful activity, picking and choosing among the different possible interpretations of it available to them. If the parties to the interaction create widely divergent interpretations because they start from different assumptions about the nature of things, they can nevertheless continue to think their definitions are shared until evidence to the contrary no longer fits a hypothesis of consensus. At such points, actors can either renegotiate a consensual definition (oh, you meant X; I thought you meant X'. Now I get it), or they can terminate the relationship, charging the other parties with noncooperation, malfeasance, or inscrutability. Puzzlements or vague feelings of social discomfort are often crucial evidence of nonconsensus, but they may not be recognized as such for extraordinarily long periods of time.

Anthropological field workers try to reduce the inherent indeterminancy of research relationships in ways that are beneficial to them and designed to maintain these relationships. They often present themselves to the people they work with in terms that they think the people will understand and accept, but they also take covert positions—not necessarily out of a desire to dissemble—which their informants know nothing about. At the same time, the identical process is characteristic of their informants' relationships with them and each other (Berreman, 1962). This often leads to nonconsensual interpretations of interaction. Informants' expectations about how certain categories of people behave in their own society will be transferred to the field workers, and if the field workers are not careful, they will do the same.

At the level of nonverbal presentations of self, these attributions and the inferences derived from them can lead to all manner of confusions, which may be difficult to correct. The discovery of mutual nonconsensus is rendered difficult because social actors assume that their definitions are shared and ignore evidence that runs counter to their assumptions. The failure of field workers to monitor the social aspects of their interactions can have serious effects on the integrity of research reports issuing from their interactions, particularly when the parties involved construct tacit and nonparallel hypotheses about the distribution of power and interest in the interaction.

Power and interests are dimensions of all social relationships, including field work relationships. In order to produce their research relationship, anthropologists acquire a practical knowledge of the local organization of power and interests. They are also interested, however, in producing accounts that analyze the role of power and interests in the production of social relationships. This requires them to examine the patterning or distribution of power, in both meaningful and causal terms. For native actors, the distinction between cause and reason, for example, is not necessarily relevant to their conduct. This is because they must incorporate causes into the reasons for their action, even if this is done in a manner which mystifies the cause (see Bhaskar, 1980). Clifford Geertz (1973) tells us that "cultural actions, the construction, apprehension and utilization of symbolic forms are social events like any other; they are as public as marriage and as observable as agriculture." We take this to mean that the performance of cultural acts serves to define situations in terms that are drawn from the repertoire of actors, and to make one or another aspect of the actor's identity relevant or irrelevant. Thus, the timing and selection of the cultural act performed is not necessarily the result of a desire to communicate, but may be a byproduct of the pursuit of interests. By extension, some actors will be constrained to act in a culturally prescribed manner not so much because of their own self-interest, but because they are unable to impose their own definition on a situation they do not control.

We do not mean to imply either that actors are necessarily aware of the degree to which they acquiesce in granting others the power to define their social world, or that definitions of situations are simply outcomes of successful strategies in ideological power games.

Weber (1958) argues that beliefs and values as components of social action act as no more than switching devices, directing action into one or another path in a course to a preexisting goal. It is possible to make this argument even stronger. The organization of interests in a given society, the distribution of power, and the constraints exercised as consequences of prior actions affect the pattern of action and the pursuit of goals in particular times and particular societies. Hence, a given action may be affected by factors that are either external to the consciousness of actors or only imperfectly understood by them.

Many social and behavioral science explanations of the causes of action depend upon the assumption that actors are unaware and cannot be as aware of the factors that produce their action, or, alternatively, that such accounts assume rather than try to discover the interior logic of native actors. In some versions, actors are presumed to think in terms of an economic calculus; in others, they are the unthinking products of the conditions of their existence.

Because patterns of action can be shown to have consequences external to the consciousness of actors, or to be the product of calculations of cost and benefit, or to be the result of the imposition of some person's will on another, some anthropologists have found it easier to ignore natives' expressions of thoughts and intentions altogether and to substitute accounts derived from a general theory of human behavior instead. There is nothing particularly wrong with causal explanations that describe behavior as the result of unapprehended factors, as long as a peculiar form of explanatory short-circuiting does not occur. Asserting or demonstrating that human actions may be *caused* does not absolve anthropologists from describing how actors account for their own behaviors, and how these accounts figure in the production of subsequent actions.[9] We need to know what actors intend by what they do and how they go about realizing their intentions if we are to have an adequate explanation of action. Actors' constructions of their own behaviors are not irrelevant data, no matter how curious or beside the point they may seem. Even if they are not true reflections of interior states, or full explanations of action, they have to be examined critically. This is so because there is always the chance that other actors will take such reports at face value and act upon them. "Untrue" interpretations may become true by virtue of their consequences. Explanations presented primarily in causal terms represent attempts to avoid confronting the problem of the observer's consciousness and its relationship to the explanations.

If anthropologists or other social scientists finally begin to make sense out of their research objects' behavior, they are then faced with problems of proving that this inspired guesswork, these interpretations of behavior, actually conform to some underlying reality. In this sense, they face a problem similar to the one members of the society being studied face, i.e., how to reconcile one's own interpretation of other people's behavior with other people's accounts. It is not that the others' behavior does not make sense; it is that the explanations they give of their behavior are sometimes irreconcilable with one's own. In many circumstances it is

difficult to establish whether other actors' self-reports are valid representations of their thoughts and intentions, instances of false consciousness,
attempts to dissemble, or some combination of these.

What then justifies the ethnographer's attempts to account for native
systems of knowledge if they cannot reproduce what goes on inside the
native's head? The justification seems to be that there are aspects of
behavior which are both internal and external to actors. We may thank
Durkheim for pointing out long ago that there must be aspects of the
ideas that people share that are publicly accessible and publicly validated;
what he called "collective representations" are interpreted and validated
in public circumstances. The knowledge of "other minds" on which these
interpretations are based is always provisional and ambiguous. The ambiguities are not only the necessary conditions in terms of which social
adjustments can be made, they are the necessary conditions of social life;
for if they provide the space out of which social order can emerge, they
also provide the material for innovation and change. If order is not completely determined, then it becomes possible to institute changes in the
very process of recreating that order (Moore, 1976).

The ambiguous nature of the symbols used in communication—their
relationship to both order and change—leads to a significant methodological point, namely, that the indeterminacy and uncertainties ethnographers perceive as features of the social relations to which they relate
their analyses are, at the same time, features of the social world to which
actors must orient themselves. The interpretive procedures through
which natives render their experiences intelligible are just that, interpretive procedures. They no more provide actors with true statements about
the internal states of others than they provide anthropologists with true
pictures of "what the natives really think." The shared idiom of social
interaction consists of symbols, or collective representations, whose function is to mediate between private experience and its public expression.
Since this is true, anthropologists seem entirely justified in pursuing their
attempts to describe native systems of thought and action in terms of the
meanings with which actors construct cultural worlds, even if they (the
anthropologists) must realize the contingent nature of the knowledge that
both they and the natives produce (see Geertz, 1973, 1976).

Social relationships or systems of social relationships have a dual
quality. Actors negotiate them on the basis of their inferences about other
actors' intentions, and, simultaneously, they are the products of factors
that are more or less remote from the consciousness of the actors. Giddens (1976) describes *structure* as having a dual quality in this same

manner. Structure, he tells us, is both the medium in terms of which action takes place and the unintended consequence of action.

Conclusions

In his account of the religion of the Nuer, Evans-Pritchard raises a fundamental paradox of anthropological field workers: that their activities are situated in a social field that encompasses radically opposed requirements in terms of which they formulate accounts.

> Nuer are not confused, because the difficulties which perplex us do not arise on the level of experience but only when an attempt is made to analyze and systematize Nuer religious thought. Nuer themselves do not feel the need to do this. Indeed, I myself never experienced when living with the Nuer and thinking in their words and categories any difficulty commensurate with that which confronts me now when I have to translate and interpret them. I suppose I moved from representation to representation, and backwards and forwards between general and particular, much as Nuer do and without feeling that there was any lack of coordination in my thoughts or that any special effort to understand was required. It is when one tries to relate Nuer religious conceptions to one another by abstract analysis that the difficulties arise [1956, p. 106].

The very idea of the "participant observer" incorporates in itself a number of paradoxes. First, there is the distinction that must be drawn between an observer's orientation to the social world which, as Bourdieu (1977) rightly concludes, leads the anthropologist to treat social life as a drama or spectacle in which the actors play already written parts. On the other hand, the actors themselves are not concerned with playing roles. Their activities are practical and purposive. For them, society is often a means to an end, and not the goal of their action.[10]

This paradox shades into a second. A key assumption of our study is that society is the product of knowledgeable actors (Giddens, 1979). Yet we have also argued that field workers often articulate their accounts in terms that are not recognized in the same way or the same form as the accounts formulated by the native actors themselves. This paradox is resolved through the distinction Giddens draws between practical and discursive consciousness. Unlike Giddens, we do not regard practical consciousness as fully reflexive. Practical knowledge must certainly lead to reflection, but a genuinely reflexive orientation to the social world is, in our opinion, destructive rather than productive of social order. Reflexivity incorporates both an understanding of how to produce order and of the very conditions of the existence of order itself. In an ideal, typical sense, the discursive consciousness of the field worker recognizes not only those factors that are discursively unavailable to the members of a society, but also that the knowledge produced by the field worker is subject to similar determinations as well. Often, field workers are able to confront the social determination of their own knowledge through the "shock" of accounting for the consciousness of the objects of their research. The natural stance which is so destructive of reflexivity is more difficult to sustain under conditions of conflict and contradiction.

The first datum of the field anthropologist is the expressed consciousness of the members of a society. Only by understanding the accounts people give of themselves can an anthropologist follow through and show them to be "false," "inadequate," or "incomplete" in some way. The notion of false consciousness, which we think stands at the very center of anthropological analyses of behavior, depends upon prior discovery of forms of consciousness that exist in a given social formation.[11] The lessons that should be drawn from this are obvious. First, if social analysts take seriously native accounts and try to reconcile them with higher-order explanations, they must also surely have to come to grips with the shifting sand beneath their own feet—i.e., they have to face the very real possibility that the meanings they assign to others' behaviors are influenced by factors outside of their *own* consciousness. They must, in other words, develop a reflexive stance insofar as it is possible, according to which they may examine critically the analytic procedures through which they constructed their explanations.

If the primary datum of field anthropology is the native's consciousness, and the second consists of the external factors that affect this native consciousness, then surely the tertiary data is the analyst's own consciousness and his or her reflections on it. This means that the anthropological image of a society should be characterized by an almost exquisite degree of self-consciousness when compared to that of the members of a society. The anthropologist's competence, or knowledge of organizing principles, is at once more comprehensive and less detailed than the native's. It must necessarily be so, because it is acquired in a very different fashion and is put to very different uses.

The dialectical relationship between discovery and validation may help to throw some light on the nature of anthropological accounts.[12] The repertoire of data elicitation devices, the systematic presentation of evidence, and the logic of hypothesis confirmation are not characteristic of what Georg Simmel might call the "practical reality" of everyday life. Everyday life is organized in terms of what phenomenologically oriented social scientists have referred to as the "natural stance," and by "natural" we take them to mean unreflective as well. The culture of anthropologists and the interests they have in surviving and succeeding in that culture require that the natural stance of native worlds be subjected to critical evaluation. They require as well that both the inferences of meaning and the description of the causal factors that produce behavior be confirmed in terms that are not drawn from the cultural world under investigation. In this sense, anthropologists' accounts face in two directions. On the one hand they must be faithful to the members of the society that is being studied, and on the other hand they must conform to the criteria of the scientific community of which the anthropologist is a member.

This is not an easy task. All too often the delicate balance is lost. That the scale tips in favor of the scientific community in most cases and not in favor of the natives may tell us something about the relative balance of power in the world. That anthropologists justify the obliteration of meaning from their accounts on the grounds of the logic of validation may tell us something about the triumph of an ideology of technical rationality. Finally, that anthropologists seem all too unaware that their accounts are as grounded in their own social situation as those of the natives is an indication of their failure to develop a reflexive anthropology. We do not mean to suggest that anthropology is unreflective. The attention to detail of good ethnography is a genuine indication of reflectiveness, but this is not the same thing as claims to knowledge which turn back upon themselves and recognize the contingent nature of the experience on which they are based.

Field work is that experience. It is like other social experiences, and yet it is unique. Field workers are persons who both affirm and deny the validity of native conceptions of existence. They know less than natives, but claim to know more. Yet their accounts must conform to community norms as much as those of the natives. Field workers present themselves to the objects of their research in one set of terms and to the scientific community in others. They must of necessity experience their mode of existence as profoundly alienated. To the degree that they deny the alienated nature of their existence, they will produce knowledge that is alienated in another sense; it is loosed from any sense of the very conditions of its existence. It is in this sense that T. O. Beidelman (1970, pp. 527-528) refers to social anthropologists as "a fascinating cultural puzzle: that of men standing within and without the objects they must understand. In this respect, it may not be unduly dramatic to suggest that the greatest of social anthropologists, those from whom we learn most, appear as the most alienated and therefore perhaps the freest but most troubled of the social scientists."

Notes

1. These reactions could be dismissed as manifestations of what is commonly called "culture shock," although doing so fails to reveal the source of the disequilibrium. *Culture shock* describes emotional discomfort in the face of alien or unfamiliar behaviors and beliefs. The initial experience of the novice field worker is actually more akin to "stage fright," i.e., the sensation of helplessness or anxiety brought on by having to perform a role in front of an audience whose willingness or ability to appreciate that role is unknown. It is the experience of not knowing what to expect, except in the most general ways (see Lyman & Scott, 1970).

The people among whom the anthropologist settles may have similar difficulties fitting him or her into their frame of reference, which leads to puzzlements, and to questions about the differences between the anthropologist and themselves. In formulating answers to such queries, anthropologists construct presentations of self that they think their hosts will comprehend, i.e., they try to translate the aims of anthropological research and the role of the field worker into categories intelligible to the indigenous peoples. These "accounts to the native" are constructed both for the anthropologist's benefit and for their non-anthropological audiences.

2. We do not deny that social life is structured. Problems arise from the tendency of social scientists to attribute an *actual* as opposed to a *virtual* existence to structure. In our point of view, social structure can be examined as a process of *structuration;* it is continually reproduced in action (see Giddens 1976, 1979). In social anthropology, this perspective has been consistently championed by Meyer Fortes, as when he describes the lineage system of the Tallensi as "a configuration of processes in time and space" (see especially the essays in his *Time and Social Structure and Other Essays,* 1970).

3. In one of the most insightful accounts of field work, Gerald Berreman (1962) draws attention to the parallels between field work and Erving Goffman's concept of "impression management" (1959). Berreman's point is that impression management, the presentation of self to achieve desired ends from significant others, is a two-way affair. Both the subjects of anthropological inquiry and anthropologists themselves play a game of mutual impression management.

In the heterogeneous community that he studied, Berreman was able to take advantage of the different ends desired by different segments of the community to acquire information about "backstage areas" that some groups would have preferred to keep hidden. Berreman's account is valuable both for its honesty and because he exposes the essentially political nature of anthropological field work. At the same time, it is also somewhat limiting. The presentations of self produced by actors in the field work drama are accounts, and as such they both affect and are affected by different fields in which the actors participate. The strategies utilized by the anthropologists and their informants are related to social contexts outside the immediate research situation. For the anthropologist, this includes the scholarly community of which he is a part. For the novice anthropologist, this scholarly community manifests itself in the form of a dissertation committee. Because of the radical separation between the social fields in terms of which anthropological presentations of self are made, anthropologists may experience severe difficulties in reconciling the space between the self as presented and the self as experienced. Many of the analogies between the field worker and other social roles presented below are attempts to present this radical disjuncture.

Another difficulty that arises out of the radical separation of the domains of scholarship and research can have significant consequences for analysis. The indexical quality of expressions allows indigenous concepts to be glossed under a variety of translation labels. If the term is used differently by a number of groups, the interaction between anthropologist and informant may result in the reinforcement of error rather than its elimination. Michael Herzfeld's examination of the concept *prika* in two Greek villages shows that the meaning of "dowry" which anthropologists attributed to the term tended to conform to its usage in the national legal code, and that the indigenous meaning attributed to the term was exactly the opposite of its legal definition. Furthermore, because the villagers had to accommodate themselves to the legal system, the context of questions and answers that Herzfeld initially used reinforced the mistaken impression that he brought to the field situation (in press).

The problem is, of course, one of translation, of "presenting the coherence of the thought of one people in the thought and language of another," as the anthropologist Godfrey Lienhardt describes it (1956). See the essays in B. Wilson, Ed., *Rationality* (1970) for a discussion of these issues. M. Crick's *Explorations in Language and Meaning* (1976) discusses the semantic nature of anthropological inquiry.

4. This returns us again to the problem of drawing boundaries in field work, but from a different perspective. In this instance, the difficulty emanates from the scholarly community of which the field worker is a member, and not from the field situation. It becomes a matter of deciding whether to "stick to one's last" or not. See Gluckman (1964) for a discussion of the issues with respect to social anthropology.

5. Burnett (1976) examines the literature on socialization and field work in considerable detail.

6. See the discussions of "implicit meaning" and "practical knowledge" in Douglas (1975) and Giddens (1979). Nash (1963) takes a psychological tack in his essay and concludes that field work is a stressful activity better handled by certain dispositions.

7. Anthropologists often obscure the relative freedom from constraint they experience in field work and romanticize the participation. F. H. Cushing is an early 20th-century anthropologist widely believed to have "gone native" and died as a full member of Pueblo Indian Society. Actually, he was removed from his field situation by his employers, the Smithsonian Institution, and died on an archaeological dig (Grunewald, 1972).

8. Alan Hoben (n.d.), in an insightful article on field work, describes ethnographic discovery as based on a "trial and blunder" method.

9. The radical separation between a reason for an action and the cause of an action that we made earlier in this section requires modification at this point. Because actors and their actions intervene between cause and effect, causes become incorporated, often unknowingly, into reasons. We find the distinction between cause and reason a useful analytical tool, not an observable feature of the social world (see Bhaskar, 1980, for a discussion of the relationship between cause and reason).

10. Anthony Giddens (1976) terms this participation of the social scientist in two life-worlds a "double hermeneutic," but if the social scientist is genuinely reflexive about his practice, then the hermeneutic may be *triple,* not double!

11. The concept of false consciousness is tricky, because it is subject to so many interpretations. Obviously it is tied to the critique of ideology, and there are notorious difficulties in the definition of the concept of ideology. We do not mean to suggest by our use of the notion of false consciousness that there is a fixed "true consciousness," in terms of which other forms of consciousness may be rendered false. In his comparison of true and false forms of consciousness, Bernstein states the issues nicely:

The concept of ideology of "false consciousness" is reciprocally related to the concept of a non-ideological understanding or a "true consciousness." *I do not think that there is any fixed criteria by which we can, once and for all, distinguish "false consciousness" from "true consciousness."* The achievement of "true consciousness" is a regulative ideal of the critique of ideology, and the relation between "false consciousness" and "true consciousness" is asymmetrical. This does not mean that we must remain intellectually agnostic, that we are never in a position to evaluate and judge the ways in which ideology is systematically distortive and reflects reified powers of domination. On the contrary, since every ideology is based on beliefs and interpretations that make the claim to validity, we can examine these claims to validity and show their falsity. We can show the falsity of an ideology without claiming that we have achieved a final, absolute, "true" understanding of social and political reality [1976, p. 109, emphasis added].

12. This distinction has been elaborated in a defense of the positivist position made by Nagel (1961). The difference in our account is that we would argue that discovery and validation are dialectically related; as procedures, they lead to new forms of socially produced knowledge that transcend the context of their production. This position is compatible with a realist philosophy of the social sciences (Bhaskar, 1980), as well as with conventionalist or phenomenological positions. "By dialectic, I understand the view that explanation and understanding would not constitute mutually exclusive poles, but rather relative moments in a complex process called interpretation" (Ricoeur, 1978, p. 150).

References

Asad, T. (Ed.). *Anthropology and the colonial encounter.* London: Ithaca Press, 1973.

Bateson, G. *Steps to an ecology of mind.* New York: Ballantine, 1970.

Beidelman, T. O. Some sociological implications of culture. In E. A. Tiryakian & J. McKinney (Eds.), *Theoretical sociology.* New York: Free Press, 1970.

Berreman, G. D. Behind many masks. *Monographs of the Society for Applied Anthropology,* 1962, No. 4.

Bernstein, R. J. *The restructuring of social and political theory.* Philadelphia: University of Pennsylvania Press, 1976.

Bhaskar, R. *The possibility of naturalism.* Sussex: Harvester Press, 1980.

Bourdieu, P. *An Outline of a theory of practice.* Cambridge: Cambridge University Press, 1977.

Brim, J. A., & Spain, D. H. *Research design in anthropology.* New York: Holt, Rinehart & Winston, 1974.

Burnett, J. H. On the analogy between culture acquisition and ethnographic method. In J. Roberts & S. K. Akinsanya (Eds.), *Educational patterns and cultural configurations.* New York: David McKay, 1976.

Carr, E. H. *What is history?* New York: Random House, 1961.

Crick, M. *Explorations in language and meaning: Towards a semantic anthropology.* New York: Halsted Press, 1976.

Douglas, M. *Implicit meanings.* London: Routledge & Kegan Paul, 1975.

Eco, U. *A theory of semiotics.* Bloomington: Indiana University Press, 1976.

Evans-Pritchard, E. E. *Nuer religion.* Oxford, Eng.: Clarendon Press, 1956.

Evans-Pritchard, E. E. Some reminiscence and reflections on fieldwork. Appendix IV in *Witchcraft, oracles and magic among the Azande* (Abridged). Oxford, Eng.: Clarendon Press, 1976.

Firth, R. From wife to anthropologist. In S. Kimball & J. Watson (Eds.), *Crossing cultural boundaries.* San Francisco: Chandler, 1972.

Fortes, M. *Time and social structure and other essays.* London: Athlone, 1970.

Fortes, M. Strangers. In M. Fortes & Sheila Patterson (Eds.), *Essays in African social anthropology.* London: Academic Press, 1975.

Geertz, C. Religion as a cultural system. In M. Banton (Ed.), *Anthropological approaches to the study of religion.* (ASA Monographs No. 3.) London: Tavistock, 1965.

Geertz, C. *The interpretation of cultures.* New York: Basic Books, 1973.

Geertz, C. "From the native's point of view": On the nature of anthropological understanding. In K. Basso & H. A. Selby (Eds.), *Meaning in anthropology*. Albuquerque: University of New Mexico Press, 1976.

Giddens, A. *New rules of sociological method*. London: Hutchinson, 1976.

Giddens, A. *Central problems in sociological theory*. Berkeley: University of California Press, 1979.

Gluckman, M. (Ed.). *Closed systems and open minds*. Chicago: Aldine, 1964.

Goffman, E. *The presentation of self in everyday life*. New York: Doubleday, 1959.

Grunewald, S. Did Frank Hamilton Cushing go native? In S. Kimball & S. Watson (Eds.), *Crossing cultural boundaries*. San Francisco: Chandler, 1972.

Herzfeld, M. The dowry in Greece: Terminological usage and historical reconstruction. *Ethnohistory*, in press.

Hoben, A. *Community study guide*. Unpublished manuscript, n.d.

Jongmans, D. G., & Gutkind, P. C. W. (Eds.). *Anthropologists in the field*. New York: Humanities, 1967.

de Josselin de Jong, P. E. The participants' view of their culture. In D. G. Jongmans & P. C. W. Gutkind (Eds.), *Anthropologists in the field*. New York: Humanities, 1967.

Karp, I. *Fields of change among the Iteso of Kenya*. London: Routledge & Kegan Paul, 1978.

Karp, I. Beer drinking and social experience in an African society. In I. Karp & C. Bird (Eds.), *Explorations in African systems of thought*. Bloomington: Indiana University Press, 1980.

Kendall, M. G. Radical grammars: Interplay of form and function. In H. Giles & P. Robinson (Eds.), *Social psychological perspectives on language*. London: Pergamon, in press.

Köbben, A. J. F. Participation and quantification: Fieldwork among the Djuka (Bush Negroes of Suninam). In D. G. Jongmans and P. C. W. Gutkind (Eds.), *Anthropologists in the field*. New York: Humanities, 1967.

Lienhardt, G. Modes of thought. In E. E. Evans-Pritchard et al. (Eds.), *The institutions of primitive society*. Oxford: Basil Blackwell, 1956.

Lienhardt, G. *Divinity and experience*. Oxford: Clarendon Press, 1963.

Lyman, S. M., & Scott, M. B. *A sociology of the absurd*. New York: Appleton-Century-Crofts, 1970.

Maquet, J. J. Objectivity in anthropology. *Current Anthropology*, 1964, 5, 24-55.

Moore, S. F. Uncertainties in situations: Indeterminacies in culture. In S. F. Moore & B. Myerhoff (Eds.), *Symbol and politics in communal ideology*. Ithaca, NY: Cornell University Press, 1976.

Nagel, E. *The structure of science*. New York: Harcourt Brace Jovanovich, 1961.

Nash, D. The ethnologist as stranger. *Southwestern Journal of Anthropology*, 1963, 19, 149-167.

Pelto, P. J. *Anthropological research*. New York: Harper & Row, 1970.

Richardson, M. Anthropologist—The myth teller. *American Ethnologist*, 1975, 2 (3), 517-533.

Ricoeur, P. Understanding and explanation. In C. E. Reagan & D. Stewart (Eds.), *The philosophy of Paul Ricoeur*. Boston: Beacon Press, 1978.

Schumann, J. H. The implications of interlanguage, pidginization, and creolization for the study of adult second language acquisition. *TESOL Quarterly*, 1974, 8, 145-152.

Schumann, J. H. Second language learning: The pidginization hypothesis. *Language Learning*, 1976, 26, 391-408.

Schutz, A. The stranger: An essay in social psychology. In A. Broderson (Ed.), *Collected papers* (Vol. 2). The Hague: Martinus Nijhoff, 1964.

Simmel, G. *The sociology of Georg Simmel*. New York: Free Press, 1950.

Weber, M. The social psychology of world religions. In H. Gerth & M. C. Wright (Eds.), *From Max Weber*. New York, 1958.

Wilson, B. (Ed.). *Rationality*. New York: Harper & Row, 1970.

Zaner, R. M. *The way of phenomenology*. New York: Pegasus, 1970.

CHAPTER 14

Emergence, Explanation, and Emancipation

ROY BHASKAR

In this chapter I want to consider the forms of explanation appropriate to the ontological setting of the human sciences; to outline a heuristic for the understanding of social life; to criticize a prevalent assumption in the metatheory of the human sciences; and to advance a counterposition. The ontological features stem from the *internally complex, preinterpreted,* and *transient* character of social objects, which entails that we are dealing with sciences that are (at least partially) concrete, in the sense of Husserl; hermeneutical, in the sense of Dilthey; and historical, in the sense of Marx. These characteristics at once differentiate the human sciences from the abstract, objectivistic, and nomological sciences of physics and chemistry and explain the total eclipse of the D-N Model in the human sphere (see Donagan, 1966). I shall call the heuristic the *transformational model of social activity* (Bhaskar, 1978b, 1979). In it, the social structure is reproduced or transformed by agents in the conduct of their everyday lives. This seems to me to be a conception implicit in much recent social thought, as well as in aspects of Marx; and similar heuristics have recently been independently proposed by Pierre Bourdieu (1977), Anthony Giddens (1976, 1977, 1979), and others.

The assumption that I wish to criticize is that of the *incorrigible*, because *constitutive*, character of agents' interpretations or accounts, which carries the implication of the neutrality of social science. In contrast, I want to argue that social science is non-neutral in a double sense: It

AUTHOR'S NOTE: I am extremely grateful to Roy Edgley, William Outhwaite, and Kate Soper for their comments on the discussion draft of this chapter.

consists of a *practical intervention* in social life, and it *logically entails* value judgments. In particular, the possibility of a *scientific* critique of lay (and protoscientific) ideas, grounded in explanatory practices based on respect for the authenticity and epistemic significance of those ideas, affords to the human sciences an essential emancipatory impulse. Such a conatus does not license an unmediated transition from factual appraisals to practical imperatives in particular situations. But, subject to the operation of various ceteris paribus clauses, we do nevertheless pass securely from statements about "what is" to statements about "what ought to be."

I want, then, to examine the forms of scientific explanation proper to an essentially configurational subject matter (see Elias, 1974), the types of content necessitated by the pre-given but activity-dependent nature of social forms, the relations between explanations or accounts, whether scientific or lay, and actions and practices, and between scientific and lay accounts of social reality. My overall argument is that it is only if social phenomena are genuinely *emergent* that realist *explanations* in the human sciences are justified, and that it is only if this condition is satisfied that there is any possibility of human self-*emancipation* worthy of the name; but that, conversely, emergent phenomena require realist explanation, and realist explanations in the human sciences possess emancipatory implications. Emancipation depends upon explanation, which depends upon emergence. Given the phenomenon of emergence, an emancipatory politics (or therapy) depends upon a realist science. But, if and only if emergence is real, the development of both are up to *us*.

Emergence, Explanation, and Complexity.

The fundamental methodological problem of any human science lies in the division [découpage] of the object of study. . . . Once this division has been made and accepted, the results will be practically predictable. [Goldmann, 1970, p. 250].

Perhaps the most significant type of event in the history of any science is that in which it defines—redefines—its object of inquiry. Normally such redefinition, or *object-constitution,* is bipolar in structure, resulting in the reorganization of *knowledge* on the basis of the (actual or anticipated) discovery of some significant feature of the *world,* most characteristically the generative structure known or presumed to explain the phenomena organizing (or disorganizing!) the previous level of inquiry. Typically, this process will involve a science, or rather some scientists, breaking free—perhaps under the stimulus of "crisis" (Kuhn, 1970)—of the "tissue of tenacious truisms" currently congealed in their field (Bachelard, 1938). Creatively exploiting their cognitive and technical legacy (Harré, 1970), they may succeed in identifying a hitherto unknown kind of generative mechanism, so for the first time elucidating a pattern of determination already efficacious in the world, an achievement which will normally necessitate the more or less drastic "recasting" of the accumulated knowledge of their science—the transformation of their "transmit" (Toulmin, 1973), the very legacy they used. Post-Humean philosophy, by virtue of its implicit or explicit commitment to the undifferentiated and unstratified ontology of empirical realism, cannot think this process of object-constitution. This metaphysical failure reflects and reinforces a methodological one, as—on empirical realist reconstructions—the human sciences appear to be beset by chronic interconnected problems of definition, verification, and application. Thus, within the ontology of empirical realism, undifferentiated events become the object of only conventionally differentiated sciences, every theory finds confirming and disconfirming instances with equal facility, and there seems to be a non-arbitrary connection between pure and applied science (or, more generally, theory and practice). The upshot is a scandal for theoretical and practical reasons, indicated by the absence of a defeasible organon for either of them. Clearly, if we are to make any headway on the problem of object-constitution in the human sciences, we must start afresh on the basis of a new, non-empiricist ontology.[1]

Transcendental analysis of experimental (and applied) activity in natural science shows that the objects of scientific investigation are structures, not events, and that such structures exist and act independently of the conditions of their identification, and in particular in open and closed systems alike—that is, whether or not empirical invariances obtain (Bhaskar, 1978a). These structures are non-empirical but empirically identifiable, transfactually efficacious but only contingently manifest in particular outcomes, and they form the real ground for causal laws. Moreover, it follows from this analysis that the world, *as we actually know it* (i.e., under the descriptions in terms of which it is known to science), is characterized by situations of dual and multiple control and by the phenomenon of emergence (ibid., esp. chap. 2.5). On this conception, then, reality consists of partially interconnected hierarchies of levels, in which any element e at a level L is in principle subject to the possibility of causal determination by higher-order, lower-order, and extra-order (external) effects, as well as by those (which define it as an element) of L.

Such an *integrative* (or structured) *pluralism* (Bunge, 1973) recognizes both *distinctions* and *connections* between the various objects of scientific inquiry. In this way it is differentiated from ontological monism and epistemological reductionism (e.g., physicalism, biologism, individualism) on the one hand, and from ontological (monadic) pluralism and epistemological "separatism" or "eclecticism" on the other. The former denies a priori the possibility of a distinction and is characteristic of positivistic philosophies of science; in the human sciences it easily leads to reification, and more generally to neglect of the subjective aspects of praxis and thought. The latter denies in a more or less a priori manner the possibility of a connection or material grounding, and is characteristic of idealist and romantic philosophies of science; in the human sciences it readily encourages hypostatization, and more generally neglect of the interdependencies between, and material bases of, the various aspects of human life. Metaphysically, it is most importantly manifest in the various forms of post-Cartesian dualism and immaterialism (e.g., vitalism, Alexandrine "emergentism," Bergsonian "intuitionism"); but epistemologically its result is an eclectic empiricism of effects. The most plausible form that integrative pluralism takes in the human sciences is that of a *synchronic emergent powers materialism* (Bhaskar, 1979).

Scientific Explanation and "The Concrete"

The absence of (epistemically significant) empirical invariances in the human sciences entails that social phenomena only occur in open systems. And it follows as immediate consequences of this that:

(1) criteria for theory assessment and development in the human sciences cannot be predictive, and so must be exclusively *explanatory;* and
(2) social phenomena in general must be seen as the product of a multiplicity of causes, so that social events will be "conjunctures" and social things (metaphysically) "compounds."

However, these considerations do not in themselves necessitate a difference in the pattern of either theoretical or practical (concrete, "historical," or applied) explanations in the human sciences. Thus, assuming there are structures producing phenomena analogous to the causal mechanisms of nature, theory will have the analogical-retroductive form identifiable in the natural sciences (Hanson, 1965; Harré, 1970; Hesse, 1974) and be subject to the same constraints of empirical adequacy, consistency, coherence, nonredundancy, independence, and so forth. Moreover, the explanation of concrete social events will reveal the RRRE pattern characteristic of natural events too: *resolution* of a complex event into its components; theoretical *redescription* of those components; *retrodic-*

tion, via independently validated normic (or tendency) statements, to possible antecedents of the components; and *elimination* of the alternative possible causes (Bhaskar, 1978a, 1979). Thus, if theoretical explanation involves retroduction from the concrete to the abstract, practical (including historical) explanation will involve the reverse passage from the abstract to the reconstructed concrete (see Marx, 1973, pp. 100-102; D. Sayer, 1979). Transcendental realism differentiates itself from transcendental idealism, of course, in seeing the aim of the first, analogical-retroductive transition as the apprehension (in thought, and if possible, in experimental actuality) of a transfactually efficacious pattern of determination, co-generating the concrete; so that "the abstract," though non-empirical, may nevertheless designate what is real.

It has often been claimed that social objects are, or may be, internally complex or *holistic.* Certainly this seems empirically plausible, and it is in fact an implication of the heuristic to be proposed below. To the extent that this is the case, the explanatory schemata outlined above will need to be modified. I shall call a combination of structures a *system* and a combination of features or aspects (e.g., of an event) a *nexus* when the combination coheres as a whole, in that:

(1) the form of the combination causally co-determines the elements; and
(2) the elements causally co-determine (mutually mediate or condition) each other, and so causally co-determine the form.

Figures 14.1 and 14.2 contrast the determination of events within a system and of features within a nexus in normal "open-systemic" cases. In case II the mechanisms, and in case IV their effects, are modified. Clearly, both may operate simultaneously. In general, the determination of events within a system will result in their constitution as a nexus. But the modification of effects within a nexus may affect the mode of operation of the mechanisms themselves. It should be noted that causal interdependency between structures does not exclude, but rather presupposes internal relations between them; and that symmetrically internal relations between the elements of a system are consistent with differential causal roles in the operation of the system, so that in particular, existential parity is consistent with ontological depth.

If (some of) the structures generating social phenomena combine as a system, then an abstraction may be found wanting either if it fails to grasp a necessary connection or if it isolates such a connection from others essential to its existence or functioning. And if (some) social systems are historically developing, then it is easy to see how this kind of illicit abstrac-

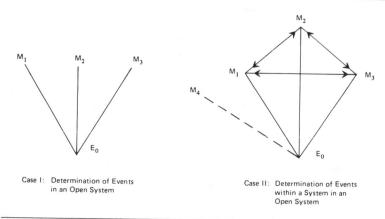

Case I: Determination of Events
         in an Open System

Case II: Determination of Events
          within a System in an
          Open System

Figure 14.1

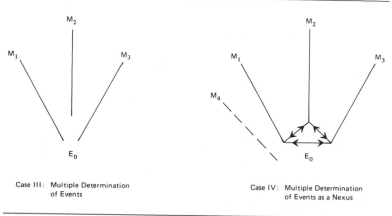

Case III: Multiple Determination
           of Events

Case IV: Multiple Determination
          of Events as a Nexus

Figure 14.2

tion may result in the eternalization of the present, the false universalization of particular historically conditioned states (Lukács 1971). If the concrete is a "condensation" of several necessities, the nature of that condensation is contingent and can only be determined in particular cases by specific empirical research (A. Sayer, 1981). To the extent, however, that the features of the concrete episode (object, event, and so on) are qualitatively modified by the character of the episode as a whole, the resolution involved in practical explanations cannot be a simple "mechanical" one. And to the extent that redescription of the features of the episode is necessary, practical explanations may unearth potentially new totalities in that sphere of social life. It is this possibility of discovering a new totality in a nexus that accounts for the configurational quality of social phenomena, just as it is the continuing unfolding of the possibilities of social objects in time that necessitates the continual rewriting of their histories. (If the history of an object is "finished," then writing it no longer depends upon the mutual mediation of time, but takes the bare form of a chronicle.)

Between *abstract sciences* and the reconstructed concepts of *concrete objects,* one needs in the human sciences to range *concrete* and *intermediate sciences.* Concrete sciences are sciences which systematically connect up and synthesize into a structured order the ensemble of significant truths about a given thing as a more or less unique natural kind within an empirical genus (see Husserl, 1970, pp. 230-231). Intermediate sciences explore the *intersection* (interaction) of two or more types of *determinations* in a given kind of thing or system. Economics and linguistics are abstract sciences, revolutions and people concrete phenomena; history and biography concrete sciences, and economic history and social biology intermediate ones. It is important to remember that in the human sphere, abstract sciences always have a concrete mooring in history and biography (a mooring which must be understood as a condition for the application of any particular theoretical explanation). Thus, in the human sphere relations of causal priority do not reflect degrees of ontological independence.

The Human Sciences and the Natural Order

Integrative pluralism suggests that we see the objects of the human sciences as distinct (and perhaps emergent) from but connected to, and in particular grounded in, nature. More particularly, I am going to propose that they are taxonomically and causally *irreducible* but *dependent* modes of matter (see Collier, 1979):

(1) *dependence*—The objects of the human sciences are unilaterally, existentially dependent on those of the natural sciences.[2]

(2) *taxonomic irreducibility*—The natural sciences are at present unable to explain the human world under *human descriptions.*

(3) *causal irreducibility*—Reference to properties *not* designated by physical theory is (apparently) necessary to explain some *physical* states (for example, those resulting from intentional action).

In SEPM (synchronic emergent powers materialism), human phenomena are consistent with and constrained (but not exclusively determined) by, natural laws. SEPM does not require the postulation of any substance other than matter as the bearer of the emergent powers, and it is consistent with a diachronic explanatory reduction, i.e., an explanation of the coming-into-being, in time, of the emergent powers. It is vital to note that only an emergent powers naturalism is consistent with a realist interpretation of nonphysical (psychological, sociological) explanations of human phenomena. Ontologically speaking, we are faced with a stark choice between reductionist physicalism and an emergent powers theory. Of course, explanatory realism may still be justified as a temporary (or more or less permanent) expedient, pending the physicalist reduction of the human sciences—and this indeed seems to have been the official position of Freud and possibly Marx.[3] But the interpretation of social and psychological theory as "elliptical" suffers from formidable problems: ontologically, the higher-order phenomena appear underdetermined under appropriate descriptions; and epistemologically, any choice of higher-order explanation appears arbitrary.

Does the unilateral, ontological dependence of the objects of the human on those of the natural sciences provide grounds for granting an explanatory priority to man's interaction with nature in the organization of his social life? Marx and Engels tended to speak as if it did. But if it does, as it is not implausible to suppose that it might do (but see Harré, 1979), the nature of the grounding must be made more precise than in slogans of the "as man is only human, he must eat before he can think" variety (see Collier, 1979, p. 44).

All human phenomena have a natural form. But it is clear that just as man is more directly implicated in some segments of space-time than others, such as those that bear his causal imprint, so nature is more directly implicated in some (e.g., medical) than other (e.g., political) practices; and that the effects of such transcategorical interactions are typically materialized in society as particular technical and cultural products (see Soper, 1979).

The study of such products, marking the confluence of two heterogeneous orders of determination, belongs in principle to linking intermediate sciences of technology, on the one hand, and social biology and social geography (or ecology) on the other. The type of natural/social relationship involved in the former may be contrasted with that involved in the latter. If technology studies the ways in which man may appropriate nature, social biology and ecology study the way in which nature, so to speak, reappropriates man. Or, we could say that whereas in the case of technology, nature, as it were, provides the content for a social form, in the cases of social biology and ecology, society generates the content for

TABLE 14.1

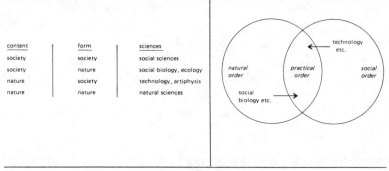

content	form	sciences
society	society	social sciences
society	nature	social biology, ecology
nature	society	technology, artiphysis
nature	nature	natural sciences

Figure 14.3

an essentially natural form (see Table 14.1). If the intersection of the natural and the social defines the practical order, then the relationships between these intermediate sciences can be depicted as in Figure 14.3. Note that whereas natural laws set the boundary conditions for the social natural sciences (such as social biology), it is economic (political, and the like) laws that set the boundary conditions for the natural social sciences (such as technology).

In principle, then, one can distinguish natural from mixed from social determinants of concrete human phenomena, as in Figure 14.4. But it seems unlikely that the natural causes of social phenomena (such as the forms of manifestation of eating, sexuality, aging, illness, or play) can rarely be *wholly* explained in physical or biological terms, so that in general one will be dealing with cases of type B rather than A. Indeed, Kate Soper (1979, p. 75) has convincingly argued that Timpanaro (1975), in his important reemphasis of the role of nature within historical materialism, tends to systematically conflate the socially mediated effects of biological determinants with the determinants themselves, thus reducing mixed to purely natural determination. In effect, this drives Timpanaro into an essentially Feuerbachian position, invoking once more an abstract, ahistorical human condition.[4]

On the Transformational Model of Social Activity

Talk of "emergence" can easily become vague and general, if not indeed laced with frankly idealist or romantic overtones. What is needed is a specification of precisely those properties of the allegedly emergent object inexplicable in terms of different sets of conditions of purely natural

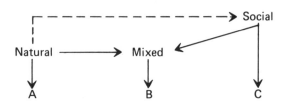

Figure 14.4

laws. This is the role of the transformational model of social activity (TMSA). It may be established either by a transcendental argument from intentional action or by a process of imminent reconciliation of the antinomies of social theory. And it may be regarded as an attempt to specify the formal conditions for substantive object-constitution in the domain of the social sciences via a specification of what must be the case for a sui generis science of social objects to be possible.

The principal historical forbears of the model, as I understand it, are Aristotle, Durkheim, and Marx. In the TMSA, the logical structure of human activity or praxis is conceived, following Aristotle, as consisting in the transformation by efficient (intentional) human agency of pre-given material (natural and social) causes. The social may be differentiated from the purely natural material causes by the property that, though necessarily pre-given to any particular agent (Durkheim, 1965) and a condition for any intentional act, they exist and are reproduced only by virtue of human agency (Marx, 1973). If there are to be *social* explanations for social phenomena (that is, if a *social* science of social forms is to be possible), then what is designated in such explanations, the social mechanisms and structures generating social phenomena, must be themselves *social products,* and so must be given to and reproduced in human agency, like any other social object. And from this important recursive feature of the TMSA, entailed by the possibility of any nonreductionist realism, flows a series of ontological differences between the objects of social and natural scientific inquiry. Elsewhere (Bhaskar, 1979), I have tried to show how it is just by virtue of these emergent properties, which may be summarized as the activity-, concept-, and space-time-dependence of social structures, that a sui generis social science is possible.

In the TMSA, then, society is conceived of both as the ever-present *condition* and the continually reproduced *outcome* of human agency. This is the duality of structure (Giddens, 1976). And human agency is conceived both as work, i.e., (normally conscious) *production,* and as *reproduction* of the conditions of production, i.e., society. This is the duality of praxis. Thus, agents reproduce in their substantive motivated productions the unmotivated conditions governing (and employed in) those productions, and society is both the unconscious medium and nonteleological product of this activity. In the TMSA, society and agents are seen as *existentially interdependent* but *essentially distinct,* for whereas society exists only by virtue of human agency and human agency (or being) always presupposes (and expresses) some or other definite social form, they cannot be reduced to or reconstructed from one another. Thus they mark the sites of potentially independent sciences, consistent with and conditioned by each other, but referring to different generative aspects of the same concrete flux of social life. The objects of these distinct sciences cannot, of course, actually be isolated, so there is no question of a predictive testing of the cognitive abstractions required to grasp them. The *social* sciences abstract from human agency to study the structure of reproduced outcomes, the enduring practices and their relations; the *social psychological* sciences abstract from these repro-duced outcomes to focus on the rules governing the mobilization of resources by agents in their interactions with one another and nature. The transformational model and the connections between structure and praxis are represented in Figures 14.5 and 14.6 below. In Figure 14.6, 2 and 4 represent the duality of structure and praxis respectively, and 1 (1′,

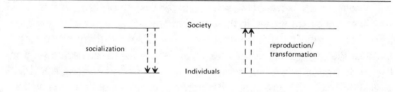

Figure 14.5

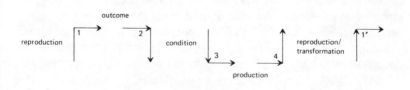

Figure 14.6

and so forth) and 3 represent the focus of the social and social psychological sciences, respectively.

The transformational conception allows us to pinpoint a double set of
errors: the ontological errors of reification and voluntarism, and the epistemological ones of social determinism and methodological individualism. And it allows us to situate the affiliated weaknesses of the substantive
traditions of structuralism and functionalism, on the one hand, and the
action-oriented and interpretive sociologies on the other. Thus, society is
not the unconditioned creation of human agency (voluntarism), but neither does it exist independently of it (reification). And individual action
neither completely determines (individualism) nor is completely determined by (determinism) social forms. In the TMSA, unintended consequences, unacknowledged conditions, and tacit skills (see 1, 2, and 4 in
Figure 14.6) limit the actor's understanding of the social world, while
unacknowledged (unconscious) motivation limits one's understanding of
oneself.

The various special sciences of social objects are concerned with the
mechanisms generating particular kinds of social practices (whether the
practices consist of the conscious following of rules or the unconscious
enactment of effects). But sociology itself may be conceived, in opposition to the prevalent individualist and collectivist conceptions, as quintessentially the science of *social relations* (Bhaskar, 1979). It is within such
relations (between the positioned practices that agents reproduce or
transform) that any human action or social effect must occur, so that
sociology—in the sense of the science of the system of relations between
practices—is presupposed in the giving of any concrete social or psychological explanation. But just as it would be a mistake to identify sociology
as the study of the social simpliciter, so it is a mistake to see psychology as
the study of the individual in the sense of the concrete, acting self (Mischel, 1977). On the one hand, the individual consists of bodily as well as
mental processes, and is constituted in part by his social relations and the
social skills and resources available to him. And, on the other, one needs
general theories of psychological phenomena, including the ways in
which individuality is experienced. It follows from this that although the
form of psychological, i.e., mental, phenomena and processes (whether
conscious or not) may be universal (species-general), their specific content will always be intrinsically social (see Toulmin, this volume), i.e.,
acquired, maintained, and transformed in the course of social life. Thus,
intermediate, historically specific sciences of social psychology will always
be required to identify the conditions for the application of psychological
(including psychoanalytical) theories to particular situations.

Problems of Topology

> Anyone who sets out in this field to hunt down final and ultimate truths . . .
> will bring home little, apart from platitudes and commonplaces of the
> sorriest kind; for example, that generally speaking man cannot live except
> by labor [Engels, 1969].

The transformational model immediately secretes two connected problems:

(1) How do we identify, and especially individuate, social practices?
(2) How are the (individuated) practices connected with one another—in
particular, should we attempt to articulate them into a unified explanatory
framework (such as historical materialism)?

The problem of individuation may be broached by reference to agents'
own accounting procedures, but agents may have no clear conception of
the interconnection of their activities.

Integrative pluralism suggests that here again we need to be able to
think the simultaneity of distinctions and connections, so that the various
practices are conceived as non-identical but causally connected, and
internally related, to each other. And here once more it seems mandatory
to insist in principle against both *monism,* whether in essentialist or reductionist guise, which would scout the distinctiveness of the practices,
and *eclecticism,* whether of an empiricist, rationalist (e.g., structuralist),
or idealist sort, which would efface their connections.

This is, of course, familiar in historical materialism as the problem of
reconciling the notion of the relative autonomy of superstructures with
that of their ultimate determination by the base. Althusser's influential
work consists in an uneasy synthesis of two kinds of resolution of this
problem, one "mechanistic," the other "holistic" in form: (1) the formula
that the economy determines the "weightings" of the levels of the social
structure, and in particular which level is dominant (Althusser, 1969); and
(2) the formula that the elements of the social structure are determined by
the configuration of the structure itself (which may of course be asymmetrically weighted; Althusser & Balibar, 1971). Neither provides, it seems to
me, a wholly adequate resolution of the problem within the topography
of historical materialism or in its more general aspect. Clearly, both need
to be further explicated in concrete models of causal determination applicable to particular areas of research (Wright, 1978). But this leads to a
more general difficulty with any such schema, for it is an implication of the

TMSA that there can be no general ahistorical theory of articulation (see Marx, 1975, p. 294), that the relations between the elements of the social totality (including perhaps even the forms of causal determination involved) change along with the elements themselves. It is a consequence of this that regional theories—in the sense of Poulantzas (1973)—must always be historically specific, intermediate sciences, and that if social theory develops by constructing nets which, when thrown over reality, continually augment our understanding, the best net at any moment of time will be continually changing.

Social practices of course, unlike the social totality, must already be conceptualized in experience. Thus we can reason retroductively from those conceptualizations reflecting the "self-understood forms of social life" (Marx, 1976, p. 75) to the conditions and mechanisms that account for them. Such an analysis may, of course, once completed, reveal a systematic discrepancy between the individuation of practices entailed by theory and that implicit in the experience of the agents concerned. There cannot, therefore, be a final resolution of the problem of individuation outside that of the problem of articulation; and the resolution of both problems depends in practice upon the construction of substantive theories which maximize their total explanatory power. This is the only kind of "organon" (Popper, 1969) available to the human sciences.

On the Corrigibility of Agents' Accounts

The history of "First Philosophy" is the history of an attempt to establish an incorrigible ground for knowledge, free from the possibility of error or the effect of ignorance, and impervious to every form of Cartesian doubt. Thus, in a recent empiricist avatar, scientific knowledge was seen as grounded in (or even exhausted by) subjective or objective sense-experience, or measurement. Of course, we now know that there are no foundations of knowledge, that there is no uniquely privileged level, moment, or type of operation, that there are no brute data; that the facts already contain a certain "sedimented" reading of the world (that natural facts are social institutions), and that the relationship between theories and facts is that between the contents of two interdependent kinds of conceptual schemes, one of which is taken as referring to objects given in experience. In short, we now know that the facts are theory-dependent and changeable, and that science itself appears, as one might anticipate from the TMSA, as a historical process of levels and connections, a weighted network, without foundations, developing in time. This view does not dispute the epistemic value of experience. However, it interprets this not as the absolute privilege of a content, but as dependent upon the ontological and social *contexts* within which the significant experience occurs (Bhaskar, 1978a).

Inasmuch as there has been a "coupure" in the recent philosophy of the human sciences, it lies in the recognition of the significance of the condition that man is a self-interpreting and self-motivating animal whose language and beliefs are in some manner necessary for and productive of his behavior, so that human reality faces the protoscientist as already preinterpreted, as linguistically and cognitively "done," as it were, prior to any scientific investigation of it. These preinterpretations are *not* externally related and contingently conjoined to what happens in social life, but internally related to and constitutive of it (see Taylor, 1971). It was natural, then, in the wake of this understanding, to suppose that these interpretations (and beliefs) would constitute the base or foundations of social knowledge; to regard them as consisting, as it were, in *brute interpretations* (or beliefs), whether such data were viewed positivistically as immediately available to the investigator, or conceived dialogically as dependent upon work within one's own culture. Thus one had a transposition of the familiar thematics of First Philosophy in a hermeneutical key — more plausible than in the original, perhaps, because nature is not self-interpreting, but little different in logical form or epistemological effect.

Both the reductionist thesis that social knowledge is *exhausted* by, and the milder position that it is *rooted* in (and so must be *consistent* with) self-interpretations lead inexorably to a displaced hermeneuticized scientism and a consequent "disavowal of reflection" (Habermas, 1972). In either variant, the doctrine of the incorrigible, because ontologically constitutive foundations of social knowledge secretes, like its positivist prototype, an inevitable corollary, the notion of the *neutrality* of the social sciences. This doctrine and its corollary extend, in one mode or another, throughout the schools of interpretative sociology (phenomenology, hermeneutics, existentialism, ethnomethodology, and the like); and there are analogues of the doctrine in both historicist and structuralist interpretations of historical materialism (in which the privileged level is defined by the revolutionary action of the proletariat and the self-validating practice of theory, respectively), as well as in our culture quite generally.

Of course, Hegel (1949) had already demonstrated that this procedure is both incomplete and circular, in that it not only cannot demonstrate its own legitimacy (see Gödel, 1962), but must already presuppose an (implicit or explicit) unvalidated content to work on. And it is clear that in these respects, any Viconian facimus must share the same limitations as the Cartesian cogito, for just as Descartes must already supply some content to initiate his axiomatic play, so for Vico, God or man must already possess some matter to make their worlds, and what an agent does not make, it has no privileged understanding of (just as what an ego cannot demonstrate—what it must presuppose to prove, take to make— it must remain uncertain of). On the transformational model, of course, we do not make the conditions or consequences, skills or motives of our intentional making, so that our beliefs about, or interpretations of, our actions cannot be constitutive in the requisite sense.

There are two main types of argument for the doctrine of social foundations. The *Viconian argument* contends that one and the same knowledge is used to generate and explain (account for, justify) behavior, that the stock of knowledge we use to act is just the stock we use to think (and explain) that action—a condition that may be related back to some notion of the identity (or very close relationship) of our powers to control and to monitor behavior (see Harré & Secord, 1972), so, as it were, superimposing a transcendental unity of action on that of thought. The *hermeneutical argument* maintains that interpretations are uniquely and completely constitutive of social reality or human actions, that what is social about social reality just consists, in the final analysis, in the agents' interpretations of it, just as what distinguishes a human action from a mere physical movement is its meaningful or intentional character. From this ontic standpoint, if we are to save the reality we are attempting to explain, it can only be done by offering an explanation of it in terms of interpretations, meanings, or intentions—for it is these features alone that ultimately differentiate it from a mere assemblage of physical events.

In considering the Viconian argument, it is important to distinguish the knowledge used in action from the beliefs (motives) that prompt or rationalize it. Both are important, for we are only concerned with the intentional domain, and so with the human sciences, inasmuch as an agent has a *belief* that his action manifests a certain property. This belief may be unconscious, and it may be wrong, but it must be there, or we are indeed dealing with a purely natural phenomenon. Second, all actions— even so-called basic ones—utilize or consist in the exercise of *skills*— practical knowledge or know-how, whether learned or innate. And the motivating belief or reason that prompts the action may be regarded as setting an initial condition for the exercise of the ability displayed in action. But of course, just as it is not a condition for an intentional action that the action does in fact possess the property for the sake of which it is performed, so it is not necessarily, and indeed will perhaps only exceptionally be the case that what is exercised in action can be expressed in speech. We need not be able to say how we do what we know very well how to do (and sometimes we are not even able to say what it is that we do)—even, as Chomsky has made abundantly clear, when the first-order skills are themselves verbal, discursive ones. Practical abilities do not commute into theoretical knowledge (or vice versa): To know how to do is not the same as to know how to think about how to do.

Of course, the agent has a special role in the verification of accounts, both of the mechanisms utilized in practical abilities, and of motives. At least the agent knows how to do something, and such practical knowledge (or competence) forms a partial epistemic analogue of experience in the natural sciences—indeed, it is experience in the social sphere. It should be noted that the assumption of relative privilege for an agent's account of his or her reasons (motives) depends upon the notion of the causal efficacy of the agent's beliefs—otherwise, there would be no reason to prefer it to an outsider's account. I have argued elsewhere that reasons must be causes if any discursive or practical thought is to be possible, or if the concept of agency is to be saved, and that the concept of the corrigibility of descriptions of states of consciousness is a necessary condition for any discursive thought (Bhaskar, 1979). Once it is accepted that an action is distinguished from a mere movement by the condition that it has a belief for its cause, then it is easy to see that some of an agent's belief *must* be efficacious, and that unless most of our everyday beliefs were in fact efficacious, and we were in general able to identify *which* of them were, communication and interaction generally would be impossible.

However, three things do not follow from this. First, that the beliefs are true. Second, that any *particular* belief about whether or not a belief is causally efficacious (or generative) or not is true, since there is always, in principle, a gap between any causally efficacious belief and any description of it (even where the description has the character of an expression). And such a gap may—for a variety of well-rehearsed reasons—sometimes be easier for an interlocutor to bridge than for the agent whose belief it is. Third, it does not follow that our beliefs about the causes of (which may include reasons or grounds for) the causally efficacious beliefs are true. It is one thing, to be sure, that an agent is intentionally washing his/her hands or car, but quite another to be sure about *why* he is doing so. Of course, this distinction between, as it were, immediate and underlying causes of actions (between causes, and causes of causes, of actions) is relative to our normal ways of identifying and describing actions, but these in turn are relative to our normal ways of acting, i.e., to

the types of acts we do in fact intentionally perform. Thus, in a psychoanalytic community, for instance, the distinction will be shifted only to
the extent that its members successfully act on analytic theories!

In considering the hermeneutical argument for foundations, it is important to distinguish the meaning of an act (or utterance) from the
agent's intention in performing it. The meaning of an act is a social fact
which, to the extent that the act is intentional, is utilized by the actor in the
production of his performance. But the reason that the act is performed
by the agent is a fact about the person which cannot be read off or
deduced from its social meaning. The question, "why is X exchanging
rings with Y?" is not exclusively or exhaustively answered by reference to
the fact that this is part of the ceremony (act) of getting married. I want to
argue that an agent's belief as to the reasons for an action may be expli-
cably false (and in particular, both false and necessary), and that both the
agent's statement or assessment of the meaning of the action, and the
meaning itself, may be in interesting ways incorrigible.

It is clearly the case that for any action, the agent N may be unaware of,
or misdescribe (before, during, or after) his real, i.e., the causally efficacious, whether underlying or immediate, reason, say s, for Ψ. Such a
misdescription, say p, of the motivating stimulus, s, for Ψ may, of course,
itself be a necessary (releasing) condition for Ψ. p, then, is *false* inasmuch
as it misdescribes s (so rationalizing Ψ), but *necessary for* Ψ, in that
without it (or perhaps some other suitable releasing condition),[5] Ψ would
not occur. And in a simple depth-psychological model, p might be *necessitated* (generated) *by* s, sp jointly co-determining—as stimulus and
releasing condition—Ψ (i.e., $s \rightarrow p$; $sp \rightarrow \Psi$). This paradigm may easily
be extended to include "outer" as well as "inner" causes, with outer
causes in principle covering all causes besides agents' reasons—e.g.,
social and natural conditions (including both "inner" and "outer" nature). Thus we might have that sp would not have occurred but for the
misdescription of some social structure in I, where that social structure is
itself necessary for I. Clearly, various combinations of inner and outer
causes are possible.

And what of meanings? If acts are what are performed in or by actions,
then it is uncontentious: first, that an agent may be unaware of some of
the acts (s)he (intentionally or unintentionally) performs; and second,
that acts, as well as actions, may come to be redescribed in history
(indeed, this is a consequence of the TMSA). By an extension of the
argument of the previous paragraph, it can be seen how lack of aware-

ness may be a causally necessary condition for action. But in what ways can the attribution of meaning by an agent to his act be wrong; in what ways can meanings be positively misidentified (misdescribed)? Meanings at the ordinary level cannot be systematically or generally misattributed within a culture, but they can be misattributed by a particular agent or for a class of acts, or at the level of the "underlying" reasons or grounds for (or more generally, causes of) everyday behavior. Here we have the possibility of what I shall call a "metacritique," that is, not of sets of ideas or institutions, but of the capacity of the language in terms of which the ideas or institutions are described (and which may of course be internally, and causally, related to those ideas and institutions) to adequately express those institutions or ideas, or more generally the structure of the total phenomena of that society. Such a metacritique seeks to pinpoint precisely what cannot be said *in* a particular language about what is said or done or known *by means of* it.

In general, then, the generative role of actors' (and social) beliefs (and meanings) must be recognized, and their authenticity respected, without lapsing into an "interpretative fundamentalism" by conferring incorrigibility upon them. But how do we isolate agents' beliefs and social meanings in the face of the corrigibility of statements of them? Agents' accounts are more than just evidence; they are an internally related aspect of what they are about. Hence, any resolution of this problem must be two-way, it being incumbent upon the social investigator to avoid both the extremes of arrogant dismissal of, and of fawning assent to, avowals (see Bernstein, 1976). But agreement between agent and investigator hardly seems either a necessary or sufficient criterion for an adequate interpretation. Rather, it would seem that the adequacy of any interpretation, or more generally of any act of self-understanding, can only be shown, in relation to the point of the interpretation (or understanding),[6] in the always more or less contingently circumscribed context of an agent's self-formation (see Habermas, 1972), that is, his total developing life activity (and not just, pace Habermas, his discourse).

The problem of identifying social meaning—again in a dialogical fusion of "horizons" (Gadamer, 1975)—raises the more general problem of the indeterminacy of translation. This can only be resolved in practice by selecting that translation (or, more generally, interpretation) which is *explanatorily most adequate* (whether or not it is the most "charitable") in the context of what is already known about the organization of the particular society in question (and societies in general). The most adequate explanation will save the maximum of significant phenomena in the society or domain under study, showing in that society or domain precisely the degree and type of irrationality that exists.

Explanation and Emancipation

The world has long possessed a dream of things which it has only to possess in consciousness in order to possess in reality [Marx, 1967].

Science is meaningless because it gives no answer to our question: the only question important for us, "what shall we do and how shall we live" [Tolstoy].

From the beginning we are unlogical and therefore unjust beings and *we can know this:* this is one of the greatest and most insoluble disharmonies of existence [Nietzsche].

In this section I want to show that social science is necessarily non-neutral; that it is intrinsically critical (both of beliefs and of the objects of beliefs) and self-critical; that accounts of social objects are not only value-impregnated but *value-impregnating;* and, in particular, that they both causally motivate and logically entail value judgments ceteris paribus (CP). I will not be concerned with the way in which factual and theoretical judgments are predisposed by value and practical considerations. This is partly because this connection has been widely recognized (see Taylor, 1969), but mainly because I want to address myself more to an aspiration than what is characteristically misconceived of as a "difficulty": the hope that the human sciences might yet come to be in a position to cast some light on what we *ought* to do and say, feel and think. In fact, of course, one is dealing with a fact-value helix here (Bhaskar, in press), which is a rationally developing one precisely to the extent that there is a sense in which factual judgments nontrivially entail value judgments but not vice versa.

My core argument is very simple. It turns on the condition that the subject matter of the human sciences includes both social objects (including beliefs) and beliefs about those objects. Philosophers have characteristically overlooked or concealed the internal relations uniting these aspects—empiricists by objectivizing beliefs, idealists by bracketing away objects. These relations, which may or may not be intradiscursive (depending upon whether the first-order object is itself a belief), are *both* causal and cognitive. In the ontological or intransitive dimension we are concerned with relations of generation; in the epistemological or transitive dimension, of *critique*. However, it is the causal relation of generation that grounds the epistemological program of critique.

I am going to contend that if we possess (1) adequate grounds for supposing that a belief P (about some object O) is *false* and (2) adequate grounds for supposing that S(co-) *explains* P, then we may (and must) pass immediately to (3) a negative evaluation of S(CP) and (4) a positive evaluation of action rationally directed at the removal of S(CP). To elaborate, inasmuch as we can explain, that is, show the (perhaps contingent) necessity for some determinate false consciousness, or perhaps just some determinate consciousness under the determinable "false," then the inferences to a negative evaluation of its source(s) and a positive evaluation of action oriented toward their dissolution are ceteris paribus mandatory. It should perhaps be stressed straight away that such action can only be rationally justified ceteris paribus to the extent that there are grounds for supposing the source to be dissoluble, and that the TMSA does not in itself license the supposition of a society without some false consciousness. The notion of false consciousness here involves simply the notion of disjuncture, mismatch, or lack of correspondence between belief and object.

In principle, this pattern of inference applies equally to beliefs about natural, as well as social objects, on the condition that the relevant *source* of false consciousness, S, is itself a social object. But in this case, S cannot be the same as O, and neither S nor P can be causal conditions for the genesis or persistence of O (or any other aspect of the object-domain so related to O), as in the more interesting forms of psychological rationalization and ideological mystification. Only in the case of beliefs about social objects can the illusory (or more generally defective) character of consciousness be a condition of what it is about (although inasmuch as beliefs about nature are social objects, *all* the modalities of false consciousness may clearly apply to our beliefs about nature, i.e., to our understanding of—as distinct from *in*—science).

I shall call (1) the critical and (2) the explanatory condition. Of course, even if the critical condition alone is satisfied, we also pass immediately to a negative evaluation of P(CP), and of action based on or informed by P(CP). But I want to distinguish this kind of "criticism" which, although it formally violates and so refutes "Hume's Law," remains silent on the causes of error, from an *explanatory critique*. In particular, if emancipation is conceived of as *the transformation of the sources of determination from unwanted to wanted ones*, it is clear that only a discourse in which the explanatory as well as the critical condition is satisfied can be intrinsically emancipatory. The structures of the various types of depth-explanation are considerably more complicated than those depicted in the bare form of an explanatory critique, but the transition from fact to value is effected in essentially the same way. The possibility of an explanatory critique constitutes the kernel of the emancipatory potential of the human sciences. To fully illustrate the possibilities here, I want to develop the argument on a series of levels, which may be regarded as so many ratchets of reason.

At the first two levels, no attempt is made to question the logical heterogeneity (and impenetrability) of facts and values. Despite this, the human sciences may still have emancipatory implications by virtue of (1) their use as sheer technique and (2) their effects in the context of relations of domination, exploitation, and oppression.

Level I: Technical Rationality

Patently, the human sciences may be used, like any other sciences, to achieve (more or less consciously formulated and justified) ends which may of course be adjudged equally good or bad. In particular, explanatory theories may be used, in conjunction with statements of particular initial conditions, to generate technical imperatives akin to "Put antifreeze in the radiator (if you want to avoid it bursting in winter) CP." If such imperatives ever appear to depart from the ends-means schema, it is only because they already presuppose a context of human purposes in the domain of their intended applications.

Level II: Contextually Situated Instrumental Rationality

The human sciences, even at the level of instrumental rationality, are not symmetrically beneficial to the parties involved in relations of domination and the like. In the first place, explanatory knowledge increases the range of known real (non-utopian) human possibilities. This may mean, of course, decreasing the range of assumed or fancied ones. But ceteris paribus, this will tilt the "state of (in a broad sense) political argument" against the status quo. This is quite consistent with the existence of only a simple external connection between knowledge and politics.

Second, even using an instrumental interpretation, explanatory knowledge appears as a necessary condition for rational self-emancipation, whether from the oppression of individuals, groups, classes, organizations, systems of relations, structures of interaction, and so forth or from the oppression of conscious or unconscious systems of ideas in which the agent is entrapped. Hence, the dominated, exploited, oppressed, repressed, and so forth have an *interest* in knowledge (in the straightforward sense that it facilitates the achievement of their desires). And the dominating, inasmuch as their interests are antagonistic to those they dominate, possess an interest in the ignorance of the dominated (and perhaps even in their own ignorance of the nature, or even the fact, of their dominance). Thus, the human sciences, and at a remove philosophy, cannot be regarded as *equally* "a potential instrument of domination," as of "the expansion of the rational autonomy of action" (Giddens, 1976, p. 159). The human sciences are not neutral in their consequences.

Level III: Intradiscursive (Non-Explanatory) Critical Rationality

The point has been made (see especially Edgley, 1976, 1979) that any science involves intradiscursive criticism, i.e., criticism of other actually or possibly believed (and therefore potentially efficacious) theories, hypotheses, and the like. Acceptance of some theory T entails, ceteris paribus, a series of negative evaluations: on theories incompatible with it, on beliefs such theories underpin, on actions they sustain or inform. Granted that "X is false" does not just *mean* "Don't believe (act on) X," it certainly ceteris paribus entails it. It is only if one denied any ontological connection between beliefs and action or theory and practice that one might have grounds for supposing that a change in theoretical does not entail a change in practical judgments (ceteris paribus). But denying such a connection makes practical discourse practically otiose. Again, this point is consistent with a contingent relationship between a science and its subject matter; and it applies, quite indifferently, at the level of intradiscursive, critical rationality, to all sciences alike.

Level IV: Explanatory Critical Rationality

All the sciences make judgments of truth or falsity on beliefs about their object domain. But the human sciences, by virtue of the distinguishing feature of their object domain, that it includes beliefs about inter alia social objects, also make (or at least entail) judgments of truth or falsity on (aspects of) that domain. And such belief/object correspondence, or lack of it, appears immediately as a legitimate object of social scientific explanation. But inasmuch as the natural sciences are also concerned in their own substantive critical discourse not just to isolate, but to comprehend (i.e., causally explain) illusory or inadequate beliefs about the natural world, then they too, assuming the second-order standpoint of the intermediate science (to use the terminology of the second section) of the natural sociology (or psychology) of belief, may come to explain false consciousness of nature at least partially in terms of human causes (e.g., faulty instruments, inadequate funds, superstition, the power of the church, state, or corporations). By virtue of their explanatory charter, then, the human sciences *must,* and the natural sciences *may* (mediately, via the natural sociology of belief), arrive at value judgments, inasmuch as they are in a position to give explanations of false consciousness.[7]

To recapitulate the central argument, then, if we have a consistent set of theories T which (1) shows some belief P to be false, and (2) explains why that, or perhaps some such false (illusory, inadequate, misleading) belief is believed, then the inferences to (3) a negative evaluation of the object S (e.g., system of social relations) accounting for the falsity of the belief (i.e., mismatch in reality between the belief P and what it is about O) and (4) a positive evaluation of action rationally directed at removing (disconnecting, or transforming) that object, i.e., the source(s) of false consciousness, certainly seem mandatory, ceteris paribus. This could be represented, informally, in the inference schema below as:

$$I.S.1 \ (1) \ T > P; \ (2) \ T \exp I(P) \rightarrow (3) \ -V(S \rightarrow I(P)) - (4) \ VO_{-S}{}^8$$

and we certainly seem to have derived value conclusions (ceteris paribus) from purely factual premises.

Now for some possible objections:

(1) It might be objected that "P is false" is not value-neutral. But if it is not value-neutral, then the value judgment "P is false" can be derived from premises concerning the lack of correspondence, mismatch, or disjuncture of objects and beliefs (in the object domain). Moreover, assuming that such judgments are intrinsic to *any* factual discourse, we are nevertheless able to infer from them, together with explanatory premises, conclusions of a type which are *not* intrinsic to *every* factual discourse, such as those specified in (3) and (4). Hence, we do have a transition here that goes against the grain of Hume's Law, however precisely that is supposed to be here interpreted or applied. On the other hand, if "P is false" is value-neutral, then the inferences to "P ought not be believed (CP)" and "Don't believe (act upon) P(CP)" certainly seem inescapable.

(2) The suggestion that science itself presupposes or embodies commitment to certain values, such as objectivity, openness, integrity, honesty, veracity, consistency, coherence, comprehensibility, explanatory power, and so on should certainly be welcomed—suggesting, as it does, that the class of the "value-neutral" is as empty as that of Austin's (1963) original "constatives." But it does nothing either to rescue Hume's Law or

to deny the validity of inference types (3) and (4), which turn on the special feature of the sciences of belief that commitment to truth and explanatory power entails the search for theories which will possess value implications that cannot be regarded as conditions of, or already implicit as anticipations in the organization of, scientific activity in general.

(3) It might be maintained that, although inference type (3) is valid, (4) is faulty, so that no commitment to any sort of action is entailed by the critical explanatory theory. But this is not so. For one can reason straight away to action directed at removing the sources of false consciousness, providing of course, one has good grounds for supposing that it would do so, that no ill (or sufficiently overriding ill) effects would be forthcoming, and that there were no better course of action which would achieve the same end. Of course, the inference scheme does not itself, conceived of as a philosophical reconstruction, determine what such practical ("critical-revolutionary") action is. That is the task of substantive theory. Of course, "remove (annul, defuse, disconnect, dissolve, transform) sources of false consciousness" does not specify *what* the sources are, any more than "lying is wrong" says which statements are lies.

Behind this objection, however, lie two considerations of some moment. First, the kind of theory underpinning (4) may be different from that informing (3). Diagnosis is not therapy. We may know that something is causing a problem without knowing how to get rid of or change it. Second, an explanatory critique of this type does not in general specify how we are to act after the source of mystification (false consciousness) is removed. It focuses on action which frees us to act, by eliminating or disconnecting a source of mystification acting as an unwanted source of (co-)determination, replacing that source with another wanted (or perhaps just less unwanted) one, so achieving (absolute or relative) liberation from one stream of constraints or compulsions inherited from, as the causalities (and casualties) of, the past. But it does not tell us what to do, if and when (and to the extent that) we are free. Thus, emancipated action may, and perhaps must, have a different logical form from emancipatory action.

The human sciences then must make judgments of truth and falsity, and these, in the context of explanatory theories, entail value judgments of types (3) and (4). Mutatis mutandis, similar considerations apply to judgments of rationality, consistency, coherence, and so forth. Thus, I.S.1 can be generalized in the cognitive direction represented in I.S.2 below, where C(P) stands for the contradictory character of some determinate set of beliefs:

I.S.2 $T \to P$; $T \exp C(P) \to -V(S \to C(P)) - VO_{-S}$

But the human sciences are, of course, not only concerned with explaining what might be called "cognitive ills." Their manifest includes the explanation of the "practical ills" of ill health, misery, repression, and so forth; and in between such ills and the cognitive ones, what might be called the "communicative ills" of deception (including self-deception), distortion, and so on.

This indicates two further lines of consideration. First, I.S.1 can be straightforwardly generalized to deal with the explanation of such non-cognitive ills, with a corresponding deduction of value judgments, as in I.S.3, where I-H stands for ill health:

I.S.3 $T \exp$ I-H; $-V(\text{I-H}) \to -V(S \to \text{I-H}) \to VO_{-S}$

However, as will be immediately obvious, this deduction, despite its evident social and epistemic power, is now no longer from purely factual premises, nor from what is immediately or self-evidently constitutive of purely factual discourse. Thus, it cannot be used to achieve a formal refutation of Hume's Law. It is precisely upon this rock that most previous attempts at its refutation, including Searle's notorious attempted derivation of an "ought" from the rather tenuous institution of "promising" (Searle, 1964, 1979), have broken. But further reflection shows another possibility here; namely, that there are *noncognitive* conditions, such as a degree of good health and the absence of marked asymmetries in political, economic, and the other modalities of power, for discourse (including factual discourse)-in-general to be possible. If this is correct, then a formal derivation of an "ought" can proceed as in I.S.4:

I.S.4 $T > P$; $T \exp (\text{I-H} \to I(P)) \to -V(S \to \text{I-H}) \to VO_{-S}$

Is there a sense in which I.S.1 and I.S.2 are epistemically prior to their noncognitive generalizations? Yes, inasmuch as empirically controlled retroduction to explanatory structures always occurs in the context of, and typically (in science) assumes the form of, criticism of beliefs (consciousness)—scientific, protoscientific, lay, and practical.

Level V: Depth-Explanatory Critical Rationality

The most thoroughly explored applications of I.S.1 and I.S.2 involve the phenomena of psychological *rationalization* and *ideological mystifi-*

cation. These phenomena are characterized by a doubling of necessity between misrepresentation (P) and source (S), and an internal relationship between source (S) and object (O), so that they do not apply in an unmediated way to beliefs about nature (what is misrecognized here is always a human phenomenon). The distinctive mark of these modes of false consciousness is, then, that the, or some similar, misrepresentation (P) is not only causally necessitated by, but causally necessary for, the persistence or modulation, reproduction, or limited (nonessential) transformation of its source (S); and that what is misrepresented (0) is either nothing other than, or at least causally dependent upon, the source of the misrepresentation (S).

Thus, in the simplified model introduced in the fourth section, we had

I.S.5 $s \rightarrow p$; $sp \rightarrow \Psi$

where N misdescribed the real (i.e., the causally efficacious) reason, s, for Ψ, by p; where p was itself a contingently necessary releasing condition for Ψ; and where p was itself generated, in context, by s.

To explain this, we now posit a structure S such that Ψ is (perhaps contingently) necessary for its persistence or modulation, as in:

I.S.6 $S \rightarrow (s \rightarrow p; sp \rightarrow \Psi) \rightarrow S^1$

Given $s \neq p$, the deductions proceed as in I.S.1.

This paradigm may be extended to include the self-mystification of forms of social life or systems of social relations in ideologies. Thus, the contradictions which mystify Colletti (1975) turn simply on the necessary coexistence in social reality of an object and a (categorially) false presentation of it, where it is the inner (or essential) structure of the object which generates the categorially false presentation (or appearance). I.S.7 is isomorphic with I.S.5:

I.S.7 $E \rightarrow A$; $EA \rightarrow P$

and I.S.8 is isomorphic with I.S.6:

I.S.8 $R \rightarrow (E \rightarrow A; EA \rightarrow P) \rightarrow R^1$

where E = essence, A = appearance, P = practices, and R, R^1 the modulated reproduction of some system of social relations (such as the capitalist mode of production).

Are there any general conditions on the internal structure (E) of a self-reproducing system (T) which generates and contains within itself (i.e., T) a functionally necessary misrepresentation (A) of itself? It seems plausible to suppose that E must possess at least sufficient internal differentiation to justify attributing to it a *"Spaltung"* or split; and that if T is to be capable of endogenous (essential) transformation, rather than merely modulated reproduction, the split must constitute, or be constituted by, *antagonistic* (opposed) *tendencies.* But apart from the *Colletti*-style *contradiction* built into the notion of the system's misrepresentation of itself, it seems a priori unlikely that what the human sciences may empirically discover about the various structural sources of false consciousness will justify the application of a single unified category of "contradiction" to those structures. Instead, one might conjecture a galaxy of concepts of contradiction clustered around the core notion of the axiological indeterminacy generated by the logical archetype (together with the evaluative connotations this secretes), with the specific concepts of contradiction achieving their individuation in the constraints they impose upon such indeterminacy, and in their theorization of its form.

Perhaps the most famous depth-critique, Marx's *Capital,* has the structure of a triple critique: of theories, of the practical consciousness such theories reflect or rationalize, and of the conditions explaining such consciousness. But in Marx, and the Marxist tradition generally, the criticized (discursive and practical) consciousness is regarded not just as false but as "ideological"—where ideology is counterposed to science. In addition to the *critical* and *explanatory* conditions, one thus finds a further set of *categorical* conditions. Here, beliefs are typically criticized for their *unscientificity* simpliciter, or for their inadequacy in sustaining the (irreducible) *specificity* of the subject matter of their domains. Thus, in reification, fetishism, hypostatization, voluntaristic conventionalism, organicism, and so forth, social life is presented, in one way or another, in an asocial mode—a condition rooted, for Marx, in the alienation and atomization characteristic of capitalism as a specific form of class society. For example, on Marx's analysis, the wage-form collapses a power (labor power) to its exercise (labor), and the value-form presents social relations in the guise of natural qualities. The critique of these categorical errors may be represented as

I.S.9 (1) $T > P$; (2) $T \exp I(P)$; (3) $T \exp -S_c (P) \rightarrow$ (4) $-V (S \rightarrow -S_c I (P)) \rightarrow$ (5) VO_{-S}; and

I.S.10 (1) $T > P$; (2) $T \exp I(P)$; (3) $T \exp -S_o (P) \rightarrow$ (4) $-V(S \rightarrow -S_o I(P)) \rightarrow$ (5) VO_{-S}

where $-S_c$ and $-S_o$ stand for the nonscientific and asocial character of belief-forms.

Level VI: Depth-Rationality

Given that clear paradigms exist in the human sciences of the inference schemes outlined above, most notably in the traditions inaugurated by Marx and Freud, but also in some of the work of the theorists of the life-world *(Lebenswelt)* of social interaction, is there a sense in which the *application* of these inference schemes, and hence of the type of explanatory critique they presuppose, is transcendentally necessary?

Assume two interlocutors, X and Y. Suppose X believes himself to possess a rational argumentative procedure, R_A, a reasoned argument A_r, and a conclusion Q; but that Y does not or cannot (perhaps "in spite of himself") accept or act upon R_A, A_r, or Q. (The reverse conditions may apply symmetrically to X, but we can ignore this complication here.) What is to be done when rational argument fails? Clearly, there are three general kinds of possibility here:

(1) Y continues to mistakenly believe (and act upon) Q;
(2) some nondiscursive procedure (e.g., force, medication) induces in Y a belief in Q; or
(3) X and Y jointly initiate an inquiry into the conditions blocking or compelling Y's beliefs.

Acceptance of solution (1), i.e., stoic acceptance of irrationality, error, and the like is a counsel of despair. Moreover, it cannot be generalized to the first person case of doubt (or more generally, choice) without vicious axiological regress. Solution (2) can be ruled out on the grounds that drugs, force, and so forth can only simulate the acceptance of A_r or R_A. Further, it is not emancipatory, in that it does not replace an unwanted with a wanted source of determination, but merely counteracts the effects of one unwanted source of determination with another. This has the corollary that inasmuch as the original source of determination is not defused, it may continue to exercise a latent power.

The alternative (3) of a *depth-investigation* (D-I) is possible where reason fails but has not yet exhausted its resources; and it is practicable where Y's beliefs are generated or underpinned by unreflected (unacknowledged) processes, and where Y seeks to understand, in order to undermine or abrogate, these processes. A depth-investigation may be defined generally as any cooperative inquiry, which includes the agent, into the structure of some presumed set of mechanisms, constituting for that agent an unwanted source of determination (which, whether cognitive or not, will always possess some cognitive manifestation), with a view to initiating, preserving, or restoring that agent's ability to act and think rationally.

Four points must be made immediately about this definition. First, what is rational cannot be stipulated a priori, but must itself be discovered, in relation to antecedent notions of rationality (its nominal essences so to speak), in the context of the explanatory critique such as D-I presupposes. Second, although the concept of a depth-investigation has been introduced as an idiographic, practically oriented *application* of some or other determinate explanatory critique, the *theory* at the heart of the critique itself depends crucially for its own development and empirical confirmation on such investigations (whether on living or reconstructed, e.g., historical, materials). It follows from this that the link between theory and practice, or pure and applied research, although not abrogating their distinction, is bound to be tighter than in the natural sciences. Third, corresponding to the different types of inference scheme outlined above, there will be different forms of D-I. These must not, however, be hypostatized, for of course the explanation of cognitive ills will in general involve reference to practical and communicative ills, and vice versa. Finally, the desire for emancipation which motivates the D-I can neither be posited a priori as a universal nor predicted in historicist fashion on the basis of some particular theory of individual development or history. But as a socially produced social object, it will of course be a critical topic for metainvestigations, which must be reflexively incorporated into the substantive theory of the practice (and such) from or for which emancipation is sought.

The structure of a simplified D-I may be elucidated as follows:

(1) Y is not capable of O; scientific realism suggests there is a mechanism M preventing this.

(2) General theory T investigates the structure of blocking/compelling mechanisms, under the control of empirical data and researches.

(3) The application of T to Y depends upon the agent Y, as well as co-investigator X, for it is Y's interpretations, actions, and determinations that are at issue.

Subjectivity in the human sciences is not an obstacle; it is (an essential part of) the datum. But ontological authorship does not automatically carry over into epistemological authority. The Y-dependence of the D-I means that Y must have a motive or interest in disengaging M, or in a range of acts that M prevents. And that co-investigator X must not have an interest in the distortion of M-descriptions. Concretely, this raises the question of the costs of emancipation for Y and of the conditions under which emancipation may be a second-best solution; for X, it presupposes both the willingness to learn (in the general spirit of Marx's "Third Thesis on Feuerbach") and the continuing development of X's own self-understanding. At a deeper level, the success of the detailed investigation of the modus operandi of M on Y must depend upon an *internal differentiation* within the experience of Y, so that the empiricist/utilitarian notion of emancipation as a process of the alteration of the circumstances of atomistic individuals must be rejected. Moreover, it should be reiterated that cognitive emancipation will in general depend upon noncognitive (and extradiscursive) conditions, and that cognitive emancipation is necessary but insufficient for full emancipation (as shown by the example of the slave who knows very well he is a slave but still remains a slave, i.e., unfree).

In fact, *dissonance,* not liberation, may be the immediate result of enlightenment. And such dissonance may lead either to "revolutionary-critical" activity or to despair. Moreover, constraints upon cognitive emancipation itself are imposed by the preformation of thought contents (in psychoanalysis), the projects of others (in social phenomenology), and the nondiscursive aspects of social reality (in historical materialism). Hence, emancipation cannot be conceived either as an internal relationship within thought (the idealist error) or as an external relationship of "educators," "therapists," or "intellectuals" to the "educated," "sick," or "oppressed" (the empiricist error).

I want to propose that the possibility of a depth-investigation is a transcendental condition for any science of man, and hence (at a remove) for any science at all; that in particular, *to inquire into the nature of the real grounds for beliefs is the same thing as to inquire into the possibility of rationalization, self-deception, deception of others, counterfinality, and systemic mystification;* and that to inquire into the conditions of possibility of these cognitive-communicative malaises immediately raises the question of the conditions of the possibility of practical ones—from ill health to brutal oppression. The issue of the causes of belief and action, presupposing a distinction between *real* and *possible* (including assumed or fancied) *grounds,* can only be taken up by the depth human sciences. But a moment's reflection shows that this distinction, and hence the possibility of a depth-investigation at the analytic, phenomenological, and historical levels, is a condition of every rational praxis or authentic act of self-understanding at all. It is necessitated by the existential intransitivity and enabled by the causal interdependency of the phenomena of sociality. Thus, in the human sciences the problem of error (oppression, and so on) must make way for the problem of its causes, as part of the program of the systematic investigation of the generative structures producing the manifest phenomena of social life.

The object of the D-I is *emancipation.* Emancipation may be conceived either as the process of the transformation of one mode of determination, D_1, into another, D_2, or as the act of switching from D_1 to D_2, both D_1 and D_2 enduring but D_1 in an inactivated state. If the emancipation is to be *of* the human species, then the powers of emancipated man must already exist (although perhaps only as powers to acquire or develop powers) in an unactualized state. The key questions for substantive theory then become: What are the conditions for the actualization of the powers? Are they stimulating (see the socialist tradition); or releasing (see the anarchic/liberal traditions)? Do they lie in social organization or individual attitudes, and so forth?

Conclusion

Can anything be said about the conditions of the possibility of emancipatory practices in general? I think that, for emancipation to be possible, four general types of condition must be satisfied.

First, *reasons must be causes,* or discourse is ontologically redundant (and scientifically inexplicable). But the potentially emancipatory discourse, given the TMSA and the general conception of an open world, can only codetermine action in an already prestructured, practical, and collective context.

Second, *values must be immanent* (as latent or partially manifested tendencies) in the practices in which we engage, or normative discourse is utopian or idle. I think that Marx, in conceiving socialism as anticipated in the revolutionary practice of the proletariat, grasped this. And it is on this feature that Habermas's deduction of speech-constitutive universals also turns (Habermas, 1973, 1976). But if there is a sense in which the ideal community, founded on principles of truth, freedom, and justice, is already present as an anticipation in every speech interaction, might one not be tempted to argue that equality, liberty, and fraternity are present in every transaction or material exchange; or that respect and mutual recognition are contained in the most casual reciprocated glance? It is an error to suppose that ethics must have a linguistic foundation, just as it is an error to suppose that it can be autonomous from science or history.

Third, critique must be *internal to* (and conditioned by) *its objects,* or it will lack both epistemic grounding and causal power. But it follows from this that it is part of the very process it describes, and so subject to the same possibilities, of unreflected determination and historical supercession, that it situates. Hence, continuing self-reflexive autocritique is the sine qua non of any critical explanatory theory.

Finally, for emancipation to be possible, *knowable emergent laws must operate.* Such laws, which will of course be consistent with physical laws, will be set in the context of explanatory theories elucidating the structures of cognitive and noncognitive oppression and the possibility of their transformation by women and men. Emancipation depends upon the untruth of reductionist materialism and spiritualistic idealism alike. On reductionism: If the physical process level is L_p, and the level at which emancipation is sought is L_e, then either L_p completely determines L_e and no qualitative change is possible; or qualitative change is possible, and the laws of L_p are violated. On idealism: either emancipation is entirely intrinsic to thought, in which case it is unconditioned and irrationality is inexplicable; or if it is conditioned, it cannot be intrinsic to thought.

The possibility of emancipation is not, of course, the reason that an emergent powers theory, if it is, is true. It is, rather, that if human beings, and social forms in general, are emergent from but conditioned by nature, then there is at least the possibility that the human sciences, provided they "do not anticipate the new world dogmatically, but rather seek to find the new world through criticism of the old" (Marx, 1967, p. 212), could still be of some benefit to the greater majority of mankind.

Notes

1. From this point of view, Smith's exchange-value/use-value distinction (at least in Marx's interpretation of it), Saussure's langue/parole distinction, Chomsky's competence/performance distinction—and perhaps Durkheimian facts, Paretian residues, and Weberian types (together with their respective contrasts)—may all be seen as so many attempts at "découpage": that is, to conceptualize in opposition to the empirical mélange a stratified subject of inquiry, designating the proper object of scientific investigation. William Outhwaite has usefully distinguished between epistemic and ontological object-constitution in the human sciences (Outhwaite, 1982). In my terminology, the former relates to the transitive and the latter to the intransitive dimension. It is clear that epistemic constitution—the constitution of some appropriate object of knowledge (in thought) in the human sciences—will always be grounded in some conception of the constitution, in social reality, of the

intransitive object of that knowledge; and that such a découpage will normally precede a "coupure" (in the sense of Bachelard and Althusser).

2. It follows from this that any social object presupposes the existence of some natural object, but not vice versa; any social change entails a natural change, but not vice versa; and a social phenomenon may be realized or represented in a number of different natural modes (see, e.g., Putnam, 1976), but not necessarily vice versa—if emergent causality operates.

3. Freud's biologism is well-known. But Marx's commitment to the project of a unified science—"Natural science will one day incorporate the science of man, just as the science of man will incorporate natural science; there will be a *single* science" (1974, p. 85)—which he never repudiated, is consistent with the notion of a reconciliation, or rapprochement, between the two epistemic orders, rather than a physicalistic reduction.

4. Contrast Marx on the historically developed nature of needs: "Hunger is hunger, but the hunger gratified with cooked meat eaten with a knife and fork is different from that which bolts down raw meat with the aid of hand and nail and tooth" (1973, p. 92); and of social forms generally: "A negro is a negro. He only becomes a slave in certain relations. A cotton-spinning jenny is a machine for spinning cotton. It becomes *capital* only in certain relations. Torn from these relations it is no more capital than gold is itself *money* or sugar the price of sugar" (1968, p. 81). Could hunger exist for the human species, as naturally endowed, without any social relations? Or is the analogy between hunger and capital exact? Is natural man *intrinsically* social? Marx claims that "only within these connections and relations does our action on nature, production, take place" (loc. cit.). Should we add "reaction to nature" also, so symmetrizing natural liabilities and natural powers?

5. In this event, p is only contingently necessary for Ψ.

6. In the next two sections, the extent to which such apparently arbitrary normative standpoints can themselves be grounded in exploratory theory will be considered.

7. It might be argued from a positivistic (or hermeneutistic) standpoint that, although judgments of truth and falsity can be straight away deduced from the propositioned content of the human sciences, such deductions are gratuitous and extraneous to the legitimate descriptive (or interpretative) tasks of the human sciences. However, inasmuch as the human sciences are conceived, in a realist mode, as being concerned not merely with describing (and/or interpreting) but with *explaining* their object domain, the situation is radically changed, for the match or mismatch of beliefs and subject matter not only appears as an interesting topic for explanation, but may itself enter necessarily into the explanation of those beliefs and perhaps that subject matter (e.g., if a rationalization or mystification is necessary for it). Mutatis mutandis, analogous considerations may be adduced to motivate the possibility of an explanatory critique in the natural sciences.

8. An explanatory critique in the natural sciences could be represented as follows:

$I.S.1'$ (1) T > P (2) T exp $I(P_N) \rightarrow$ (3) $-V(S_S \rightarrow I(P_N)) \rightarrow$ (4) VO_{-S_S}

References

Althusser, L. *For Marx.* London: Allen Lane, 1969.

Althusser, L., & Balibar, E. *Reading capital.* London: New Left Books, 1971.

Austin, J. Performative-constative. In C. Caton (Ed.), *Philosophy and ordinary language.* Urbana: University of Illinois Press, 1963.

Bachelard, G. *La formation de l'esprit scientifique.* Paris: Vrin, 1938.

Bernstein, R. *The restructuring of social and political theory.* Oxford: Blackwell, 1976.

Bhaskar, R. *A realist theory of science* (2nd ed.). Atlantic Highlands, NJ: Humanities Press, 1978. (a)

Bhaskar, R. On the possibility of social scientific knowledge and the limits of naturalism. *Journal for the Theory of Social Behaviour,* 1978, *8*(1). (b)

Bhaskar, R. *The possibility of naturalism.* Atlantic Highlands, NJ: Humanities Press, 1979.

Bhaskar, R. Scientific explanation and human emancipation. *Radical Philosophy.* 1980, 26.

Bourdieu, P. *An outline of a theory of practice.* Cambridge: Cambridge University Press, 1977.

Bunge, M. *Method, model and matter.* Dordrecht: D. Reidel, 1973.

Colletti, L. Marxism and the dialectic. *New Left Review,* 1975, *93.*

Collier, A. Materialism and explanation. In J. Mepham & D. Ruben (Eds.), *Issues in Marxist philosophy* (Vol. 2). Brighton: Harvester Press, 1979.

Donagan, A. The Popper-Hempel theory reconsidered. *Philosophical analysis and history.* New York: Harper & Row, 1966.

Durkheim, E. *Rules of sociological method.* New York: Free Press, 1965.

Edgley, R. Reason as dialectic. *Radical Philosophy,* 1976, *15.*

Edgley, R. Marx's revolutionary science. In J. Mepham & D. Ruben (Eds.), *Issues in Marxist philosophy* (Vol. 3). Brighton: Harvester Press, 1979.

Elias, N. The sciences: Towards a theory. In R. Whitley, (Ed.), *Social processes of scientific development.* London: Macmillan, 1974.

Engels, F. *Anti-Dühring.* London: Lawrence & Wishart, 1969.

Gadamer, H. G. *Truth and method.* London: Sheed & Ward, 1975.

Giddens, A. *New rules of sociological method.* London: Hutchinson, 1976.

Giddens, A. *Studies in social and political theory.* London: Hutchinson, 1977.

Giddens, A. *Central problems in social theory.* London: Macmillan, 1979.

Gödel, K. *On formally undecidable propositions.* New York: Basic Books, 1962.

Goldmann, L. *Marxisme et sciences humaines.* Paris: Gallimard, 1970.

Habermas, J. *Knowledge and human interests.* London: Heinemann, 1972.

Habermas, J. *Theory and practice.* London: Heinemann, 1973.

Habermas, J. Towards a theory of communicative competence. *Inquiry,* 1976, *13.*

Hanson, N. *Patterns of discovery.* Cambridge: Cambridge University Press, 1965.

Harré, R. *Principles of scientific thinking.* London: Macmillan, 1970.

Harré, R. *On social being.* Oxford: Blackwell, 1979.

Harré, R., & Secord, P. *The explanation of social behaviour.* Oxford: Blackwell, 1972.

Hegel, G. *The phenomenology of mind.* London: Allen & Unwin, 1949.

Hesse, M. *The structure of scientific inference.* London: Macmillan, 1974.

Husserl, E. *Logical investigations* (Vol. 1). London: Routledge & Kegan Paul, 1970.

Kuhn, T. The structure of scientific revolutions (2nd ed.). Chicago, 1970.

Lukács, G. *History and class consciousness.* London: Merlin Press, 1971.

Marx, K. *Writings on philosophy and society.* New York: Anchor Books, 1967. Originally published 1843.

Marx, K. Wage, labour and capital. *Selected works.* London: Lawrence & Wishart, 1968. Originally published 1847.

Marx, K. *Grundrisse* London: Harmondsworth, 1973. Originally published 1857.

Marx, K. *Selected writings in sociology and philosophy.* London: Harmondsworth, 1974. Originally published 1844.

Marx, K. *Selected correspondence.* London: Lawrence & Wishart, 1975.

Marx, K. *Capital* (Vol. 1). London: Harmondsworth, 1976. Originally published 1867.

Mischel, T. *The self.* Oxford: Blackwell, 1977.

Outhwaite, W. *Concept formation in social science.* London: Routledge & Kegan Paul, 1982.

Popper, K. Science: Conjectures and refutations. *Conjectures and Refutations.* London: Routledge & Kegan Paul, 1969.

Poulantzas, N. Political power and social classes. London: New Left Books, 1973.

Putnam, H. The mental life of some machines. In J. Glover (Ed.), *Philosophy of mind.* Oxford: Oxford University Press, 1976.

Sayer, A. Abstraction: A realistic interpretation. *Radical Philosophy,* 1981, 28.

Sayer, D. *Marx's method.* Brighton: Harvester Press, 1979.

Searle, J. How to derive "ought" from "is." *Philosophical Review,* 1964, 73.

Searle, J. *Speech acts.* Cambridge: Cambridge University Press, 1979.

Soper, K. Marxism, materialism and biology. In J. Mepham & D. Ruben (Eds.), *Issues in Marxist philosophy* (Vol. 2). Brighton: Harvester Press, 1979.

Taylor, C. Neutrality in political science. In P. Laslett & W. Runciman (eds.), *Philosophy, politics and society* (3rd series). Oxford: Blackwell, 1969.

Taylor, C. Interpretation and the sciences of man. *Review of Metaphysics,* 1971, 25(3).

Timpanaro, S. *On materialism.* London: New Left Books, 1975.

Toulmin, S. *Human understanding* (Vol. 1). Oxford: Oxford University Press, 1973.

Toulmin, S. The genealogy of "consciousness." This volume.

Wright, E. *Class, crisis and the state.* London: New Left Books, 1978.

CHAPTER 15

Epilogue

PAUL F. SECORD

Here we return once again to the core theme of this book to ask whether our contributions, taken as a whole, have moved us forward and, if so, to ask in which directions. First, it seems desirable to emphasize that it can no longer be doubted that the knowledgeable activities of conscious agents must have a place in any adequate psychology or sociology. In emphasizing them, symbolic interactionists, along with many anthropologists, ethnomethodologists, phenomenologists, and various other critics of behaviorism and mainstream sociology have surely been right. Mainstream sociology has, by and large, taken the behaviors of individuals as a kind of "empirical reality" which remains unexamined in the study of groups and institutions. But in so doing, it has stripped individuals of their most human qualities, slighting intentional action and its subtleties in a mistaken conception of the nature of science.

On the other hand, symbolic interactionists and other critics of mainstream sociology have sometimes acted as if the intentional actions of conscious agents were the whole of sociology. They have slighted the other side of human action—those routines and themes which stem not from the intentions of actors, but from unacknowledged sources. These include the unrecognized conditions of settings in which actions take place, as well as subtle feedback from unintended consequences of actions. Much human action springs from tacit rather than conscious knowledge, and certainly some actions are unconsciously motivated. Ultimately, then, both of these polar views have something right about them, but neither should be emphasized at the expense of the other. They oversimplify too much, and as our contributors have shown, these apparently incompatible views can only be articulated by constructing a more complex model of social life.

Another theme, explicit in the contributions of Bhaskar, Giddens, and Manicas, but also reflected in various ways in most of the other chapters in this volume, concerns the nature of social science. The dominant conception here represents a "new" philosophy of science emerging from significant contributions in that field occurring over the last two decades or more, and it constitutes a radical departure from traditional social science views. Traditional sociology has viewed social institutions, for example, as "empirical realities." The approach has been to identify recurring regular patterns of action and their "causes." This is consistent with a Humean view of causality which has prevailed in science for over two centuries. This view emphasizes regular concomitance between two or more variables as fundamental to causal inferences. But the new philosophical view favors what has been termed efficient cause or a singularity view of cause. Under this perspective, causes are "natural necessities." A given set of conditions *must* produce the effect. This differs sharply from the Humean view, which holds that there could not be a necessary connection between cause and effect—that cause could be inferred only from the regularly occurring concomitance of antecedents and consequents. Under the natural necessity theme, what science discovers is necessary connections in the real world—generative mechanisms or structures. But these are *not* usually observable under ordinary conditions; they can only be grasped through a combination of theory and experiment. It is for this reason that readily observable, naturally occurring regularities in the world are apt to be rather sterile, misleading indicators of causal mechanisms.

Clearly, what gives impetus to the central question of this volume is the parochial nature of the various social science approaches. Each exaggerates the value of its own position in providing explanations of the social world and slights other approaches that often encompass a whole domain of knowledge. Given this state of affairs, it is not surprising that those social scientists who have recognized the poverty of parochial approaches have tried to develop more encompassing social theory that would enable us to articulate the diverse sources that produce and shape social behavior. Many of the chapters in this book have contributed to such articulation.

Yet one possibility, perhaps even a likelihood, is that very little of a *general* nature can be said about the articulation between consciousness, behavior, and social structure. Certainly this articulation must depend upon the domains of behavior and social structure that are under consideration. Even the Bhaskar/Giddens thesis, that structure is reproduced and provides at the same time the enabling conditions for such reproductions, may well apply only to less durable structures. An inquiry here into what makes structures endure might provide valuable insights. Are certain structures especially suited to human nature (e.g., the family) and thus virtually universal? Are other structures an inevitable consequence of the economic necessity for commerce among human beings? And why are some structures ephemeral (e.g., those underlying communes)?

Another argument in support of the nongeneral nature of any theoretical articulation between consciousness, behavior, and social structure is that surely no behavior articulates with all existing structures. Likewise, no one structure bears on the entire set of behavior domains. We can think of a particular behavior domain as being relevant only to a few selected structures. Both the behavior domain and the structures may be of a kind quite different from another domain.

Nothing said so far is meant to imply that such specialized pursuits as ethnomethodology, or even behaviorism, are unproductive in contributing to our understanding of human behavior. Rather, it is that their explanations typically are critical of other "ologies" and are presented as if they are complete forms. Components of the individual/social structure complex that are omitted from consideration are not merely ignored but positively rejected. This is just the opposite of what is needed for an adequate representation of a particular behavioral or structural domain. Without articulation among components of the whole pattern, the described behavior domain may not only be grossly distorted, but actually may not exist. If we think of behaviors as constantly tempered by the social context in which they occur, describing them as they are enacted in some artificial or truncated context leaves us in the dark as to the form that they would take in situ. Similarly, descriptions of social structures that are not in some way articulated with the nature and behavior of individuals are also incomplete. Such descriptions cannot avoid making implicit assumptions about the nature of the participating individuals. Since these are only implicit, a part of the explanation remains murky.

What might be a reasonable (but difficult) task for the theorist interested in the problem of specifying the relation between individual behavior and social structure would be to lay out what the components might be in two extreme cases:

(1) that case or domain where the number of elements articulated is at a maximum; and

(2) that case or domain where the number of elements articulated is at a minimum.

What is needed in addition, however, is a large number of adequately worked out explanations that are specific to particular behavioral and structural domains. But this is precisely what parochial approaches do not do; indeed, they positively discourage such efforts. At present, too little of social science knowledge is secure enough to form a base for more general theory.

A final thought: The present volume suggests that the boundaries conventionally drawn between the various social sciences act to inhibit the formulation of more adequate explanations of social behavior. Conceptualizations that are confined to the language of a particular discipline are bound to be sharply limited in their generality. This is not an indictment of any of the disciplines; each is a necessary part of the whole enterprise of social science. But social science will only reach maturity when we arrive at a stage where some practitioners have become master social scientists who can weave together all of the necessary components to arrive at a complete explanation of particular social phenomena.

AUTHOR INDEX

SUBJECT INDEX